Unleash the power of
Corel*DRAW!*

Skill Sessions

If you need to learn about a specific feature of CorelDRAW!, go right to that skill session. In it, you will learn the ins and outs of that topic—why you'd want to use it, how to use it, and a few examples. The Skill Sessions are grouped in a series of workshops that cover everything from the basics to more advanced topics.

> Basic Skills Workshop
> Manipulation Workshop
> Effects Workshop
> Advanced Skills Workshop
> Text Workshop
> Bitmap Workshop
> Output Workshop
> Graphics Toolkit Workshop
> Advanced Topics Workshop

Companion Software and Hardware Workshops

You can increase the versatility of CorelDRAW! by using it in tandem with other software and hardware pieces. These two sections review some of the more popular companion pieces, including Adobe Photoshop, Fractal Design Painter, Pixar Typestry, the Kurta XGT Tablet, and Syquest Removable Drives.

The Color Pages

CorelDRAW!4 Unleased contains two 16-page full-color inserts filled with original art created in CorelDRAW! and its companion software pieces. Browse through these sections to get a better idea of the artistic power that you can obtain from CorelDRAW!.

Projects

The best way to learn is to tackle real-world projects, so this section gives you the opportunity to follow along as the authors use CorelDRAW! to design and create useful examples.

Project 1	Creating a Map Using the Layers Option
Project 2	Creating a Chrome Effect
Project 3	Creating a Gem Box Package Design
Project 4	Polygons and Stars
Project 5	Ortho to ISO
Project 6	Landscape
Project 7	Gallery
Project 8	Layouts for Business Cards, Letterheads, and Envelopes

What's on the CD-ROM

You'll find a treasure chest full of software on the CD-ROM included with this book. Here's a sample of the types of software you'll find:

> Commercial demos
> Clip art
> Graphics
> Fonts
> Programs and utilities
> Sound clips
> Video and animation clips
> Corel tech support files

For more information about the CD-ROM, see Appendix B.

CorelDRAW!™
Unleashed 4

Corel

Corel

CorelDRAW!™
Unleashed

Foster D. Coburn III
Carlos F. Gonzalez
Pete McCormick

SAMS
PUBLISHING

A Division of Prentice Hall Computer Publishing
201 West 103rd Street, Indianapolis, Indiana 46290

Overview

Contents

XVII

Contents

XXVii

Introduction

This book represents a milestone for the authors, as we consider ourselves users just like most of you. Although we have all written articles and provided training on Corel Draw in the past, this book was a tremendous undertaking.

We consider this book a living project. A program like Corel Draw usually has more than one way to accomplish a particular task and has many hidden features. We have purposely omitted complicated illustrations in most of the skill sessions. We believe Corel Draw users want to know how to use the different effects rather than seeing an author's intricate drawing that they may never have a need to create themselves. Once you understand how to use the effects, you can put your own creative talents to work. We have done our best to cover everything, but we have no doubt missed something in the process. If you find something we didn't mention, feel free to contact us and let us know. This will help us produce an even better book the next time.

There are many people who must be thanked in helping to get this project finished. Most important are our wives, friends, and families who wondered why we were always so tired for the past few months. Their patience has been most appreciated.

The Font Company not only provided some excellent fonts for the book and the CD-ROM, but most important was their flexibility and their equipment, which aided in the production of this book.

Ray Litman did a fantastic job of putting us on the moon and finding our every flaw with his great photography. We may not be his best models, but we did the best we could for rank amateurs.

Bill Cullen and Rus Miller of Corel's quality assurance team were bombarded by questions and bug reports throughout the production of this book and bent over backwards to get everything straightened out. Their hard work and diligence is much appreciated. Mike Daschuk and John Scarlett of Corel's technical support staff handled many more questions posted on the CompuServe forums and their assistance was invaluable.

All of the other lurkers on CompuServe provided wit, wisdom, and ideas throughout the whole process. Thanks, guys, and we'll talk online soon.

Last and most important, we thank you, the reader, for purchasing our book. If we have turned on the light of understanding, inspiration, and creativity, we have done our job.

Part

I

Skills Workshops

Corel DRAW!

Part I

Basic Skills Workshop

Workshops

Basic Skills Workshop

Installing CorelDRAW! for Windows

The *Installation Guide* that comes with Corel Draw is excellent and should be read before installing the programs included in Corel Draw.

Most users like to jump right in and start the installation process. This practice should definitely be avoided when installing this multi-application program. Taking the time to read the *Installation Guide* will eliminate several problems you can encounter by not following instructions.

Special Tips

- If you have either a Syquest or Bernoulli tape drive, consider installing Corel Draw to its drive letter. This will save 34 MB of hard drive space and run almost as fast.

- If you have Corel Draw 3.0 installed on your system, be sure to follow the instructions under "Notes" on page 6 and all of page 13 in the *Installation Guide.*

- Prior to starting the actual install process, take time to pick the fonts you want to install from the front of the clip art manual. During the install process, you will be asked to choose the fonts you want installed. You are limited to 50 fonts whether you do a custom install or a full install. Knowing the ones you want ahead of time will make it easier. If for some reason, you do not have enough room on the hard drive to install all the fonts you selected, you can eliminate those that are less important.

- If you're short on hard drive space, perform a custom install and install only the programs you have room for. The Install program will keep a running count on the amount of space you need for the programs you select for installation.

- Be sure to read the README files for any update information on the install process. Early versions of Corel Draw 4 had some problems with the install program.

- When installing from a CD, you may get a message saying you need 60 KB of free disk space before you can install the program. If you get this message, you need to create a RAM drive of 60 KB or more. See your Windows documentation for instructions on creating a RAM drive.

Basic Skills Workshop

Starting and Exiting CorelDraw!

Starting Corel Draw

To start Corel Draw, click on the CorelDRAW! balloon icon in the Corel 4 program group displayed on the Windows screen. Press Enter or double-click the icon (see Figure 2.1).

Figure 2.1. The CorelDRAW! icon.

When you launch Corel Draw, the main Corel Draw screen appears. Figure 2.2 shows the Corel Draw screen and illustrates the components that make up the screen.

Status Line

The status line is blank until you select an object. The status line is a very important element of the Corel Draw screen, as it provides information about every object in your drawings.

Figure 2.3 shows two rectangles; one has only an outline and one has a color fill. The first rectangle is selected. Notice the small box at the far right of the status line. This box tells you what basic attributes the selected object has applied to it. In this case the box has an × in the center, which means the selected object does not have a color fill. The text line tells you it has an outline of .02 points.

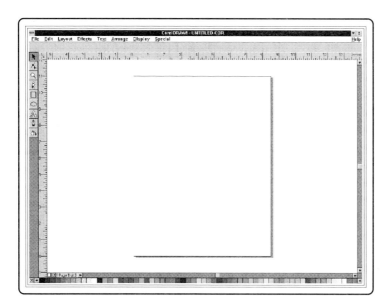

Figure 2.2 The Corel Draw initial screen.

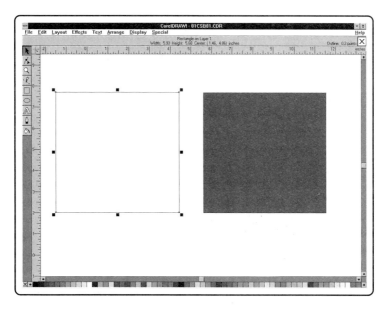

Figure 2.3. The rectangle on the left has been selected.

Figure 2.4 shows the same two rectangles with the second rectangle selected. The status line now tells you that it has a fill of Red and no outline.

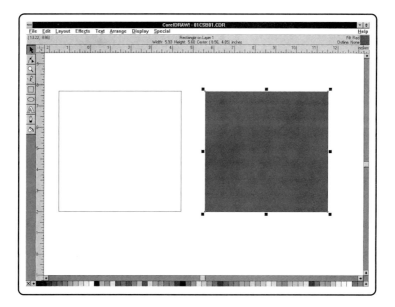

Figure 2.4. The rectangle on the right is selected.

Figure 2.5 shows the second rectangle being rotated. Notice that the status line shows the degree of rotation being applied. During this operation, the Color and Outline box does not appear.

In Figure 2.6, two different effects have been applied to each rectangle. The first rectangle has had a Contour effect applied to it. For the second rectangle, a smaller rectangle was added in the center, and the two were blended with the Blend effect. The two original rectangles now appear exactly alike.

When the left object is selected, the status line shows that it is a contour group (Figure 2.6). When the right object is selected, it shows that it is a blend group (see Figure 2.7).

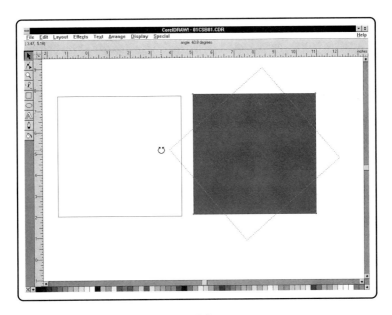

Figure 2.5. Rotating the rectangle on the right.

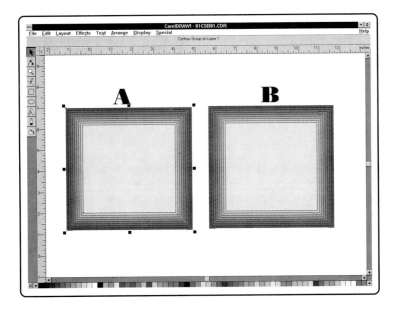

Figure 2.6. The rectangle on the left is a contour.

Basic Skills Workshop

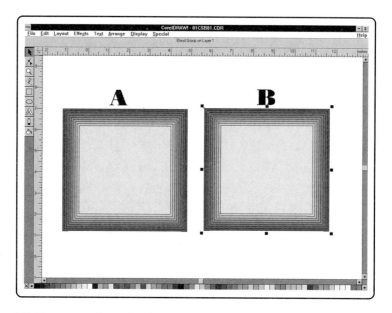

Figure 2.7. The rectangle on the right is a blend group.

The purpose of this illustration is to point out the importance of referring to the status bar during your projects. If you had tried to split the first object because it looks like a blend (see Skill Session 19, "Blending"), you could not do it. Because it certainly looks like a blend, you might wonder why the Split command doesn't work. This could lead to an unnecessary and expensive (as well as embarrassing) call to Tech Support.

Title Bar

The title bar displays the name of the file you are working on. By dragging the title bar, you can move the entire Corel Draw window to a different position on-screen.

Rulers

You can display rulers on-screen by selecting Show Rulers in the Display menu. When rulers are displayed, you can use them to align elements in your drawings and measure distances. If you drag the alignment aid icon, located at the top left where the rulers intersect, you can change the zero point of the rulers. The zero points are defaulted to line up with the page dimensions of the page size you select.

Menu Bar

The menu bar displays the names of the nine pull-down menus. When you click on a menu name, a list of commands or effects is displayed. Figure 2.8 shows eight of the menus as they appear when they are selected. The ninth menu is the Help menu located at the far right on the menu bar.

Figure 2.8. Some of the Corel Draw drop-down menus.

Tool Box

The tool box provides the basic tools for drawing and filling objects in your projects. Table 2.1 lists the tools provided, beginning at the top.

Table 2.1. The tool box tools.

Tool	Used For
Pick tool (▸)	Selecting and transforming objects
Shape tool (⸝)	Node-editing and shaping objects

continues

Table 2.1. continued

Tool	Used For
Zoom tool (🔍)	Changing the viewing window
Pencil tool (✏)	Drawing lines and curves, Power Lines, and dimension lines
Rectangle tool (□)	Drawing rectangles and squares
Ellipse tool (○)	Drawing ellipses and circles
Text tool (𝔸)	Adding text and symbols
Outline tool (♀)	Setting outline attributes
Fill tool (✍)	Setting fill attributes

Printable Page

The printable page is the area defined by the page border. The page border can be turned on or off in the Page Setup dialog box accessed through the Layout menu. Even if you turn off the page border, your drawings will print only within the page dimensions that you set in the Page Setup dialog box.

Window Border

By dragging this border, you can resize the Corel Draw window. This is useful if you are running more than one program at a time.

Page Counter

The page counter displays the number of the page you are working on if your project consists of multiple pages.

Color Palette

Use the color palette to select fill and outline colors for objects. To permanently display it at the bottom of the screen, select Show Color Palette from the Display menu.

Scroll Bars

The scroll bars allow you to move the image view you are working on up or down and left or right. This feature comes in handy when you are zoomed in.

Basic Mouse Techniques

Using a mouse or pen in Corel Draw is mandatory for creating objects in your projects. Certain functions can be done with the keyboard described in "Basic Keyboard Techniques."

A standard two-button mouse has left (primary) and right (secondary) buttons. The primary and secondary buttons can be reversed by changing the setting in the Windows Control Panel. The primary button is used for almost everything you will do. The secondary button is used for changing the color of an object's outline or to leave an original behind when moving an object. The secondary mouse button can also be assigned a special function command by clicking on the Mouse button in the Preferences dialog box accessed through the Special menu. For example, you might want to assign Edit Text to the right mouse button if you will be using a lot of text in your projects.

The mouse can be used for everything except typing text in dialog boxes. Use the mouse to draw, to scroll up or down in parameters boxes to change a number value, to select colors from the color palette, and so on.

Basic Keyboard Techniques

The keyboard in Corel Draw is primarily used for typing text on the screen and typing names and numbers in dialog and parameter boxes. Many users may take exception to this statement. These are the users who prefer to use the many shortcut key commands available in Corel Draw (see Part V, "Command References").

The numbers of shortcut key commands are so many that the average user will learn a few special ones for his or her style of working.

For example, a few favorite keyboard shortcuts are:

- Pressing the spacebar to toggle between the last two tools used in the tool box.

- Tabbing with the Tab key to select objects on the screen.
- Using Ctrl-Q to convert text to curves.
- And of course, using the favorite Delete key to remove objects.

Exiting Corel Draw

To exit the Corel Draw program, select Exit from the File menu. Or press Alt-F4 if you want to use the shortcut method.

If you've forgotten to save your work, a message appears asking if you want to save your work. If you select Yes, a dialog box will appear allowing you to name your file, if you haven't already done so. If the file has a name the file will be saved when you choose Yes. If you choose No, Corel Draw will exit, and any changes you have made to a new or existing file will be lost.

Basic Skills Workshop

Using Menus and Dialog Boxes

The menus in Corel Draw are comprised of eight separate menus plus the Help menu. When you click on a menu heading, a drop-down list of commands appears. Each command can be selected either by clicking on the command or by using the keyboard.

To use the keyboard technique, press the underlined letter of the command. This method is a variation of the shortcut key technique. The full shortcut method involves activating the command without using the menus. For example, press the Alt key, then press L, and then P to accesses the Page Set-Up dialog box. To learn all the shortcut keys refer to Part V, "Command References."

You can also choose options in dialog boxes with either the mouse or the keyboard. Choosing with the mouse is usually a matter of clicking an item in a list or scrolling in a list box to locate an item to click. If the option is executable, you can double-click the option instead of taking the extra step of clicking OK to speed things up. For example, you can double-click a file name in the Open dialog box found in the File menu.

You can maneuver around in dialog boxes from the keyboard by using the Tab key to go from one section to another within the dialog box. You will also use the letter, number, and arrow keys.

Changing Dialog Box Settings with the Keyboard

Figure 3.1 shows the Grid Set-Up dialog box. In order to change settings in this dialog box, you would do the following after you have highlighted each selection using the Tab key:

1. Set for Global Units: Press the letter G to add or remove the check for the check box (always look for the underlined letter in check-box situations).

   When the number is highlighted in the left parameters box, type in the desired number.

   When Inches is highlighted in either of the next two parameters boxes, use the ↓ key to change the selection. When you've made a selection, press the Tab key again to make the selection permanent. (You can change these parameters only when Set for Global Units is checked.)

2. Grid Frequency: Type the desired numbers in both the Horizontal and Vertical parameters boxes.

   When Inches is highlighted in the Horizontal or Vertical parameters boxes, use the ↓ to make a selection and press the Tab key again to make the selection permanent. (You can change this setting only when Set for Global Units is not checked.)

3. Grid Origin: Type the desired numbers when the parameters boxes are highlighted.

4. Show Grid: When Show Grid is highlighted type the underlined S in **S**how to add or remove a check mark from the box.

5. Snap to Grid: When Snap to Grid is highlighted, type the Underlined letter N in **Sn**ap to add or remove a check mark from the box.

6. When either the OK or Cancel button is highlighted, press Enter.

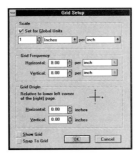

Figure 3.1. The Grid Setup dialog box.

The Windows Control Menu

The Windows Control menu is accessed by clicking on the icon in the top left of the title bar above the File menu. To access it from the keyboard, hold down the Alt key and press the spacebar (see Figure 3.2).

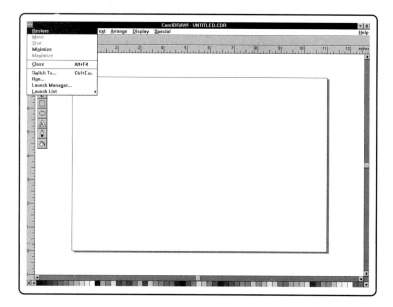

Figure 3.2. The Windows Control menu.

When you click Switch To, the Task List pops up (see Figure 3.3). Here you have several more choices. If you want to switch to another active Windows application, select that application and click the Switch To button.

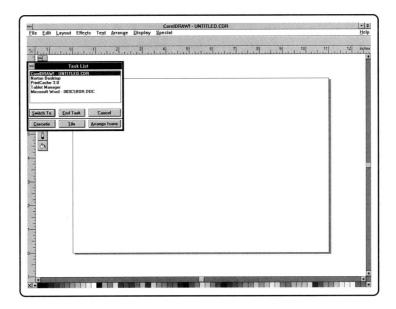

Figure 3.3. The Task List dialog box.

Basic Skills Workshop

The Pick Tool

The Pick (⬚) tool is the first tool in Corel Draw's toolbox. It is also the most versatile tool in the toolbox. Choose the ⬚ tool by either pressing the spacebar (except when in text editing mode) or by clicking on it in the toolbox.

Selecting Objects

The Pick tool is primarily used for selecting objects. The easiest way to select an object is to click once on its outline with the ⬚ tool.

Corel *NOTE!*

When in preview mode, you can also select filled objects by clicking anywhere inside the object.

You will see a set of eight squares surrounding the object's perimeter. These are called the *object handles.* An example is shown in Figure 4.1. Notice that the status bar changes to show that an object has been selected. The status line indicates what type of object is currently selected, where it is located, the fill color, the outline width, and the outline color.

To select multiple objects, hold down the Shift key while you click on additional objects. When you select multiple objects, the status line indicates how many objects are selected, and the object handles surround the perimeter of all objects selected, as shown in Figure 4.2. Click a second time on a selected object while continuing to hold down the Shift key to deselect the object.

Another way to select multiple objects (or even a single object) is by *marquee selection.* Use the ⬚ tool to draw a box around all objects you want to include in the selection group. As you draw the box, a blue, dotted line is shown on-screen (see Figure 4.3). If you select more objects than you want, use the Shift key in conjunction with the ⬚ tool to deselect those objects.

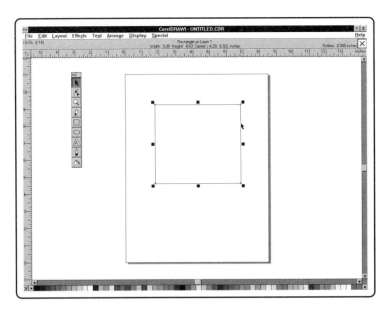

Figure 4.1. Object handles surrounding a selected rectangle.

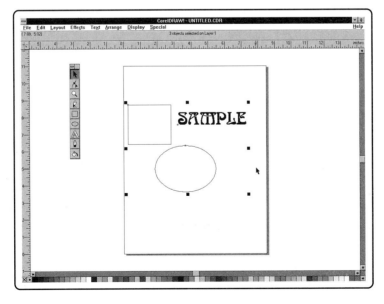

Figure 4.2. Selecting multiple objects.

Basic Skills Workshop

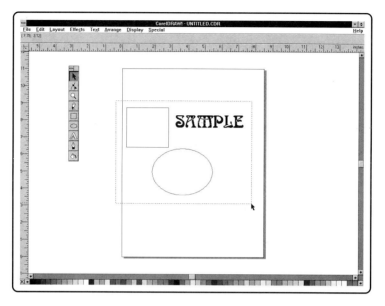

Figure 4.3. Marquee selection using the Pick tool.

Corel*NOTE!*

Using marquee selection is a great way to select objects that may be hidden behind other objects.

In previous versions of Corel Draw, once an object is grouped with other objects, it is impossible to work with that object unless the group is first ungrouped. Corel Draw 4 allows you to select objects within groups by holding down the Ctrl key and clicking on the object. The status line then indicates that a child object has been selected, and the object handles will be round instead of square (see Figure 4.4). This method works with groups and extrude groups (see Skill Session 21), but not blend groups (see Skill Session 19) or contour groups (see Skill Session 53). Those groups must first be separated, and then this new method will work.

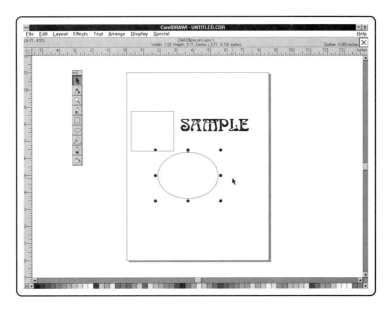

Figure 4.4. Selecting objects within a group.

The Tab key can be extremely useful for finding objects. Each time you press Tab, the current selection moves forward one object in the drawing. Press Shift-Tab to move backward one object. To deselect all objects, press Esc or click in a blank part of the drawing window.

Manipulating Objects

Once you have selected an object or objects, you can use the Pick tool to manipulate them. Probably the most important use is to move objects into different positions. Select the object(s), click on them with the ▸ tool, and drag them to the new position. The objects may jump to the grid or guidelines depending on what you specified in the Layout menu. For more accurate positioning, it is usually best to place a guideline exactly where you want the object to go. Press the numeric keypad + (plus) key or click the secondary mouse button to make a copy of the selected object(s). Another way to quickly duplicate an object is to press Ctrl-D (for *duplicate*). This places an identical object behind the original object, offset by the amount you specified in Preferences.

Corel*NOTE!*

Due to a bug in Corel Draw, clicking on the secondary mouse button does not work with certain tablets.

When moving the object by dragging isn't accurate enough, the arrow keys can come in quite handy. Use the ←, →, ↑, and ↓ keys to move the object in the indicated direction precisely the amount set as the nudge factor in the Preferences dialog box. The default setting is .1 inch, although you might want to set this to .01 inch for smaller nudges.

Distorting Objects

While an object is selected, you can distort it by manipulating the object handles. As the Pick tool moves over an object handle, it changes to a +|- cursor, as shown in Figure 4.5. With the +|- cursor, the object can be distorted simply by clicking and dragging until the object is the desired size and shape. Each of the corner handles allows the object to be scaled both horizontally and vertically while the top, bottom, and side handles allow changes in only one direction. Several examples of these changes are shown in Figure 4.6.

Hold down Ctrl while stretching and scaling to constrain movement to 100-percent increments. This constraint is also a great way to horizontally or vertically mirror an object—drag a center handle across the object in the direction that the object is to be mirrored. Hold the Shift key to stretch and scale from the center point out; hold Shift and Ctrl to invoke both constraints at once. Figure 4.7 contains examples of each type of constraint.

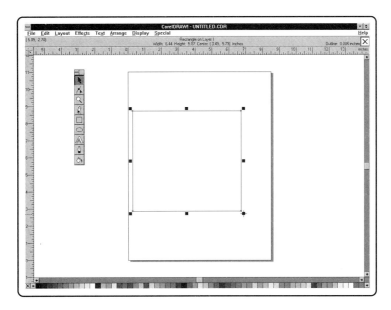

Figure 4.5. Grabbing an object handle with the crosshair cursor.

Rotating and Skewing Objects

Click a second time on the object's outline (or its fill if you are in Preview mode) to bring up the rotate and skew handles. The four corner handles change to arced double-headed arrows and the center handles change to double-headed arrows, as shown in Figure 4.8. At the center of the object, there is a circle surrounding a point representing the center of rotation. You can move this point freely by clicking on it and dragging it to the location you want. If you hold down the constrain key (Ctrl), it will snap to any of the eight handles or the true center of the object.

29

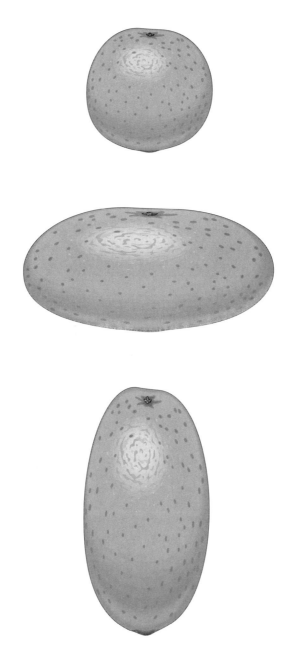

Figure 4.6. Sizing and shaping an object with the Pick tool.

Figure 4.7. Stretching and scaling with constraints.

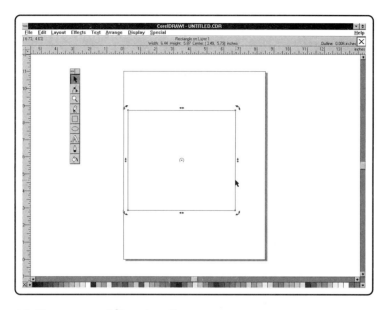

Figure 4.8. The rotate and skew handles.

Drag a corner handle to rotate the selected object freely around the center of rotation. Hold down the Ctrl key while rotating to constrain the rotation to the amount set in Preferences. This amount defaults to 15 degrees. While the object rotates, a dotted outline represents where the object will redraw when you release the mouse button. The status line always displays the amount of rotation that has been applied. An example is shown in Figure 4.9.

Click on a center handle of a selected object to skew the object in the directions that the two arrows point. The Ctrl key also limits the skewing angle to what is set in Preferences. The status line displays the amount of skew that has been applied, and a dotted outline represents the new shape. Figure 4.10 provides an example of skewing. For more information about rotating and skewing, see Skill Session 16.

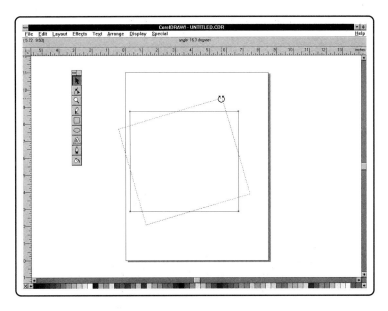

Figure 4.9. Rotating an object.

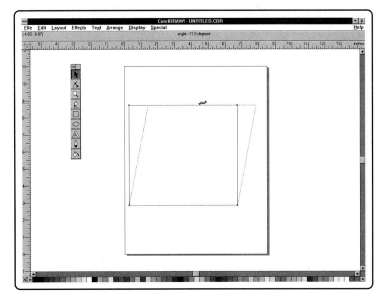

Figure 4.10. Skewing an object.

The Object Menu

The Pick tool can also be used to pop up the Object menu by clicking on an object with the secondary mouse button. Use the Object menu to define styles or apply them to an object. It also allows the creation of the object database, so that other information can be attached to an object. For more information about the Object menu, see Skill Session 52.

Basic Skills Workshop

The
Shape Tool

Selecting Nodes

The Shape (⋏) tool is perhaps the most useful tool in Corel Draw because of the many things that it does. It seems to act with each type of object differently, and, used in conjunction with the Ctrl and Shift keys, it can do even more.

To choose the Shape tool, click once on its icon (the second one down in the toolbox) or press F10. Next, select the object you wish to modify, just as with the Pick tool. Notice that each of the object's nodes has changed into an enlarged round or square point (as shown in Figure 5.1). The status bar reports how many nodes exist on the selected path.

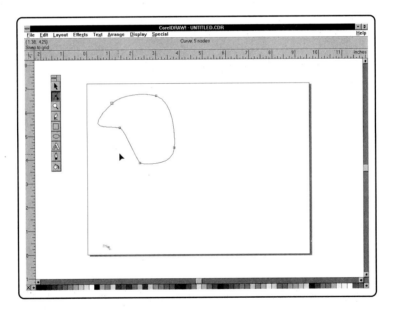

Figure 5.1. Selecting an object with the Shape tool.

To highlight the individual nodes, click on them with the ⋏ tool. The highlighted node will be filled if it belongs to a linear segment or hollow if it belongs to a Bézier curve segment. For nodes on a Bézier curve, the status bar indicates whether the node is a cusp, smooth, or symmetrical node, and two Bézier control points protrude from the node. Figure 5.2 shows an example of linear, cusp, smooth, and symmetrical nodes and their associated Bézier control handles.

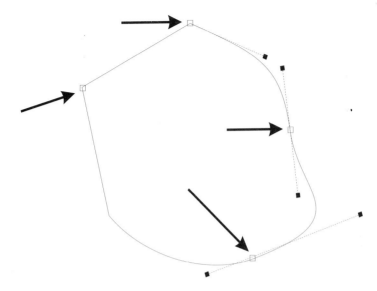

Figure 5.2. A selected object showing linear, cusp, smooth, and symetrical nodes.

Corel*NOTE!*

> There are times when a Bézier control handle is hidden by the node
> itself. In order to adjust that handle, deselect all nodes, hold down the
> Shift key and drag the Bézier control handle.

To select multiple nodes, press and hold down Shift while clicking on the
nodes to be selected. Click on a previously selected node to deselect it.
To marquee-select multiple nodes, drag an imaginary rectangle around
all the nodes to be selected. Always check the status bar to see whether
you've selected the appropriate number of nodes, as it reports the
current number of nodes selected.

For an example of exactly how nodes work, try the following steps:

1. Choose the rectangle tool and draw a rectangle that fills most of the
   page similar to the one shown in Figure 5.3.

2. Convert it to curves by choosing Convert To Curves in the Arrange menu or pressing Ctrl-Q.

3. The status bar should now read "Curve: 4 nodes."

4. Click on each of the four nodes and watch the status bar. The node in the corner where the rectangle originated will say "First node of a closed curve," while the other nodes will say "Selected node: Line Cusp."

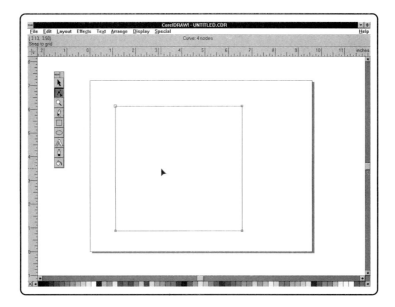

Figure 5.3. A simple example for understanding nodes.

Node Edit Roll-Up

To bring up the Node Edit roll-up, double-click on any selected node. Figure 5.4 shows the rectangle object with a node selected and the Node Edit roll-up active.

Not all the functions in the Node Edit roll-up are currently active. Click on Add (+) to add a node to the rectangle. Click on Delete (−) to change the rectangle to a triangle. Click on Break to break the curve at the currently selected node. Examples of all three are shown in Figure 5.5. The Bézier control handles have been moved slightly so that they are visible in the figure. They actually sit right on the line.

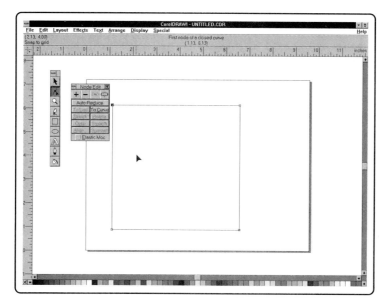

Figure 5.4. The Node Edit roll-up.

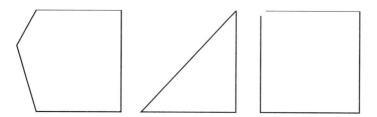

Figure 5.5. Using Add, Delete, and Break.

For this example, the Auto-Reduce button has no effect because there is no way to reduce the number of nodes making up the rectangle. The To Curve button changes the currently selected segment to a curve, and Bézier control handles appear, as shown in Figure 5.6. Again, the Bézier control handles have been moved slightly for clarity.

Basic Skills Workshop

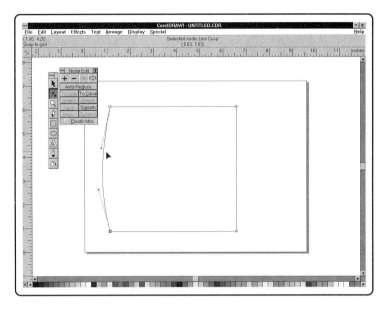

Figure 5.6. Using To Curve.

Notice that the node type is cusp. This means that the Bézier handle can be moved anywhere, and the Smooth button is now available. Choose Smooth to automatically move the Bézier handle so that it is collinear to the adjoining straight segment. You can move the handle back and forth along that line segment, but you cannot rotate it (see Figure 5.7).

Select all the nodes of the rectangle by dragging a marquee box around all four nodes. Click on the To Curve button, and all of the line segments become curves instead of lines. Each of the nodes is still a cusp, but by clicking on just one node and selecting Smooth, notice that the Bézier handles align with one another. Moving the handles in and out has no effect on the opposite handle, but rotating one handle also rotates the opposite handle. Now click on Symmet to change that same node to a symmetrical node, and try the same procedure. Moving one Bézier handle will have the exact same effect on the opposite Bézier handle.

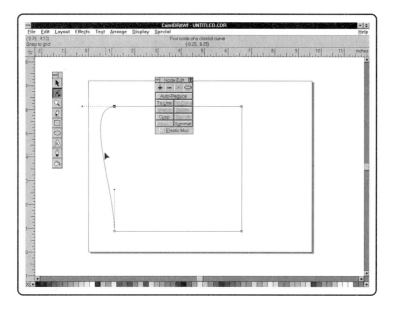

Figure 5.7. Using Smooth.

Repeat the above process, but this time start with an ellipse. Be sure to convert the ellipse to curves; otherwise the Shape tool will create a totally different effect (see "Shaping Rectangles and Ellipses," later in this Skill Session). Notice that different parts of the Node Edit roll-up are highlighted and that each of the nodes begins as a symmetrical node instead of a cusp node.

Draw another circle, but this time use the ℓ tool. Figure 5.8 shows a circle drawn with the mouse using the Pencil tool. Notice that the edges are very rough and the status bar indicates 26 nodes. This is due mostly to the difficulty of drawing precisely with a mouse and partly to the fact that, for demonstration purposes, freehand curve tracking is set to 1, producing the large number of nodes.

Select all the nodes on the hand-drawn circle by marquee-selecting them. Double-click on a node if the Node Edit roll-up is not already active.

Basic Skills Workshop

Click on the Auto-Reduce button; many of the extraneous nodes should go away without affecting the shape of the circle. By adjusting Curves Auto-Reduce in the Preferences dialog box, you can change the distance between deleted nodes. Figure 5.9 shows the same circle after using Auto-Reduce. Notice that there are now seven nodes instead of 26.

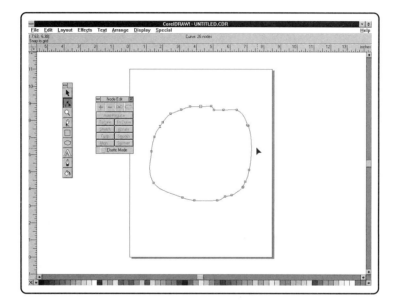

Figure 5.8. A circle drawn with the Pencil tool.

Corel*NOTE!*

Auto-Reduce is not active unless the Shape tool is selected.

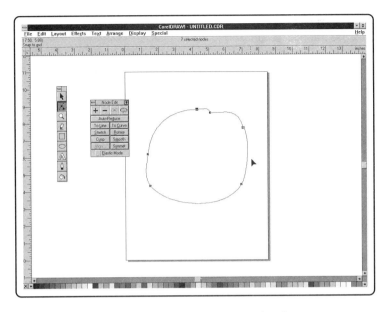

Figure 5.9. Using Auto-Reduce to reduce the number of nodes.

Adding and Deleting Nodes

To add a node, double-click where you want the new node and click on the Add (+) button in the Node Edit roll-up.

Corel *TIP!*

Here's another way to add nodes: Select an existing node. Click on the Add button, and a node is added exactly halfway between the selected node and the next node on the path. To tell which segment is considered the highlighted segment (and thus the one where the new node will be added), press Shift-Tab and the selected node moves to the next node on the path. Tab back to the previously selected node and then press Add.

Corel *NOTE!*

Node ordering seems to be the reverse of object ordering, in that Shift-Tab goes to the next node and Tab goes to the previous node. The previous node is not necessarily any particular direction from the current node. The node ordering is dependent on the direction in which the object was drawn and can seem to make no sense whatsoever (although after a while some of it will make sense).

If you select more than one node, new nodes appear in the middle of each node's segment. A great example of this is to make an octagon from a circle (see Figure 5.10).

1. Create a circle using the ⬭ tool. Hold down Ctrl to constrain it to a perfect circle.
2. Convert the circle to curves by using Arrange Convert To Curves.
3. Switch to the ⟋ tool and select all the nodes by marquee selection.
4. Double-click one of the nodes, and the Node Edit roll-up appears if it hasn't already.
5. Click the Add button. The circle now contains eight equidistant nodes.
6. Again select all the nodes. Click To Line in the Node Edit roll-up. The object should be a perfect octagon.

Earlier we described the Auto-Reduce function as one way to delete nodes. Another way is to select the nodes to be deleted and either click on the Delete (−) button or press Delete on the keyboard. This provides control over which nodes are deleted. The best way is to delete most nodes using the Auto-Reduce function and then selectively delete other extraneous nodes using the Delete function.

Shaping Curves

The Shape tool's most beneficial feature is the capability to shape curves until you create just the right effect. You can do this two different ways:

- Physically move nodes to different locations.
- Adjust the Bézier handles to alter the curvature entering and leaving that node.

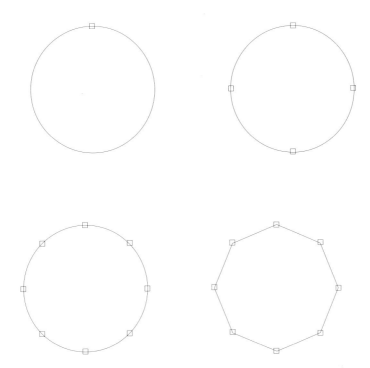

Figure 5.10. Converting a circle to an octagon by adding nodes.

You can move nodes individually or in groups. Much like a dining room table can be expanded by putting in extra leaves, an object can be stretched by choosing all the nodes on one end and pulling them away from the other end. This method does not distort curves the way that stretching the whole object does. Figure 5.11 shows the same object stretched using these two different methods. Note that using the Ctrl key while moving nodes will constrain movement to either horizontal or vertical.

Corel Draw 4 includes the extra benefit of elasticity. When you choose this feature (by checking the box labeled Elastic Mode), all nodes selected do not necessarily move a uniform distance and angle. They move a relative distance. Figure 5.12 shows the same stretch as Figure 5.11, but this time using Elastic Mode.

Figure 5.11. Stretching with the Pick tool versus the Shape tool.

Figure 5.12. Stretching with Elastic Mode turned on.

Nodes can be aligned by selecting two nodes and clicking on the Align button in the Node Edit roll-up. Figure 5.13 shows the Node Align dialog box that appears when you click on the Align button.

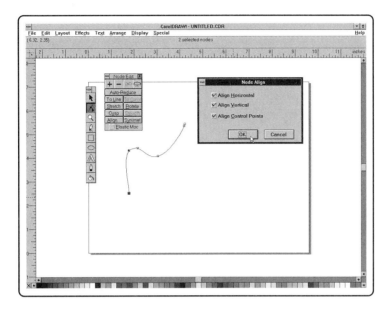

Figure 5.13. The Node Align dialog box.

You have three options in this dialog box: Align Horizontal, Align Vertical, and Align Control Points.

- Choose horizontal only to align the nodes to each other on a horizontal path from the first node chosen.
- Choose vertical only to align the nodes on a vertical path from the first node chosen.
- Choose both horizontal and vertical to place the second node selected on top of the first node (the line between them may stick out).
- Choose horizontal, vertical, and control points to align the Bézier control handles with the first node selected.

Examples of each of these are shown in Figure 5.14.

You can create other interesting effects by stretching a group of nodes. Figure 5.15 shows a word that has been converted to curves and that same word distorted using the node stretching technique. This is a great way to give a logo added interest.

Basic Skills Workshop

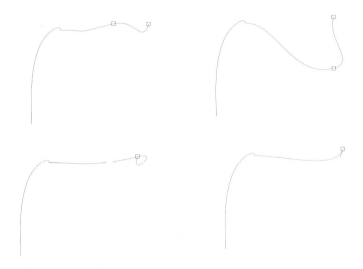

Figure 5.14. The effects of the Align Node dialog box options.

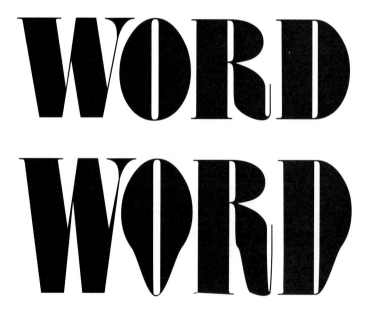

Figiure 5.15. Distorting text by stretching groups of nodes.

Shaping Rectangles and Ellipses

By using the Shape tool with rectangles and ellipses, you produce drastically different results than with those same objects after having been converted to curves. In all previous examples we specified that these objects must first be converted to curves. In this section, the objects will be modified first.

Create a rectangle by dragging out an area with the □ tool. Switch to the ⚲ tool and click on the node in the upper left corner. Drag this node towards the right and notice that the corners of the rectangle are now rounded. The status bar shows the corner radius of each corner. Note that this radius is distorted (as indicated in the status line) if the original rectangle is tranformed in any way. To avoid this, the rectangle must be completely redrawn in the desired shape. Figure 5.16 shows four examples: a rectangle, the rectangle after having the corners rounded, the rectangle stretched before the corners were rounded, and a rectangle that was redrawn to the same size and then had its corners rounded.

Depending on where you move the node, using the Shape tool on an ellipse can create either arcs or wedges . Each ellipse has just one node. It is found at the top for ellipses drawn from the top down and at the bottom for those drawn from the bottom up.

Draw an ellipse with the ○ tool and switch to the ⚲ tool. Select the ellipse with the ⚲ tool and then click on its node. Drag the node around the circle on the outside, and the ellipse changes to an arc. Drag the node on the inside of the ellipse, and the ellipse changes to a pie wedge. Hold down the Ctrl key while dragging the node to constrain the node to angles that are a multiple of the constrain angle set in Preferences. Figure 5.17 gives an example of an ellipse before making any changes, after creating an arc, and after creating a pie.

Basic Skills Workshop

Figure 5.16. The effects of stretching and rounding a rectangle with the Shape tool.

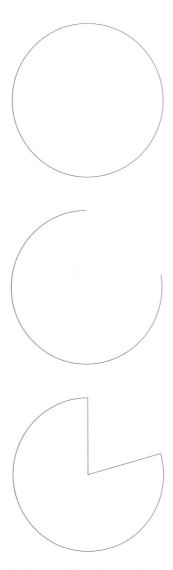

Figure 5.17. Using the Shape tool on an ellipse to create arcs and wedges.

Shaping Envelopes

The process of shaping envelopes (see Skill Session 22) is very similar to shaping other polygonal objects. Nodes can be moved by clicking and dragging them (like any other node). For any of the first three envelope types (line, single curve, and double curve) the Ctrl and Shift keys constrain the node you are moving:

- Hold down the Ctrl key to move both the selected node and the opposite node in the same direction.
- Hold down the Shift key to move the opposite node in the opposite direction, but the same distance from the start point.
- Hold down both Ctrl and Shift to move either all four center nodes the same amount or all four corner nodes the same amount in opposite directions.

Figure 5.18 shows a rectangle that has been modified first with just the node movement, with Ctrl and node movement, with Shift and node movement, and with Shift-Ctrl and node movement.

Cropping Bitmaps

You can use the Shape tool with a bitmap to crop the bitmap. This should be used carefully because the bitmap still takes up the same amount of space on disk. Sometimes the best method is to just rescan the bitmap until it is the correct size for the space.

Manually Kerning Text

You can kern text manually using the Shape tool. Enter a word of text and switch to the ⋏ tool. Select the object, and nodes will appear to the left of each character in the string. These nodes can be dragged in any direction; the character will follow. To select more than one character, hold down the Shift key while clicking on additional nodes or draw a marquee box around all desired nodes.

It is usually a good idea to hold down the Ctrl key while dragging character nodes as it will constrain all movement to the baseline. Another option is to use the Align to Baseline command in the Text menu after kerning the text as this removes any vertical shifts that occur. The Ctrl key constraint applies even to text that has been fit to a path.

Figure 5.18. Using Shift and Ctrl to constrain node movement.

You can also adjust text spacing by using the Shape tool in conjunction with ⫽ and ≑. Click and move ⫽ to adjust the spacing between characters; hold down Ctrl to adjust the word spacing. Use ≑ to adjust the line spacing for Artistic text. Used in conjunction with the Shift key, the line spacing adjustment applies to paragraph text. Ctrl-≑ adjusts the space between paragraphs.

Editing Character Attributes

When a character's node is selected, its attributes can be changed as if it were a separate object. Click on a color in the color palette with the primary mouse button to change the character's color. Use the right mouse button to change its outline color. Double-click on the node to bring up the Character Attribute dialog box (see Skill Session 29).

Basic Skills Workshop

The Zoom Tool

By using the Zoom (🔍) tool in conjunction with the scroll bars, you have the ability to look at a drawing in almost any view imaginable. You can zoom many ways—the Zoom tool actually has five different variants. You can zoom the screen in as tight as approximately 1/2 inch by 1/2 inch on the rulers. You can zoom out to show as much as 30 inches by 48 inches. (These numbers are approximate and may vary slightly from system to system.)

Zoom In

The Zoom In tool (🔍) is used similarly to marquee selection with the Pick tool. When you click the Zoom tool, a fly-out menu appears. The first button on the fly-out menu is the Zoom In tool. Click this tool and the cursor changes to a magnifying glass. Drag a marquee rectangle around the area to be zoomed and the screen is redrawn showing just the marqueed area. Figure 6.1 shows the screen before the zoom occurred. Figure 6.2 shows the marquee rectangle being drawn around the objects. Figure 6.3 shows the screen after the zoom occurred.

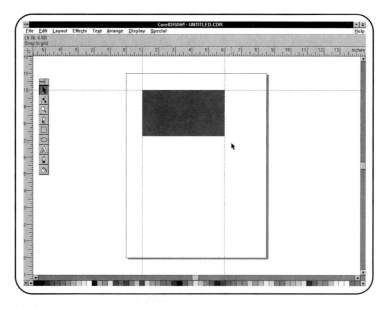

Figure 6.1. An unzoomed view.

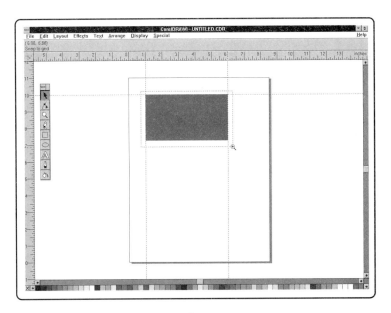

Figure 6.2. Marqueeing the area to zoom in on.

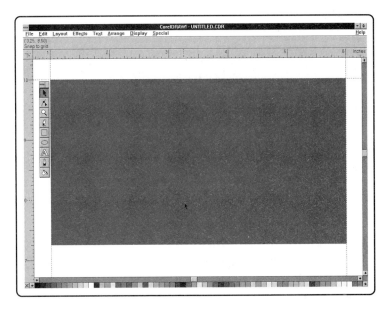

Figure 6.3. The zoomed view.

Zoom Out

The Zoom Out (🔍) tool returns the screen to the view before the last Zoom In. If you used one of the other Zoom tools, it zooms out to show twice the area previously showing.

Zoom Actual Size

Zoom Actual Size attempts to zoom so that the objects on-screen are exactly the same size as their size shown in the status bar. Corel Draw does this by attempting to guess the resolution (in dots per inch) of the display on which it is being run. You can't count on this because the same VGA screen resolution (640 by 480) could be on a laptop with an eight-inch screen or a large, 21-inch monitor. Therefore, you shouldn't use this particular zoom level for accurate measurement. Use the rulers instead. Figure 6.4 shows the same objects as Figure 6.1 after Zoom Actual Size was chosen. The rectangle measures six inches by the rulers, but on the monitor it measured nine inches.

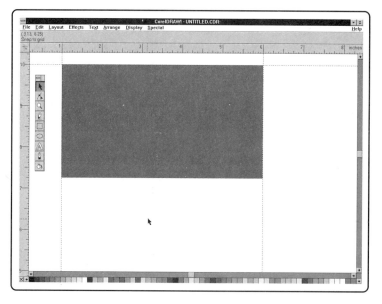

Figure 6.4. Using Zoom Actual Size.

Zoom All Objects

Zoom All Objects ( ) zooms to show every object in the drawing. This can achieve the same effect as using the Zoom In tool when there are just several small objects to be enlarged. It can also be very handy for finding objects that have disappeared from view either because the screen is zoomed in very tight or the objects are off the page. The Zoom All Objects tool does not necessarily Zoom In or Zoom Out; it always changes the view to fit all the objects in one screen. Figure 6.5 shows the effect of the Zoom All Objects when there are several objects outside the defined page size.

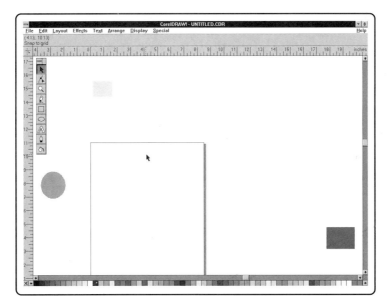

Figure 6.5. Using Zoom All Objects.

Zoom Full Page

Zoom Full Page ( ) zooms so that the defined page fills the whole screen. Again this is not any exact size, but rather the page size as defined in Page Setup. If you display the Page Frame, you will find this concept a little easier to understand. Figure 6.6 shows a screen that has several objects displayed in the middle of a page. After you choose Zoom Full Page, the screen will look like Figure 6.7.

Basic Skills Workshop

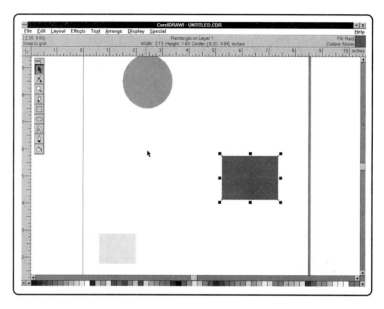

Figure 6.6. Before using Zoom Full Page.

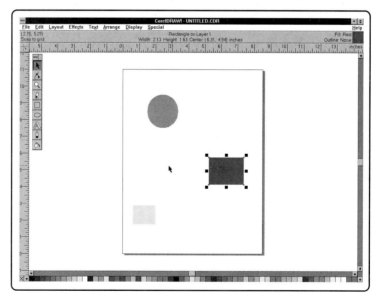

Figure 6.7. After using Zoom Full Page.

Basic Skills Workshop

The Pencil Tool

Basic Skills Workshop

The Pencil tool (ℓ) is actually five tools in one. It can be used to draw freehand curves using two different methods and three different types of dimension lines. You can select each of these methods from the fly-out menu that appears when you press and hold down the primary mouse button while selecting the ℓ tool as shown in Figure 7.1. Then select any of the five tools by dragging the cursor to the desired tool and releasing the mouse button.

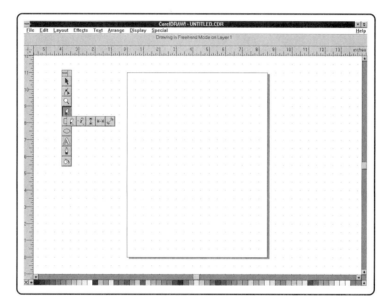

Figure 7.1. The Pencil tool fly-out menu

The tool on the far left of the fly-out is the Freehand Pencil tool. When it is selected, the status bar indicates "Drawing in Freehand Mode on Layer *x*." By holding down the primary mouse button and dragging the mouse in various directions, you create a line that follows the path of the mouse. As soon as you release the mouse button, the line ends. The number of nodes on the new line is related to the accuracy specified in the Curves section of the Preferences dialog box. Figure 7.2 shows a line drawn with the Pencil tool in Freehand mode.

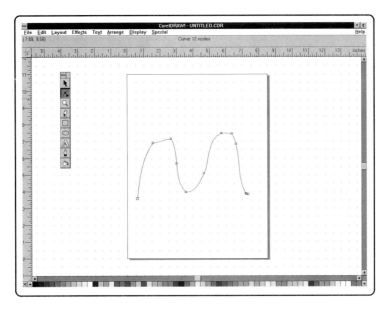

Figure 7.2. A line drawn with the Pencil tool in freehand mode.

You can draw straight lines by clicking the primary mouse button on the starting point of the line and then clicking again on the endpoint of the line. Hold down the Ctrl key while drawing a straight line, to constrain it to the angle set in Preferences. Figure 7.3 shows two straight lines, one of which was constrained by holding the Ctrl key.

The Pencil tool is also used for auto-tracing bitmaps. If a bitmap is selected when the Pencil tool is chosen, the Pencil tool will be used as an autotrace tool. For more information about using this method and others to autotrace bitmaps, see Skill Session 39.

Bézier Tool

The second tool of the fly-out is the Bézier ( ) tool. Bézier mode allows the creation of lines by connecting the dots. Since this gives complete control over where the nodes are placed, the lines tend to be less complex and more accurate. By holding down the primary mouse button when the node is placed, Bézier control handles will appear so that the curve can be shaped as well. Figure 7.4 shows a curve being created with the Bézier tool.

Basic Skills Workshop

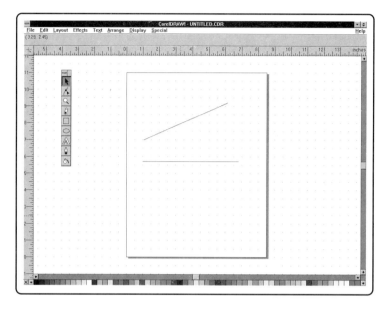

Figure 7.3. A straight line and a constrained straight line.

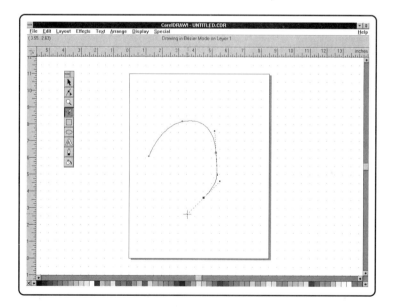

Figure 7.4. Creating a curve with the Bézier tool.

Dimension Lines

Dimension lines are new to Corel Draw 4. They allow you to assign various types of measurements to objects. This comes in very handy for CAD-like drawings that need to show sizes of objects. Three types of dimension lines are provided for drawing horizontal, vertical, and diagonal lines. The main difference between dimension lines and regular lines is that each end of the dimension line has a tic mark to indicate the endpoints, and in the middle of the line is the measurement of the line itself. Figure 7.5 shows a sample drawing with vertical and horizontal dimension lines.

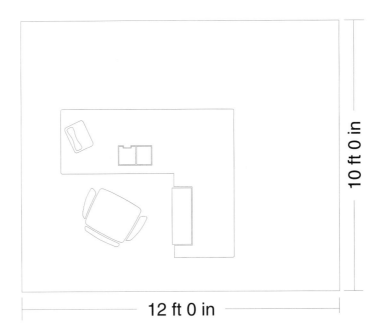

Figure 7.5. Sample drawing with corresponding dimension lines.

Corel NOTE!

For dimension lines to work properly, the rulers must be set for inches regardless of what measurement system is used for the dimension lines.

Basic Skills Workshop

Creating dimension lines is a three-step process. The first step is to click where the line begins, then click where the line ends, and finally click in the middle of the line. To measure an object accurately, use Snap To Objects to allow the dimension line to snap on the end nodes of the object being measured. The dimension measurement can be displayed in many different formats according to what is set in the Preferences dimension settings. For more information on choosing the dimension format, see Skill Session 60.

Dimension line text can be formatted just like any other text. Select the text by clicking on it, and the status bar indicates that control text is selected. Once it has been selected, it can be edited just like any other Artistic text.

Dimension lines are flawed in that the dimension is only measured the first time the line is drawn. If the line is adjusted to a different length, the dimension text will not change. So, when using dimension lines, be careful that they are the last items drawn. While this can be useful when a whole drawing is to be scaled to fit within a particular page size, it is extremely frustrating when the line has to be redrawn several times to get it to just the right size. The optimal method is to lock the dimensions once the lines are correct by placing them on a Dimension Layer.

Basic Skills Workshop

The Rectangle Tool

The Rectangle (□) tool is used to create rectangles, squares, rounded rectangles, and rounded squares. When you use it with the Ctrl and Shift keys, you can create many different effects.

Rectangles

Use the Rectangle tool in its standard configuration to draw rectangles of any size and shape by holding down the primary mouse button, dragging from one corner of the rectangle to the opposite corner, and then releasing the mouse button. The status bar indicates the height, width, and center location of the rectangle. Figure 8.1 shows a rectangle and the accompanying information on the status bar.

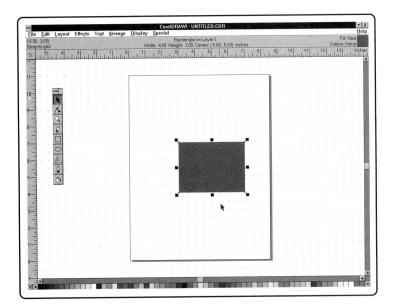

Figure 8.1. Drawing a rectangle.

While you can create squares using the standard Rectangle tool and watching the status bar closely, it is much easier to hold down the Ctrl key with the primary mouse button while dragging out the appropriate square. Be sure to release the mouse button first and then the Ctrl key. If you release the Ctrl key first, the Rectangle tool creates a standard rectangle instead. Figure 8.2 shows a square and the accompanying information on the status bar.

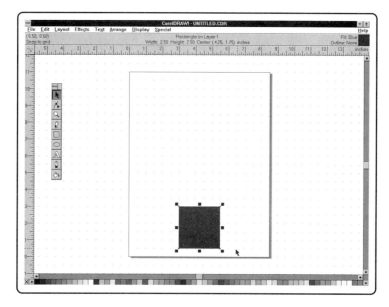

Figure 8.2. Drawing a square.

You can use the Rectangle tool in conjunction with the Shift key to produce yet another set of effects. The Shift key causes the rectangle or square to be drawn from the center out rather than from corner to corner. To test this, draw a rectangle while holding down the Shift key and drag in any direction. Note that the rectangle's center is exactly where the cursor was when the mouse button was first depressed, and the vertical and horizontal movements are symmetrical on each side of the center. Figures 8.3 and 8.4 were drawn in the exact same manner as Figures 8.1 and 8.2 except that the Shift key was held down.

Basic Skills Workshop

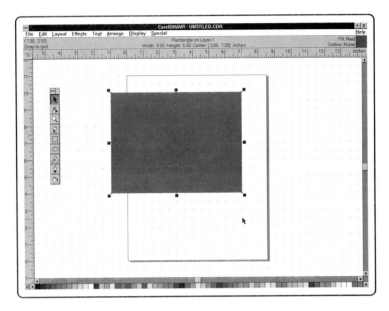

Figure 8.3. Drawing a rectangle from the center out.

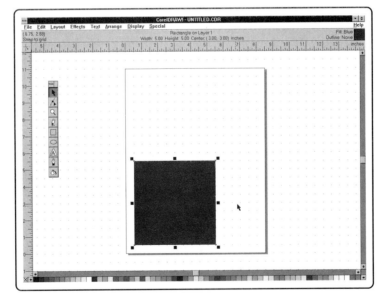

Figure 8.4. Drawing a square from the center out.

You can create rounded rectangles and squares by using the Shape tool in conjunction with a preexisting rectangle or square. This is covered in depth in Skill Session 5. Figure 8.5 shows an example of each of these shapes.

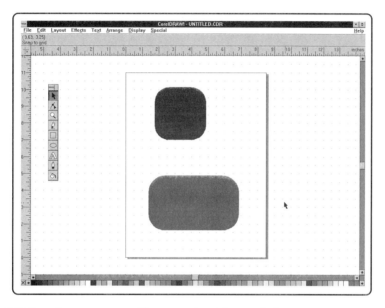

Figure 8.5. Drawing a square and a rectangle with rounded corners.

Exact Sizing and Placement

One of Corel Draw's deficiencies is that the exact sizes of rectangles and squares cannot be specified somewhere in a dialog. That means to create an object with exact sizing, you must carefully monitor the status bar to ensure that the sizes match what you want. Even so, those sizes may change by the time the mouse button is released. One way around this is the careful use of guidelines and a grid. The grid can be used for snapping either the rectangle itself or guidelines if the desired measurements will fall on the grid. As guidelines can also be placed at exact locations, they can be used for oddly shaped rectangles. Skill Sessions 26 and 27 describe how to use guidelines and grids in depth.

Basic Skills Workshop

Once you've drawn the rectangle in the correct shape, you can use the Move Absolute Coordinates command to put the new shape into the position you want (see Skill Session 18).

Basic Skills Workshop

The Ellipse Tool

You use the Ellipse (◯) tool to create ellipses, circles, arcs, and wedges. With a little ingenuity, the Ellipse tool is also very useful for creating many free-form shapes.

Corel *NOTE!*

Ellipses, circles, arcs, and wedges are all surrounded by an imaginary rectangle that is tangent to each of the extreme points.

To draw an ellipse, click on the ◯ tool and hold down the primary mouse button while dragging from one corner of the ellipse to the opposite corner. While you hold the mouse button down, the status bar indicates the height, width, starting point, current point, and center locations. After you release the mouse button, the status bar shows the height, width, and center location only. Figure 9.1 shows an ellipse being drawn and Figure 9.2 shows the ellipse after releasing the mouse button. Notice the changes in the status bar.

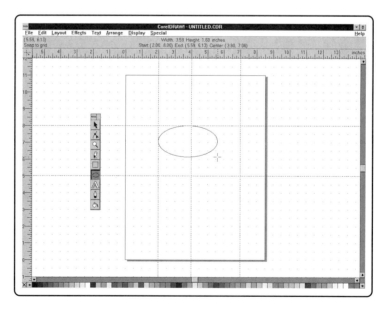

Figure 9.1. Drawing an ellipse.

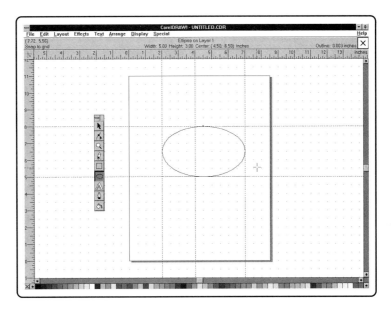

Figure 9.2. The completed ellipse. Note the status bar.

Just as with the Rectangle tool, you can constrain the Ellipse tool to fully symmetrical objects (that is, circles) by holding down the Ctrl key. Remember not to release the Ctrl key until after you release the mouse button, or the object may revert to an ellipse. Figure 9.3 shows a circle.

You can use the Shift key to draw both ellipses and circles from the center out rather than from corner to corner. To draw an ellipse from the center outward, hold down the Shift key while dragging the cursor from the center point outward in any direction. All movement in either the horizontal or vertical direction is mirrored on the other side of the center point. Release the mouse button and then the Shift key. For a circle, hold down both the Shift and Ctrl keys while dragging outward from the center point. Figure 9.4 shows an ellipse drawn with the same starting and ending points as Figure 9.2 and Figure 9.5 shows a circle drawn with the same starting and ending points as Figure 9.3. Notice the differences in drawing these objects with and without the use of the Shift key.

Basic Skills Workshop

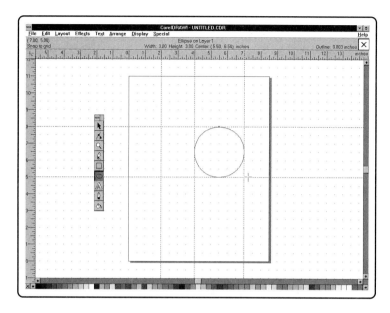

Figure 9.3. Drawing a circle.

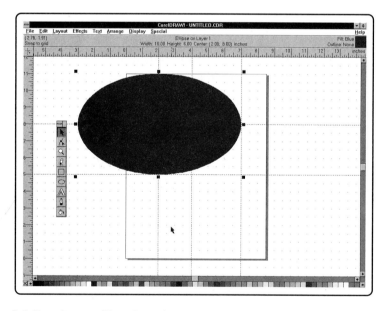

Figure 9.4. Drawing an ellipse from the center out.

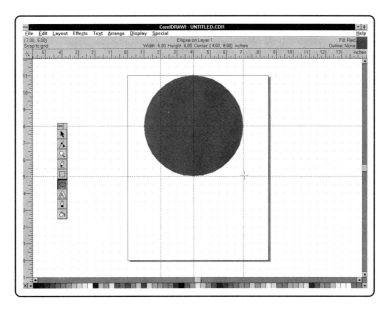

Figure 9.5. Drawing a circle from the center out.

You can create arcs and wedges from circles and ellipses by using the Shape tool. First draw the appropriate shape with the ○ tool; then switch to the ⋏ tool and adjust the node to get either an arc or a wedge. See Skill Session 5 for more information about how to create these shapes. Figure 9.6 shows an example of each.

You can also use the Ellipse tool to create objects of a more free-form nature. This creates much smoother objects than if they were drawn free-form with the Pencil tool. First draw an ellipse of an approximate size and shape. Then convert the ellipse to curves and switch to the ⋏ tool. Use the ⋏ tool to add and place nodes until the object is the correct shape.

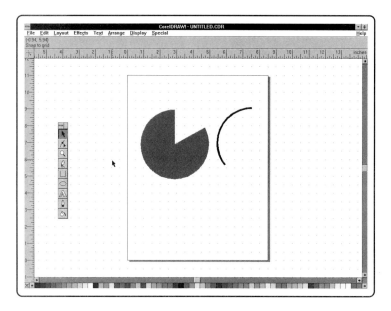

Figure 9.6. Drawing an arc and a wedge.

Exact Sizing and Placement

It is sometimes very important to know the exact radius and center of a circle. Since Corel Draw doesn't provide this capability directly, you must perform some tricks to achieve the same results. The best way to do this is with a good set of guidelines and a well-defined grid. The most accurate way to draw circles is from the center out, where the center point is either at the intersection of two guidelines or at a well-spaced grid point. Place a guideline at the correct radius and *voila!*—a perfectly sized and placed circle. Ellipses are much more difficult because there is no real way to know where the foci are located and what the radii are. If the circle or ellipse is drawn but not correctly located, use the Move Absolute Coordinates command to put the object at an exact position. This is described in Skill Session 18.

Basic Skills Workshop

The Text Tool

The Text ($\mathbb{A}$) tool, like some of the other tools, is actually three tools in one. It can be used to add Artistic text, Paragraph text, and symbols. Each of these has a different tool on the Text fly-out menu shown in Figure 10.1.

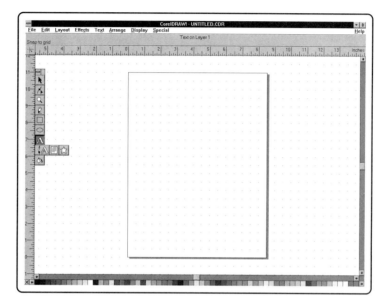

Figure 10.1. The Text tool fly-out menu.

Artistic Text

Artistic text is limited to text strings no longer that 250 characters. This allows the text to be manipulated like any other graphic object within Corel Draw, including Blends, Extrudes, and special text functions like Fit Text to Path. To add Artistic text to a drawing, choose the $\mathbb{A}$ tool and then click the cursor on the page where the new text string should begin. Once you've placed the cursor, just type the desired text right on the page. Note that by changing a setting in CORELDRW.INI, it is possible to have the Edit Text dialog box appear immediately (see Skill Session 61, "Understanding INI Files"). Once the text has been entered, the Edit Text dialog can be brought up by choosing Text Edit Text. Figure 10.2 shows the Edit Text dialog box.

Figure 10.2. The Edit Text dialog box.

The Edit Text dialog box allows you to set many of the basic text attributes, such as font, style, point size, justification, and spacing, through the Spacing dialog box. The point size can range from a miniscule .7 points to a humongous 2,160 points. Only existing styles are shown in the Style drop-down box, but some TrueType weights are not available because Corel Draw sees only Normal and Bold. Note that this does not affect any of the fonts which come packaged with Corel Draw. The spacing attributes are set through the Spacing dialog box shown in Figure 10.3.

With Artistic text, you can adjust only character, word, and line spacing. Character and word spacing are both specified as a percentage of the space character's width. Line spacing can either be specified as a percentage of a character's height or in points (which is the method most familiar to typographers).

Figure 10.3. The Spacing dialog box.

The Text roll-up provides access to many of the same attributes that are available in the Edit Text dialog box. Figure 10.4 shows the Text roll-up. Figure 10.5 shows the Paragraph dialog box, which is accessed through the Text roll-up. It contains many of the attributes of the Edit Text dialog box.

Paragraph Text

The Paragraph text tool ( ) is the middle tool on the text fly-out menu. It should be used for blocks of text longer than 256 characters or when no effects will be applied to the text. Each paragraph is limited to 4,000 characters and no more than 850 paragraphs can be contained in a file. The text may either be typed directly into a frame created by dragging out the appropriately sized rectangle with the primary mouse button, or by importing a file using the File Import command.

Figure 10.4. The Text roll-up.

Figure 10.5. The Paragraph dialog box.

Corel *NOTE!*

Don't confuse the File Import command with the Import button found in
the Edit Text dialog box. The Import Button is able to work only with
ASCII text files, while File Import can work with most popular word
processor formats. This is a major design flaw in Corel Draw.

When importing text using File Import, pages will be added to accommodate all the text contained in the file. The size of the text frame is determined by the page size in the word processor file, and will almost always
need to be manually adjusted on each and every page.

Text can also be entered in the Paragraph Text dialog box, which is
accessed by using the Text Edit Text command. This dialog box is
shown in Figure 10.6. It may seem that not all the text is showing, but
the dialog box shows only one paragraph at a time. The up and down
arrows are used to move between paragraphs. Again, this seems like a
major design flaw.

Figure 10.6. The Paragraph Text dialog box.

The Text roll-up can also be used with Paragraph text. Figure 10.7 shows the same dialog box as Figure 10.5, but with Paragraph text, fewer options are grayed out.

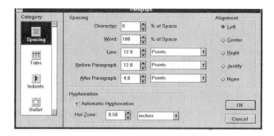

Figure 10.7. The Paragraph dialog box.

The many options available in the Paragraph dialog box and the Frame Attributes dialog box will be covered in depth in Skill Session 30.

Symbols

The Symbol (☆)tool is found on the far right of the Text tool fly-out. When you select it, the Symbol roll-up (shown in Figure 10.8) appears, and the Text tool will default back to the tool that was previously selected.

Corel Draw includes a library of over 5,000 symbols in many different categories. You can add other symbols to the roll-up either by creating them (using Special Create Symbol) or by adding a .WFN or TrueType font that is a symbol font. Unfortunately, there is no way to add PostScript fonts to the Symbol roll-up.

Figure 10.8. The Symbol roll-up.

Basic Skills Workshop

The Outline Tool

The Outline tool is as important to understand as the Fill tool (see Skill Session 12), as outlines are usually attached to new objects you create. The Outline tool also determines the look of straight and curved lines that are not outlines of objects but rather lines you have drawn. You might think of the Outline tool as a tool that determines certain attributes of lines which are also used as outlines. The reason for this approach is that you are dealing not only with line widths and colors, but also dashed lines and lines with arrowheads. These lines don't outline an object but are objects in and of themselves.

Setting Outline Defaults for Graphic Objects

Follow these steps to set the default outline width and color for graphic objects. Text and paragraph text defaults should be set separately because you normally would not want outlines on text.

1. Deselect all objects before setting defaults.

2. Click the ♦ tool icon in the toolbox.

3. Click the outlinepen icon in the fly-out menu (see Figure 11.1).

   When you click this icon with nothing selected, a small Outline Pen dialog box appears with a message telling you nothing is selected and to which objects the default will apply (see Figure 11.2).

Select Graphic; leave the Artistic Text and Paragraph Text boxes blank. Click on OK. A larger Outline Pen dialog box appears (see Figure 11.3).

Corel *TIP!*

The Outline Pen dialog box presents several options. You are setting the default settings, so remember the settings you choose will apply to every object you draw. You can access this same dialog box by selecting an object first and then clicking on the outlinepen icon. When you use this method, you are changing the settings only for the individual object you selected.

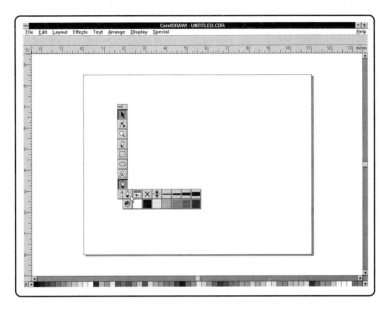

Figure 11.1. The Outline tool fly-out menu.

Figure 11.2. The initial Outline Pen dialog box.

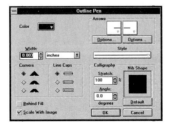

Figure 11.3. The Outline Pen dialog for setting graphic defaults.

Basic Skills Workshop

The first thing you should do is set the default color. Click the Color button and a color palette appears (see Figure 11.4). Choose the color for all your outlines. You can access custom colors by clicking on the More button at the bottom of the color palette.

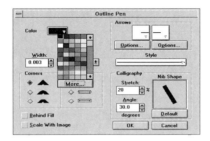

Figure 11.4. Setting the default outline color.

Line Width

The next step is setting the default line width. You have the following choices of units of measure:

- Inches
- Millimeters
- Picas, Points
- Points

Select the units of measure and enter a value in the parameters box.

Corel *NOTE!*

> Normally, the only settings you'd set as defaults are the Line Width and Color. All the other settings in the Outline Pen dialog box are used for specific attributes you want to assign to a specific object's outline.

Setting Outline Defaults for Text

Most users prefer not to have an outline when entering text or importing paragraph text. This is because, if the defaults were set too wide, the outlines would cover the text, and all you would see is a black blob. If the outline color defaulted to white, there is a chance you wouldn't be able to see the text. Figure 11.5 illustrates these possibilities.

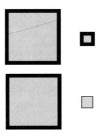

Figure 11.5. Using outlines with text may cause problems.

The correct way to set the outline defaults to no outline is to click the pen icon in the toolbox and then click the X icon in the top row of the fly-out menu (see Figure 11.6).

The small Outline Pen dialog box appears. Select both Artistic Text and Paragraph Text. Do not select Graphic. Click OK. That's all there is to it. Your text will not have an outline when it is typed or imported.

Corel*NOTE!*

> If you were to try to set the default to no outline using the Outline Pen icon as you did with Graphics defaults, you would be given an "Invalid Width" error message in the Outline Pen dialog box, telling you the width must be between 0.1 and 288.0 points.

Basic Skills Workshop

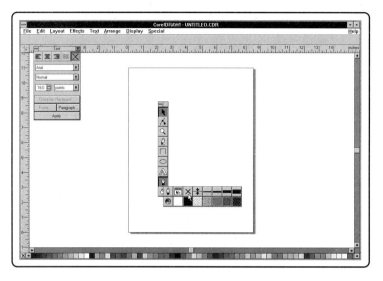

Figure 11.6. The Pen fly-out menu, showing the X icon.

Optional Settings for Outlines

The Outline Pen dialog box provides many choices of settings to apply
to outlines. To change outline settings, first select the object you wish
to change. Click the pen icon in the tool box and then click on the
outlinepen icon in the fly-out menu. This brings up the Outline Pen dialog
box just as you saw when setting defaults. However, the changes you
make here will affect only the object selected.

Corel *TIP!*

If you knew you were going to use a certain outline setting other than
the defaults for an entire project, you might want to make these options
the defaults. But be sure to reset those changes when you're through
with the project.

Corners

There are three choices for setting Corner attributes:

- Square corners. This is the most often used option because it provides a look that fits most shapes.
- Rounded corners.
- Beveled corners.

Figure 11.7 shows all three options applied to a rectangle.

Figure 11.7. The three styles of corners.

Line Caps

There are three choices for setting line caps. Line caps determine how far the end of a line extends beyond the termination point of the line. Figure 11.8 shows all three options applied to a straight line.

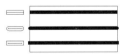

Figure 11.8. Three styles of line caps.

Behind Fill

You should check Behind Fill when using text with an outline. The reason for this is that normally an outline is drawn after the object is drawn. This means the outline is placed on top of the object. When you check the Behind Fill box, the outline is drawn first and then the object is drawn. The benefit of this for text is that the original design of the text is not altered by the outline. If you use a high-quality font or a very stylized font, all the original attributes are still there. Figure 11.9 illustrates the use of behind filling text. Notice that for the letter *B,* even though the outline of the behind-filled letter is double that of the letter with the outline on top, the appearance of the behind-filled letter is better.

Figure 11.9. Behind-filled text versus text without behind fill.

Scale with Image

Check Scale with Image if you will be changing the size of objects throughout your projects. If this box is not checked, the outline of objects remains the same size when the object is resized. You will get some very distorted effects by not checking this box. Figure 11.10 shows the effect of the use of Scale With Image.

Figure 11.10. Using Scale With Image.

Arrowheads

Adding arrowheads to the ends of single lines can be very useful in your designs. The dialog box offers a left and right selection box. The left box is for selecting an arrowhead at the start of a line, the right box for the end of a line. Click on one of the boxes and a menu appears allowing you to choose a specific arrowhead design (see Figure 11.11).

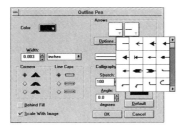

Figure 11.11. Choosing an arrowhead.

Below the selection boxes are two Options buttons. When you click one of the option boxes, a pull-down menu appears providing three options (see Figure 11.12). The first option is Swap. This option comes in very handy when you accidentally put an arrowhead on the wrong end of the line. When you click Swap, the arrowhead switches to the other end of the line.

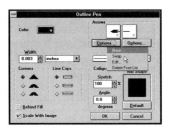

Figure 11.12. The Options pull-down menu.

The second option is Edit. This option brings up the Arrowhead Editor
dialog box (see Figure 11.13), which allows you to change the size of the
arrowhead. You can also create a mirror image of the arrowhead by
clicking on the reflect buttons.

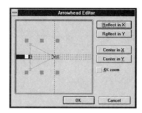

Figure 11.13. The Arrowhead Editor dialog box.

Corel*NOTE!*

To create your own custom arrowheads, choose the Create Arrow
command in the Special menu.

The third option is Delete From List. When you select this option, a
message box appears asking you to verify that you want to delete the
current arrowhead displayed in the selection box. If you click this option
by mistake, don't worry—you are given the chance to say No to deleting
the arrowhead.

Style

The Style option box is a long narrow box with a solid line running
across it. Click this box and a pull-down menu appears (see Figure 11.14)
giving you a choice of dotted and dashed lines. If you want to change
back to a solid line choose the solid line at the very top of the dialog box.

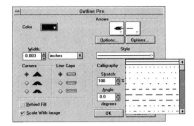

Figure 11.14. The Style option box and pull-down menu.

Calligraphy

The Calligraphy settings allow you to change the rectangular shape and angle of a line. Changing from the default setting of Square can allow you to add calligraphic effects to outlines. Figure 11.15 illustrates the use of these effects.

Figure 11.15. Adding calligraphic effects.

The Stretch parameter box allows you to scroll or type a new number below 100. You will notice the height of the square is shortened as the numbers are reduced.

97

Basic Skills Workshop

The Angle parameter box allows you to scroll or type a number to change the angle of the rectangle or default square. Figure 11.16 shows the Stretch and Angle parameter boxes.

The best way to determine the effect you desire is to try different settings until you achieve the desired result.

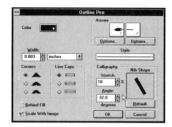

Figure 11.16. The Outline Pen dialog box showing the Stretch and Angle parameter boxes.

Outline Roll-Up

The Pen roll-up offers quick access for changes to outline attributes. To access the roll-up, click on the Roll-Up icon in the Outline fly-out menu.

Line Width

The top window of the roll-up is the Line Width setting. It defaults to a Hairline width (see Figure 11.17). To change the default Hairline width, click on the Edit button in the roll-up. This will bring up the normal Outline Pen dialog box where you can change the minimum width.

Figure 11.17. The default line width setting.

You can also use the scroll arrows on the roll-up to change the line width. Scrolling all the way down causes the box to display a × in the window; this represents no outline (see Figure 11.18).

Figure 11.18. The Pen roll-up with No Outline selected.

Scroll up, and the line width increases with a visual representation of the line and the measurement either in inches, or points, and so on (see Figure 11.19).

Figure 11.19. A 13-point line width in the Pen roll-up.

Arrowheads

Just below the Line Width window are the Arrowhead settings. They function just as they do in the main Outline Pen dialog box. The left button is for adding an arrowhead to the beginning of a line (see Figure 11.20), and the right for the end of a line. If you need to swap ends or edit the arrowhead, click on the Edit button in the roll-up.

Basic Skills Workshop

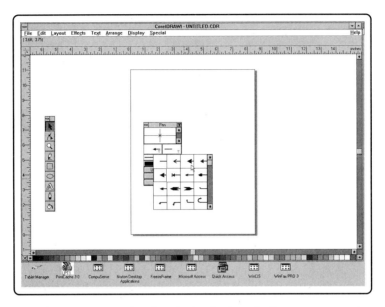

Figure 11.20. Adding an arrowhead to the beginning of a line.

Dots and Dashes

The long narrow box below the arrowheads is for changing from a solid line to dots and dashes. Click this box and a pull-down menu appears (see Figure 11.21) with a choice of line styles. The very top of this menu is the default solid line.

Color

The next choice you have is changing the outline color. Click the solid black box just above the Update From button. A color palette appears (see Figure 11.22), allowing you to choose an outline color. Click the More button at the bottom of the palette to access the Select Color dialog box. The Select Color dialog box lets you choose custom colors as well as custom palettes.

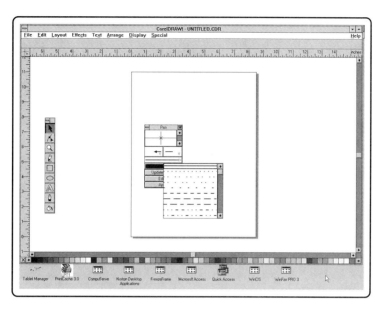

Figure 11.21. Changing the line style.

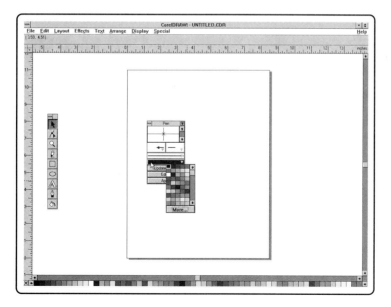

Figure 11.22. Selecting an outline color.

Basic Skills Workshop

Update From

Use the Update From button to copy the outline attributes from one object to another. Select the object you want to modify and click on the Update From button. An arrow appears on screen in place of the normal cursor. Use this arrow to click the object from which you want to copy outline attributes (see Figure 11.23). Your first object will now take on the outline attributes of the target object.

Edit

The Edit button can be used at any time to edit the objects outline. Click on this button to bring up the Outline Pen dialog box (see Figure 11.24). This is the same box referred to many times in this skill session.

Apply

The Apply button is the most important button of all in the roll-up. You can make all the changes you want, as described above, but none of the your changes will take effect until you click on Apply.

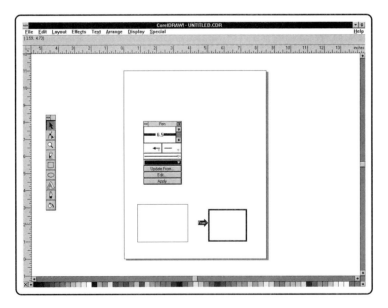

Figure 11.23. Copying the outline attributes from one object to another.

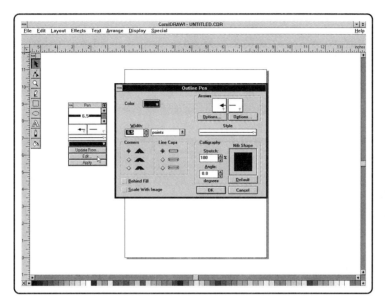

Figure 11.24. Accessing the Outline Pen dialog box from the Pen roll-up.

Basic Skills Workshop

The Fill Tool

The Fill tool could be the most important tool in terms of learning Corel Draw. The various options offered and how you use them determine how your finished project will look. Making the right choices in selecting the colors, gradient fills, textures, shading, and patterns can make the difference between mediocre and superb. You can create the perfect design and layout and use the perfect Font, but if the color, shading, and texture scheme are poor, the results are a disaster. Corel Draw 4 includes fill features that can make anyone an artist. Your only problem could be choosing between 32,768 different textures.

Because the Fill tool deals with colors, a discussion on the various palettes precedes this session.

Setting the Default Palette

To change the default palette, click on the ⊛ icon found in the fly-out menu of the Fill tool in the toolbox (see Figure 12.1).

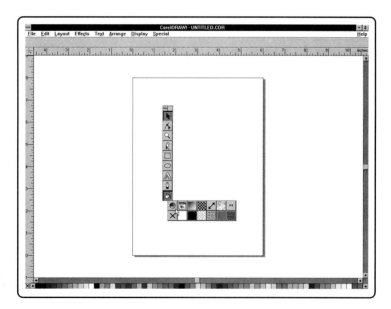

Figure 12.1. The Fill tool fly-out menu.

When you click this icon with nothing selected, a small Uniform Fill dialog box appears with a message telling you nothing is selected and to which objects the default will apply. In this case, choose all three options. Click OK. A larger Uniform Fill dialog box will appear (see Figure 12.2). Click the Custom Palette button in the lower left corner. A small pop-up menu appears.

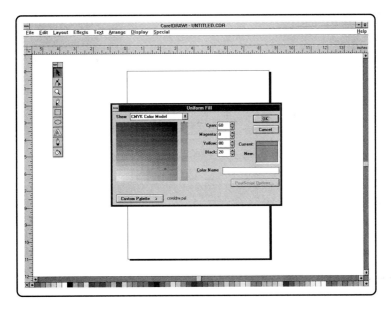

Figure 12.2. The Uniform Fill dialog box.

From this menu choose Open. The Open Palette dialog box appears (see Figure 12.3).

This dialog box allows you to choose several more custom palettes by scrolling with the up and down arrows in the File Name box. You can also choose at this time whether you want spot or process colors by clicking on the down arrow in the List Files of Type box. After making your selections click OK.

Basic Skills Workshop

Figure 12.3. The Open Palette dialog box.

Before you leave the Uniform Fill dialog box, you are presented with another choice. When you click on the Show Color Names check box, the name of the Spot and the name and number of the Pantone and Trumatch Process colors display in place of the actual colors themselves (see Figure 12.4). This is handy if you know the actual colors you want to use. If you choose Show Color Names, the Color Name box changes to Search String. You can now simply type the name or number of the color you want for that given palette.

Corel NOTE!

Whatever Palette and color you choose is now your default. This means whenever you draw an object or type text for the first time, the object or text will be filled with this color.

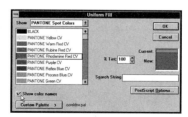

Figure 12.4. Showing color names in the Uniform Fill dialog box.

Fill Tools

Access the Fill tools from the Bucket icon at the bottom of the tool box. A fly-out menu appears when you select the icon. The first icon on the top half of the fly-out menu is the Color Wheel icon (see "Setting the Default Palette"). The second icon, the Fill Roll-Up icon, activates the Fill roll-up. The next five icons bring up dialog boxes for (from left to right) Fountain Fill, Two Color Pattern, Full Color Pattern, Texture Fill, and PostScript Texture (see Figure 12.5).

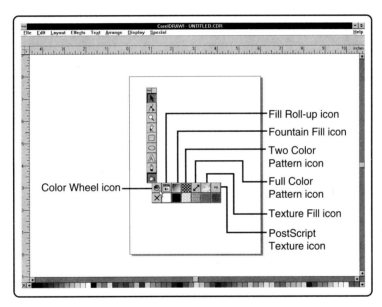

Figure 12.5. The Color Wheel, Fill Roll-Up, Fountain Fill, Two Color Pattern, Full Color Pattern, Texture Fill, and PostScript Texture icons.

Uniform Fill

Use the Uniform Fill dialog box (see Figure 12.6) to change the values of colors. Select a filled object that you want to modify. Click on the ⊗ icon (if you've selected an object with no fill, choose a color from the palette at the bottom of the dialog box). This palette corresponds to your default palette. The fill color of the selected object is displayed in a preview square on the upper right side of the box. The square is divided into two sections, Current and New. You change the values of the selected color in the boxes adjacent to the preview square. These boxes are labeled as the four process colors: Cyan, Magenta, Yellow, and Black. To change any of the individual colors, type a new value or use the up and down arrows. When you change any of the values, the preview square adjusts to your changes. It shows the changes made and the current color (the one you started with). After making changes, click on OK. The changes are reflected in the selected object.

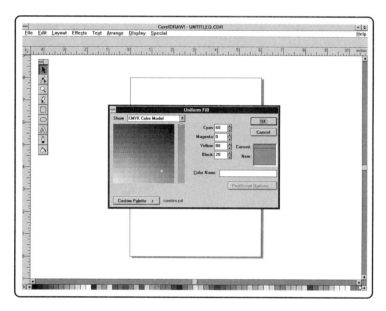

Figure 12.6. Changing a color in the Uniform Fill dialog box.

These instructions are based on a CMYK palette. If you change to the HSB Color Model in the Show box, the boxes adjacent to the preview square change to Hue, Saturation, and Brightness. If you use the RGB Color Model, the boxes list Red, Green, and Blue. If you change to

Pantone Spot Colors in the Show box, a Tint box displays next to the preview square. You can scroll with the arrows to tint your selected color or type in a specific value.

Corel *NOTE!*

> The Pantone Process and the Trumatch Process palette in the show box have no adjustment boxes because these palettes already have the complete range of values in them.

Fountain Fill, Two Color Pattern, Full Color Pattern, and Texture

The Fountain Fill, Two Color Pattern, Full Color Pattern, and Texture icons function the same as their counterparts in the Fill roll-up (see "Fill Roll-Up" later in this Skill Session for more information).

PostScript Fills

The PostScript Texture is the last icon (identified by the letters PS) in the Fill fly-out menu. When you select this icon, the PostScript Texture dialog box (see Figure 12.7) appears, with a menu listing texture names. Appendix F in the Corel Draw User Manual shows the texture for each name. Appendix A shows how changes made in the Parameter boxes affect the default textures. The textures do not display on-screen; objects filled with a PostScript texture instead display a series of PSs. PostScript fills will print only on a PostScript printer.

Fill Roll-Up

The Fill roll-up (see Figure 12.8) allows you on-screen access to most of the icons in the Fill fly-out menu. Click on the Fill Roll-Up icon (the second icon in the Fill fly-out menu) to display the Fill roll-up. The Fill roll-up incorporates everything in the Fill fly-out menu except the PostScript icon and the Uniform Fill icon. To change the color of a uniform (solid) filled object, use the color palette at the bottom of the screen.

Basic Skills Workshop

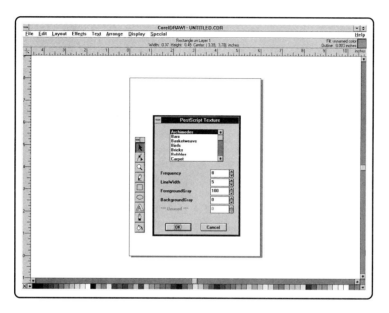

Figure 12.7. The PostScript Texture dialog box.

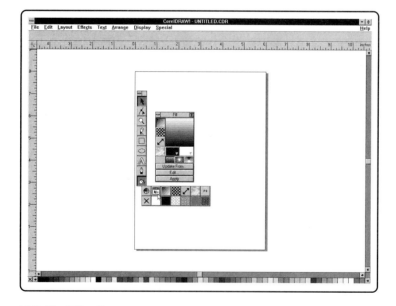

Figure 12.8. The Fill roll-up.

Starting at the top left, the first icon in the Fill roll-up is the Fountain Fill icon. This is the default icon. The preview window adjacent to the icons always displays the last fill created using the Fill roll-up.

Corel*NOTE!*

It is important to differentiate the Fill roll-up settings and the settings in the Uniform Fill dialog box. If an object is filled using the Uniform Fill dialog box, its fill does not show in the preview window of the roll-up when the object is selected. Conversely, a fill created using the Fill roll-up does not appear in the Uniform Fill dialog box. Choose one method to work with as your primary method to help eliminate confusion when working with fills.

Fountain Fill Icon

The Fountain Fill icon (located at the top left of the Fill roll-up) offers three varieties of fountain fill. You must select the fill icon you plan on using to make sure you have the right one. *Remember, the last fill used will appear in the preview box.* Choose which variety of fountain fill from the buttons directly under the preview window. The first button on the left is for linear fills. The second button is for radial fills and the third button is for conical fills.

Each fountain fill can be modified for color and direction. If you want to change just the direction of the fill (for example, left to right instead of bottom to top), place the cursor in the center of the preview box and drag. A line appears allowing you to rotate the direction of the fill. For radial and conical fills, a cross hair replaces your cursor in the preview window. Drag the cross hair to change the center point. Hold down the Ctrl key to constrain movements to 15-degree increments. Use the secondary mouse button to constrain the angle of fill in a conical fill. You can use a light color in the center and a dark color on the outside while creating a radial fill to produce the illusion of a sphere with a highlight.

Corel *NOTE!*

> You must remember to click on the Apply button in the Fill roll-up for any changes to take effect in the selected object.

Editing Fountain Fills

You can have fun editing fountain fills and produce some interesting effects. To edit a fountain fill, click on the Edit button. The Fountain Fill dialog box appears (see Figure 12.9), offering some of the same options as in the Fill roll-up, such as changing color and choosing Linear, Radial, or Conical fill. The added options allow you to manually enter the center offset of radial, linear, and conical fills. You can also change the angle of the fill in the Angle parameter box. The Steps parameter box shows the number of steps in the fountain fill. The number showing is the default number, and it is grayed out. To change the number of steps, click on the Lock icon next to the word Steps. This allows you to change the number of fountain stripes you want in the fill. You can choose between 2 and 256. The parameter box under the Steps box is called Edge Pad. Setting this number greater than zero determines how much of the beginning and ending colors of a fill will remain solid before they start to blend with the next color in the fill.

Figure 12.9. The Fountain Fill dialog box.

Custom Fills

The Options button is located beneath the Color buttons in the Fountain Fill dialog box. Click on this button, and the Fountain Fill Color Options dialog box appears (see Figure 12.10), offering more variations. You can create some very unusual and beautiful effects in this dialog box.

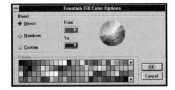

Figure 12.10. The Fountain Fill Color Options dialog box.

You have three fill blending methods to select from in the Color Options dialog box. The first is Direct; this is the same as what you could do in the original roll-up. The only difference is that the color wheel on the right displays a line showing the color spectrum the fill passes through when you select colors from the From and To selection buttons.

The second method is Rainbow (see Figure 12.11). When you select this option, two icons appear depicting rotation. The top icon shows a counterclockwise direction while the bottom icon shows a clockwise direction. When you select colors from the From and To selection buttons, an elliptical line displays the direction of the blend on the Color Wheel. You will be able to see what color spectrum the blend will pass through. The color at the top or bottom determines the path direction. If you choose Orange to Red the blend will pass through the entire color spectrum.

Figure 12.11. The Fountain Fill Color Options dialog box with Rainbow selected.

The third method is Custom. Select Custom to bring up a different display, which shows the From and To buttons as before, but with new options (see Figure 12.12). The first thing you notice is a long rectangle displaying the fountain fill going from the first color to the second, horizontally. At the bottom left and bottom right corners is a small black square. These squares represent the starting point of the fill and cannot be moved. If you click on one of the squares, a triangular pointer appears next to it. These pointers allow you to add multiple colors to the fountain fill. You can add as many pointers as you want by double-clicking just below the fountain fill itself. (Do not click in the actual fountain fill.)

Figure 12.12. The Fountain Fill Color Options dialog box with Custom selected.

Each time you add a pointer, you can change to a different color by selecting the new color from the color palette in the dialog box. You do not need to click on one of the black squares to begin adding pointers. You can drag the pointers along the path of the fill and place them wherever you want. The Position parameter box at the upper right corner of the dialog box allows you to select a pointer and manually enter its position along the path. Custom fills can be applied to linear, radial, and conical fills. (Figures 12.21 through 12.26, later in this skill session, show various fills using the above methods.)

Two-Color Pattern Fills

The second icon in the Fill roll-up is the Pattern icon. When you select this icon, the preview window displays a blank page with a diagonal line and a small triangle in the bottom right corner. Click on the preview window to bring up a menu of patterns to choose from. At the top of the pattern menu are three buttons: File, OK, and Cancel. You select File to open a pattern from a source other than the default directory. The OK button confirms your selection from the pattern menu (you can also double-click on the selected pattern). Click on the Cancel button to return to the roll-up without selecting anything.

Editing Patterns

After you have filled an object with a pattern, click on the Edit button in the Fill roll-up. The Two-Color Pattern dialog box appears (see Figure 12.13).

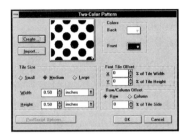

Figure 12.13. The Two-Color Pattern dialog box.

The first options at the top left of the dialog box are Create and Import. Click on the Create button to bring up the Two-Color Pattern Editor (see Figure 12.14). This editor allows you to create your own patterns, a pixel at a time, and save them as custom patterns. The editor provides three choices of bitmap size. These sizes represent the total size of the finished pattern. The Pen size represents the number of Pixels applied with one mouse click while you actually create the pattern.

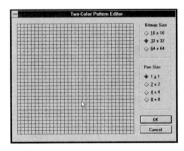

Figure 12.14. The Two Color Pattern Editor.

The Import button allows you to import patterns stored in other directories.

Corel*NOTE!*

Use the entire screen grid when making a pattern. This ensures the pattern size matches the bitmap size you selected.

Tiling Patterns

To tile patterns means to put more than one complete image of the pattern within the object you are filling. First, select a pattern and click on Apply in the Fill roll-up. This puts your pattern in the selected object on the screen. Click on Tile and then click on Apply again; two small squares appear in the upper right corner of the object you just filled. Click on the node at the bottom center of the squares and drag down and to the right (see Figure 12.15). You will notice that the squares get larger. The two squares represent the size of the pattern tile. The smaller the size of the squares, the more times the selected pattern will be tiled in the object. If you drag the squares so that the left square is the only square covering your object the pattern will only appear once. Try dragging so the squares are long and narrow to create different effects.

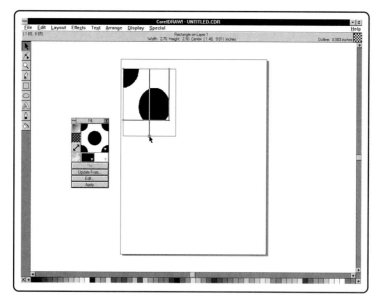

Figure 12.15. Tiling a pattern.

Editing Tiled Patterns

After you have tiled a pattern, click on the Edit button in the Fill roll-up. The Two-Color Pattern dialog box appears, allowing you to offset the tiles to create another effect. You are also presented with a choice of tiling in rows or columns as well as changing the size of the bitmap that makes up the pattern. Select either Small, Medium, or Large. You can also enter specific sizes in the parameter box.

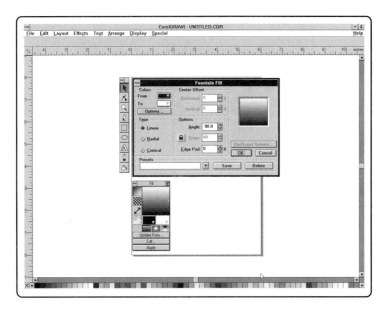

Figure 12.16. Editing a tiled pattern.

Full Color Patterns

The Full Color Pattern icon is identified by a double arrow.

Choose different patterns by first clicking in the preview window. A fly-out menu appears, showing all patterns available. Double-click on the pattern you want to bring it into the preview window. You can edit (with the exception of color) and size them just like two color patterns when you click on the Edit button in the Fill roll-up. Click on the Load button in the Full Color Pattern dialog box (see Figure 12.17) to select a pattern by name. Use the Import button to access patterns that might be located in directories other than the default directory. Full color patterns can also be tiled like two-color patterns.

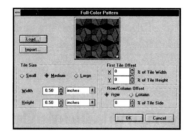

Figure 12.17. The Full Color Pattern dialog box.

Changing Colors in Full Color Patterns

A full color pattern is a vector image and therefore is not unlike a basic .CDR file you create. The pattern was originally made as a .CDR file and saved with a .PAT extension by using the Create Pattern command in the Special Menu (see how to create patterns in Part V, "Command References," "Special Menu Commands").

You cannot change the colors of a full color pattern from the dialog box like you can with two color patterns. To change the colors in a full color pattern:

1. Open the pattern you want to edit by using the Open command in the File menu.
2. Choose Pattern file *.Pat in the List Files of Type scroll box.
3. Using the Directories list in the Open dialog box, change to the directory where the pattern files are located. The default is Coreldrw\Custom.
4. Select the pattern by name from the list.
5. Click OK.

The pattern you choose opens like a normal .CDR file. You can now change the color scheme just as you would a .CDR image. The pattern will open on screen as a group, so you need to ungroup the objects in the pattern before making changes. Do not resize the original pattern unless you have a specific reason for doing so. After you have made your changes, select Save in the File menu. This method permanently changes the color of the default pattern. If you want to keep the colors in the default pattern, choose Save As in the File menu to assign a new name to your edited image. The next time you look for your new pattern it will appear at the bottom of the pattern display in the Fill roll-up.

Texture Icon

The Texture icon is the last icon in the Fill roll-up. It works like the Pattern icon with one exception. If you know the name of the texture you want to use, you can select it by name from the scroll box beneath the Styles scroll box, located under the preview window (see Figure 12.18). The word Styles in the Styles scroll box is the only name listed. This is because all the default textures are located in the Styles library.

To visually select a texture, click on the preview window. A fly-out menu appears displaying the textures you can choose from. Use the scroll bar to select the texture you want. Double-click on a texture, and it will

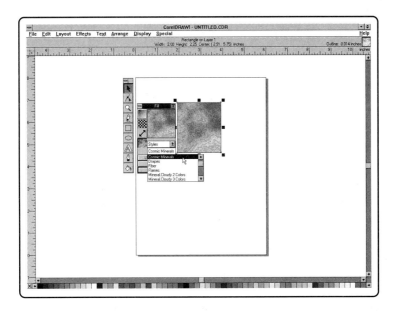

Figure 12.18. Selecting a texture.

appear in the roll-up's preview window. Click on Apply to place the texture in the selected object. You can modify the look of a texture by clicking on the Edit button.

Editing Textures

Select one of the default textures and click on the Edit button in the Fill roll-up. The Texture Fill dialog box appears (see Figure 12.19), showing the selected texture in a preview window. The dialog box also contains a number of numeric parameter selection boxes allowing changes to various attributes of the selected texture. Each texture contains one common selection box. That box shows the identification number of the displayed texture. You can scroll or type any number from 1 to 32,768. By combining the total choices of textures with the other choices (such as color), you will never be at a loss for discovering a different look. You must click on the Preview button to view any changes you make in the selection boxes.

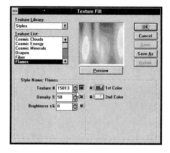

Figure 12.19. The Texture Fill dialog box.

When you edit a particular texture and want to save it for future use, click on the Save As button to give your new texture a new name and a new library name.

Corel *NOTE!*

You cannot save an edited texture in the default Styles library.

Enter a name for your texture in the Texture Name box and then type a new library name in the Library Name scroll box (see Figure 12.20). Any textures you edit in the future can then be added to this new library. For example, you could give all new textures you create your own descriptive name and save them in library called CUSTOM. You can overwrite an existing texture after it has been edited by using the Save command.

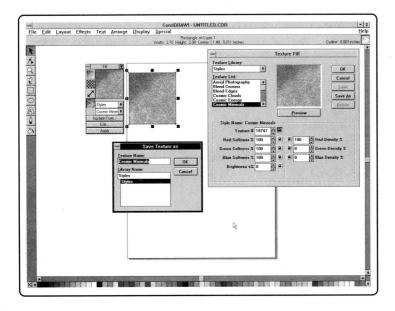

Figure 12.20. Saving a new texture.

Corel*NOTE!*

Remember, you must always click on the Apply button in the roll-up after selecting or editing textures before they can be applied to the selected object.

Deleting Textures

You cannot delete a texture from the Styles library. You can only delete textures that you have created and placed in a custom library.

Sample Fills

Figures 12.21 through 12.30 show a few examples of the different uses of fills. These examples are very basic, but with some imagination you can create some spectacular effects.

Figure 12.21. Linear, radial, and conical fills.

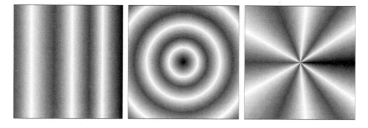

Figure 12.22. Linear, radial, and conical fills with added custom stripes.

Manipulation Workshop

Object
Ordering

Order

Use this command to arrange objects in relation to each other. Select Order from the Arrange menu to bring up a fly-out menu (see Figure 13.1) offering five choices:

■ Select To Front to move the selected object in front of all other objects. For example, you could use this command to move text previously placed on-screen in front of a new object.

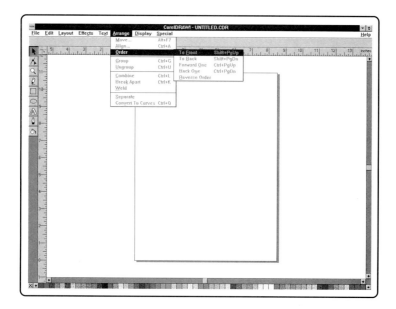

Figure 13.1. The Order fly-out menu.

■ Select To Back to move the selected object behind all other objects. For example, suppose you create a background for an illustration as an afterthought. By creating the background last, you place the background in front of everything else. To solve this dilemma, select the new background and choose Order, To Back from the Arrange menu.

Figure 13.2 illustrates the use of To Front and To Back.

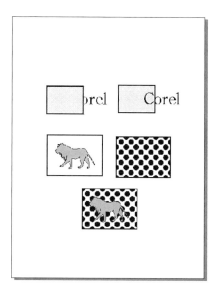

Figure 13.2. Using To Front and To Back to position objects.

■ Select Forward One to move the selected object one place forward at a time. This command comes in handy when there are many objects on-screen and you want to move a specific object to a specific place in a sequence. For example, suppose there are 20 objects on-screen, and you create a new object that you want to place just in front of the background. The quickest way to do this would be to select the new object and move it to the back using the To Back command and, while the object is still selected, choose Forward One.

Corel *NOTE!*

If you somehow deselected the object after you placed it to the back it would be hidden by the background. To select the object again hold down the Shift key and press Tab. As you continue to press the Tab key, each object will be selected in order from back to front.

Manipulation Workshop

- Back One accomplishes the opposite of Forward One.
- Select Reverse Order to reverse the order of two objects or groups of objects. Imagine two objects, one in front of the other. Select the two objects either by marquee selection or by holding down the Shift key and clicking on each object. Choose Reverse Order from the Arrange menu and the two objects exchange places (see Figure 13.3).

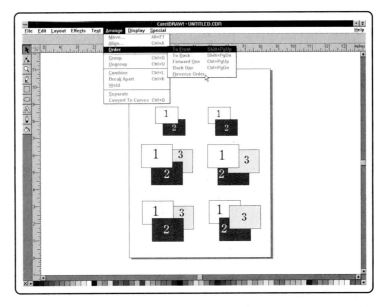

Figure 13.3. Using Reverse Order.

Manipulation Workshop

Grouping and Ungrouping

Grouping single objects and groups of objects in Corel Draw is one of the most common commands you will use. Grouping joins objects that are common to each other. This includes all of the individual objects that make up a particular image you have drawn. It could also include all objects common to a specific part of the overall design. For example, you could group all icons in a border you have created (see Figure 4.1). Each icon would be a group made up of individual objects; the border would be a second group including all icons. The value of grouping becomes evident when you want to reposition objects in a drawing.

Figure 14.1. Grouping objects in a drawing.

Corel*NOTE!*

A complicated drawing can become cluttered with individual objects if you don't take advantage of the Group command.

Grouping objects is very simple:

1. Select two or more objects you want to group either by marquee selection or by clicking on each object with the ⬧ tool while holding down the Shift key.

2. Pull down the Arrange menu and select Group.

Corel*NOTE!*

> To ungroup a group, select the group by clicking on it, pull down the Arrange menu, and select Ungroup.

Editing Objects Within a Group

Corel Draw 4 has added the capability to edit individual objects within a group. This feature eliminates the need to ungroup a group to make changes. It also removes the problem of trying to select all the previously grouped objects to regroup them.

To edit any object within a group:

1. Hold down Ctrl and click the object you want to edit.

   The selected object shows eight round handles instead of the customary square handles.

2. The status line shows that the object is a child object.

3. Release the Ctrl key. The object remains selected. You can now change the object with many of the features that Corel Draw offers to any single object, such as rotate, shape, size, fill, color, and so on.

Clip Art Groups

Most clip art is imported as a single group. You will discover, once you ungroup the clip art group, that what remains are additional groups and curves. If you plan to edit the clip art, you will need to determine which parts of the clip art need to be ungrouped to get you to the place that you want to edit. Some clip art suppliers advertise that their images are logically grouped. This is important because it makes it much easier to modify the clip art. For example, you could take the head that has been grouped with one image and put it on a different image (see Figure 14.2).

Figure 14.2. Modified clip art.

Manipulation Workshop

Combining
and Breaking

The Combine command in Corel Draw has a number of applications. The function of the Combine command is to take two or more objects and make them into a single object. The resulting single object becomes a curve, and it can be manipulated as any other curve.

Creating Masks

Figure 15.1 illustrates how combining one object on top of another creates a transparent hole in the bottom object. This is commonly referred to as *creating a mask*. The purpose of a mask is to allow an underlying object behind the hole to show through. To create a mask, follow these steps:

1. Create an object that you want to make as your mask. This will become the object with the hole in it.

2. Create a second object and place it on top of the first object.

   The second object becomes transparent; it must be on top of the first object. If the second object was created prior to the first object, select the second object to bring it to the front: Pull down the Arrange menu and select Order; then select To Front.

3. Select both objects either by marquee selection or by clicking on each object while holding down the Shift key.

4. Pull down the Arrange menu and select Combine.

5. With the new mask selected, choose a fill color for the mask, with or without an outline.

6. Place the mask on top of the image that you want to show through the hole or holes in the mask.

Figure 15.1 illustrates a bitmap beneath a mask. Text was placed on top of a rectangle and combined to create a mask. The bitmap beneath the mask shows through the transparent text.

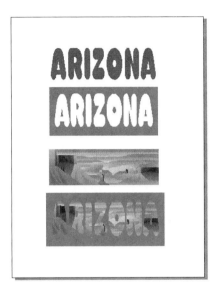

Figure 15.1. A bitmap is visible beneath the overlying mask.

Figure 15.2 uses three masks to create the illusion of looking into a house, seeing a couple dancing, and then seeing through the back window to the trees. The following steps take you through the process:

1. Create a background (in this case the sky and trees). Group these objects together.

2. Draw the back wall of the room by drawing two rectangles and combining them to create the transparent window (mask). Draw two crossed lines to form the window panes. Group these objects together.

3. Place the back wall group over the top of the background objects so that the objects show through the window.

4. Create something to put in the room and place it in front of the back wall.

   The dancing couple in this illustration is part of the Symbols clip art library.

5. Draw an outside wall just like the one in Step 2.

Manipulation Workshop

6. Group these new objects together and place the outside wall over everything else. Adjust the window if you like.

7. Create some shutter slats by drawing a series of narrow rectangles and lining them up in a vertical row. Create another mask for the shutter frame. Do this the same way you made the windows, but make the second rectangle almost as big as the first rectangle.

   Place the shutter frame over the shutter slats and group them together.

8. Place the shutters over the outside window.

The Perspective effect was used on the right-hand shutter in the illustration to create the illusion of being opened.

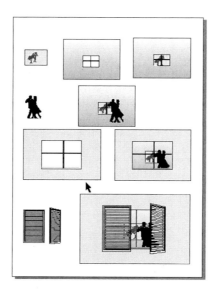

Figure 15.2. Combining masks to create depth.

You can also use the Combine command to create multiple holes in masks (see Figure 15.3). As long as you put the shapes you want to become holes inside and on top of the mask object, you can make as many holes as you want. You must not, however, use the Combine command until all the holes have been put on the mask. When this is done, marquee-select all the objects, including the mask shape, and then select Combine from the Arrange menu.

Figure 15.3. Creating multiple holes in masks.

Creating Effects

You can create different and unusual effects with the Combine command. Figure 15.4 shows different objects combined together to change the look of the original objects. Chapter 16 illustrates even more uses of the Combine command along with the Rotate command.

The Break Apart Command

Knowing how Combine and Break Apart work is important when editing clip art. Some clip art is made up of combined objects. This is because the clip art was originally scanned from original art or created in other programs and then auto-traced. This method causes problems when you want to make changes to the clip art. The primary problem occurs when you change the color in a particular section of a clip art drawing. The area you want to change may be combined with an area you don't want to change. This is when the Break Apart command in the Arrange menu becomes valuable.

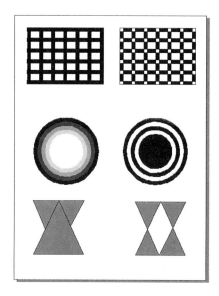

Figure 15.4. Combining objects for different effects.

The quickest way to find out which objects are combined is to click on a particular section of clip art you want to change and then change its color (make sure you have ungrouped the clip art first.) If more objects are affected by the color change than the object you want to change, you know you have to use the Break Apart command.

The clown in Figure 15.5 is a simple example of the use of the Break Apart command. In the original clip art, the clown's collar and buttons are combined. The dark portion of the collar is combined with the dark portion of the buttons, and the white portion of the collar with the white portion of the buttons. If you change the color of the buttons you also change the color of the collar. Follow these steps to change the button and collar color separately:

1. Click on the white part of the buttons and select the Break Apart command from the Arrange menu.

   The white parts of the collar and buttons are now separate objects.

2. Click on the dark part of the buttons and select the Break Apart command from the Arrange menu.

   The dark parts of the collar and buttons are now separate objects.

This is a very simple illustration. Most clip art will require much more use of the Break Apart command if you decide to make changes.

Figure 15.5. Using the Break Apart command to edit clip art.

Manipulation Workshop

Rotating, Skewing, and Stretching

Manipulation Workshop

The Rotate and Skew commands are found in the Effects menu. These commands enable you to explore your creative talents. Figures 16.1 through 16.5 show just a few samples of an endless number of different effects you can create.

The basic use of these two effects is to change the angle or shape of a particular object. You must first select the object and then, while the object is still selected, click once more on the object to change the handles to double-headed arrows. Inside the arrows is a small circle with a dot in the center. This is the *center of rotation*.

Notice that when you move the cursor over any one of the arrows, it changes to a cross hair. Put the cursor on one of the corner arrows and drag; the object rotates around its center of rotation. If you put your cursor on one of the side arrows and drag up or down, you skew the object. If the constrain angle is set to the default setting of 15 degrees in the Preferences dialog box, you can rotate or skew an object by this increment by holding down Ctrl while you drag. Another way to set the rotate and skew increment is via the Rotate & Skew dialog box brought up when you select Rotate & Skew from the Effects menu.

By changing the center of rotation of an object and making duplicates until you reach 360 degrees, you can produce some unexpected and beautiful results. For the figures, I used different types of objects to illustrate different effects. The possibilities are endless. Try using text, Symbols clip art, or any freehand shape you create.

Each of the sample patterns was created by rotating or skewing an object at a specific angle and duplicating each step until a complete circle was formed. The quickest way to do this is to follow these steps:

1. Select an object to rotate or skew.
2. Move the center of rotation by putting the cursor on the circle located in the center of the object. Drag the circle to any point on the object that you want the object to rotate around.

Corel*NOTE!*

In Figure 16.1, the center of rotation is positioned at the top of the guitar and at the bottom of the ice-cream cone.

3. Set the Rotation Angle or Skew in the Rotate & Skew dialog box.

4. Click the Leave Original box.

5. Click OK.

6. While the objects are still selected, press Ctrl-R. This repeats the last action you perform.

7. Repeat Step 6 (without releasing the Ctrl key) until your circle is complete. You can also experiment with completing only a partial circle.

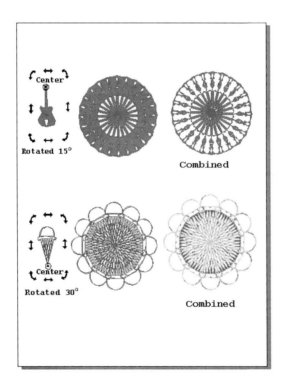

Figure 16.1. Rotating clip art.

Figure 16.1 uses objects from the Symbols clip art library. The guitar and the ice-cream cone have a large number of nodes in them, which can lead to problems when printing at high resolutions. If you use complex objects, decease the number of nodes in the original object before you begin duplicating and combining. The following steps take you through the process of removing nodes from an object.

1. Select the object with the ▸ tool and then change to the ⩘ tool.
2. Marquee-select the entire object with the ⩘ tool.
3. Double-click one of the nodes to bring up the Node Edit dialog box.
4. Click the Auto-Reduce button to reduce the total number of nodes.

Corel*NOTE!*

In rare cases, this action could change the original shape of the object to a point that is not acceptable. If this happens, you should delete individual nodes one at a time until you have reduced the total node count without changing the appearance of the original.

5. Change back to the ▸ tool. The object remains selected.
6. With the number of nodes now reduced, you can start rotating and duplicating as shown in Steps 1 through 7 above.

In Figure 16.1, as in all the sample patterns, you can achieve a different effect by using the Combine command on the completed circle. The first pattern is created by following Steps 1 through 7 above. To create the second pattern, marquee select all the newly created objects, and then pull down the Arrange menu and select Combine.

Corel*NOTE!*

This second procedure causes the new objects to become a single object that contains all the nodes from the individual objects. This is why it is important to reduce the number of nodes of the original object before you begin.

Figure 16.2 shows in the first two examples how objects will look when the original object is skewed before rotating. In the third example, the original has an envelope effect applied to it before rotating (see Skill Session 22, "Enveloping").

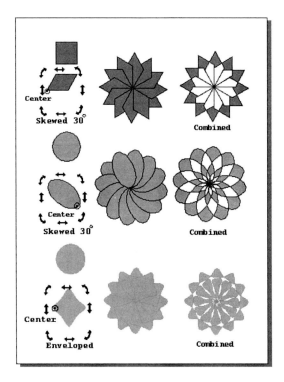

Figure 16.2. Skewing and rotating simple shapes.

Figure 16.3 shows how the use of text can create interesting and appealing patterns. With all the typefaces available today, the possibilities are endless.

149

Figure 16.4 uses another piece of clip art from the Symbols library. The second and third examples show the same freehand shape rotated from different centers of rotation.

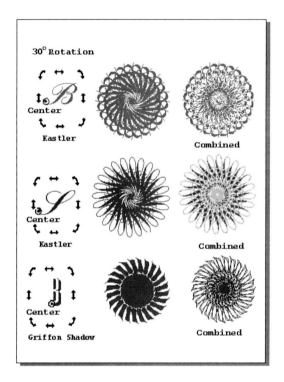

Figure 16.3. Rotating text.

Figure 16.5 illustrates how multiple objects look when the pattern technique is applied. In the first example, I used a piece of clip art. As with most clip art, which is made up of multiple objects, the objects have been combined to form a single object. The resulting pattern is very pleasing.

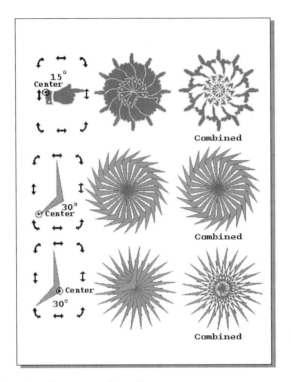

Figure 16.4. Changing the center of rotation.

The second example shows how the pattern is changed if you break apart the single object (using the Break Apart command on the Arrange menu) and return it to its original state of multiple objects. The results are very different. What happens is that each of the eight objects rotates around the center of rotation on a different axis.

In the third example, the eight objects are grouped together (using the Group command) and rotated around a single point.

151

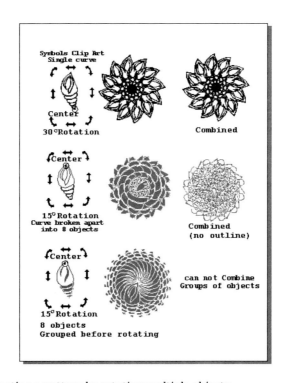

Figure 16.5. Creating a pattern by rotating multiple objects.

17

Manipulation Workshop

Aligning Objects

Manipulation Workshop

In the Arrange menu, you will find the Align command, used for aligning various selected objects. You can align any selected object(s) to the center of the page as well as to the grid. When aligning to the grid, Corel Draw uses the grid setup that you have set (using Grid Setup in the Layout menu).

You can also align objects to each other. When you use the Align command, it is important to remember that objects will align themselves to the last object you select.

You can override this feature only by selecting Align to Center of Page or Align to Grid. Figure 17.1 shows three different selected objects; notice that they are all in different positions on the screen (see Figure 17.1).

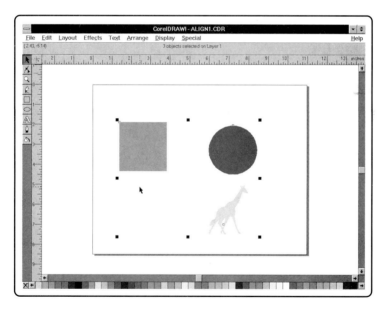

Figure 17.1. Three objects in different locations on the page.

To invoke the Align dialog box, pull down the Arrange menu and select Align (see Figure 17.2).

The Align dialog box appears. From here you can select various options for aligning the objects you have selected (see Figure 17.3).

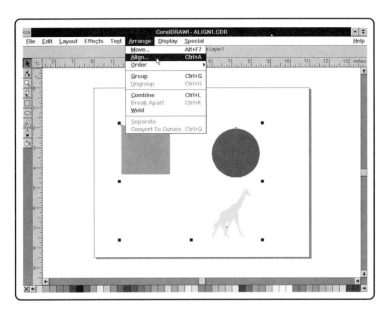

Figure 17.2. The Arrange menu pulled down showing three objects selected on-screen and the Align command highlighted.

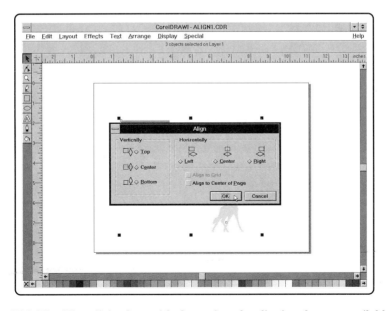

Figure 17.3. The Align dialog box with the options for aligning that are available.

Manipulation Workshop

For now, choose Align to Center of Page. Notice that the Center options in both the Vertically and Horizontally sections are enabled. Choosing Align to Center of Page automatically enables these options (see Figure 17.4).

Figure 17.4. The Align dialog box with the Align to Center of Page box checked.

Figure 17.5 shows what effect Align to Center of Page has to the three selected objects.

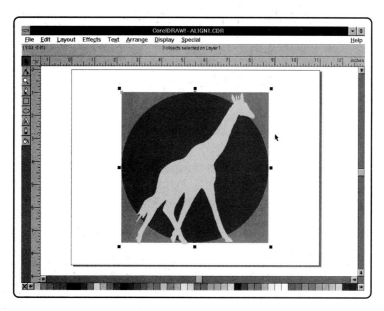

Figure 17.5. The three objects after they have been centered to the page.

You can also align objects to the grid that you set up. This option works in much the same way as aligning to the center of the page. The Snap to Grid or Show Grid options found in the Layout menu do not have to be enabled for this option to work. For this example, the grid is set up at 1-inch increments.

Figure 17.6 shows the Align dialog box with the Align to Grid box checked. The center vertical and horizontal settings are also enabled, but you can set these independently of the Align to Grid option. With these settings enabled, the centers of the objects should align to the grid.

Figure 17.6. The Align dialog box with the Align to Grid option enabled.

Corel *NOTE!*

You must check one of the alignment boxes before the Align to Grid option can be enabled.

Figure 17.7 illustrates the difference between the Align to Grid option and the Align to Center of Page option. The objects have been aligned to the grid, which is set at 1-inch increments. The grid is also being displayed. The centers of the objects have been aligned to the grid in this instance.

Figure 17.8 shows the three objects again but in different positions. Suppose you want to align them all across the top. The other objects will align to the circle, so you will select it last. First select the other objects; then select the circle and invoke the Align dialog box.

Manipulation Workshop

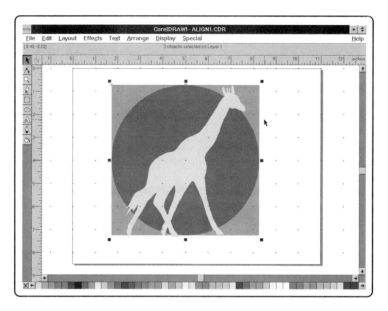

Figure 17.7. Three objects aligned to the grid. The grid is set at 1-inch increments, horizontal and vertical, and is displayed on-screen.

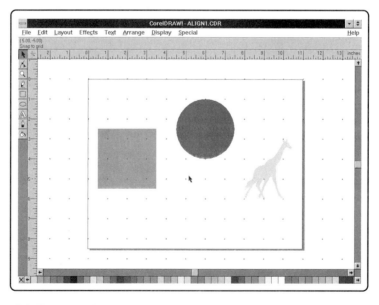

Figure 17.8. The three objects; the circle is closest to the top of the page.

In the Vertically section, select Top and then click OK (see Figure 17.9). The two other objects are now aligned across the top with the circle (see Figure 17.10).

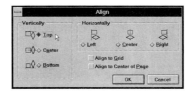

Figure 17.9. The Align dialog box with Top enabled in the Vertically section.

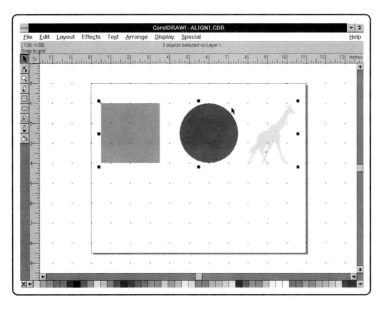

Figure 17.10. The other two objects aligned to the circle. Select the circle last before you invoke the Align dialog box.

In Figure 17.11, notice that two of the objects have been reduced: the giraffe and the circle. The rectangle is kept the same size. This will make it easier for you to see the effect of the available alignment options.

Manipulation Workshop

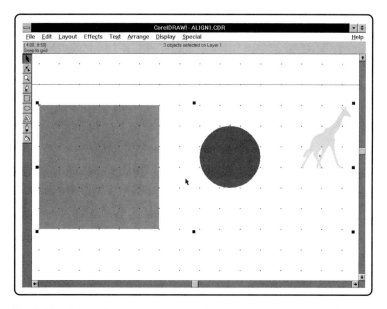

Figure 17.11. The three objects with the giraffe and the circle reduced.

First select the giraffe and the circle. Select the rectangle last, and bring up the Align dialog box. In the Vertically section, select Top. In the Horizontally section, select Left. Click OK (see Figure 17.12).

Corel*NOTE!*

In the Align dialog box, you can select two options, one from the Vertically section and one from the Horizontally section. You cannot enable two or more options from within either section at the same time.

Figure 17.13 shows what happens after the options in the dialog box are applied to the three selected objects.

Figure 17.12. The Align dialog box with Vertically Top and Horizontally Left selected. Only one option in each section can be enabled.

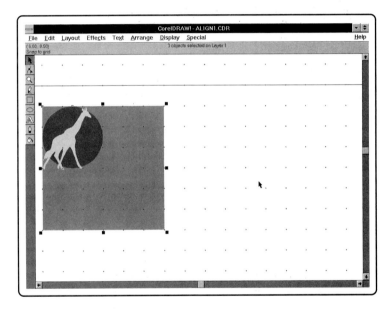

Figure 17.13. The three objects after being aligned.

In Figure 17.14, the three objects have been duplicated seven times and each set of three objects has been aligned differently.

161

Manipulation Workshop

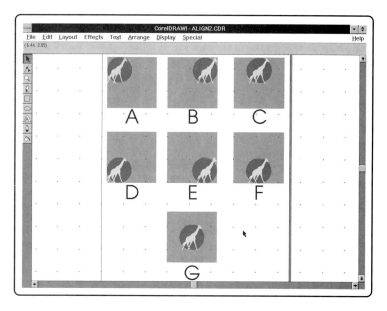

Figure 17.14. Seven sets of three objects aligned in various ways.

Corel*NOTE!*

> Remember that you can align more than just three objects. Three objects have been used in these examples for the sake of simplicity. You can also align one or more objects either to the page or to the grid that you set up.

Manipulation Workshop

Moving

Manipulation Workshop

The Move command is important when you need to move objects precisely and accurately. When you select Move from the Arrange menu, a dialog box appears allowing you to enter the exact location you want the object to move to (see Figure 18.1). If you check the Leave Original box, a copy of the object moves to the new location, leaving the original object in place. The boxes to the right of the parameter boxes allow you to choose one of the following units of measure:

- Inches
- Millimeters
- Picas,Points
- Points

Figure 18.1. The Move dialog box.

Table 18.1 shows the approximate conversion values for inches, points, and picas.

Table 18.1.
Converting inches, points, and picas.

Unit	Approximate equivalent
1 inch	6 picas
1 pica	12 points
1 inch	72 points

If you want to move an object 1/4 inch using Picas,Points, type 1,6 in the Parameters box. You must separate the two numbers with the comma.

Check the Absolute Coordinates box to move the object to a position on the page relative to the rulers. When you check the Absolute

Coordinates box, nine boxes appear in the lower left of the dialog box (see Figure 18.2). These boxes represent the points on the object and where they should be placed in relation to the rulers.

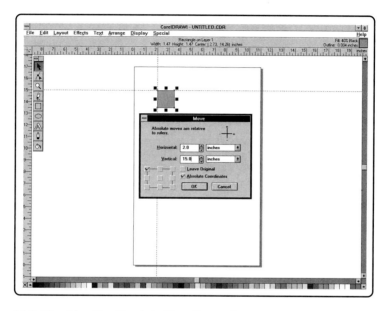

Figure 18.2. Checking the Absolute Coordinates box.

Corel*NOTE!*

Important: When you select an object and check the Absolute Coordinates box, the Parameters box displays a set of numbers, both horizontal and vertical. These numbers represent where the object you selected is currently positioned relative to your current rulers. If you check any one of the nine boxes, the numbers will change. If you then check OK, the object doesn't move. The reason the object doesn't move is that when you check a different box, the center box for example, the numbers only reflect the position of the center point of the object to the current rulers.

Manipulation Workshop

To actually move an object using Absolute Coordinates, you must
enter the new numbers in the parameter boxes. For example,
suppose you want to move an object so that the upper left corner is
positioned exactly two inches in and two inches down from the left-
hand corner of the page. Type **2** in the Horizontal box and **2** in the
Vertical box. When you click OK, the object moves to its new position.

Figures 18.3 through 18.6 show different examples using Absolute
Coordinates.

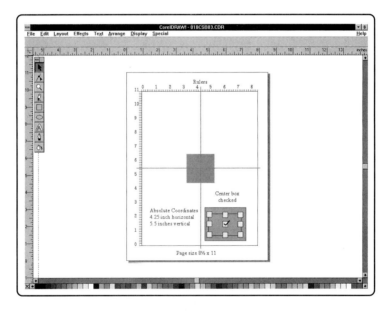

Figure 18.3. Moving by Absolute Coordinates with the center box checked.

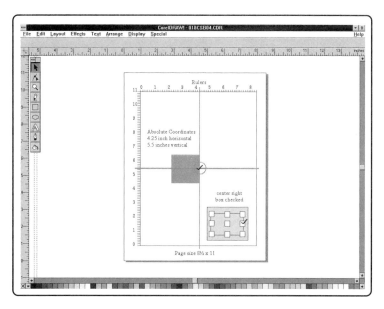

Figure 18.4. Using the same coordinates, but with the center right box checked.

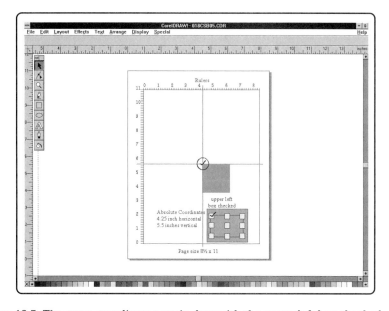

Figure 18.5. The same coordinates again, but with the upper left box checked.

Manipulation Workshop

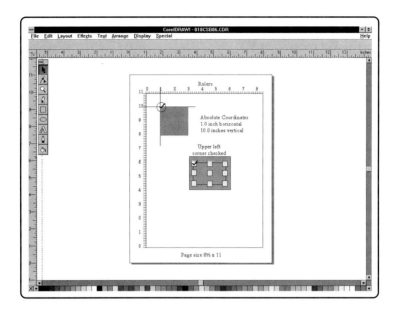

Figure 18.6. Keeping the upper left box checked while changing the coordinates.

You might think we went to a lot effort to describe the use of Absolute Coordinates, but we've found that very few users know how to use this feature. It can be confusing at first, but with a little practice it will become second nature to you.

Effects
Workshop

Workshops

Effects Workshop

Blending

The Blend feature in Corel Draw does a great deal more than simply blend one object into another. It is important to first understand the separate parts of a blend and the difference between single blends and multiple blends. Blends can also be used in ways that are not commonly associated with the normal artistic use of blending. They can be used to make grids, graphs, or anything that requires evenly spaced objects to illustrate an idea or message.

The Basic Blend

Figure 19.1 illustrates how to achieve a basic blend. Select two objects either by marquee selecting or by holding down the Shift key while clicking on each object. Pull down the Effects menu and select the Blend Roll-Up command. In the Blend roll-up, click on the top icon, which depicts three objects. This icon allows you to choose the number of steps you want in a blend. In the illustration, five steps were chosen. Next, click on Apply at the bottom of the dialog box. Corel Draw creates a five-step blend.

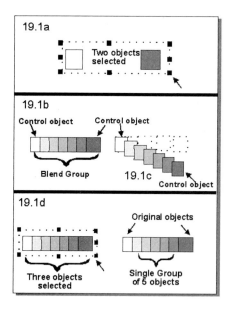

Figure 19.1. The basic blend: (a) selecting two objects; (b) a blend group with control objects; (c) dragging a control object; (d) a basic blend group consists of three objects.

The Parts of a Blend

If you click the center of the newly created blend, the status line tells you that it is a *blend group* (see Figures 19.1b and 19.1c). A blend group is not the same as a normal Corel Draw group. When you click on the first or last object of the blend group, the status line tells you that it is a control object—a rectangle, curve, ellipse, and so on. A blend group is made up of three parts (see Figure 19.1d).

You can change the direction of a basic blend from beginning to end by clicking one of the control objects and dragging it to a new position (as shown in Figure 19.1c).

There will be times when you will want to separate a blend group. To do this, click the blend group and then select the Separate command from the Arrange menu. Once you separate a blend group, it becomes three different objects. The first and last objects return to their original form—rectangle, curve, ellipse, and so on. The middle objects are now a group of objects, which represents the number of steps you originally selected for the blend group. This group of objects is now like any normal Corel Draw group, and you can ungroup it with the Ungroup command in the Arrange menu.

Blend Variations—Fitting a Blend to a Path

Making a blend follow a specific path is one of the easier blend variations. The purpose of making a blend follow a path is to create various effects that would otherwise be difficult to do manually. Figure 19.2 shows two effects using this method. To fit a blend to a path, follow these steps:

1. Make a basic blend using any shape you want.
2. Create a path for the blend to follow, for example, a wavy line or ellipse.
3. Select the Fit to Path tool from the Blend roll-up (see Figure 19.2a).
4. A fly-out menu appears. Select New Path.
5. The cursor changes to an arrow. Use the arrow to click the path you created.

Effects Workshop

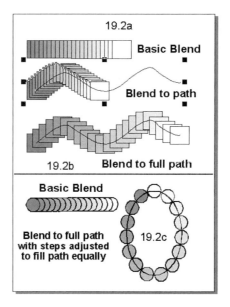

Figure 19.2. Fitting a blend to path: (a) the basic blend; (b) same blend fitted to a path; (c) adjusting the number of paths.

The blend follows the new path. The number of steps in your blend will determine how far along the path the blend will travel. If you want the blend to go from the beginning to the end, click on the Full Path box in the Blend roll-up (see Figure 19.2b). If this causes your blend to "break apart," increase the number of steps in the blend until you get the desired effect. You can create evenly spaced objects along your path by selecting the right amount of steps (see Figure 19.2c.)

The blend and the path have been linked together. This allows you to slide the control object of the blend along the path to make the blend travel a specific distance along the path. This is in effect a variation of the Full Path choice you made earlier.

Keep in mind that you can blend many different types of objects. Here are just a few ideas: clip art, text, symbols, and freehand objects (see Figure 19.3).

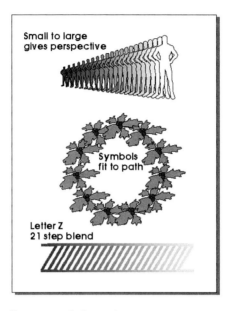

Figure 19.3. Blending clip art, symbols, and text.

Making Grids and Charts

Grids (see Figure 19.4) are easy to make with the Blend feature:

1. With the ✎ tool, draw a horizontal line across the top of your page and a second horizontal line at the bottom of the page.
2. Select the two lines and blend with the number of steps you need.
3. To complete the grid, draw a vertical line from the top to the bottom of the page on the left and right sides and blend these two lines with the number of steps you need.

Corel*NOTE!*

Use the rulers and guidelines to help you make the corners square.

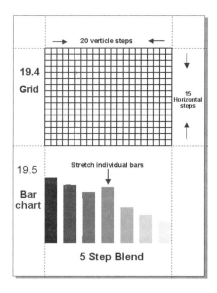

Figure 19.4. Creating a grid with the Blend feature.

Bar charts (see Figure 19.5) are equally easy to create:

1. Create a long rectangle and a short rectangle, and then blend the two together using the number of steps you need.

2. To make the middle bars different lengths, separate and ungroup the blend and stretch the bars that need to be changed.

Split Blends

Splitting blends can provide some very interesting effects (see Figure 19.6). You make a split blend by taking a normal blend group and converting one of the objects within the group to a new control object. By selecting the new control object with an entirely new object you can create a second blend that is connected to the first blend. You can continue to add new blends one at a time; there is no limit to the number of blends you can create.

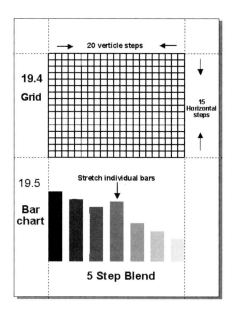

Figure 19.5. Creating a bar chart with the Blend feature.

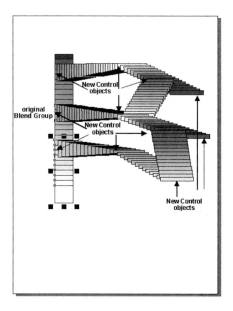

Figure 19.6. Splitting blends to create multiple blends.

To split a blend, follow these steps:

1. Start with a normal blend.
2. Add a new object to blend to.
3. Click the Clock icon in the group of three icons in the Blend roll-up box.
4. Click the Split button. Your cursor changes to an arrow.
5. Click the arrow anywhere in the original blend group where you want to start your second blend.
6. The object you clicked on is selected, and the status bar indicates that the object is a control object.
7. Hold down the Shift key and select the new object.
8. Click the Apply button, and your new blend is drawn. The number of steps will be the number that you last used. You can change the number of steps as with any other blend.

Adding Additional Split Blends

To continue adding new blends to the first two, perform the following steps:

1. Add a new object to blend to.
2. Press and hold both the Ctrl and Alt keys and click in any of the previous blends where you what to create a new control object.
3. The previous blend changes from a compound object to a blend group.
4. Click the Split button and proceed as for splitting a normal blend.

Corel *TIP!*

If you forgot to add a new object to blend to before you performed a new split, it might be difficult to find the new control object. A quick way to find the new control object is to use the Tab key. Tabbing selects each object or group on the page in the sequence it was made. When your new control object is highlighted, hold down the Shift key and select the new object you want to blend to.

The Fuse Command

The Fuse command recombines split blends. Follow these steps to fuse split blends:

1. Hold down the Ctrl key and click the blend group you want to fuse.
2. Click whatever Fuse button is highlighted.
3. If the start and end object is shared by three or more blend groups, a special pointer replaces the cursor.
4. Click an intermediate object at least one object removed from the start or end object you want to fuse with. The status line indicates that you now have a compound object again.

Neon Effects

You can create the look of neon as shown in Figure 19.7. Use the following steps:

1. Type some text on the screen (See Skill Session 10). Use your favorite font.
2. Remove the fill from the text (see Skill Session 11) and change the outline width to 6 or 8 points (see Skill Session 12).
3. Change the outline color to Neon Red. This color is in the default palette.
4. Make a duplicate of the text and place it directly on top of the first text. The easy way to do this is to set zero values in the Place Duplicate dialog box in the Preferences menu.
5. Change the outline of the duplicate to a width of .001.
6. Change the outline color to White.
7. Marquee select the two objects and blend with a 20-step blend.
8. You can experiment with different line widths to get different effects.

Effects Workshop

Figure 19.7. Creating a neon effect with Blend.

Blends with Rotation

Rotating blends can create even more ways to illustrate an idea. Corel Draw 4 includes a new feature called Loop that is used to rotate a blend. Figure 19.8 shows an example of two rotated blends using the Loop feature.

1. Start with a normal blend using as many steps as you want.
2. Select the blend group, and enter −90 degrees in the Blend roll-up.
3. Click the Loop box and then click Apply.
4. You can move either of the control objects to vary the effect.

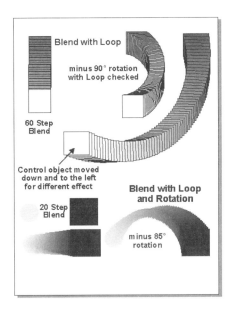

Figure 19.8. Using the Loop feature with rotated blends.

Mapping Nodes

You can create more effects when blending by changing the node order that Corel Draw normally uses. Figure 19.9 illustrates three variations of blending with the node order changed.

1. Select two objects to blend and then click on the Map Nodes icon in the Blend dialog box.
2. The cursor changes to a curved arrow.
3. Click one of the highlighted nodes on one of your control objects.
4. The curved arrow appears again, upside down, and the nodes on the other control object are highlighted.
5. Select a node that does not correspond to the first set of nodes in the first control object.
6. Click Apply. The new blend is drawn.

Effects Workshop

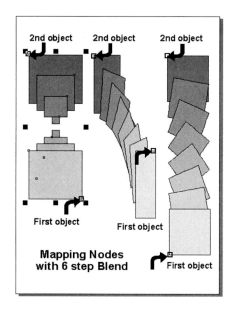

Figure 19.9. Changing the node order while rotating a blend.

Experiment with different node selections for different effects.

Effects Workshop

Perspective

Effects Workshop

Adding perspective to a drawing is a fundamental way of adding depth to a drawing. The perspective effect in Corel Draw can be used on individual objects or groups of objects. To illustrate the illusion of a road lined with trees going toward the horizon requires the use of perspective. As the road gets farther away, the width of the road narrows and the trees gets smaller. Figure 20.1 illustrates this basic example. The road is made up of two rectangles grouped together. The group of two objects is shown at the top of Figure 20.1; the bottom of the figure shows the group with perspective applied. The actual process of applying perspective to an object is as follows:

1. Select the object or group of objects.
2. Click Add Perspective in the Effects menu.
3. The ⋏ tool is automatically selected for you, and a selection box appears around the object with four handles.
4. For one-point perspective, drag either horizontally or vertically on the handles to achieve the desired perspective. You can hold down the Ctrl key to constrain your motion according to the settings in the Preferences dialog box. (If you hold down the Ctrl and Shift keys together, the opposing handles will move either in the opposite direction or the same direction.)

   When you drag straight across toward the middle, an × appears representing the vanishing point. You can click and drag on this × to change the perspective even more.
5. For two-point perspective, drag inward toward the center of the object. Two vanishing point ×s appear in this case, allowing you to change vanishing points individually.
6. When you release the mouse button after dragging on a handle or vanishing point, the object will be redrawn with the new perspective.

The perspective effect cannot be used on the trees (see Figure 20.2) because they would appear to be laying down. Instead the trees are duplicated and made smaller as they recede toward the background. To make sure the trees follow the same perspective as the road, draw a guideline from the top of the foreground tree to the horizon. Adjust the heights of the individual trees so they do not exceed the height of the guideline.

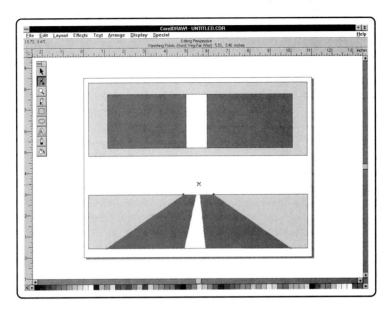

Figure 20.1. Adding perspective to a road.

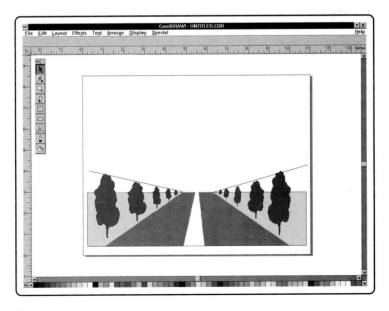

Figure 20.2. Adding trees in perspective.

Figure 20.3 illustrates the use of perspective on text. Notice how, through the use of perspective, you can show shadows receding toward the horizon and give the illusion of the text coming toward and going away from the viewer.

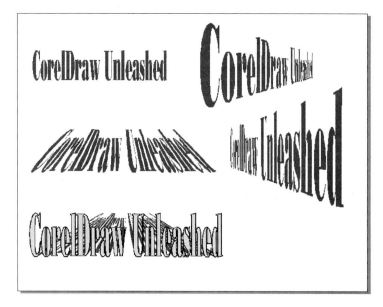

Figure 20.3. Various uses of perspective on text.

When adding perspective to text, you can still change its attributes (for example, change the font from Arial to Bahamas). However, you cannot change the attributes of an individual letter.

Figure 20.4 illustrates the use of perspective on a checkerboard pattern. This is a very good way to show depth on a floor.

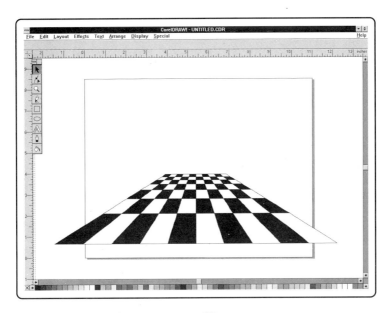

Figure 20.4. Using perspective on a pattern fill.

You can always revert to an object's original shape by selecting Clear Perspective from the Effects menu.

Effects Workshop

Extruding

The Extrude feature of Corel Draw allows you to add a three-dimensional effect to objects. To use this feature, click on the Effects menu and select the Extrude roll-up option. The roll-up menu must be on-screen and rolled down in order to apply an extrude to an object.

Corel NOTE!

Before any changes can take effect with roll-up menus, you must click on the Apply button.

Let's start with a simple extrude applied to a square. The default setting is Small Back. A preview of this effect is shown in the preview window when the top icon is highlighted. The default depth of Extrude is 20. The larger the number, the farther back the object will be extruded. Figure 21.1 shows the effect of the default setting when applied to a square. No fill was applied to the square so that you can see the outlines of the four sides of the box.

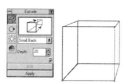

Figure 21.1. A basic extrude.

Figure 21.2 shows the box filled with a solid color.

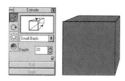

Figure 21.2. A basic extrude filled with solid color.

Notice the × on the page. This is the vanishing point. If you click and drag on the ×, you can change the shape of the box (see Figure 21.3).

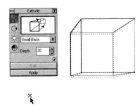

Figure 21.3. Changing the shape of an extruded object.

Figure 21.4 shows the results of changing the vanishing point and filling the box with a solid color.

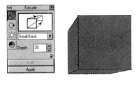

Figure 21.4. A modified extrude filled with color.

The next option in the Extrude roll-up is Rotate. Its icon is represented by a circle with an arrow. When this icon is selected, the preview window displays a sphere with directional arrows. If you click on any of these arrows, the object rotates in the direction of the arrow. Figure 21.5 shows a dotted-line display of what takes place by clicking on the center down arrow.

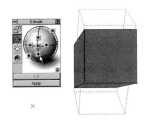

Figure 21.5. Rotating an extruded object.

Effects Workshop

Figure 21.6 show the final result when the object is filled with a solid color.

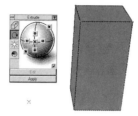

Figure 21.6. The rotated extrude filled with solid color.

The next option you have in the Extrude roll-up is the Light Source icon. When you click on this icon, the preview window displays a sphere inside a transparent box. To activate the light source, click on the On button. You can change the direction of light by clicking on one of the intersecting lines of the box. After you have made your selection, click on Apply, as always, to have the lighting take effect. Figure 21.7 shows the results of the lighting effect.

Figure 21.7. The extruded object with lighting applied.

The last effect option you have is Color Shading. The Color Wheel icon at the bottom changes the dialog box, giving you three choices of color to apply. The Shade button allows you to pick colors to shade the extruded portion of the object. The default is White and Black. When you click on the Color button, a palette of colors appears. Figure 21.8 shows the effect of a shaded box.

Figure 21.8. The extruded object with shading applied.

Figure 21.9 shows the effect of extruding text. The word "Unleashed" has been extruded using the default command. As you can see, the vanishing point is located now in the top left of the rectangle, rather than in the center of the page. This is because all the settings you make to your last extruded object become the default settings for all new objects you want to extrude. In order to have the default settings revert to their original settings, you must close the roll-up and then reopen it again. This phenomenon occurs in version 3.0 as well. Corel Draw does not consider it a bug, so you will have to live with it. Just be aware of it.

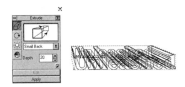

Figure 21.9. Extruding text with depth set at 20.

Figure 21.10 shows the effect on the extrude by changing the number in the depth parameters box to 80 instead of the default number of 20.

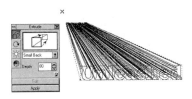

Figure 21.10. Extruded text with depth set at 80.

Effects Workshop

In Figure 21.11 the vanishing point is moved to line up with the center of the text still using the depth figure of 80.

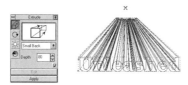

Figure 21.11. Vanishing point moved to center.

Figure 21.12 shows the completed extrusion with the extrusion shaded from black to white and the text itself colored black.

Figure 21.12. Finished extrude with shading.

Figure 21.13 shows the effect the Extrude command has on four squares that were extruded with the vanishing point in the center of the page. Notice the direction of each extrude goes to the center.

Figure 21.14 shows these same objects, only each has been rotated toward the center at 25 degrees. Lines have been drawn to illustrate the effect.

Figure 21.15 illustrates how using the same text object and extruding it at different angles can create an interesting effect. Notice that the vanishing point is almost off the page and the extrude at the bottom right has not been brought into place.

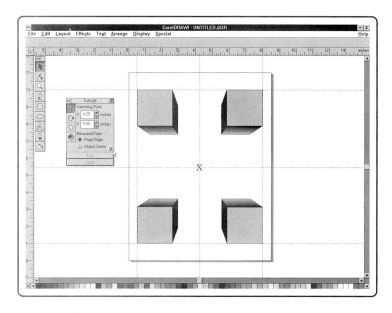

Figure 21.13. Four boxes extruded to center.

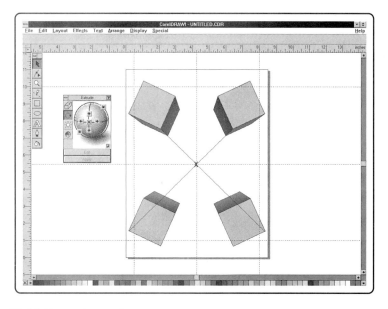

Figure 21.14. Rotated extrudes.

Effects Workshop

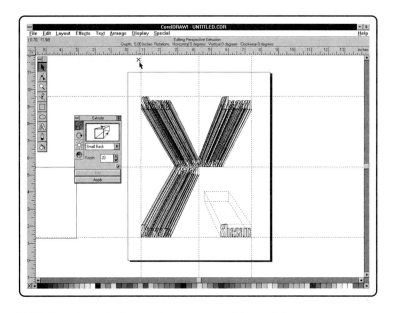

Figure 21.15. Running out of space to move vanishing point.

This problem is overcome by zooming out on the page to allow you to move the vanishing point high enough to finish the extrude. Click on the Magnifying tool in the tool box and select the Minus tool. If you still cannot move the vanishing point to where you need it, select the Minus tool again and zoom out even farther. Figure 21.16 shows the effect of zooming out once. Notice that you still can't see the vanishing point.

Figure 21.17 shows the effect of zooming out twice.

Figure 21.18 shows the completed effect with an extra extrude thrown in.

Although most users think of the Extrude feature as applying only to text and basic shapes, there are more uses for this amazing feature. Figure 21.19 shows how simple shapes for the symbols library in Corel Draw can look when they are extruded.

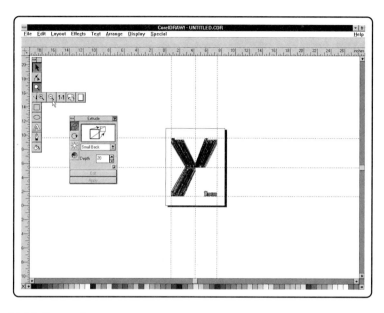

Figure 21.16. Zoomed out once.

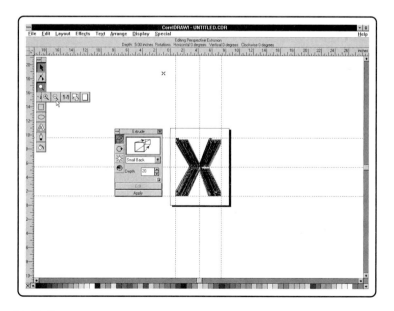

Figure 21.17. Zoomed out twice.

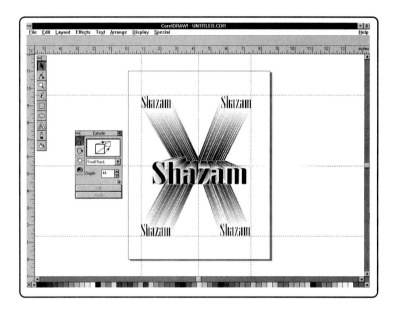

Figure 21.18. The final drawing.

Figure 21.19. Extruded symbols.

Experiment with different objects and shapes. Try extruding a single curved line. You will be surprised at what effects you can create.

Effects Workshop

Enveloping

Enveloping is an effect in Corel Draw that allows you to reshape objects. Distort might be a better description. To access the Envelope feature choose Envelope Roll-Up from the Effects menu.

All enveloping effects are applied to objects using the different options in the roll-up. Envelopes can be applied to any object or group of objects except bitmaps. Corel Draw's new texture fills, although technically bitmaps, can have envelopes applied to them.

When you apply envelopes to Paragraph text you can reshape the frame to flow text around or inside objects. Text reshaped with an envelope will remain as text. This means you can edit it and change its attributes, but you cannot change the attributes of individual characters.

As with all other roll-ups in Corel Draw, you must click on the Apply button before the effect can be applied.

Basic Shapes

Let's start with a simple rectangle, as in Figure 22.1. Select the rectangle and then choose Add New from the roll-up (you must always click on Add New before applying an envelope). Now choose an envelope type from the choices just below the Create From button (these are called Editing Mode buttons). In this case the third mode button was selected. Notice the buttons show the basic shape that can be created by choosing them. The fourth button, depicting the Shape tool, is the Unconstrained mode; all the handles move freely and have control points that can be used to fine-tune the shape of the envelope.

With the rectangle and mode button selected click on apply. A marching-ants selection box with eight handles is applied to the rectangle. Notice that the Shape tool is automatically selected. This is the same tool you use when doing any node editing. Click on the top center node of the rectangle and drag upward. The outline of the selection box begins to form the shape of the mode you selected. Continue dragging until you reach the desired effect. Click on Apply and the effect is applied. This particular mode allows you to drag all of the center nodes of the rectangle, and the same effect will be applied to each side. If you drag on a corner node you will move the two adjacent center nodes together, in a stretching manner.

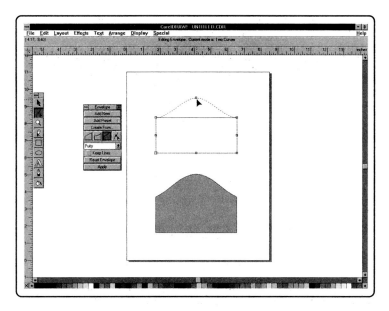

Figure 22.1. Beginning a basic envelope effect.

Figure 22.2 shows what enveloping does to a rectangle using the unconstrained mode.

Enveloping allows you to add or take away nodes just as you can when node editing any curve. Figure 22.3 illustrates how by double-clicking on the curve the Node Edit roll-up appears, allowing you to add or delete nodes. In this case, a new node was added.

Figure 22.4 shows the results of adding the extra node and using it to further change the shape of the envelope.

Figure 22.5 shows the final result after clicking on the Apply button.

Effects Workshop

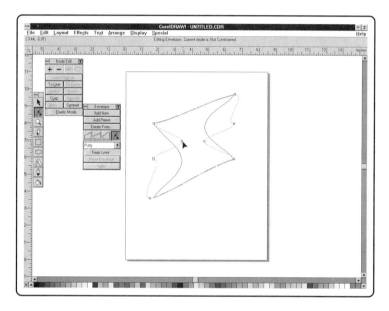

Figure 22.2. Enveloping in unconstrained mode.

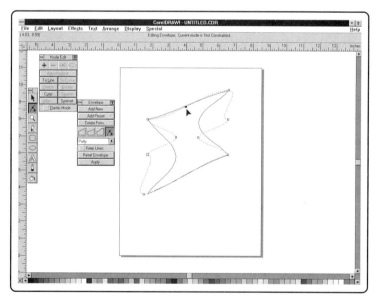

Figure 22.3. Adding a node to an envelope.

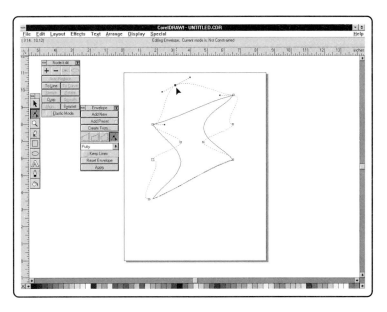

Figure 22.4. Reshaping an envelope with an added node.

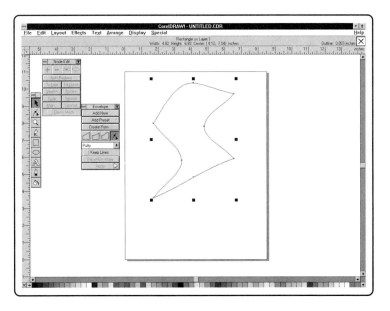

Figure 22.5. The final result after reshaping.

203

Create From

The Create From button lets you force a source object to take on the
shape of another object. Figure 22.6 illustrates how Paragraph text
was made to conform to the outline shape of an elephant.

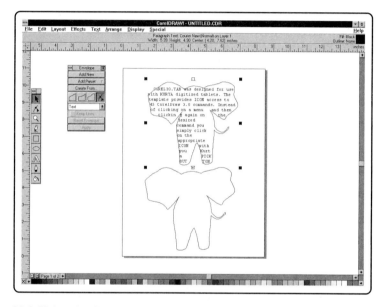

Figure 22.6. Using the Create From command.

The process is extremely simple. Create a target shape, your own or
a shape from the Symbols library. In Figure 22.6, a silhouette of the
elephant was taken from the Symbols library.

Select the source object you want to change—in this case the paragraph
text—and click on the Create From button in the roll-up. A black arrow
with the word *From* on it will appear on screen. Move the arrow until it
touches the outline of the shape you have chosen. Click once with the
primary mouse button. The source object will now have a selection box
around it in the shape of your target object. Click on Apply and your
shape will now follow the shape of the target object.

In Figure 22.7, the target object was moved behind the new object and
given a black fill. The text was changed to white for a different look.

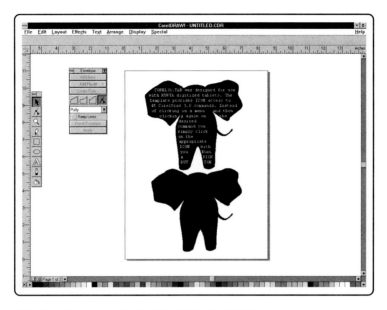

Figure 22.7. Creating a new look with white on black.

Preset Shapes

When you click the Add Preset button, a fly-out displays a selection of preshaped envelopes. Click the one you want; then select an object on-screen and click on Apply. Note that when applied to Paragraph text, the preset envelopes are stretched proportionally to fit the text frame. For other types of objects, they are stretched non-proportionally.

Figure 22.8 shows Paragraph text that has been selected. The fly-out menu from the Add Preset button shows a heart shape selected.

Figure 22.9 shows the results of applying the preset heart shape to the text.

Notice the heart is squeezed horizontally. The reason for this is because not all of the paragraph has been displayed on-screen. The Paragraph text was purposely cropped for this example. If the entire paragraph were displayed the heart shape would appear correct. When the situation calls for cropping a portion of Paragraph text you can still make the correct shape by node-editing the envelope. Figures 22.10 and 22.11 illustrate node-editing this particular shape. Again, you must click Apply before your changes take effect.

Effects Workshop

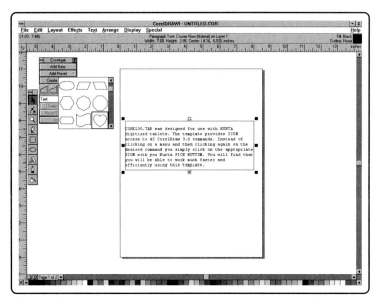

Figure 22.8. Preparing to add a preshaped envelope.

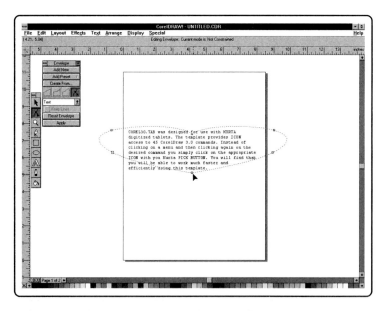

Figure 22.9. Paragraph text with a preset shape applied.

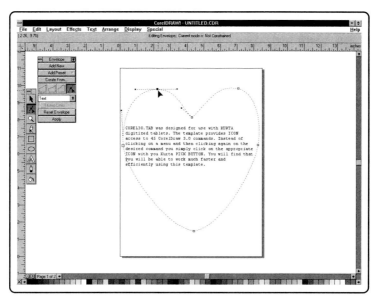

Figure 22.10. Adjusting the shape of the envelope.

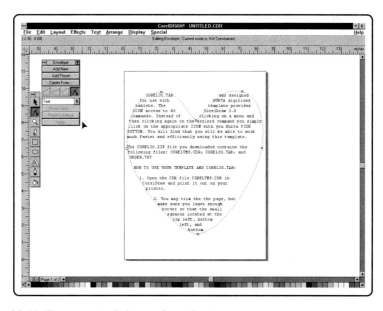

Figure 22.11. The corrected shape after adjustment.

Simple Text Enveloping

This example illustrates enveloping the word *BUBBLE* to a circle, as shown in the following steps:

1. Type the word *BUBBLE*.
2. Create a circle with the ⬭ tool (see Figure 22.12).
3. Select the text again.
4. Select New from the roll-up.
5. Click the Create From button.
6. When the From arrow appears, click on the circle.
7. Click Apply. (The result you get will not be what you see in Figure 22.13).

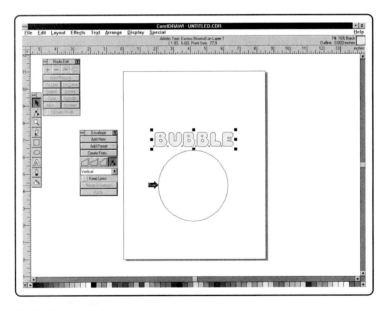

Figure 22.12. Preparing to envelope text to a circle.

The reason your text appears slanted is that there is one step that was left out. There is a Mapping Modes parameters box with the word Putty as its default. Use the down arrow in this box and scroll down until you reach Vertical. Now when you click on Apply, your text will be as shown in Figure 22.13. Try different settings for different effects.

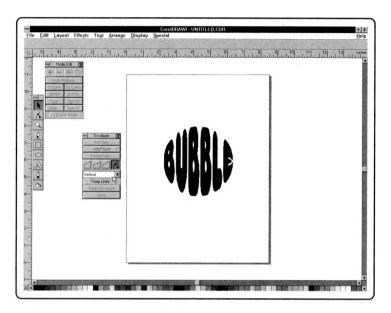

Figure 22.13. Text enveloped to a circle.

Keep Lines

The Keep Lines check box just above the Reset Envelope button can be very useful in certain circumstances. When you put a check mark in the Keep Lines box, Corel Draw will not convert straight lines in the object to curves. Figure 22.14 illustrates the two different effects. The top object is the original object that is being enveloped in all four directions. The middle object is the result of this enveloping with Keep Lines checked. The bottom object is the result with Keep Lines not checked.

Reset Envelope

Reset Envelope undoes any changes to the envelope since it was last applied.

Effects Workshop

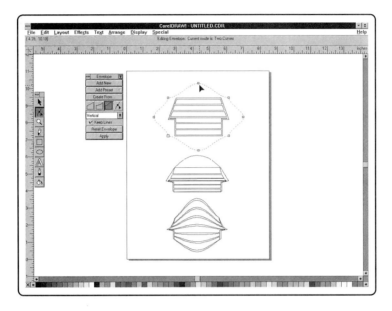

Figure 22.14. Enveloping with Keep Lines on and off.

Special Project

The image in Figure 22.15 was done using the Envelope feature on Paragraph text enveloped to fit inside the star shape from the symbols library. Texture fills were applied to the backgrounds and an embossed effect was created for a three-dimensional look. (see Text Special Effects in Skill Session 32).

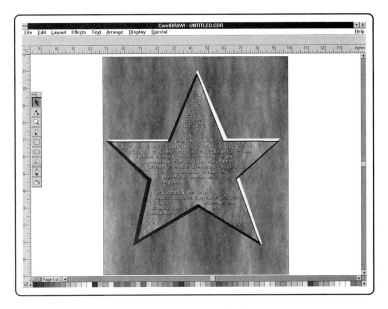

Figure 22.15. Enveloping with special effects added.

Caveats

If you select an unacceptable object, such as a bitmap, an information box will appear telling you so.

Effects Workshop

Separating

The Separate command has a special purpose. It is used only on certain
effects in Corel Draw. It precedes the Ungroup command whenever it is
used. Its function is to separate the different parts of objects that have
had an effect applied to them.

Corel *TIP!*

It is important to know when to use the Separate command. You use the
Separate command only when you want to edit the following effects:
Blend (including fitting Blends to Path), Contour, Extrude, Power Lines,
Fit Text to Path, and Clones.

When you apply one of the above effects to an object, the object could
include several different parts making up the effect. When you want to
separate those parts for editing, first use the Separate command. All
the effects except Cloning will have a group of objects remaining. For
example, when you create a Blend, it becomes a blend group. When you
use the Separate command on the blend group, the parts remaining are
the two original control objects, which are now normal objects, and the
center of the blend, which is now a normal group of objects. This group
of objects is made up of the number of steps you put in your blend. To
edit the objects within this group, choose the Ungroup command in the
Arrange menu. You must always perform this sequence of separating
and Ungrouping to have complete editing control over all objects within
the effect (see Figure 23.1).

Corel *NOTE!*

Separating clones is different. To separate all clones at once, you must
select them all either by clicking on them separately while holding the
Shift key down or by marquee selecting. When you select a clone object
individually and choose Separate, only that clone object is separated
from the other clones. This is handy if you are modifying the original
and don't want the changes to affect a particular clone (see Fig 23.2).

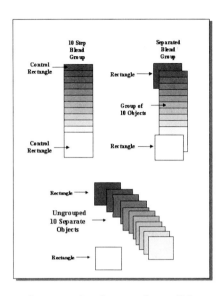

Figure 23.1. Separating and ungrouping for complete editing control.

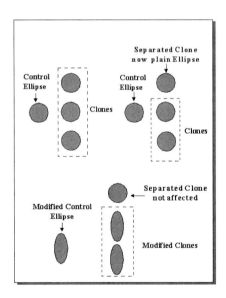

Figure 23.2. Separating and modifying clones.

Advanced Skills
Workshop

Advanced Skills Workshop

Welding

Advanced Skills Workshop

The Weld feature, new to Corel Draw 4, allows you to create effects that are not possible with earlier versions of Corel Draw.

Welding differs from the Combine feature in many ways. Welding is an additive process, while Combine falls more in the catagory of a subtractive process.

To weld one object to another, place one object so that it touches or covers a portion of the other object. Select the two objects either by marquee selecting or separately clicking on the objects while holding down the Shift key. Select Weld in the Arrange menu. The new object created is a single curve object with nodes that can be manipulated with the Shape tool.

Notice in Figure 24.1 that welding a circle on top of a square produces a single object with a new shape.

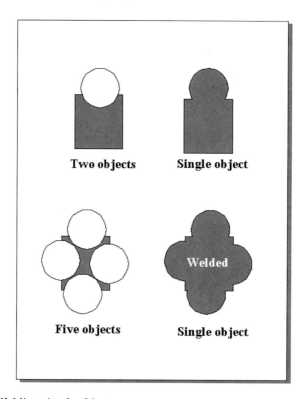

Figure 24.1. Welding simple objects.

Corel *NOTE!*

The fill color of a welded object is determined by the fill color of the last object selected.

Figure 24.2 illustrates other variations of welds.

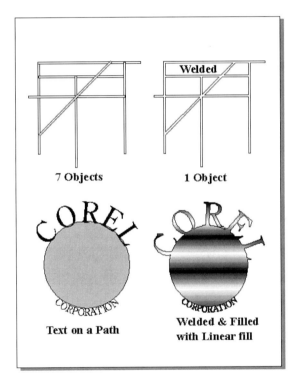

Figure 24.2. Using the Weld feature to create street maps. Welding and filling to create a logo.

Corel*NOTE!*

There are instances where welding an object on an angle across other objects that are already welded can cause a knockout effect similar to the Combine effect. To prevent this, weld the angled object to the other objects in a single weld, not one object at a time.

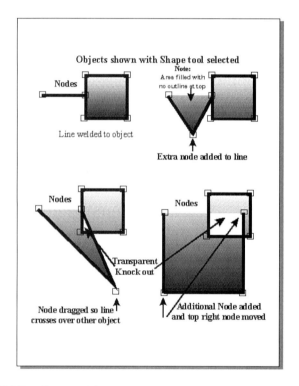

Figure 23.3. Welding lines to objects.

Welding lines to lines produces a similar effect to grouping. For example, if you weld three intersecting lines, they become one object, but they still maintain nodes at the end of each line. As a single object, they can be moved as a unit like any other single object.

You can also weld lines to objects. Figure 24.3 shows what effect welding a line to a square can produce and what happens when additional nodes are added and moved.

Figure 24.4 illustrates welding several objects to create an interesting shape that can be made into a pattern. You can then add the new pattern to your library of patterns for future use. Follow these steps to create the pattern shown in Figure 24.4:

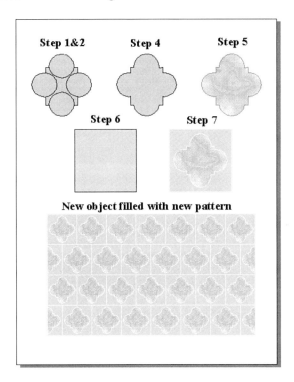

Figure 24.4. Welding simple shapes to create a pattern.

1. Draw a rectangle.
2. Draw four circles and place them on top of the rectangle.
3. Select the rectangle and circles by marquee selection.
4. Choose Weld from the Arrange menu.
5. Fill the new shape with a texture fill.

6. Draw a square and fill with the color you want.

7. Place the new shape on top of the square you just made.

8. Select Create Pattern from the Special menu.

9. The Create Pattern dialog box appears. Check the Full Color and High Resolution boxes and click OK.

10. When the cross hairs appear on screen, place the intersecting lines on the top left of the square; then drag to the bottom right corner and release the primary mouse button.

11. A dialog box appears asking whether you want to create a pattern from the selected area. Click OK.

12. The new pattern will now be available the next time you choose the Full Color Pattern icon in the Fill tool fly-out menu or the Fill roll-up.

Advanced Skills Workshop

Converting to Curves

Most objects when originally drawn in Corel Draw are either ellipses, rectangles, text, or freehand. Many effects can be applied to these objects in their original state, but the original object still maintains its original identity. For example, if you applied an extrude to a rectangle, the original rectangle would still be a rectangle even though it would be referred to as a Control Rectangle in the status line. If you used an ellipse to blend to a rectangle, the selected ellipse would show in the status line as the Control Ellipse and the rectangle would show as the Control Rectangle. If you applied an envelope to some text the new shape is still text. The point of all this is that although you can change the shape and look of these basic objects with different effects, you can change them even more if you convert them to curves. The one exception to this are objects that have been drawn freehand. Freehand objects are created as curves from the beginning, and they can be manipulated without converting them to curves again.

Figure 25.1 illustrates the effect of Convert to Curves on basic objects.

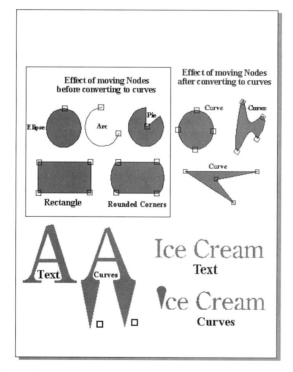

Figure 25.1. Converting some basic objects to curves.

A basic ellipse has only one node. When you convert it to curves, it has four nodes. If you tried to move the single node of the basic ellipse you would create either an arc or a pie shape. When you convert the ellipse to curves, you can change the shape completely using the four nodes. You can even add extra nodes to continue manipulating the shape (see Skill Session 5, "The Shape Tool").

A basic rectangle has a node at each corner. When you convert it to curves, it still has the same four nodes, but they affect the shape in a different way. If you move any one of the nodes in a rectangle before it's been converted to curves, you round the corners of the rectangle. After you convert it to curves, each node can be moved independently to create a new shape. You can add extra nodes (as with the ellipse) to create any shape you can imagine.

Converting text to curves can provide some interesting looks. Figure 25.1 includes a simple illustration of manipulating text after it has been converted to curves. Even though there seems to be an unlimited number of fonts to choose from in Corel Draw, you can vary the look of each one to be different from the rest.

Corel *TIP!*

Unless you are absolutely sure that your printer or the person you are sending your files to has the same fonts you used in your document, get in the habit of converting all your text to curves even if you don't plan on manipulating it. If the person printing your file does not have the font you used in your document or drawing, it will be printed using the printer's default font. If this happens, all the effort that went into that special font will go up in smoke.

Advanced Skills Workshop

Using Grid
Setup

Advanced Skills Workshop

With Grid Setup, you can set a grid to whatever specifications are required to complete almost any project. Drawings that need to have exact measurements, such as blueprints, maps, or electronic schematics, can be accomplished faster using Grid Setup. To activate the Grid Setup dialog box, select Grid Setup from the Layout menu. You can also activate the Grid Setup dialog box by double-clicking the rulers with the cursor (see Figure 26.1).

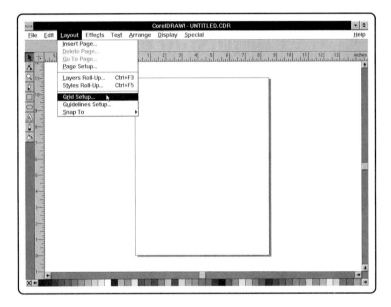

Figure 26.1. The Layout menu with the Grid Setup option highlighted.

In the Grid Setup dialog box (see Figure 26.2), there are options for setting the grid frequency, grid origin, showing the grid, and snapping to the grid. Under the Scale heading, you can set the global units. This option comes in handy for drawings that have objects in them that are not drawn to scale, such as the roads on a map. You can set your measurements in ratios, for example, 1 inch could be set equal to 3 miles.

If you don't already have your rulers on, pull down the Display menu and select the Show Rulers option. A check mark will appear next to the Show Rulers option when they are enabled. The rulers now appear on-screen (see Figure 26.3).

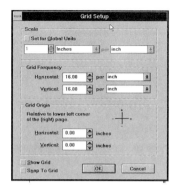

Figure 26.2. The Grid Setup dialog box with its available options.

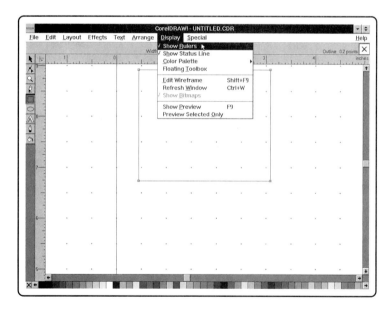

Figure 26.3. The Display menu with Show Rulers enabled and the rulers on-screen.

Advanced Skills Workshop

If you want, you can display the grid on-screen. the grid is represented by a series of dots. To enable this option, select Grid Setup from the Layout menu. The Show Grid option is located at the lower left section of the Grid Setup dialog box (see Figure 26.4).

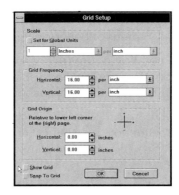

Figure 26.4. The Grid Setup dialog box with the Show Grid option disabled.

Just below the Show Grid option is the Snap To Grid option. This option is helpful when you know what size you want to draw certain objects. A rectangle that needs to be 2×3.5 inches can have a grid that is set up in 0.50-inch increments. It will be easier to attain that specific requirement with the Snap To Grid option enabled than to draw that rectangle freehand.

When accuracy counts, you will find that setting up the grid and then enabling the Snap To Grid option will speed up drawing time and ensure that the sizes of objects that you draw are what they need to be. The Snap To Grid option can also assist you when you need to align various elements (see Figure 26.5).

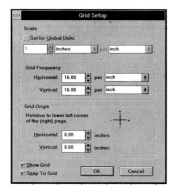

Figure 26.5. The Grid Setup dialog box with the Show Grid and the Snap To Grid options enabled.

Draw a rectangle with the Snap To Grid option off. Draw a second rectangle with the Snap To Grid option on. Notice how the second rectangle clings to the grid as you draw (see Figure 26.6). Another method of enabling or disabling the Snap To Grid option is to press Ctrl-Y.

You can also turn the grid on or off using the Layers roll-up (see Skill Session 28, "Layers"). To turn the grid on or off, double-click Grid in the Layers roll-up; in the Layer Options dialog box, enable or disable the Visible option (see Figure 26.7).

There is one other method of turning the Snap To Grid option on or off, found at the bottom of the Layout menu. Select Snap To, and a cascading menu with Grid, Guides, and Objects appears. Select Grid from the list (see Figure 26.8).

Advanced Skills Workshop

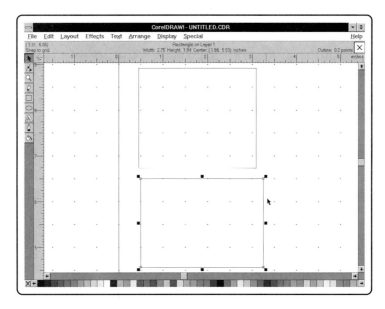

Figure 26.6. The selected rectangle is drawn with the Snap To Grid option enabled.

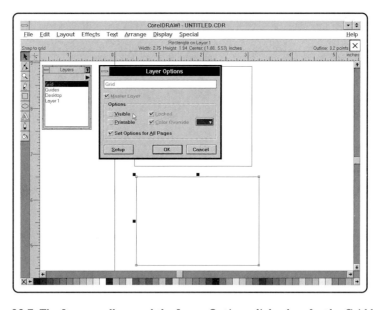

Figure 26.7. The Layers roll-up and the Layer Options dialog box for the Grid layer with the Visible option disabled.

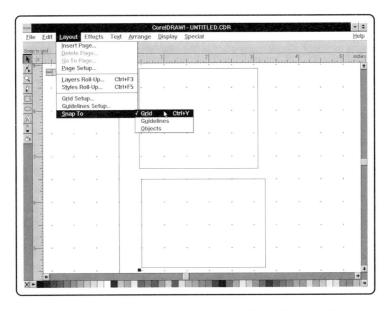

Figure 26.8. The Layout menu with Snap To selected and the cascading menu with the Grid option enabled.

Draw a rectangle with the Snap To Grid option enabled. Make it 2 inches wide and 1 inch high. If you need to draw an object to scale, you can use ratios (for example, a 1:10 ratio can be set at 10 inches equal to 1 mile) for building schematics or maps. You can use the Scale option in the Grid Setup dialog box.

Bring up the Grid Setup dialog box. At the top in the Scale section, enable the Set for Global Units option. In the first box at the left, change the number of inches from 1 to 7. In the second box from the left, change inches to feet. Leave the third box at the right set at inches (see Figure 26.9).

Select the 2×1-inch rectangle, and notice that the status line now reflects the changes that were made in the Grid Setup dialog box. The status line now tells you that the rectangle is 14×7 feet (see Figure 26.10).

Advanced Skills Workshop

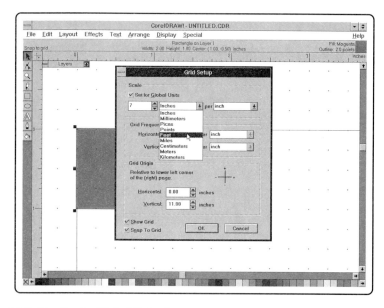

Figure 26.9. The Set for Global Units Option in the Grid Setup dialog box enabled.

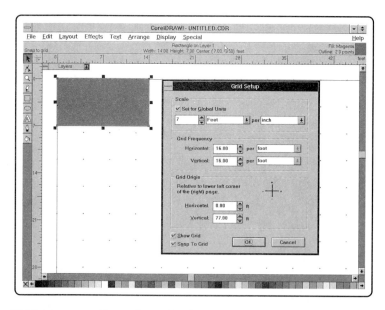

Figure 26.10. The status line reflects the change made in the Grid Setup dialog box.

In the Grid Setup dialog box, you change the grid frequency by entering new values in the horizontal and vertical sections. Type a value or use the up and down arrows. You can change the measurement system from inches to millimeters, picas, or points.

Corel*NOTE!*

When you open a new file, it retains the grid setup information used for the last document. If the Snap To Grid option is enabled in one file, that option will carry over into the next file until you disable that option.

The grid origin tells you where the grid is placed relative to the lower left corner of the right page. You can also change values by retyping them or using the up and down arrows. By using the grid and its available options, you can quickly create a grid to your specific measurements (see Figure 26.11).

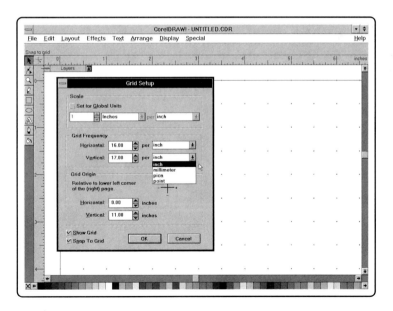

Figure 26.11. The Grid Frequency and Grid Origin can be changed to different values from the default setting.

Advanced Skills Workshop

Guidelines

Advanced Skills Workshop

In the Layout menu, you will find the Guidelines Setup command (see Figure 27.1). Use guidelines for aligning objects. On-screen, the guidelines appear dashed. Place as many guidelines as you need in your document. The guidelines will not print. Corel Draw saves the guidelines with the file.

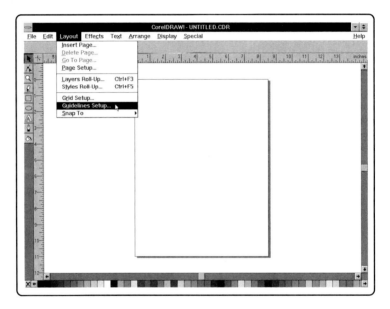

Figure 27.1. The Layout menu with Guidelines Setup highlighted.

You can also snap objects to guidelines. In the Layout menu, select Snap To. A cascading menu appears; choose Guidelines from the list (see Figure 27.2).

To set the guidelines, click and hold the mouse button on either of the vertical or horizontal rulers and drag a guideline away from them. A guideline appears on-screen. You can use the rulers to place the guidelines, or you can invoke the Guidelines dialog box and set precise positions for the guidelines.

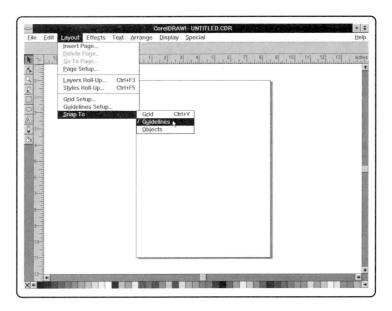

Figure 27.2. The Layout menu with Snap To highlighted and the cascading menu with Guidelines selected.

There are several options in the Guidelines dialog box. The first section is Guideline type. You can choose horizontal or vertical guidelines. The second section is Ruler Position. You can change the position of the guideline by typing in a new value and clicking on the Move button. It uses the measurement system set up by the Grid. The figure displays inches as the current measurement system. Below that section you find the Snap To Guides option; enable this option.

There are five buttons beneath the Snap To Guides option (see Figure 27.3):

Delete   This deletes the currently selected guide.

Move   You can type in a new value and then click on Move to reposition the guideline to that new area.

Add   Click on this button to add more guidelines.

Advanced Skills Workshop

Next   This rotates you through all current guidelines in your document, displays whether they are horizontal or vertical, and shows their position.

Close   This closes the dialog box.

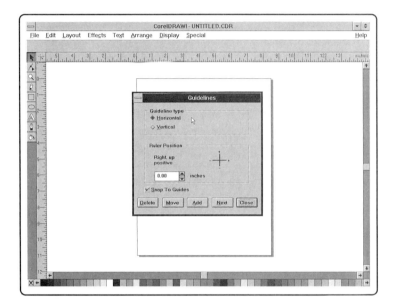

Figure 27.3. The Guidelines dialog box and its available options.

With Snap To Guides on, click on the vertical ruler and drag the guideline to the 1-inch position. Do the same with the guideline from the horizontal ruler (see Figure 27.4).

Draw a rectangle using the □ tool and move it to the guideline. Feel how it seems to stick to the guideline as you move it along. This will help you when you need to align objects to specific areas on your document. You can place a guideline at the required increment on the ruler and move any objects to that position (see Figures 27.5 and 27.6).

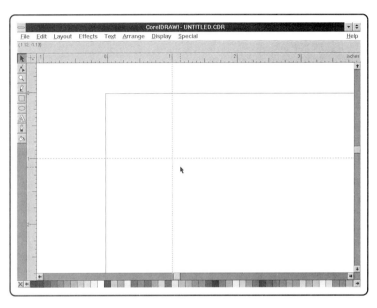

Figure 27.4. A vertical and horizontal guideline placed at the 1-inch mark on the rulers.

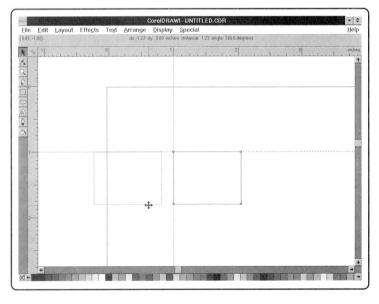

Figure 27.5. A rectangle snapping to the guidelines as it is moved.

Advanced Skills Workshop

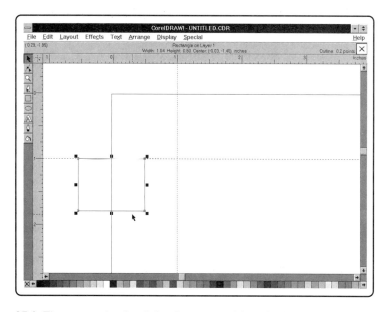

Figure 27.6. The rectangle after it has been repositioned while snapping to the guideline.

Guidelines can also be used to help create setups for projects such as company logos, letterhead, statements, business cards, or forms. Place guidelines where you want to position graphic elements and text (see Figure 27.7). Use the rulers to help you set up the guidelines.

You can use predetermined requirements to create the document. Use the Guidelines dialog box to add and place the guidelines (see Figure 27.8).

From the Layers roll-up, bring up the Layer Options dialog box for Guides. The Color Override default is set to blue. Click on the color button and a pull-down menu appears (see Figure 27.9). Select a color from the palette or click on the More button to select other color choices. After you select a new color, click on OK to see the color of the guidelines change on your screen (see Figure 27.10).

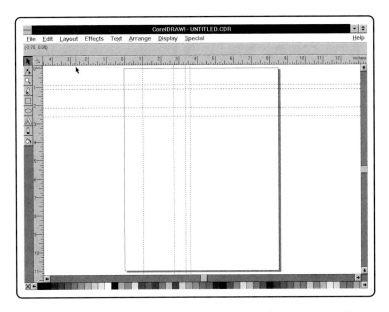

Figure 27.7. Positioned guidelines on the screen where elements are to be placed.

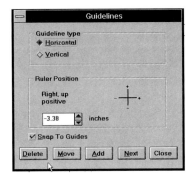

Figure 27.8. Use the Guidelines dialog box to add and place guidelines to exact positions.

Advanced Skills Workshop

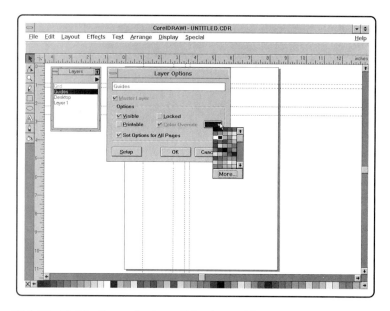

Figure 27.9. The Guides Layer Options dialog box with color selected.

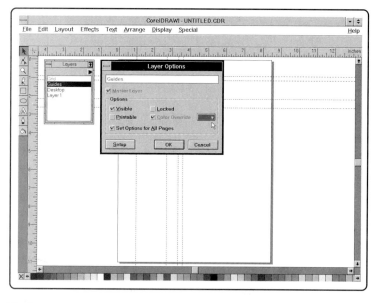

Figure 27.10. The Guides Layer Options dialog box with the new color displayed.

In the document, you can see the guidelines' color change. All guidelines on this layer will take on the same attributes.

Select Guides from the list in the Layers roll-up. New objects that are placed or drawn on this layer take on the attributes of a guideline. You can use this feature to create odd-shaped Guidelines. Drawings of objects as well as text can be placed on the Guidelines layer (see Figure 27.11).

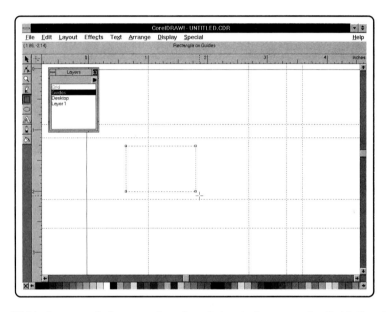

Figure 27.11. A rectangle (or any other shape) that is drawn on the Guidelines layer becomes a guide.

Corel *NOTE!*

You can import objects onto the Guides layer as well. A vector-based image, such as a .CDR or .EPS file, appears on-screen as a dashed line. However, an imported bitmap object, such as a .PCX or TIFF file, shows a dashed line only around that bitmap's bounding box.

Advanced Skills Workshop

Use the Guidelines to align text and other objects to each other. If you need to fit an illustration or logo into a specific area, use the guidelines to assist in resizing these elements (see Figure 27.12).

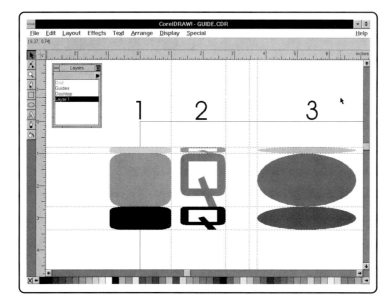

Figure 27.12. Using the guidelines to place and resize various elements.

Figure 27.13 is a close-up of a sample form. It is a statement set up using the guidelines. Elements were created and then they were positioned according to predetermined specifications.

Figure 27.14 is a full-page view of the statement. Twenty different guidelines were used to set up this statement. Once the guidelines are in place, setting the elements up to create the statement is a breeze.

Figure 27.13. A statement created by using the guidelines.

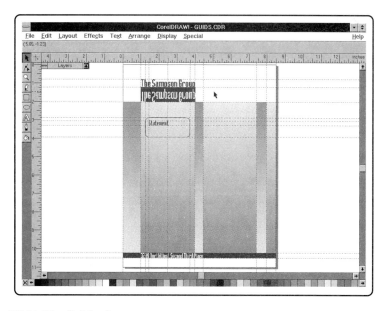

Figure 27.14. The finished statement.

Advanced Skills Workshop

Layers

Advanced Skills Workshop

With the Layers feature, you can have as many layers as your available system resources allow. You add new layers and delete and edit them through a menu. You can also delete, copy, and move objects from one layer to another. Each layer can have its own elements on them, and you can make each layer printable, visible, locked, or even change the color override. In the Layout menu, you will find the Layers Roll-Up option (see Figure 28.1).

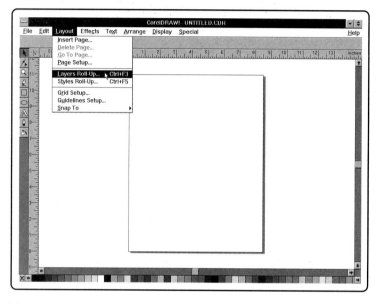

Figure 28.1. The Layout menu with the Layers roll-up highlighted.

When you select this command, the Layers roll-up appears on-screen (see Figure 28.2). There are four default settings in the roll-up: Grid, Guides, Desktop, and Layer 1.

There is also a button at the upper left corner that has a pull-down menu with these selections: Roll down, Roll up, Arrange, Arrange All, Help, and Close. In the upper right corner of the Layers roll-up there is an arrow. When the roll-up is rolled down the arrow points up (see Figure 28.3).

Figure 28.2. The Layers roll-up with the four default settings.

Figure 28.3. The Layers roll-up system menu.

Figure 28.4 shows the Layers roll-up in the rolled up position after selecting Arrange from the pull-down menu. Notice that the arrow on the top far right now points down. After you select Arrange, the roll-up is tucked into the top corner of your screen (which corner depends on how many roll-ups you have open). You can arrange one roll-up at a time, or you can select Arrange All, and the roll-ups will place themselves in the upper left and right corners.

Under the arrow at the upper right of the roll-up there is an arrowhead. Click on the arrowhead and a fly-out menu appears. Selections include New, Edit, Delete, Move To, Copy to, and MultiLayer (see Figure 28.5).

With the MultiLayer option in the fly-out menu enabled, you can be on a different layer and still work and select an object that is on any unlocked layer. Any new element, whether it is text or an object, is placed on the current layer highlighted in the Layers roll-up.

When you select New from the Layers roll-up fly-out menu, the Layer Options dialog box appears. The default name is Layer 2. You can give the layer any name you want. If you want to work on one layer, you can lock the other layers and make them invisible. By locking the layers you will not be able to accidentally select and move objects on that layer. By making a layer invisible you will have faster screen redraw times. This will also save you unnecessary confusion.

Advanced Skills Workshop

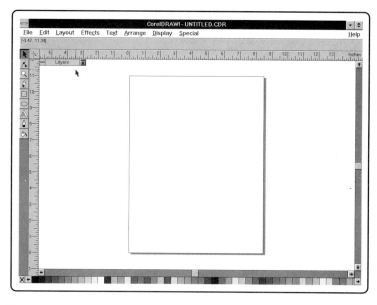

Figure 28.4. After selecting Arrange from the pull-down menu, the Layers roll-up rolls itself up and tucks itself in the upper corner of your screen.

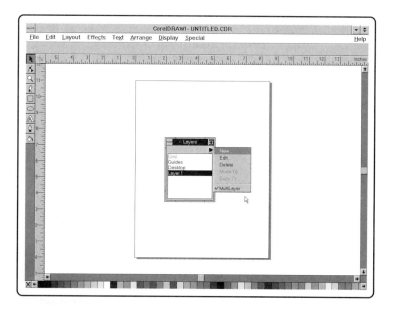

Figure 28.5. The Layers roll-up with the fly-out that selects New, Edit, Delete, Move To, Copy To, and MultiLayer.

The following options are available: Visible, Printable, Locked, Color Override, and Set Options for All Pages. These are toggles. If an option is on, there is a check mark next to it. The Color Override fly-out menu lets you select colors from the fly-out or click on More to call up the other palettes available (see Figure 28.6).

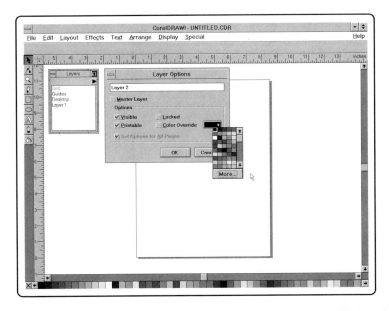

Figure 28.6. The Layers Option dialog box with the available options displayed and the Color Override Fly-out selected.

The Master Layer option allows you to have elements that repeat on every page of a multi-page document. This option is used for repeating elements such as headers or logos. A document can have more than one Master Layer.

After you click on the More button from the Color Override fly-out, the Select Color dialog box appears. You can change the current color by entering new values or by clicking on the palette display and watching the color change on the New view area.

At the lower left of the dialog box you can press the Custom Palette button. This function allows you to create your own custom palette. A fly-out menu appears that includes the following options: Add Color, Delete Color, New, Open, Save, Save As, and Set As Default (see Figure 28.7).

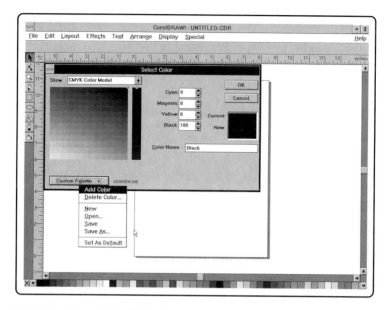

Figure 28.7. The Select Color dialog box with the Custom Palette button pressed and the fly-out menu displayed.

At the top left there is a pull-down menu of available palettes. Select from different palettes, such as PANTONE Process Colors, TRUMATCH Process Colors, as well as RGB and HSB Color Models, and others (see Figure 28.8).

In the Layers roll-up, double-click the Guides layer to invoke the Layer Options dialog box (see Figure 28.9). You can change current settings to the settings you wish to have in this dialog box. You can also bring up the Guides setup by pressing the Setup button at the lower left of the dialog box.

When you press the Setup button, the Guidelines dialog box appears on-screen (see Figure 28.10). See Skill Session 27, "Guidelines," for more information about using the Guidelines dialog box.

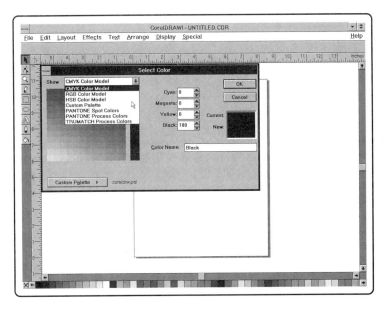

Figure 28.8. The Select Color dialog box with the pull-down menu that lets you change palettes.

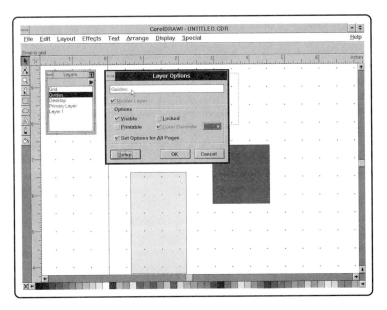

Figure 28.9. The Layer Options dialog box for the Guides layer.

Advanced Skills Workshop

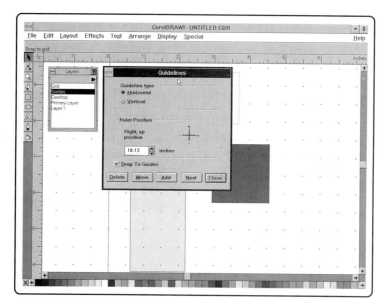

Figure 28.10. The Guidelines dialog box.

Select the Grid layer in the Layers roll-up and double-click it. This brings up the Layer Options dialog box for the Grid layer. You can also bring up the grid setup by clicking on the Setup button at the lower left of the dialog box (see Figure 28.11).

After you press the Setup button, the Grid dialog box will be displayed. There are various options you can select to change your grids (see Figure 28.12). See Skill Session 26 for more information about using the Grids dialog box.

The Grid layer is locked by default. You will not be able to make this layer active, draw, or place any objects there. If you attempt to move an object to the Grid layer, Corel Draw will prompt you with a message that says "Operation cannot be completed. The active layer 'Grid' is locked or invisible" (see Figure 28.13).

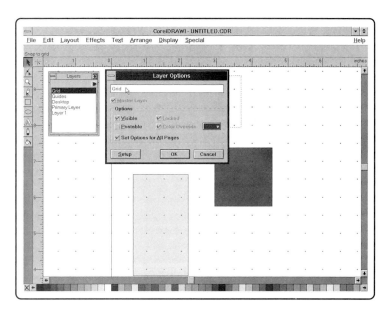

Figure 28.11. The Layer Options dialog box for the Grid layer.

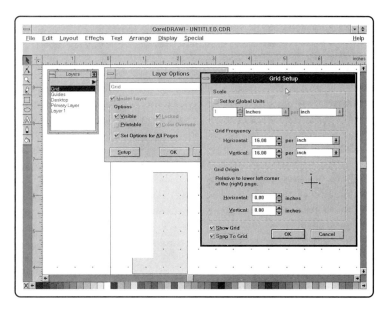

Figure 28.12. The Grid Setup dialog box.

Advanced Skills Workshop

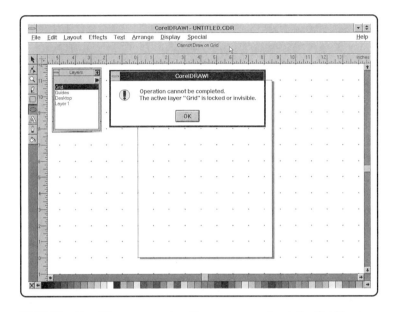

Figure 28.13. The Corel Draw prompt with a message about the Grid layer.

When you're working with layers, what you see on-screen depends on which of the two available drawing modes you're working in. The two modes are wireframe and preview. You can change the mode you are in by selecting Edit Wireframe from the Display menu or by pressing Shift-F9 from your keyboard (see Figure 28.14). A check mark appears in front of the options in the Display menu that are enabled. For more information on the Display menu see "Display Menu Commands" in Part V, "Command References."

When working in preview mode, you can't see the override color of the objects on-screen, except for the grid or guidelines.

When working in wireframe mode, you can see the override color of the objects on-screen. If the color override for the Primary layer in the example shown in Figure 28.15 is changed to orange, any object moved, placed, or drawn on this layer will take on the override color, as shown in Figure 28.16.

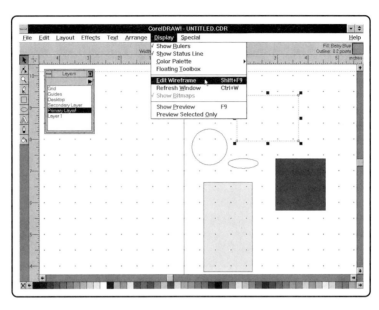

Figure 28.14. The display menu with the Edit Wireframe option off.

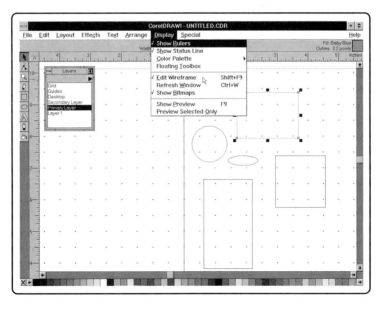

Figure 28.15. Edit Wireframe mode enables you to see the override color of each layer.

Advanced Skills Workshop

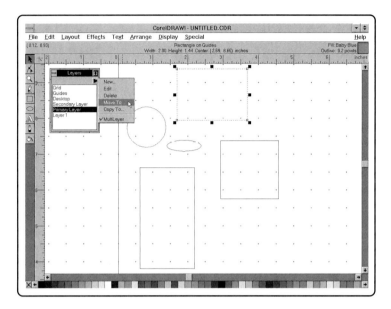

Figure 28.16. An object that has been moved to a different layer and has now taken on that layer's color override attribute.

Text

Workshop

Workshops

Text Workshop

Spacing, Kerning, and Changing Character Attributes

You can adjust text kerning and spacing in two different ways: interactively and through dialog boxes. The interactive method can be useful for adjusting spacing and kerning on short text blocks such as headlines, but can be quite maddening to use for larger blocks of text. This method uses the Shape tool and is described in detail in Skill Session 5.

You can work with the spacing dialog boxes either through the Text roll-up's Paragraph button, the Text Paragraph command, or the Edit Text dialog box's Spacing button. The dialog boxes of the first two options look exactly the same and they are shown in Figure 29.1 for paragraph text. The Artistic Text dialog box would have the Before Paragraph, After Paragraph, and Hyphenation options grayed out. Figure 29.2 shows the dialog box that appears when accessed through the Edit Text dialog box. Again, the Before Paragraph and After Paragraph options would be grayed out for Artistic text.

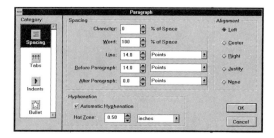

Figure 29.1. The Spacing dialog box for the Text Paragraph command.

Character spacing refers to the spacing between individual characters that make up words. It is measured as a percentage of the character space. The default value is zero. A positive value adds space between characters, while a negative value decreases the space between characters. Figure 29.3 shows the same line of type set with character spacing of –20, 0, and 20.

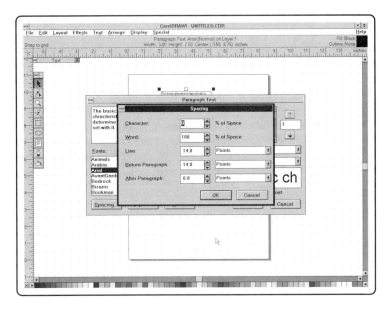

Figure 29.2. The Spacing dialog box for the Edit Text dialog box.

This is to demonstrate inter-character spacing.

This is to demonstrate inter-character spacing.

This is to demonstrate inter-character spacing.

Figure 29.3. A line of type with character spacing of −20, 0, and 29.

Word spacing refers to the width of the space character which separates words. It is measured as a percentage of its default width as defined in the font. The default value is set to 100 percent. Values above 100 percent will increase the space between words while values below 100 percent will decrease the space. Figure 29.4 shows the same line of type as Figure 29.3, but the variations are now between the word spacing. The top line is set to 80 percent, the middle line at 100 percent, and the bottom line at 120 percent.

This is to demonstrate inter-word spacing.

This is to demonstrate inter-word spacing.

This is to demonstrate inter-word spacing.

Figure 29.4. Word spacing set at 80 percent, 100 percent, and 120 percent.

While the first two settings can be substituted for kerning, they are really not the same thing as kerning. Corel Draw automatically uses the kerning pairs defined in TrueType and PostScript fonts, so if the kerning is properly defined it will not need to be adjusted very often. The most obvious times are for headlines, where the spacing between characters can be critical.

Line spacing refers to the space from baseline to baseline of a paragraph of text. It can be set as either a percentage of character height or in points. The default value is set to either 100 percent or the point size of the text itself. The most common value for body text should be the point size of the text plus 2 points. This will leave a comfortable amount of space between the lines so that they are both readable and yet conserve space. Figure 29.5 shows a paragraph of 12-point text with 10-point spacing on the left, 12-point spacing in the middle and 14-point spacing on the right.

The basic character in type design is determined by the uniform design chracteristics of all letters in the alphabet. However, this alone does not determine the standard of the typeface and the quality of the composition set with it. The basic character in type design is determined by the uniform design chracteristics of all letters in the alphabet. However, this alone does not determine the standard of the typeface and the quality of the composition set with it.

The basic character in type design is determined by the uniform design chracteristics of all letters in the alphabet. However, this alone does not determine the standard of the typeface and the quality of the composition set with it. The basic character in type design is determined by the uniform design chracteristics of all letters in the alphabet. However, this alone does not determine the standard of the typeface and the quality of the composition set with it.

The basic character in type design is determined by the uniform design chracteristics of all letters in the alphabet. However, this alone does not determine the standard of the typeface and the quality of the composition set with it. The basic character in type design is determined by the uniform design chracteristics of all letters in the alphabet. However, this alone does not determine the standard of the typeface and the quality of the composition set with it.

Figure 29.5. Paragraph of 12-point text with interline spacing of 10, 12, and 14 points from left to right.

Corel *NOTE!*

> You may hear line and paragraph spacing refered to as "leading" (rhymes with "sledding"), after the strips of lead inserted by typographers back in the days of hot metal type.

Before Paragraph spacing refers to the amount of space before each paragraph. Much like interline spacing, it can be set as either a percentage of character height or in points. It also defaults to either 100 percent or the point size of the paragraph text. It should be set at the same amount as interline spacing unless either more or less space is desired between paragraphs. This space can also be achieved by setting the After Paragraph spacing to something other than its default value of zero.

The Paragraph dialog box also allows you to turn hyphenation on or off for Paragraph text. The hyphenation is done by a hyphenation algorithm and occurs within the Hot Zone defined in the Paragraph dialog box. The Hot Zone refers to a measurement at the end of a line of text where hyphenation is allowed. The default value of .50 inches is normally fine unless you are working with either very large or very small sized type.

Character Attributes

The attributes of individual characters can be changed when using either the Text or the Shape tool. Use either tool to select the characters to be changed. With the ⅄ tool, marquee-select the characters by dragging a box around the nodes to the left of the characters. With the 𝔸 tool, select the characters by dragging the cursor over the characters with the primary mouse button. Figure 29.6 shows a sentence selected with the Shape tool and Figure 29.7 shows the same sentence selected with the Text tool.

After the text has been selected, the attributes can be changed through the Character Attributes dialog box. Either double-click on one of the selected nodes or choose Text Character to invoke the Character Attributes dialog box, shown in Figure 29.8.

Text Workshop

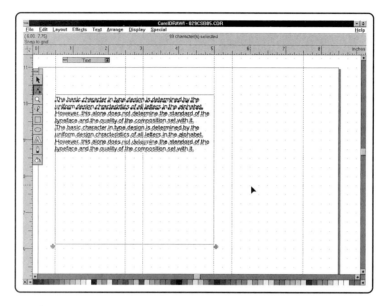

Figure 29.6. A sentence selected with the Shape tool.

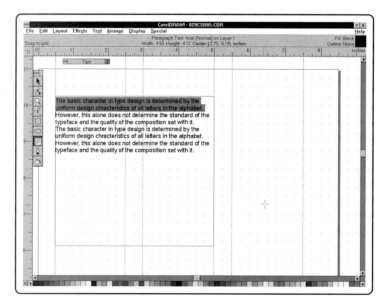

Figure 29.7. A sentence selected with the Text tool.

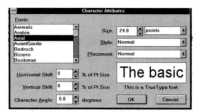

Figure 29.8. The Character Attributes dialog box.

The top half of the dialog box controls the font used, its point size, style, and alignment. These controls work exactly like the controls found in both the Edit Text dialog box and the Text roll-up. In fact, it is much easier to edit these attributes through the Text roll-up. The key difference between the Character Attributes dialog box and the Edit Text dialog box is that the you cannot work with individual characters in the Edit Text dialog box.

The three settings on the lower left of the dialog box are only found in the Character Attributes dialog box. Horizontal Shift moves the text right for a positive percentage and left for a negative percentage. Vertical Shift moves the text up for positive percentages and down for negative percentages. Character Angle rotates the text on the baseline counter-clockwise for positive angles and clockwise for negative angles.

The fill and outline of the characters can also be changed easily using all of the methods described in Skill Sessions 11 and 12. Again note that any changes you make apply only to the characters selected and not the whole text block.

It is a common misconception that Corel Draw is unable to italicize or boldface a word within a text block, because the concepts discussed in this chapter are not completely understood. This is also a great way to make things like subscripts, superscripts and other features that Corel Draw may seem to be missing. So, the next time an obvious feature cannot be found, give these methods a try and the missing feature may reveal itself.

Text Workshop

Paragraph Text Attributes

Text Workshop

Paragraph text frames have many attributes that are not available to Artistic text. One of the most important in relation to page layout tasks is the ability to set up multiple columns. To do this, select either the Text Frame command or the Frame button in the Text roll-up. Either of these will bring up the Frame Attributes dialog box, shown in Figure 30.1.

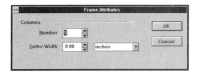

Figure 30.1. The Frame Attributes dialog box.

The number of columns can range anywhere from 1 to 8 with the default being 1. The gutter width controls the amount of gutter space placed between each column of text. This defaults to 0, but can be as large as 2 inches. Figure 30.2 shows a text frame with three columns of text.

Setting Tabs

You can easily set tabs using the Paragraph dialog box. This dialog box is accessed either through the Text Paragraph command or the Text roll-up's Paragraph button. On the left are four icons. The second icon down is the Tabs icon. When you select it, the dialog box appears as shown in Figure 30.3.

Left-aligned tabs are automatically set at half-inch increments. These can easily be changed and/or deleted. Individual tab settings can be selected from the list box in the lower middle of the dialog box by clicking on the appropriate value. They can also be chosen by clicking on the tab marker sitting on the ruler at the top of the dialog box. Once the appropriate tab has been selected, it can be deleted by clicking on the Clear button, moved by typing a new value into the list box, or dragged manually along the ruler. The tab alignment can be set by choosing an option button from Left, Right, Center, or Decimal. To clear all the tabs, choose the Clear All button.

You can add tabs by typing a new value into the top of the list box and clicking on the Set button, or by clicking along the ruler where the new tab should appear.

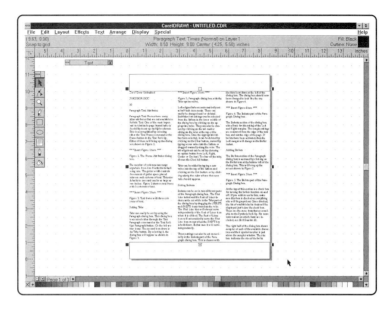

Figure 30.2. A text frame with three columns of text.

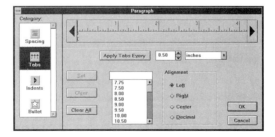

Figure 30.3. The Paragraph dialog box with the Tabs option active.

Setting Indents

Indents can be set in two different parts of the Paragraph dialog box. The First Line indent and the Rest of Lines indent can be set while in the Tabs part of the dialog box by dragging the First Line and Rest of Lines icons found on the ruler. The First Line icon will always move independently of the Rest of Lines icon when it is clicked. The Rest of Lines icon will automatically move the First Line icon except when you hold down the Shift key, in which case it moves independently.

These settings can also be set numerically in the Indents part of the Paragraph dialog box. This is chosen with the third icon down at the left of the dialog box. This dialog box is shown in Figure 30.4.

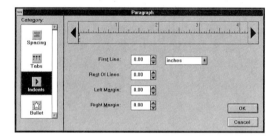

Figure 30.4. The Indents part of the Paragraph dialog box.

The Indents section of the dialog box also allows for the setting of the left and right margins. The margin settings are measured from the edge of the text box and not the edge of the page. If bullets have been activated, Left Margin changes to Bullet Indent.

Adding Bullets

The Bullets section of the Paragraph dialog box is accessed by clicking on the Bullet icon at the bottom left of the dialog box. This brings up the dialog box shown in Figure 30.5.

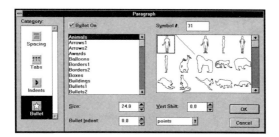

Figure 30.5. The Bullets part of the Paragraph dialog box.

At the top of this section is a check box for turning the bullets function on and off. If you want to use bullets, make sure this box is checked, or everything else will be grayed out. Once Bullets On is checked, the list of available bullet fonts is displayed just below the check box. These are the same fonts that are available in the Symbols roll-up. For more information about which fonts are included, see Skill Session 10.

The right half of the dialog box shows samples of each of the available characters, and the symbol number is just above the samples window. The size box indicates the size of the bullet character and the Bullet Indent is the same value as shown in the Indents part of the Paragraph dialog box. This value indicates the amount of space between the bullet and the rest of the text. Vert Shift indicates the amount of space above the baseline where the bullet will sit. A negative number places the bullet's baseline below the paragraph's baseline.

Styles

Most of the attributes covered in this Skill Session are best used with defined styles within a template. For more information about creating and modifying styles and templates, see Skill Session 51.

Text Workshop

Fitting Text
to a Path

Fitting text to a path involves dynamically linking the text to a specified path. The path could be an ellipse, rectangle, line, or curve. You can even use text that has been converted to curves.

You can edit the text on the path in several ways, including modifying the spacing of the text and changing the direction of the path.

Corel*NOTE!*

> You can also fit text to text. However, there is one thing you must do first. Convert the primary text to curves using the Convert To Curves command in the Arrange menu. The primary text is the text that will receive the applied text.

Fitting Text to a Circle

To begin, select Fit Text To Path from the Text menu. The Fit Text To Path roll-up appears on-screen. Follow these steps to create the Jingling Circus logo. During this session you will be shown ways to avoid doing it the wrong way as well as the correct way.

1. Type the word "CIRCUS" on-screen. The Big Top font was used in this example.
2. Draw a circle to fit your text to.
3. Select both the text and the object (see Figure 31.1).
4. From the Fit Text To Path roll-up, choose the orientation you want the text to appear on the path (the default is vertical). The text orientation box is the top box with the letters *ABC* showing.
5. Choose which side of the line your text will lay on from the next box down. By scrolling in this box, you will see several visual choices. Each choice shows how the text will fit the object's outline path. You might want the descenders to rest on the line or extend below the line. The last choice is variable. When you choose this option, you can manually move the text inside or out of the path line. For this example choose the default qrst.

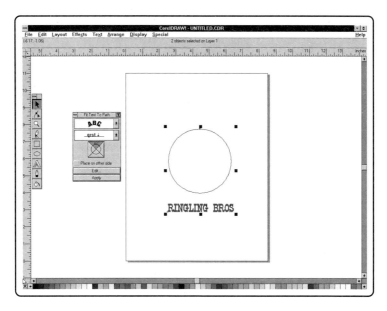

Figure 31.1. Selecting the text and the object.

6. Your next choice is whether you want your text on top of the circle or along the sides or at the bottom. The sectioned box defaults to the top section. Clicking on either of the other sections will change the setting. For this example keep the top default selection.

7. Now you can click the Apply button. Figure 31.2 shows the result.

Select the text on a path you just created and check the Place on the other side box; then click on Apply again, and see the results, as shown in Figure 31.3.

Notice that the text is now on the inside of the circle's outline and still at the top. Unfortunately, the text reads backwards. One option you have is to rotate the text around the inside of the circle using the Shape tool. Marquee-select all the nodes in the text string. Drag any node to slide the text around the circle until you have it where you want it. Figure 31.4 illustrates this technique very well. While you are sliding the text around, the cursor changes to crossed arrows and there is a "marching ants" selection box around the text. The original text stays in place until you release the primary mouse button.

Text Workshop

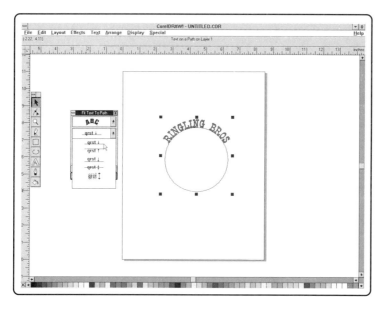

Figure 31.2. Fitting text to a path using the default settings.

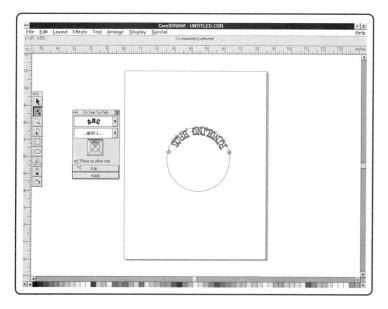

Figure 31.3. Placing the text on the other side of the path.

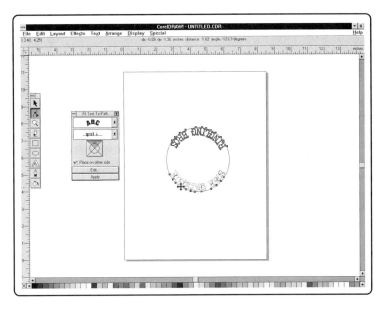

Figure 31.4. Sliding text along a path using the Shape tool.

Figure 31.5 shows the text on the circle after it has been rotated to the bottom.

When you select the text with the Shape tool, two text-spacing nodes appear. Drag the right node and the text string lengthens, allowing you to change how much of the lower half of the circle is filled with text (see Figure 31.6).

Figure 31.7 shows how you can place the text on the other side so it is right for reading. Choose the variable placement option in the placement dialog box. It is the last choice in the box. Drag the text downward with the Pick tool. A small double-arrow line appears as you drag and a circle appears that provides a visual guide to how the position of the text is changing. When you have moved the text to the desired position, release the primary mouse button.

Text Workshop

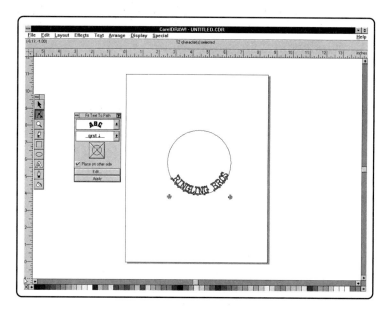

Figure 31.5. The text is now located on the bottom of the circle.

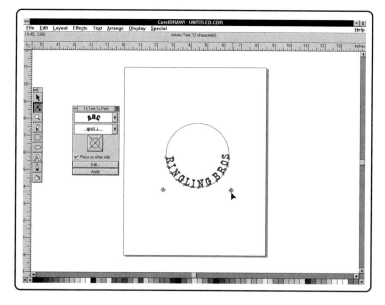

Figure 31.6. Adjusting the spacing.

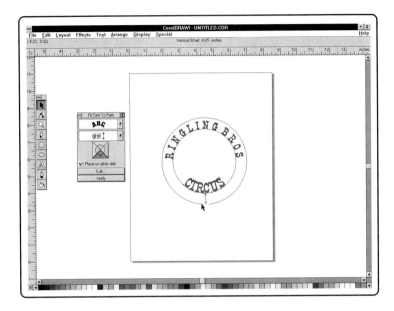

Figure 31.7. Using the variable placement option to position text.

Figure 31.8 shows the final result. Figure 31.9 shows how the final design could look. In this case, the circle was filled with bright blue and an image of a lion taken from the Symbols library was placed in the center. The lion was filled with white to provide a nice contrast. The word "JINGLING" was placed on top of the circle using the default settings as in Figure 31.2.

Fitting Text to a Single Path

Figure 31.10 shows a text string applied to a single path. Notice the first letter of the text string begins at the left side of the line. This is the default setting. When you apply text to a line, a third options box appears in the Fit Text To Path roll-up offering three choices. The first choice, abc (the default), places the text at the start of the line. The second choice places the text on the center of the line. The third choice places the text at the end of the line. In Figure 31.10 the line was originally drawn from left to right.

Text Workshop

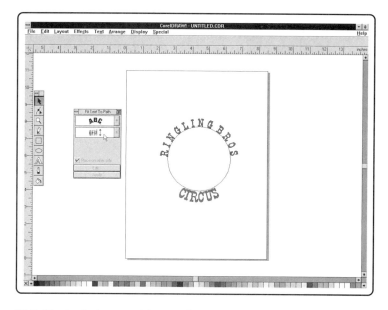

Figure 31.8. The text placement is complete.

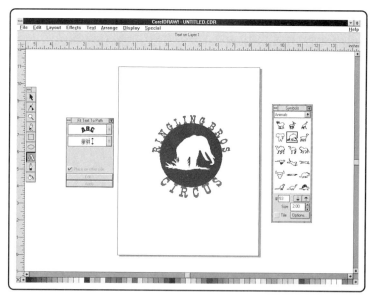

Figure 31.9. The final logo.

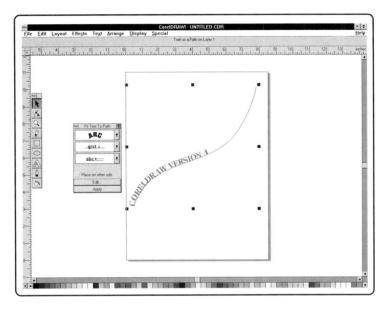

Figure 31.10. Fitting text to a single path.

Corel *NOTE!*

Left-handers take note: Had the line been drawn from right to left, the text string would have ended at the right end of the line, upside down, and below the line.

Figure 31.11 illustrates how the text can be spaced evenly over the entire length of the line. Click the ⚲ tool and then click the right-hand text-spacing node. Drag to the right to stretch the text string to the desired length.

Figure 31.12 illustrates how the shape of the line can be dynamically changed. Select the ⚲ tool and click the line. Use the nodes or handles to reshape the line.

Text Workshop

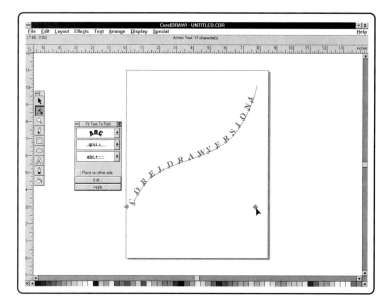

Figure 31.11. Spacing text along the length of the path.

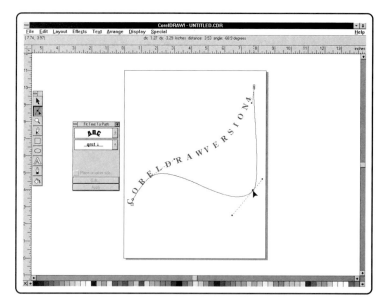

Figure 31.12. You can shape the path dynamically.

Corel *NOTE!*

> Corel Draw! 4 now lets you click anywhere on the line to reshape the line. You do not have to use the nodes or the handles.

Figure 31.13 shows the results of changing the shape of the line. Notice that the text string no longer travels the full length of the line.

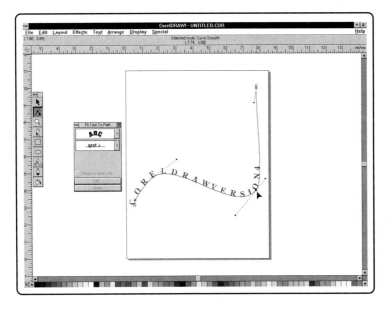

Figure 31.13. The text now follows the reshaped line.

To reposition the text along the line as in Figure 31.14, marquee-select the text "VERSION 4" with the tool. With all of the nodes selected, click on any of the nodes and drag the selection along the line to the desired position. Release the primary mouse button.

Figure 31.15 shows the same technique used on the word "CORELDRAW" to move it away from the left side.

Text Workshop

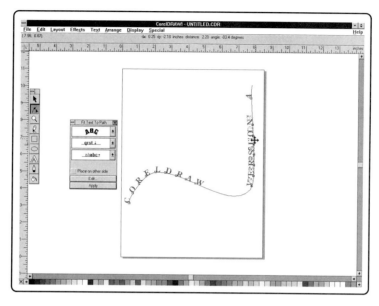

Figure 31.14. Repositioning text along the path.

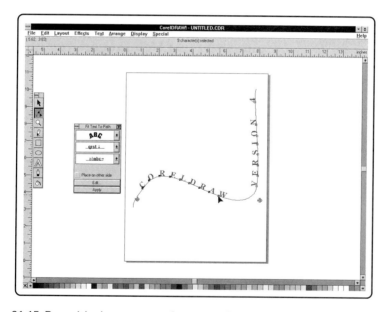

Figure 31.15. Repositioning text—another example.

Figure 31.16 shows an example of one of the many ways Fit Text To Path can be incorporated in your projects.

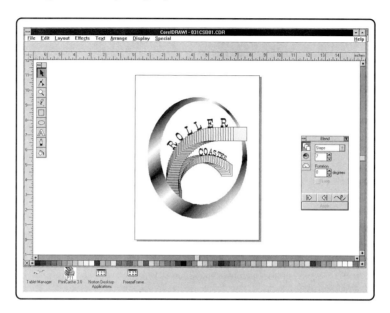

Figure 31.16. Combining Fit Text to Path with other techniques.

Text Workshop

Text Special Effects

Text Workshop

There are many special effects that can be applied to text. Some of the more popular ones are neon, embossing, debossing, and chrome. Often a client will ask for one of these special effects to be used in a project. Following the steps below will help you master these effects.

Neon

Figure 32.1 illustrates the steps involved in creating a Neon effect.

1. Type the text on the screen.
2. Remove the fill and make the outline width 6 points.
3. Make the outline color Red.
4. Select the text and copy it to the clipboard with the Copy command in the Edit menu.
5. Paste the text back on top of the original text by selecting the Paste command in the Edit menu.
6. Change the outline width of the pasted text to .1 point.
7. Change the outline color to White.
8. Select both text objects by marquee-selecting them.
9. Open the Blend roll-up by selecting it from the Effects menu.
10. Use the default setting of 20 in the Blend roll-up.
11. With both text objects still selected, click Apply in the Blend roll-up.

Figure 32.1. Neon effect.

You can change the outline colors, of course, but always make sure they contrast with each other and that the darkest color is on the bottom with the wide outline. Try using dark blue with very light blue.

Embossing and Debossing

Embossing makes your text appear to be above the background surface. Debossing makes your text appear to be below the background surface. Figure 32.2 illustrates both embossing and debossing. The top image has been given the embossing effect.

Figure 32.2. Emboss and deboss effects.

The secret to making these effects is to use three copies of the text. The following steps will take you through the process:

1. Draw and fill an object with Dark Brown for a background.
2. Type the text and place it on the background.
3. Fill the text with Light Brown. Do not use an outline on the text.
4. Select the text and copy it to the clipboard by selecting Copy in the Edit menu.
5. Change the color of the text on-screen to Chalk Yellow (very light).
6. With the text selected, open the Arrange menu and select Move.
7. Type .04 inch in the Horizontal parameters box.
8. Click OK.

Text Workshop

9. With the text still selected, select Move Again from the Arrange menu.

10. This time type in -.08 inch in the Horizontal parameters box.

11. Click the Leave Original box.

12. Click OK.

13. When the screen redraws, change the color of the selected text to Black.

14. Click the Edit menu and select Paste.

   The original text is pasted on top of the first two text objects and your project is done.

To deboss, follow all the steps above except in Step 5 change the color to Black. This will create the illusion of the text being recessed in the background.

Chrome

Creating the illusion of chrome can be accomplished in several ways. Figure 32.3 illustrates three of those ways.

Figure 32.3. Three chrome effects.

Corel*NOTE!*

> Each method produces a different look of chrome. Which you prefer is a matter of individual taste; what looks most like chrome to one does not to another. These are just three variations. You may discover still other ways of doing it.

Method 1

The first method shown is by creating multiple colored fountain fills to fill the text. Corel Draw 4 now allows you to add as many colors to a fountain fill as you wish (see Skill Session 12, "Fill Tool"). In the first illustration three shades of blue were used and the angle of stripes was set to 45 degrees.

Method 2

The second method is somewhat complicated. Follow the steps below to accomplish this effect.

1. Fill your text with a multiple colored fountain fill as in the first method above.
2. Click the Special menu and select Preferences.
3. Change the values in the Place Duplicates and Clones parameters box to 0.0.
4. Click OK and return to the page.
5. Click the Edit menu and select Duplicate. You have now placed an exact duplicate on top of the original.
6. With the new object still selected choose Convert to Curves from the Arrange menu.
7. Click the Display menu and choose Edit Wire Frame.
8. Select your text with the Move command from the Edit menu. Type 2.0 inches in the Vertical parameters box. This will move the duplicate text out of the way so you can work on it.
9. With the ⋏ tool, break apart a node on each side of the first letter of your text somewhere near the center (see Skill Session 5, " The Shape Tool").

297

Text Workshop

10. Marquee-select the remaining nodes at the top of the letter and delete them.

11. Reconnect the side nodes across the center of the letter.

12. Click the center of the crossover line and pull up or down to create a wavy line.

13. Repeat these steps with each letter.

14. Marquee-select all of the letters and fill with the darkest color you used in your multiple fountain filled first text object.

15. Choose the Move command again in the Edit menu and type –2.0 inches. This will put your edited text back on top of the first text object to complete the effect.

16. Select Edit Wire Frame from the Display menu again to bring you back to preview mode.

Figure 32.4 illustrates the steps above.

Figure 32.4. Creating a chrome effect, Method 2.

Method 3

The third method is a combination of the first and second methods. To accomplish this look, you need to extrude the back text object after you have completed the second method.

1. Click the back text object with the fountain fill.
2. Select Extrude roll-up from the Effects menu.
3. Use the default setting of Small Back.
4. Click Apply.

Text Workshop

Merging and Extracting Text

Editing large amounts of text in multiple or single page documents may be easier in a word processor. Select the Extract option in the Special menu to invoke the Extract dialog box, where you can save your file in ASCII format. This allows you to open the file for editing in most word processing programs. Once you have saved your document as a text file, choose the word processor you want to edit your file in.

Corel *NOTE!*

When editing your file in the word processor, do not change the first line at the beginning of the file or the first and last lines at the beginning of each paragraph or text string. These are codes that Corel Draw uses to interpret the text file.

If you wish to add attributes to your text, add them after you merge back the text. Not all attributes are retained in word processing programs.

Transformations or attributes (such as font type, size, character spacing, or point size) and alignment (such as justified, centered, left, right or none) will not be altered when merging back text. Text that has been fitted to a path, extruded, or blended may be altered when merging back. For more information about Extract and Merge-Back, see "Special Menu Commands," in Part V, "Command References."

Corel *NOTE!*

When your text file is merged back, the positioning of the original text of your Corel file will not change.

Artistic and Paragraph Text

You can have a mixture of Artistic and Paragraph text in the Corel file that you wish to extract (see Figures 33.1 and 33.2). If there are graphic elements in your file, they will not be extracted to the text file.

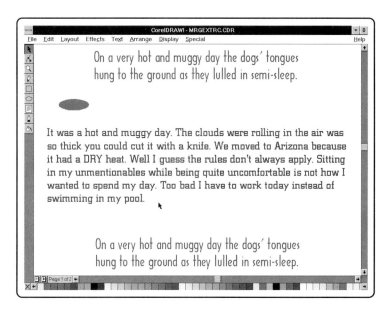

Figure 33.1. Page 1 of 2 with Artistic text, graphic element, Paragraph text and Artistic text displayed.

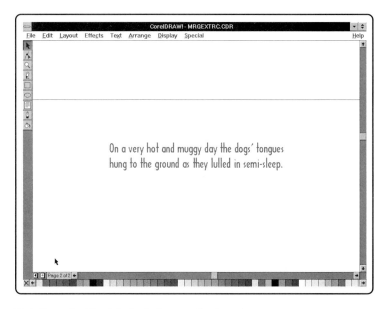

Figure 33.2. Page 2 of 2 with Artistic text displayed.

Special Extract

Select the Extract option from the Special menu to invoke the Extract dialog box (see Figure 33.3). Save your file in ASCII format. Choose a directory to save the file in.

Corel*NOTE!*

Extracting text does not require the text to be selected.

Figure 33.3. The Extract dialog box with the extracted file saved in ASCII format.

Open your text file in the word processor of your choice. This example uses Windows Write (see Figure 33.4). There are several lines of code that are used by Corel when merging back the text file. Do not change these lines of text. You will notice that the Artistic text in the word processing file is placed at the top of the screen and the Paragraph text follows it. This differs from the original order in the Corel file. This does not affect the positioning in the Corel document. The last piece of Artistic text displayed is on page 2 of the Corel document. Edit the text as needed.

Merge-Back

Select Merge-Back from the Special menu and the extracted text will replace the edited text in your file (see Figure 33.5).

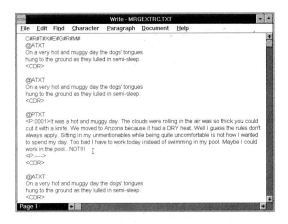

Figure 33.4. Using Windows Write to edit text.

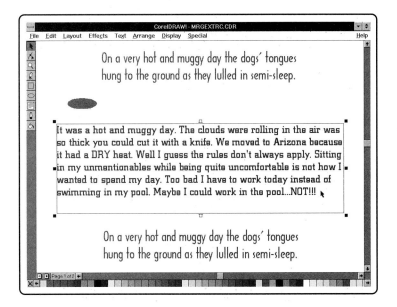

Figure 33.5. The edited text after merging back to the Corel file.

305

Text Workshop

Creating Your Own Fonts

Beginning with Corel Draw 2.0, the ability to create custom fonts was made available. This capability means that it is very easy to turn a set of simple drawings and logos into a font that can be easily used in almost every Windows program. The most difficult part of this process is creating the template used for creating the fonts.

Creating the Template

Create a new file. Select Page Setup from the Layout menu and change the Page Size to Custom. The measurement system should be changed to Points both vertically and horizontally. Set the width and height to 720 points.

720 points is approximately the same as 10 inches. This provides enough room for the detail necessary for designing a character. This is also one-half the size of the largest point size available in Corel Draw (through version 2.0).

Double-click on the rulers to bring up the Grid Setup dialog box. Change the grid frequency to 1 per point in both the Horizontal and Vertical directions. The Grid Origin should be set to 0 points Horizontal and 240 points Vertical. Ensure that Snap to Grid and Snap to Guidelines are both enabled. Insert a horizontal guideline at 480 points to indicate the cap height and another at 0 points to indicate the baseline.

480 points is used for the cap height because it is two-thirds of the 720-point design size you are using. The two-thirds of point size is a standard throughout the type foundries of Europe that provides for consistency between typefaces.

Insert a vertical guideline at 60 points to indicate the left sidebearing. This just happens to be a good round number that doesn't sit on the edge of the page; there is no real significance to this number. Deselect Snap to Grid because you won't need it.

Type the text string HOqdx. Highlight the text and change it to a font similar in design to the one you plan on creating. Choose a font that has characteristics very close to the one you are designing, for example, serif or sans serif, x-height, descenders, and so on.

Adjust the text so that it sits flush to the baseline and to the left of the guideline. Stretch the text so that the top of the *H* is even with the cap height guideline. Drag out horizontal guidelines for the x-height and the descenders. Delete the text string and save the file. This is now the template to use for creating new fonts.

In the future, most of these steps will be unnecessary if you hang on to the template file just created. A copy of this file can be found on the accompanying CD as MAKEFONT.CDR. Figure 34.1 shows the font-creation template.

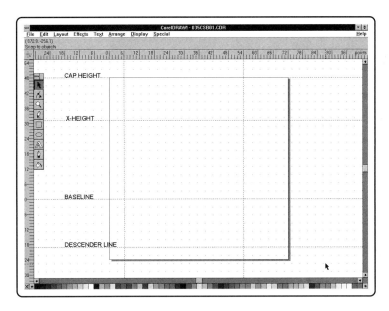

Figure 34.1. The font-creation template.

At this point, it is time to start creating some characters. Font characters can be made up of only a single object, so it is necessary to combine the pieces of characters that contain more than one path. For now, create an *O* by combining two ellipses. Enlarge the *O* so that it extends from the baseline to the cap height. Choose File Export and either the PostScript or TrueType font format. If there is more than one object on-screen, make sure to choose Selected Objects Only. When you export the first character to a new font, the dialog box shown in Figure 34.2 appears.

Text Workshop

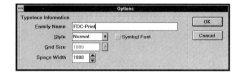

Figure 34.2. The Font Export Options dialog box.

Name the font in the Family Name field. This name will appear in the Windows font menus. This name should be no more than 32 characters long. Choose the Style of the font you are creating. Draw provides only four choices: Normal, Italic, Bold, and Bold Italic. If this font is to be used as a standard text typeface, the Symbol check box should be disabled. If you want the font to appear in Corel's Symbols roll-up, make sure this is checked. The Grid Size and Space Width should both be left at the defaults of 2048 for TrueType fonts and 1000 for PostScript fonts, unless there is an obvious reason to do otherwise. These numbers come straight from the font specifications for TrueType and PostScript Type 1. Once everything is checked, click OK. The Export dialog box shown in Figure 34.3 appears.

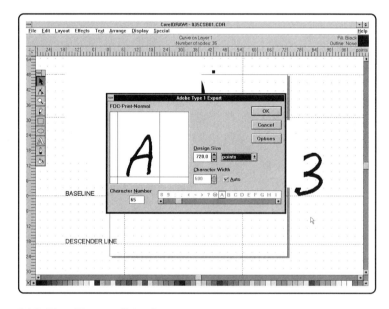

Figure 34.3. Font Export dialog box.

The Design Size should be set to 720 points because this is the size used to design the characters. If you have deviated from the instructions in this chapter, this may need to be adjusted. The Character Number indicates which position in the font that the current character will be placed. Alphabetic and other keyboard characters will display above the ANSI number. Consult the character chart that accompanies your Corel Draw package for the ANSI number of other characters. The Character Width field can be adjusted by clicking on either the up or down arrow and the right sidebearing will move accordingly. For most characters, it is much simpler to accept the default value by checking the Auto Width check box. After you've made all selections, click on Export Character.

When you export a character to a font that has an existing character, the Options dialog box like the one shown in Figure 34.4 appears.

Figure 34.4. The Options dialog box that appears for an existing font.

This Options dialog box adds a button for Load Font Metrics. The Load Font Metrics button can be used to import an Adobe Font Metrics (.AFM) file from an existing typeface to mimic its spacing and kerning. Unless the face you are creating is very close to an existing face, this is usually unnecessary. When you click on OK to export a character to an existing font, an extra dialog box appears if there is already a character in the position selected. The dialog box asks whether you want to overwrite the existing definition.

Repeat this process until all the characters you want are in the font. This font does not contain any kerning information unless the Load Font Metrics option was chosen. At this point, you may want to import the "finished" font into a program such as Altsys

Text Workshop

Fontographer (see Part II, "Companion Software Workshops," for a full description of Fontographer) to optimize the spacing and add kerning information.

Once all adjustments are made, the font can be installed either through Adobe Type Manager or Control Panel Fonts and used in any Windows program that supports scaleable fonts, including Corel Draw itself. Not only can you create fonts for yourself, but you can create them for a client so that a logo, signature, or many other symbols could be used in any of their Windows applications.

Text Workshop

Font Formats

Corel Draw supports three different font formats: WFN, TrueType, and PostScript. Each of these formats has several advantages and disadvantages. These will be pointed out as each font format is described, and the installation process for each will be described in detail.

WFN Format

This format was developed by Corel for use in earlier versions of Corel Draw. While the format is still usable by Corel Draw 4, it is not recommended because it is the least rich of the three supported formats. The symbols shipped with Corel are mostly in the WFN format, and for this purpose, the WFN format does offer some advantages.

The advantage of the WFN format is that the fonts are seen only by Corel Draw. For those who have installed a large number of TrueType or PostScript fonts, performance has undoubtedly taken a serious hit when loading Windows or applications themselves. Since the WFN fonts are seen only by Corel Draw, this is a way to avoid the performance penalty the other formats impose. Another advantage is that four different weights of a font can be included inside one WFN file.

WFN's advantages are also some of its biggest disadvantages. Since the fonts can be seen only by Corel Draw, a favorite font won't be available in other applications. Since Corel's symbols are stored mostly in the WFN format, they cannot be used by other programs in Windows. Because many of them are simply clip art, this isn't that important, but some of the dingbat-type characters may be sorely missed when using a word processor or layout package. Also, WFN fonts do not contain hinting information. This information is used to optimize the output of characters at small sizes and/or low resolutions. Unhinted type usually has fairly rough edges and can have unbalanced character weight especially when used on-screen or on a laser printer. This effect is usually negligible when outputting to an imagesetter. Probably the biggest disadvantage of the WFN format is the complete lack of kerning information. This means that text will have to be manually kerned in order to get the best output.

Installing WFN Fonts

Installing WFN fonts is a two-step process. First, copy them to the appropriate directory—the directory in which Corel Draw expects to find them.

You can locate this directory by looking in the CORELAPP.INI file for the line FontsDir =. This specifies the full path to the directory where the fonts should be stored. For more information on .INI files, please see Skill Session 61.

The next step is to add a line to CORELFNT.INI to register the font. The best way to do this is to copy the listing from an old CORELDRW.INI file from either version 2.0 or 3.0. If the font has been used in the past, it will be listed in an old .INI file. If this is a new WFN font (very rare these days), the line will have to be created from scratch. It should read as follows:

FontName=*x font*.wfn

FontName is the case-sensitive name of the font as it will appear in Corel Draw's font menus. *x* is a number that represents the weights of fonts contained within the WFN file. It is an additive number, where the normal weight is 1, the bold weight is 2, the italic weight is 4, and the bold italic weight is 8. Add the numbers for the weights contained, and this will be the number represented by *x*. *font*.wfn is the actual filename of the file that contains the fonts.

TrueType Format

TrueType was codeveloped by Apple and Microsoft to challenge PostScript Type 1's then proprietary format. Support for TrueType fonts is built directly into Windows 3.1 and higher as well as the Macintosh's System 7.0 and higher. This ensures that the format has a very large user base and has proven to be quite successful on Windows since the release of Windows 3.1. Unfortunately, the many advantages of the TrueType format are vastly underutilized by current software and, in particular, Corel Draw 4.

The biggest advantage to TrueType fonts is the fact that they are directly supported by Windows, and therefore can be used by almost all Windows-compliant applications without the need for an additional utility. At this point, that is the only practical advantage the TrueType format provides. One advantage that could be very beneficial to Corel Draw users is the ability to embed TrueType fonts in data files. This would mean that if a drawing was made that included a nonstandard font, it could be shared with other users without distributing the font (which could be illegal). This would be especially beneficial for sharing a drawing between several systems and/or sending the file to a service bureau. The embedding specifications provide for several different types of embedding, but unfortunately Corel has decided to wait until a future version to implement these important services. TrueType fonts can also define more than four weights under a font's family name. The main advantage to this feature is to shorten the font menu. The best example would be to look at the Swiss/Switzerland family that Draw provides. In the current implementation, there are 22 different families in the menu. Using TrueType to its fullest would decrease that to three or four families. It also allows the names to be more intelligent and less confusing.

Installing TrueType Fonts

Double-click on the Control Panel icon shown in Figure 35.1. It is usually located in the Main program group. Double-click on the Fonts icon shown in Figure 35.2. The dialog box shown in Figure 35.3 appears, showing all the fonts currently installed. By clicking a font name, a sample will be shown in the lower window along with the size of the disk file. To add fonts, click on the Add button on the right side of the dialog box. This presents the dialog box shown in Figure 35.4.

Control Panel

Figure 35.1. The Control Panel icon.

Fonts

Figure 35.2. The Fonts icon.

Figure 35.3. The Fonts dialog box.

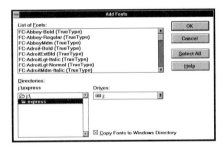

Figure 35.4. The Add Fonts dialog box.

The Add Fonts dialog box presents a list of all fonts found in the current directory. Change the Drives drop-down box so that the drive and directory containing the fonts is indicated. The List of Fonts should now show all the fonts found in the directory. Select the fonts you want to install by clicking on their names while holding down the Shift (selects all fonts between clicks) or Ctrl (selects only names clicked) key. Once all the desired fonts are selected, click on OK; the fonts will be added to your Windows installation.

PostScript Fonts

PostScript fonts were developed by Adobe Systems to be used with its PostScript Page Description language. PostScript Type 1 fonts are commonly confused with the PostScript Page Description language. The language is not necessary to use the fonts. Under Windows, Adobe Type Manager (see Part II, "Companion Software Workshops," Workshop 1) provides full use of PostScript fonts both on-screen and on the printer.

Text Workshop

For users with PostScript output devices, which range from laser print-ers to imagesetters, there is really no choice but to use PostScript fonts. While the other formats will work fine, the PostScript fonts are the native format to the output device and thus are the preferred format to use. Unfortunately, Corel Draw does not adequately support PostScript fonts. Most programs can download the font to a PostScript printer at the beginning of a job and then let the printer create the individual letters as necessary. Corel Draw either converts all characters to curves or renders them as bitmaps and then sends the bitmap to the printer. Either of these solutions causes a decrease in the quality of output and the user pays a tremendous performance price. A full page of body text can easily create a print file of over 2 MB; the same page from another application might be less than 100 KB. This means that files take longer to print and print at a lower quality.

There is a workaround to this deficiency in Corel Draw, however. PostScript fonts can be registered in the CORELFNT.INI file by inclu-ding their menu name and the internal PostScript name by which the printer references the font. This is not information that the average user has to work with, but the results are well worth the effort. The names for all fonts that are supplied with Corel Draw are provided in the CORELFNT.INI file already, so the only fonts that must be added are those from another source. For more information on adding this infor-mation, see Skill Session 61 which fully describes the CORELFNT.INI file.

Once fonts have been properly registered in CORELFNT.INI, download all the necessary fonts before printing a file. When printing the file, specify All Fonts Resident and the fonts will be requested by name instead of being rasterized or converted to curves. If a mistake has been made, Courier will be substituted for any fonts not found.

All these steps may seem to be a hassle that applies to only PostScript fonts. In reality, PostScript fonts are the only format to have such a workaround available.

The biggest advantage to PostScript fonts is the fact that they are the native format to many high-end devices. They are also the most popular format, with well over 20,000 different fonts available from numerous vendors.

One of the most interesting advantages for Corel Draw users is the fact that fewer nodes are required to render a PostScript font than a

TrueType font. Figure 35.5 shows the exact same character from a font that was supplied in both formats. When the characters were converted to curves, the PostScript version had three fewer nodes.

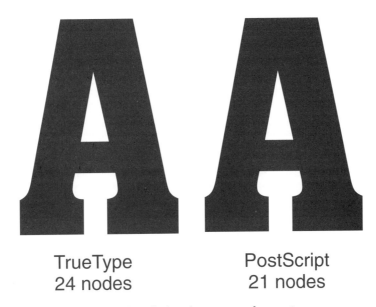

TrueType
24 nodes

PostScript
21 nodes

Figure 35.5. TrueType versus PostScript character node count.

While three nodes can seem to be a negligible difference in this case, consider that when a page full of graphics is converted to curves, the difference can be thousands of nodes. This can make a significant difference in print files and times.

The last major advantage is the fact that PostScript fonts are much more reliable at larger sizes. Due to bugs in the TrueType rasterizer, many of the more complex fonts will just blow up and characters will be represented by a hollow square. Sometimes this appears only on printout, which can be quite frustrating.

Therefore, for those who really care about their output, PostScript is the format of choice.

Installing PostScript Fonts

Since the use of PostScript fonts in Corel Draw requires Adobe Type Manager (ATM), the fonts themselves must be installed by following the directions that came with ATM. The Companion Software Workshop on Adobe Type Manager provides the appropriate instructions for installing fonts through ATM.

Text Workshop

Basic Typography

Typographical Terms

Figure 36.1 shows several characters and how they relate to some basic typographic terms. The baseline is an imaginary horizontal reference line on which the characters align. Note that some characters extend slightly below this line. The cap height line is another imaginary line that defines the height of the capital letters. Again, notice how some characters extend slightly above this line. The cap height is usually about two-thirds of the point size, but this is not true of fonts from all foundries. The x-height is defined as the height of a lowercase letter without ascenders or descenders. An ascender is a lowercase letter that extends above the x-height. Characters with ascenders include *b, d, f, h, k, l,* and *t.* A descender is a lowercase letter that extends below the baseline. The descenders include *g, j, p, q,* and *y.* In old roman typefaces the ascenders will extend above the cap height. Descenders are not necessarily always the same; some may descend farther than others.

Figure 36.1. Common typographical terms.

True Italic versus Skewing

With a program like Corel Draw, it is common to use skewing when italics are the actual desired result. Unfortunately, for many typefaces, the two are not the same. An italic typeface is meant to be the "cursive" version of the roman typeface. On a sans serif typeface, the italic is normally called *oblique,* as it is just a slanted or skewed version of the roman. But, on serif faces and some sans serif faces, the italic weight has different curves and can even have a quite dissimilar letter shape. Figure 36.2 shows examples of two different typefaces with their roman weight, a skewed version of the roman, and a true italic face. Notice in the sans serif version how there is little difference between the skewed version and the italic version. The serif version shows a dramatic difference. While sometimes it may seem appropriate to create a false italic, it should be strongly discouraged, especially on serif faces.

abciABC abciABC
abciABC *abciABC*
abciABC *abciABC*

Figure 36.2. Roman, skewed roman, and true italic typefaces.

Bold versus Outlining

Many people feel that a bold weight can be created by adding an outline to characters. Figure 36.3 shows two different faces with a roman weight, the roman weight with a thin outline, and a true bold weight. Notice how the true bold has a much crisper look than the outlined version. Corel Draw 4 also offers a contouring feature, which could be used to create a pseudo-boldface font. While the feature is available, be cautious about its use.

abciABC abciABC
abciABC abciABC
abciABC **abciABC**

Figure 36.3. Roman, roman with outlining, and true bold typefaces.

Condensed and Extended Fonts versus Stretching

By stretching Artistic text by less than 100 percent, you can create a pseudo-condensed typeface. This can come in handy when trying to fit that extra little bit of text into a tight area. Before using this feature, check whether a true condensed version of the typeface is available. Figure 36.4 shows how various characters may become distorted when they are condensed. Notice how the width of the stem on the pseudo-condensed O is not a uniform thickness when compared with the true condensed weight of the font.

The same applies to extending a font by stretching Artistic text more than 100 percent. Figure 36.5 shows the same text block in Figure 36.4 with both a true-extended and a pseudo-extended weight. Again notice how the thickness of the letterforms is not uniform on the pseudo-extended face.

Figure 36.4. Distortions may occur when you use stretching to condense a font.

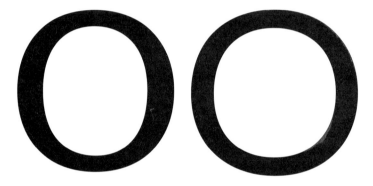

Figure 36.5. A true extended font and the same text extended by stretching.

Ligatures

Ligatures are two or more characters combined into one character for better legibility. Figure 36.6 shows several of the more common ligatures, and below are the same characters typed in the normal way. There are five different ligatures shown (*fi, ff, fl, ffi,* and *ffl*—note that Windows currently does not support these characters unless they are remapped into nonstandard locations, which is commonly the case in expert set typefaces). Ligatures were created for these characters so that they could be set closer together. They also have been shown to increase legibility. Dipthongs (see Figure 36.7) also are considered ligatures. There are occasionally several other ligatures within a typeface (such as the *ct* in Figure 36.6), but they are not very common.

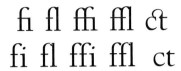

ﬁ ﬂ ﬃ ﬄ &t
fi fl ffi ffl ct

Figure 36.6. Several ligatures and their equivalents.

æ   Æ   œ   Œ

ae   AE   oe   OE

Figure 36.7. Common dipthongs and their equivalents.

Old Style Numerals

Numerals come in two styles (shown in Figure 36.8). The top example is called *old style* or *nonaligning,* and the bottom example is called *modern* or *aligning.* These should be used in a style consistent with your document. Numbers under 100 are usually spelled out, unless they relate to references, and they should always be spelled out at the beginning of a sentence. Some style books change this rule to ten and under, so consult the style book for your particular project.

0123456789
0123456789

Figure 36.8. Two styles of numerals.

Small Capitals

Small capitals (see Figure 36.9) are designed to match the x-height of a particular typeface. Many fonts do not include true small capitals and so they are created by reducing the point size by two sizes (to 80 percent). These characters often appear lighter and look out of place, as in the first

325

line of Figure 36.9. True-cut small caps are the same height as the x-height and are usually equal to the normal cap width. Small caps should be used for abbreviations of awards, decorations, honors, titles, degrees, and so on following a person's name. They should also be used for time as shown in Figure 36.9.

8 A.M. 8 A.M.

8 A.M. 8 A.M.

Figure 36.9. Reduced point size versus true small capitals.

Swash Characters

Swash characters (see Figure 36.10) are alternative characters with extra flourishes on them. They are meant to be used for an initial capital or an occasional alternate character, but they should be used conservatively.

ABCDEFGHIJKLMNOPQRSTUVWXYZ
ABCDEFGHIJKLMNOPRSTUVWXYZ

Figure 36.10. Swash characters.

Ornamental Drop Caps

Ornamental drop capitals are usually used for the first character of a large block of text to indicate the beginning of a passage. Many of these ornamental capitals are too complex to fit within the bounds of a TrueType or PostScript font. Therefore, they are provided as clip art files. This can create problems when trying to make the character fit with the rest of the text block. In Corel Draw 4, you can do this by wrapping the text block around the ornamental character. Figure 36.11 shows how this technique can be used.

 nce upon a time there was a software company in Ottawa, Canada that made an illustration package for use on a PC. Then new versions were released that enabled the software to run on many other types of computers thus making the world a happier place to live.

Figure 36.11. An ornamental drop cap.

Common Kerning Pairs

Kerning pairs are used to better fit various pairs of characters closer together or farther apart than the normal spacing allocated to the characters. Figure 36.12 gives an example of the letter pair *AV* set with the normal spacing and then kerned with the built-in kerning pair. Corel Draw 4 supports up to 1,500 kerning pairs per font. These pairs are stored within a TrueType font's .TTF file or a PostScript font's .AFM and .PFM file. An .AFM file (SAMPLE.AFM) containing a list of over 2,600 kerning pairs is included on the accompanying CD-ROM. While these pairs are not necessary for every font, they can be helpful. Decorative faces, such as script, normally do not contain kerning pairs because the exact spacing is needed to keep the letterforms connecting properly.

Tips for More Attractive Documents

Following are a few typographical tips that will help you create more attractive documents. They will also help you to avoid mistakes that will brand you a novice to typography.

Quotation marks and apostrophes. Do not use the " and ' keys to indicate quotation marks and apostrophes. Instead, use Alt-0147 for open quotation marks and Alt-0148 for closed quotation marks. The single quotation marks are Alt-095 for open and Alt-039 for closed.

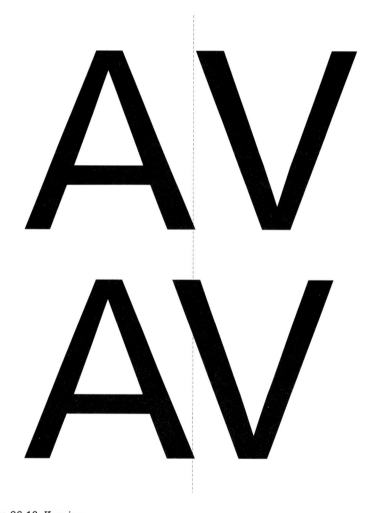

Figure 36.12. Kerning.

Corel *NOTE!*

To create extended characters, hold down the Alt key while typing the character's number on the numeric keypad. The Corel character chart shows all the keys and their numbers.

Dashes. The em dash, Alt-0151, is used to separate two thoughts in a sentence. An en dash, Alt-0150, is used to separate two dates or times. Some typographers add space before and after an em dash or an en dash. This is uncommon. If you must have space, use a thin space.

Spaces. Always put a single space between sentences. Two spaces are a good idea when using a typewriter with its monospace type, but when using proportional type it looks horrible.

All Caps and Underlining. Again, this was necessary when using a typewriter to give emphasis to a section of text. But it looks hideous when using proportional type. Use bold or italic type instead, and if you must have all caps, set them in small caps.

Bullets. No more asterisks, hyphens, lowercase *o*'s, and so on. Now you can use real bullets. But don't go overboard. Stick to bullets, circles, and squares. Avoid pointy fingers, arrows, snowflakes, and so on unless you have a good reason to use them. For example, you might use a snowflake bullet for a skiing brochure.

Numbers. Don't type a lowercase *l* when you need a one (1), or an uppercase *o* when you need a zero (0). This not only looks bad, but it creates problems for a spell checker.

Abbreviations. Spell out words rather than abbreviating them whenever possible. It's rarely necessary to abbreviate a word or state names. If you do abbreviate a state, use the postal form of two capital letters with no period.

Where to Get More Information

I've presented a brief overview of typography and several situations that often confuse electronic publishers. Should you need more information, I provide a brief list of reference works.

The Chicago Manual of Style, Thirteenth Edition. Chicago: The University of Chicago Press, 1982.

The AP Style Book.

While many companies use either The Chicago Manual of Style or the AP Style Book, others have created their own style manual

Text Workshop

which should be followed for any documents created for that company. It never hurts to ask what style manual should be followed.

Williams, Robin. *The PC is not a Typewriter.* Berkeley, California: Peachpit Press, 1992.

Romano, Frank J. *The TypEncyclopedia.* New York: R.R. Bowker, 1984. This one might be a little more difficult to find, but worth searching out if you want to learn more about type and typography.

Lieberman J. Ben. *Type and Typefaces.* New Rochelle, New York: The Myriads Press, 1978. This probably is even harder to find, but it is an excellent source for learning about the origins of type, how to identify typefaces, and to see examples of more than a thousand typefaces.

The Font Company Type Library Poster. An excellent source for examples of more than 2,000 typefaces. Call (800) 442-3668 for more information.

CorelDRAW!
Unleashed

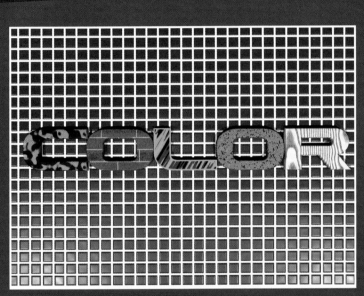

gallery

Right: Photograph of the authors superimposed on a stock photo of the moon's surface in Adobe Photoshop.

Above: This picture shows one way that images from CorelDRAW! can be used. Here they are superimposed on an actual watch face in several different variations.

Above: Here are two license plate designs created by Deborah Gonzalez, wife of co-author Carlos Gonzalez.

Above: These buttons were created by co-author Carlos Gonzalez for various organizations.

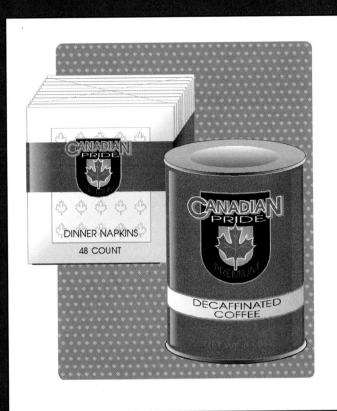

Left: Custom package design treatment drawn by Kent Looft of DesignArts, (602) 786-9411, for a cover contest sponsored by Corelation Magazine.

Below: The basketball court design was created by co-author Foster Coburn as a potential new court for his alma mater University of Kansas.

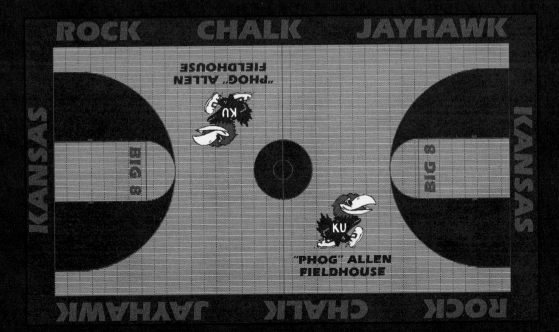

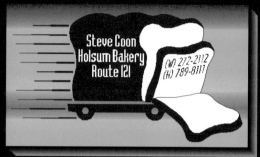

Above: Various business cards designed by co-author Carlos Gonzalez.

Right: Business card, envelope and letterhead created by co-author Carlos Gonzalez as described in Project 8.

DEBORAH L. GONZALEZ
aka *Running Changes*
(602) 555-8888
GRAPHIC DESIGN

Running Changes 7773 N. Center Lane, Suite 234, Phoenix, Arizona 10101

Running Changes 7773 N. Center Lane, Suite 234, Phoenix, Arizona 10101

Right: Banner created by co-author Carlos Gonzalez.

Right: Banner created by co-author Carlos Gonzalez and his wife.

Below: Postage stamp created in CorelPHOTO-PAINT! and CorelDRAW! by Steven A. Cousins, Stone Mountain, GA featuring his two children Juanita and Elliot. Won an Award of Excellence in Corel's Fourth Annual World Design Contest.

Above: Drawing showing the use of guidelines as described in Skill Session 27.

Right: Technical drawing done in CorelDRAW!

Below: Business card, envelope and letterhead created by co-author Carlos Gonzalez as described in Project 8.

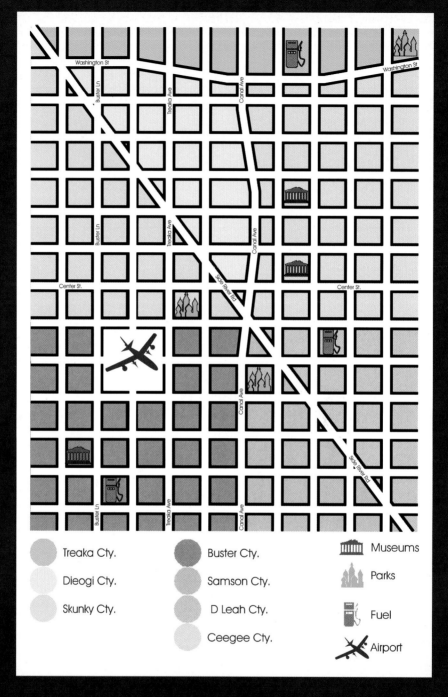

Above: Map created by co-author Carlos Gonzalez showing one particular use for layers as described in Project 1.

Right: Parody ad created in CorelDRAW! by David J. Adducci, 3441 W. Kings Ave., Phoenix, AZ 85023, (602) 993-8718.

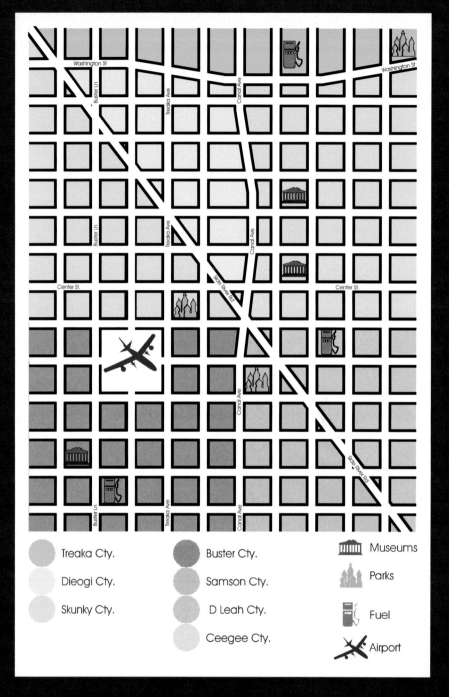

Above: Map created by co-author Carlos Gonzalez showing one particular use for layers as described in Project 1.

Right: Parody ad created in CorelDRAW! by David J. Adducci, 3441 W. Kings Ave., Phoenix, AZ 85023, (602) 993-8718.

VAT III

Boldt Brewery

BOLD

new

BOLDT

The Secret is in the Source

Homebrew at it's finest!

J. B. Boldt Homebrews of Phoenix AZ

Right: Co-author Peter McCormick's Grand Prize World winning drawing from Corel's Third Annual World Design Contest.

Below: Venice exported from CorelDRAW! as a TIFF file and modified with lighting effects in Fractal Design Painter.

Top: Created entirely in CorelDRAW! by co-author Peter McCormick as described in Project 7.

Bottom: Gallery scene exported from CorelDRAW! as a TIFF file and modified with lighting effects and color overlays in Fractal Design Painter.

DONUT SHOPPE

Above: Created entirely in CorelDRAW! by co-author Peter McCormick. Won 3rd prize in September 1991 at Corel's Third Annual World Design Contest.

Right: Created by importing a TIFF file of a photograph taken by co-author Peter McCormick into CorelDRAW! and adding mask and text.

Bitmap
Workshop

Workshops

Bitmap Workshop

Transparency and Coloring

Transparency

You can make a bitmap transparent only when using black-and-white bitmaps, and only the black pixels can be made transparent. The purpose of making part of a bitmap transparent is to allow a background image to show through.

Follow these steps to make the black pixels of a bitmap transparent:

1. Import a black-and-white bitmap into Corel Draw using the Import command in the File menu.

2. Select the bitmap and click on the X icon in the Fill fly-out menu. This is the same as removing the fill of an object.

3. Place the bitmap over any desired background. Resize as necessary.

Figure 37.1 shows the effect that making the black pixels transparent has on the underlying image.

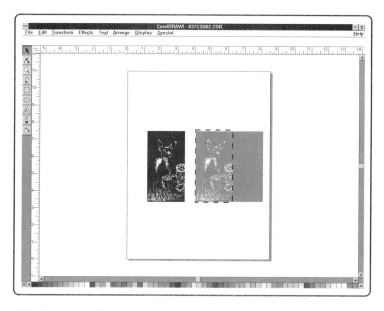

Figure 37.1. Creating a bitmap transparency.

Coloring Bitmaps

You can change the color of bitmaps only using black-and-white bitmaps. When you change colors, you change black to a different color and white to a different color.

Follow these steps to change the color of a bitmap:

1. Select the bitmap with the ⭠ tool.
2. Change the black pixels by clicking the color palette with the primary mouse button.
3. Change the white pixels by clicking the color palette with the secondary mouse button.

Figure 37.2 shows three examples of changing colors of a bitmap.

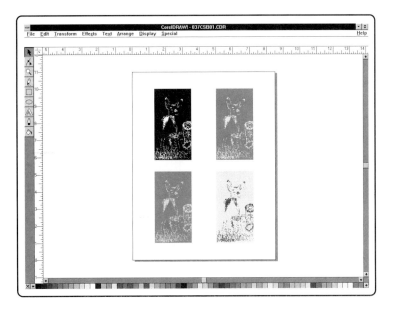

Figure 37.2. Changing the colors of a bitmap.

Bitmap Workshop

Cropping, Hiding, and Blending with Background

Cropping Bitmaps

Cropping bitmaps in Corel Draw is very simple and straightforward. When you import a bitmap into a new or existing file, it comes in as a rectangle or square. If the image does not have a definite background that fills the entire image area, the image you import will have a white square defining the area. This extra area of white background can sometimes interfere with other objects on the screen. It can also conflict with the background color (see "Blending Bitmaps with Backgrounds" later in this chapter). You can remove some of this background by selecting the bitmap and using the ⟋ tool to drag the handles in to crop out the unwanted area. Figure 38.1 illustrates how this is done.

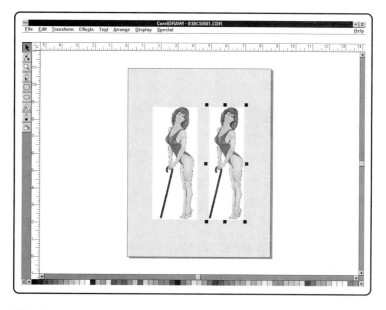

Figure 38.1. Using the Shape tool to crop excess white space from a bitmap.

Another reason for cropping a bitmap would be to crop out part of the image itself. The procedure for this is the same as removing unwanted background. Figure 38.2 illustrates this procedure.

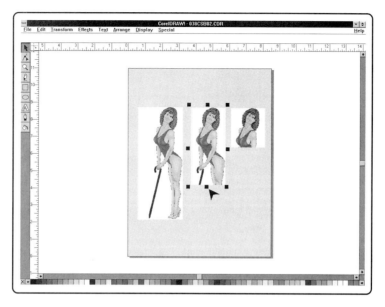

Figure 38.2. Cropping an image with the Shape tool.

Hiding Bitmaps

Hiding a bitmap means that the bitmap will not show in Preview or Wireframe mode. The reason for doing this is to speed up the screen redraw time. When hiding a bitmap, you have two options. The first method is to remove the check mark from Show Bitmaps item in the Display menu. You can only remove the check mark while in Preview mode. The bitmap will still appear in Preview mode but will be hidden in Wireframe mode. If you switch to Wireframe mode and then return to Preview mode, you must repeat the process or the bitmap will show again in wireframe. You should only use this method if you are going to spend a lot of time in Wireframe mode.

The second method requires putting the bitmap on its own layer. This is accomplished by adding a new layer in the Layers roll-up (see Figure 38.3) and moving the bitmap to this new layer. The next step is to remove the check mark from the Visible box before you leave the Layers dialog box. Because both the preview and wireframe mode is effected by this change, don't forget you still have an image on your page. (See Skill Session 28, "Layers," for information about using layers.) To preview the entire page with bitmaps, choose Full Screen Preview from the Display menu (or press F9).

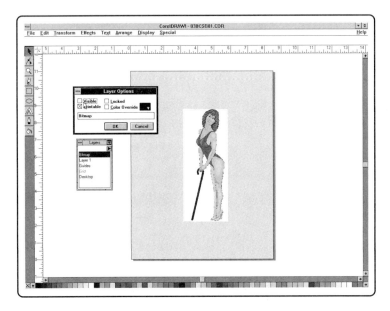

Figure 38.3. Using layers to hide a bitmap.

Blending Bitmaps with Backgrounds

One of the biggest frustrations when using bitmaps in projects is getting rid of the white background that is left over after cropping. Of course, this is not a problem if you want your background to be white.

The solution is to make the background color match the background of the page. There are two ways to approach the problem. The first method involves fewer steps but requires a steady hand. The second method requires more steps and usually works the best.

Freehand

Import the bitmap and place it on the page where you want it. Using the ℓ tool, trace around the portion of the bitmap you want to use. You can use either the freehand tool or the ℓ tool. If you use the Bézier method, select all the nodes of the finished trace and double-click on one of the nodes to bring up the Node Edit roll-up. Choose To Curve in the dialog box and click OK. Choosing To Curve puts two handles on each node, allowing you to manipulate straight lines around the shape of the bitmap. Once the tracing is complete, draw a larger rectangle, big enough to cover the original bitmap. Select the rectangle and the tracing and combine them using the Combine command in the Arrange menu. You have now created a mask over the bitmap image. Color the mask the color of the background you want to match, using the color palette. Figure 38.4 illustrates this method.

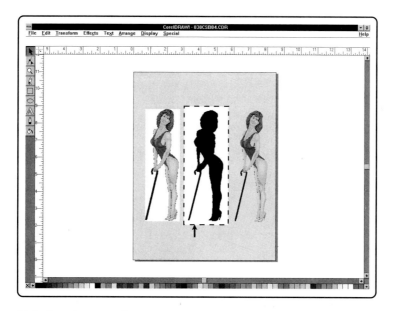

Figure 38.4. Creating a mask to cover the white bitmap background.

Matching Background in Corel PHOTO-PAINT!

Follow these steps to fill in the background color:

1. Draw a small sample rectangle and fill it with the desired background color.
2. Place this rectangle somewhere on the white space of the bitmap.
3. Export the bitmap along with the rectangle using the Export command in the File menu.
4. Select the Selected Only box in the Export dialog box.
5. Use either a .PCX or .TIF extension.
6. Start Corel Photo-Paint and open the .PCX or .TIF image you exported from Corel Draw.
7. Select the eyedropper tool from toolbox.
8. Click on the small sample rectangle that contains your fill color.
9. Select the ✋ tool from the toolbox.
10. Click on the original background of the bitmap (usually white).
11. The background will be filled with your sample color.
12. Be sure to fill any separate holes in the background (in Figure 38.5, note the hole created by the person's crossed hands).
13. Save this new image using the Save As command in the File menu of Corel Photo-Paint.
14. Start Corel Draw and open your project file.
15. Select the Import command from the File menu and import the new image you created.

You should now see your bitmap with a background matching the overall background, as shown in Figure 38.5

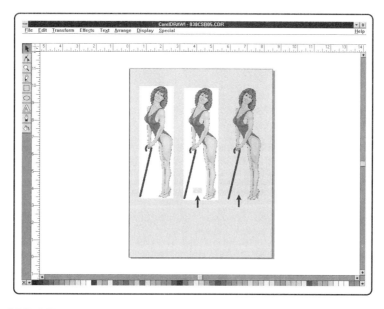

Figure 38.5. Filling in the background color in Corel Photo-Paint.

Bitmap Workshop

Manual Tracing versus AutoTracing

Manual Tracing

Import the bitmap and place it in a convenient place on the page. Using the ℓ tool, trace around the portion of the bitmap you want to use. You can use either the Freehand tool or the Bézier tool. If you use the Freehand tool, hold down the primary mouse button the entire time you are tracing. If you should release the primary mouse button while tracing, you will have to go back and connect the nodes after your trace is completed. If you use the Bézier method, click once with the primary mouse button and then move to another point on the image you are tracing and click again. Continue this point-to-point method of tracing until you finish the trace. Be sure you connect the first node with your last click of the mouse button. If you don't connect the first node with the last you will have to join them (see Skill Session 5, "The Shape Tool").

Now that you have completed your trace, marquee-select all the nodes and double-click on one of the nodes to bring up the Node Edit dialog box. Choose To Curve in the dialog box and click on OK. Choosing To Curve puts two handles on each node allowing you to manipulate your straight lines around the shape of the bitmap.

All this may sound complicated, but it really isn't. For those of you who use tablets with pens, it is a very easy thing to manually trace any object. It is more difficult to manually trace using a mouse.

AutoTracing

Unless you are tracing a very simple black-and-white bitmap, don't bother attemping to use AutoTrace. AutoTrace traces an outline of each color in a bitmap. This means that if your bitmap contains 100 colors, you'd have to click with the Shape tool 100 times to complete the trace, and you'd end up with a shape containing 100 objects.

The procedure for using AutoTrace is as follows:

1. Choose Import in the File menu.
2. Select a bitmap image to import (black-and-white only, if you want any chance of success).
3. In the Import dialog box, click on the For Tracing box.
4. Click OK.
5. When the bitmap appears on-screen, select it with the Pick tool.
6. Click the Pencil tool.

7. The Shape tool changes to a cross hair cursor with the right-hand line extended. The cross hair will not display unless the bitmap is selected.

8. Click the portion of the bitmap you want to trace.

9. An outline of the object is drawn as a vector object.

10. The lines may or may not be connected. If the lines are not connected, you will need to join them using the Node Edit dialog box.

Corel *NOTE!*

If you do not want to manually trace or AutoTrace an object, by all means use Corel Trace. It is an excellent tracing program. Version 4 has made tracing a joy to work with. It will trace everything from black-and-white to full color images with great detail.

Output
Workshop

Output Workshop

Import Filters

Vector Formats

Imported vector files can sometimes have an excess number of nodes. These can automatically be reduced through the use of the .INI file switch AutoReduceOnImport. It works the same as the Auto Reduce function found in the Node Edit roll-up. Any nodes that do not significantly alter the shape of the curve are deleted. Please see Skill Session 61 for more information on setting this switch in CORELDRW.INI.

Adobe Illustrator (AI, EPS)

Full support is provided for all Adobe Illustrator formats up to and including 3.0, Illustrator 88, and 1.1.

Imported files will come in as a group of objects that can be ungrouped using Arrange Ungroup.

AutoCAD (DXF)

AutoCAD files can be converted to DXF format using the DXFOUT utility included with AutoCAD. For 3D images, choose the view you wish to convert before running DXFOUT. Polylines should be used whenever possible rather than regular lines, as they will reduce the complexity of the file.

DXF File Complexity

DXF files that are too complex to import can be output as a Plot-To-File and then imported using the HPGL import filter.

Notes and Limitations on DXF Files

- An attempt is made to center the imported image in an 18×18-inch area. This is not guaranteed, especially with 3D images. All drawings will be scaled to fit within an 18×18-inch area.
- Dashed lines will be converted to a similar dashed line pattern.
- Dimension entities may tend to scatter when imported. In these cases, explode the dimension entities in the original AutoCAD file and re-export to DXF.
- Imported polylines will retain only their minimum line width as specified in AutoCAD. This width may be up to four inches.

- Solid and trace entities will be filled for all non-3D fills (that is, they are filled on an xy-axis view only).

- Points are imported as ellipses, while extruded points come in as a line segment with two nodes.

- If a file was exported as "Entities only," it may import incorrectly due to lack of header information.

AutoCAD Features Not Supported by Corel Draw

- Shape entities cannot be used since Corel Draw does not read .SHX files.

- Polylines including variable-width polylines, elevation (group 38), mesh M and N vertex counts (groups 71 and 72), smooth surface M and N densities (groups 73 and 74) and smooth surface type (group 75).

- 3D shapes such as cones, spheres and tori; extrusion of circles, arcs, text, polylines with width and/or dashed patterns.

- Invisible lines in 3D face entities.

- Automatic wireframes.

- Hidden lines removal.

- Extrusion direction assumed to be parallel to the z-axis.

- Binary DXF format.

- Paper space entities within a model space.

- Layers information.

Text in the DXF File

AutoCAD-generated text will show the following differences:

- The justification on text may not be preserved. Text that specifies no justification will work best.

- Due to limits in Corel Draw regarding point size and skew, Corel Draw may adjust the values to stay within those limits.

Regarding special characters in text strings:

- Control characters will be ignored.

- Overscore and underscore will be ignored.

- Characters referred to by number must be a three-digit number, such as %%065 for character 65.

■ The character %%010 is a carriage return and line feed.

■ Corel Draw replaces any nonstandard characters with a "?". These characters include the degree symbol, the +/- tolerance symbol, and the circle dimensioning symbol.

Typefaces specified in .DXF files will be remapped to Draw fonts according to Table 40.1.

Table 40.1.
Converting AutoCAD typefaces to Corel Draw typefaces.

AutoCAD Typeface	Corel Draw Typeface
Complex	Toronto
Gothic	Frankenstein
Greek	Symbols
Italic	Toronto
Monotext	Monospace
Roman	Toronto
Script	Banff
Simplex	Toronto
Standard	Toronto
Symap	Geographic
Symath	Symbols
Symusic	Musical
(other)	Toronto

Corel Draw (CDR)

Corel Draw files will import as a group of objects. You may ungroup them using the Arrange Ungroup command.

Text in Version 1.xx Files

Text that is contained in 1.xx files may import with inter-character spacing that is slightly off. This problem affects only certain typefaces and is not always noticeable. It is most noticeable when the text is close to another graphic element. It can be corrected by using the ⚲ tool to adjust the spacing. If the text is fit to a curve, straighten it and then use the Text Fit Text to Path command again.

CorelTRACE! (EPS)

CorelTRACE! files will import as a group of objects. You may ungroup them using the Arrange Ungroup command.

GEM Files (GEM)

Object Interior Fills

Objects with custom fills such as grids, hatches, and ball bearings are not supported. They will be imported with a tinted color fill corresponding to the color of the pattern fill of the original object.

Line End Styles

Caps or corners created in GEM Artline will not import. For files created in GEM Draw, the following will occur:

- ■ Round end caps will be successfully imported.
- ■ Lines with arrows import with no end caps.

Symbols

Symbols created in GEM Artline will be converted to curves when imported into Corel Draw.

Text in GEM Files

- ■ GEM Artline files will convert all text to curves. Text contained in other GEM files will come in fully editable.
- ■ Text specified as Dutch will be changed to Toronto and Swiss will be changed to Switzerland_Narrow.
- ■ The text alignment may not be exactly the same as the original file due to differences in font sizes and spacing between the formats. This can be corrected once the file is imported into Corel Draw.
- ■ Characters not supported by Corel Draw will appear as question marks. Underlined text is not supported.

Output Workshop

Computer Graphic Metafiles (CGM)

Bitmaps

Bitmaps are not supported.

Markers

Only markers supported by the CGM standard are imported; private-use markers are ignored.

Text in CGM Files

- Text is editable only if the correct options were used when exporting the file.

- The typefaces will probably change in the import process. This can be changed once the file is in Corel Draw.

Hewlett-Packard Plotter (HPGL)

Corel Draw supports only a subset of the HPGL and HPGL/2 command set. A stepping factor of 1,016 plotter units = 1 inch will be used.

Image Size

A dialog box appears that allows a drawing to be scaled when importing. If a drawing is bigger than what Corel Draw supports, it will be automatically scaled to fit with Corel Draw's maximum page size.

View

3D files should be changed to the desired view before exporting as that will be the view imported into Corel Draw.

Colors in HPGL Files

HPGL files define colors by pen numbers. The pen numbers can be mapped to a color by putting definitions in the CORELFLT.INI file. These definitions are entered in the [CorelHPGLPen] and [CorelHPGLColor] sections. Up to 256 definitions can be entered. Any pen numbers not defined will default to Black. All changes made will affect both the HPGL import and export filters.

Fills

Not all objects in an HPGL file will be filled in Corel Draw.

Line Types

HPGL dotted, dashed, and solid line types are remapped to a Corel Draw line pattern as shown in Table 40.2.

Table 40.2.
Converting HPGL lines to Corel Draw line types.

HPGL Line	Corel Draw Line Type
#0	Solid
#1	Dotted
#2	Small dash
#3	Large dash
#4,5	Dot-dash
#6	Double dot-dash
#7 and over	Same as #2

Text in HPGL Files

- Text will only be editable if the exporting application is capable of exporting text as text.
- Text will be assigned to the Monospaced font, but can be changed to any typeface and size once imported.
- Imported text will have a fill color based on its pen number, but no outline color.

IBM PIF (GDF)

Unsupported Functions

- Set Background Mix, Set Foreground Mix, Call Segment and Set Character Set orders are not processed. Objects will be overlaid in the order they are read in. Each nonoverlapping object will have its own defined color.
- Set Paper Color and Set Pattern Symbol are not supported.

PIF Line Types

- Line types 1, 3, 4, and 6 map to Corel Draw's "three-unit dash followed by a five-unit space" line type.
- Line types 2 and 5 map to Corel Draw's "one-unit dash followed by a five-unit space" line type.

Line type translations are not controlled by the CORELDRW.DOT file as all the translations are hard-coded into the PIF import filter.

Text in PIF Files

Text strings are assigned the Monospace typeface if available. In its absence, Toronto would be used next. Otherwise, the first font in the font list will be used. The font can easily be changed once the text is imported.

Lotus PIC (PIC)

Color

Colors in a .PIC file are translated into one of eight gray shades.

Text

- All text will come in as editable text.
- All Title text will map to the Toronto typeface and all non-Title text will map to the Monospaced typeface.

Macintosh PICT (PCT)

Objects

Objects with both a fill and an outline will import as a group of two objects with one being the outline and the other the fill.

Colors

Many PICT fills are actually bitmap patterns, and Corel Draw will try to maintain them as bitmap patterns.

Pattern Outlines

Pattern outlines will be converted into a solid color.

Arrowheads and Dashed Lines

Arrowheads and dashed lines are not supported.

Text

- All text will come in as editable text.
- Fonts specified as Times will map to Toronto, Helvetica to Switzerland and Symbols to Greek/Math Symbols. All other fonts will map to Toronto.
- Text may not be aligned properly due to changes in font size and spacing. This can be adjusted in Corel Draw.
- Question marks will replace all unsupported characters.
- Bold, Italic, Outline, and Shadow text styles and any combinations are fully supported. Underlined text is not supported.

Micrographx 2.x, 3.x (DRW)

- Clip regions are not supported.
- Most raster operations are not supported.
- Gradient and fountain fills will be converted to a series of polygons.

Windows Metafile (WMF)

Table 40.3 shows the font substitutions made between Windows Metafiles and Corel Draw files.

Table 40.3.
Converting Windows Metafile fonts to Corel Draw fonts.

Windows Font	Corel Draw Font	Similar To
Swiss (default)	Switzerland	Helvetica
Swiss Light	Switzerland Light	Helvetica Light
Swiss Extrabold	Switzerland Black	Helvetica Black
Roman	Toronto	Times Roman
Modern	Memorandum	American Typewriter
Script	Banff	Brush Script
Decorative	Lincoln	Linotext

WordPerfect Graphic (.WPG)

■ WPG version 2 is not fully supported.

■ Graphics Text Type 2.

Bitmap Formats

You can import black-and-white, color, and gray-scale bitmap graphics. If you save a color or gray-scale bitmap as part of a CDR file, the color and shades of gray will be retained.

GIF Bitmaps

GIF files conforming to the 87A and 89A specifications can be imported.

JPEG Bitmap (.JFF, .JTF, .JPG, .CMP)

The JPEG standard format was developed by the Joint Photographers Experts Group offering superior compression techniques, albeit in a lossy format. This allows large color files to be easily transported between a wide variety of platforms. Lead bitmaps can also be imported using the JPEG filter. These have a .CMP extension. JPEG files created in Adobe PhotoShop 2.5 may not import correctly in Corel Draw 4.0A5; these work fine in version 4.0B3.

Kodak Photo CD (PCD)

Photo CD format was developed by Eastman Kodak as a way to store 35mm photographs on a compact disc. The files contain multiple resolutions of the same picture stored in a single compressed file. This file may exceed 8 MB. When imported in Corel Draw, you will be given a choice as to which resolution photo you would like imported.

PCX, PCC Bitmaps

PCX files of specification 2.5, 2.8, and 3.0 can be imported. They may contain either 1-, 2-, or 4-color planes. Those containing 3-color planes cannot be imported.

Targa Bitmaps (TGA)

16- and 24-bit Targa files can be imported in the following variations:

- Uncompressed color-mapped images.
- Uncompressed RGB images.
- RLE compressed color-mapped images.
- RLE compressed RGB images of types 1, 2, 9 and 10 (as defined by AT&T Electronic Photography and Imaging Center).
- Some 32-bit TGAs will be imported, but the last 8 bits will be ignored.

TIFF Bitmaps (TIF)

Black-and-white, color, and grayscale TIFF files can be imported up to and including the 6.0 specification. The files can be compressed using the CCITT, Packbits 32773, or LZW compression algorithms. Loading times may be longer on compressed files as they must be decoded. Some compression algorithms may not be compatible with the TIF import filter including those that use JPEG compression or YCbCr. CMYK TIFFs can be imported by using the Four Color TIFF filter, but are immediately translated to RGB, thus destroying the CMYK information.

Windows & OS/2 Bitmaps (BMP)

All .BMP files are imported following the Windows BMP specification. Color, gray-scale, black-and-white, and even compressed bitmaps (RLE) can be imported.

If the RLE has "bands" that appear where they should not, some editing is required in CORELFLT.INI. In the CORELFLT.INI file's [CorelBMPImport] section, add the following line: Import Corel30RLE=1. If this section does not exist in CORELFLT.INI, simply create it.

Word Processing Filters

Text files that are imported will mirror the original document as much as possible, although not all formatting attributes and layout features are supported. If possible, the features will be simulated. The following features are not supported:

Output Workshop

- Header, footers, footnotes, and endnotes.
- Underlining.
- Embedded graphics.
- Columns.
- Tables.
- Macros.

Fonts and Character Sets

Corel Draw will attempt to match fonts when importing the file for any format that includes accessible font family information. The settings used to match the fonts are found in the CORELFNT.INI file.

All .RTF files will be converted into the Windows ANSI character set. The Macintosh Character Set and Standard IBM PC Code Page 437 are also supported.

Due to the differences in character sets, not all characters can be properly translated. In these cases, an underscore character (_) will be substituted for the undefined character.

Table 40.4 shows how the various word processor formats translate fonts in Corel Draw.

Table 40.4.
Corel Draw word processor font support.

Word Processor	From RTF to Corel Draw
WordPerfect 5.x	All fonts supported
Microsoft RTF	All fonts supported
Microsoft Word for DOS	All fonts supported
Ami Professional	All fonts supported
Microsoft Word for the Macintosh	Limited font support
MacWrite	Limited font support
Microsoft Word for Windows	All fonts supported

Applications that list "All fonts supported" means that Corel Draw can support all the font family information provided by that format. Those that have "Limited font support" are unable to read some of the font family information because Corel Draw cannot work with extended font families. Formats that are not listed in Table 40.4 will map to the best font available.

Proportional Fonts versus Nonproportional Fonts

Because of the spacing differences between proportional and non-proportional fonts, imported documents that specified a proportional font may have more text per page than the original.

Page Size and Margins

Imported documents will retain the page size specified in the original document regardless of the page size specified in Corel Draw. The top and bottom margins will affect the top and bottom of the paragraph text frame, but the left and right margins will have no effect.

Anchored Text and Frames

Anchored text may be properly converted from WordPerfect 5.x, Microsoft RTF, Microsoft Word for Windows, Microsoft Word for the Macintosh 4.0 and 5.0, and Ami Professional. All other formats will convert the anchored text to regular text.

Miscellaneous Formatting

- Due to the fact that Corel Draw relies upon RTF for importing, alignment of paragraphs applies to the whole paragraph and not individual lines.
- Documents containing tables of contents and indexing convert into the appropriate functions in RTF.
- Automatic outlining data converts to regular text.
- Style sheets specified in the original document will not import into Corel Draw styles, however the formatting specified by the styles will apply to the imported text.
- Text contained within a frame or a positioned object is retained.

Character Limits

There is a character limit of 4,000 characters per paragraph of Paragraph text. This limit can be smaller for complex fonts.

Output Workshop

Ami Professional 2.0, 3.0 (SAM, 9)

No special considerations.

ASCII Text (TXT)

This filter imports only true ASCII files. If your word processor is not supported by another filter, export the files to pure ASCII, specifying text only. All attributes such as bold, italics, and underlining will be ignored. Tabs and indents will be converted to spaces.

MacWrite II 1.0, 1.1 (*.*)

Graphics

Pictures will be imported as well, using the PICT format filter.

Microsoft Rich Text Format (RTF)

Unsupported Features

- Table of contents and indexing data.
- Frames/positioned objects.

Microsoft Word 5.0, 5.5 (*.*)

Endnotes or footnotes are not supported.

Microsoft Word for Mac 4.0, 5.0 (*.*)

Endnotes or footnotes are not supported.

Microsoft Word for Windows 1.x (*.*)

General Notes and Limitations

- The embedded field method for building indexes is supported, but the style-implied method is not.
- Word's Normal text style is converted to Corel Draw's default text style, Avalon (Avant Garde).
- Characters that are available in the sets Symbol or MS Linedraw will be converted to the corresponding PC character set entries when possible.

364

Microsoft Word for Windows 2.x (*.*)

Problems with Pre-Release Files

Files created in a pre-release copy of Word for Windows 2.0 may result in unpredictable conversion errors. These files should be opened in a released version of Word 2.0 and resaved.

General Notes and Limitations

- The embedded field method for building indexes is supported, but the style-implied method is not.
- Word's Normal text style is converted to Corel Draw's default text style, Avalon (Avant Garde).
- Characters that are available in the sets Symbol or MS Linedraw will be converted to the corresponding PC character set entries when possible.

WordPerfect 5.x for DOS and Windows (*.*)

General Notes and Limitations

- Text in WordPerfect's table of contents and index functions is not supported by Corel Draw.
- WordPerfect style sheets are not supported.
- Equations and formulas created in WordPerfect's equation language are converted to regular text by Corel Draw.
- Graphic features like HLine and VLine are not supported.

Other Formats

EPS Thumbnail (EPS, PS, AI)

This filter will import EPS files that cannot be imported with the regular AI EPS filter including EPS files exported by Corel Draw. They will be displayed by showing the header included within the file but cannot be edited. They may be transformed by stretching, scaling, rotating, and so on. Corel Draw 4.0A5 has some problems sizing and scaling these files properly.

Excel for Windows 3.0, 4.0 (XLS, 9)

Cell widths in Excel create a ruler line in the target file with the tab stops matching the cell widths.

Lotus 1-2-3 1A, 2.0 (WK?), Lotus 1-2-3 for Windows 3.0 (WK?)

The currency setting should be specified with the Options/Spreadsheet Currencies command in Lotus 1-2-3 before converting spreadsheets containing international currency symbols and conventions.

Cell widths in Lotus 1-2-3 create a ruler line in the target file with the tab stops matching the cell widths.

Output Workshop

Export Filters

Illustrator 88, 3.0 AI

AI versus EPS

AI is the native format of Adobe Illustrator and is a subset of the Encapsulated PostScript file format. Not all of the effects Corel Draw produces are available in the AI format. But AI files are fully editable when imported into Corel Draw unlike EPS files.

Limitations

- Fountain fills are exported as a series of filled bands much like Corel Draw's blending feature. The number of bands created is controlled by the Preview Fountain Steps in Preferences.
- Texture fills are exported as a solid gray fill.
- Arrowhead line caps are exported as separate objects.
- Fit Text to Path exports each character as a separate text string.
- Text objects containing characters with special attributes (kerning, rotation, typeface changes, and scaling) will be exported as separate text objects.

Outline Attributes

Setting the CalligraphicClipboard to 1 in your CORELDRW.INI file will accurately reproduce calligraphic outlines, corner styles, and line caps. Outlines export as a group of polygons matching the outlines in Corel Draw, but add significantly to the size of the exported file.

Bitmaps

Bitmaps are not supported.

General Notes and Suggestions

- Objects should not be combined so that the export conversion is easier.
- If the drawing will require future editing, it should be done in Corel Draw to avoid the complexities added during the conversion.
- Files that will be imported into layout packages should be exported as EPS files as they will print much better.

Text

■ Exported text can be sent as editable text if the necessary fonts are available in Illustrator. Otherwise, the text should be Sent as Curves.

Adobe Type 1/TrueType Fonts

Limitations

■ Type 1 and TrueType fonts are exported with no hinting.

■ Exported characters must be composed of only one object. This can be accomplished by combining the various pieces using Arrange Combine.

■ Fill and outline attributes are not supported.

■ Adobe Type 1 fonts can only be used with Adobe Type Manager version 2.0 and higher.

AutoCAD DXF

Unsupported Corel Draw Features

■ Calligraphic pen effects, dashed and dotted lines, and all line weights are converted to solid lines 0.003 inch thick.

■ Bitmaps are not supported.

■ Curves are exported as polyline segments.

■ Layers information is not supported.

Texture fills

Texture filled objects are filled with a solid gray fill. All other fills are not supported.

Objects with No Outlines

Filled objects that have no outlines will have an outline added when exported.

File Size

Files can grow quite large when exported from Corel Draw to the DXF format. An increase of size of more than ten times is not uncommon.

Colors

Standard Colors (7)   Matches colors in the Corel Draw file to the seven colors available in DXF.

Full Colors (255)   These files may more closely represent the original Corel Draw file, but they are heavily dependent on the video driver being used by AutoCAD.

Text

Text is exported as curves to maintain its appearance. Therefore, it is not editable.

Bitmaps

Scaling Bitmaps

Due to the nature of bitmaps, they will degrade in quality when they are enlarged. Shrinking them will usually not degrade the quality, but disk space will be wasted.

File Size

Bitmaps should be exported correctly sized for where they will be placed in their destination application. A full-page bitmap exported at 300 dpi can take over 24 MB of disk space. Many times, 300 dpi resolution is overkill for the intended use.

Compression Schemes

Compression applies only to images that are 16 color, 256 color, 16 gray, or 256 gray (that is, 4- or 8-bit images).

The following compression schemes are used:

Windows BMP RLE (Run-Length Encoding)   This format is not universally supported and may cause problems in many applications.

CompuServe GIF   LZW (GIF version 89A).

CorelPHOTO-PAINT PCX   RLE (PCX version 3.0).

Targa TGA   Either RLE-compressed color-mapped images or RLE-compressed.

RGB images (types 9 and 10 as defined by AT&T Electronic Photography and Imaging Center)   24-bit color TGA files will be exported as RLE-compressed RGB bitmaps. Compressed TGA files are supported by few applications.

TIFF   PackBits (TIFF Version 5.0). Not all applications can work with TIFF v5.0 files and, therefore, they should be exported as TIFF v4.2. The ExportToTiff42 switch found under the [CorelTIFFExport] section of CORELFLT.INI can be set to 1 to force export as TIFF v4.2. This is necessary for WordPerfect.

Fountain Fills

The number of steps in a fountain fill is controlled by the Preview Fountain Steps setting in Preferences.

GEM Files (GEM)

Saves files in a vector format usable in GEM Artline, Delrina Perform and Ventura Publisher (version 2.0 and higher).

Limitations

- Fills, outlines, arrowheads, and segments in dotted and dashed lines are exported as separate polygons.
- Fountain fills are very grainy due to the limited color availability in GEM.
- Texture fills are exported as a solid gray fill.
- Breaks may occur when outlines come to a point. This depends on the size of the objects, thickness of the outline, and the angle at which the outline meets at the point.
- Text is exported as curves and is not editable.
- Colors are mapped to the 16 colors GEM supports.
- Due to limits in the number of objects that the GEM format supports, some files will not be completely exported. Decreasing the complexity of the drawing may alleviate this problem.

Unsupported Features

- Bitmaps.
- Bitmap pattern fills.
- PostScript Textures (converted to uniform mid-gray fills).
- Corners (joins) will appear round in GEM Artline.
- Dotted and dashed lines.

Bézier Curves

Not all applications can work with Bézier curves; therefore, they are converted to line segments. Curves with more than 128 segments will be broken into smaller grouped objects.

When the objects are broken, construction lines will appear when imported back into Corel Draw. These will show only in wireframe mode and will not print.

In GEM Artline, the objects that appear to be individual are actually groups of smaller objects.

HP Plotter HPGL (PLT)

Unsupported features

- All fills will be ignored except for texture fills which are converted to a solid gray fill.
- Bitmaps.

Limitations

- Dotted and dashed lines convert to the standard HPGL line types.
- Bézier curves are converted to line segments.
- Outlines are exported with a pen width of one. Thickness and calligraphic settings are not supported.

Colors

The colors exported to HPGL files are controlled by the pen numbers assigned to the file. These pen colors can be controlled in Corel Draw's HPGL Pen Color Selection dialog box so that they correspond to the colors of the pens in the plotter.

The pen color definitions are found in the [CorelHPGLColors] section of the CORELFLT.INI file. There can be as many as 256 pens defined, although most plotters have eight or fewer pens. The color definitions affect both the HPGL import and export filters. Corel Draw's default configuration contains the eight most widely used pen colors, as shown in Table 41.1.

Table 41.1.
The default pen color definitions.

[CorelHPGLPens]	[CorelHPGLColors]
P1= Black	Black=0,0,0,100
P2= Blue	Blue=100,100,0,0
P3= Red	Red=0,100,100,0
P4= Green	Green=100,0,100,0
P5= Magenta	Magenta=0,100,0,0
P6= Yellow	Yellow=0,0,100,0
P7= Cyan	Cyan=100,0,0,0
P8= Brown	Brown=0,50,100,25

Page Size and Orientation

In order to have the image properly positioned when plotted, verify that the page size and orientation specified in Corel Draw match those of the plotter.

Unoutlined Objects

Any filled object that has no outlines will have one added when it is exported.

Text

Text will be automatically converted to curves when it is exported to maintain its appearance.

IBM PIF

Limitations

- Colors will be mapped to the best available color from PIF's 16-color palette.
- Due to the limited palette, fountain fills will not render well.
- Texture fills will be converted to solid gray fills.

Outlines Attributes

The following outline effects will be exported as polygons, provided the CalligraphicClipboard value in CORELDRW.INI is set to 1.

- Objects created using the calligraphic pen.
- Line caps.
- Custom outline thicknesses.

Unsupported Corel Draw Features

- PostScript textures.
- Bitmaps.
- Two-color and full-color pattern fills.

Text

Text will be automatically converted to curves when it is exported to maintain its appearance. This text will not be editable. The text can be exported as text by checking the Export Text As Text check box when exporting.

MAC PICT (.PCT)

Outline Attributes

The following outline effects will be exported as polygons, provided that the CalligraphicClipboard value in CORELDRW.INI is set to 1.

- Calligraphic pen effects.
- Line caps.

Calligraphic effects and line caps appear as separate objects grouped with the line they are applied to.

Unsupported Corel Draw Features

- Bitmaps.
- PostScript texture fills are exported as a gray fill.
- Two-color and full-color pattern fills.

Objects with Fills and Outlines

Filled objects with an outline export as a group of two objects. One object will be the outline and the other the fill.

Outlines on text will export only when the text is converted to curves prior to export by choosing Arrange Convert to Curves.

Fountain Fills

The number of steps in fountain fills are determined by the Preview Fountain Steps setting in Preferences.

Colors

The colors available on the Mac are dependent on the type of display being used. A display that uses 8-bit color is limited to 256 colors. A display that uses 24-bit color will display colors that are virtually identical to the original file.

Text

Text will be automatically converted to curves when it is exported to maintain its appearance. This text will not be editable. The text can be exported as text by checking the Export Text As Text checkbox when exporting.

Matrix/Imapro SCODL (.SCD)

Outline Attributes Option

The following outline effects will be exported as polygons, provided that the CalligraphicClipboard value in CORELDRW.INI is set to 1.

- Corner types.
- Calligraphic pen effects.

Output Workshop

- Line caps and arrows.
- Fountain fills.

Unsupported Corel Draw Features

- PostScript textures.
- Bitmaps.
- Two-color and full-color pattern fills.

Producing Slides with Full PostScript Effects

Agfa-Matrix offers an Adobe PostScript RIP for their film recorders. This will virtually eliminate the limitations above. Check to see if your service bureau offers this option.

Optimizing Output

Your screen display should be optimized by using one of the RGB PAN files supplied with Corel Draw.

Aspect Ratio

For proper slide output, the page size should be set to 7.33 inches by 11 inches. If the page size is set to another value, change to this option and resize the elements on the page to fit within the page borders.

Working in Portrait Orientation

To produce slides in portrait orientation, follow these steps:

1. Select Slide as the Page Size in the Page Setup dialog.
2. Select Custom and change the Orientation to Portrait. Do not change the page dimensions.
3. After completing the drawing, change the Orientation back to Landscape.
4. Select all objects and rotate them 90 degrees in the drawing.
5. Choose Export.

Encapsulated PostScript (.EPS)

Corel Draw cannot import the EPS files it creates as editable files, so always save the original CDR file if you want to edit it later.

Image Header Size

A low-resolution header adds about 2 KB to the size of a file, a medium-resolution header adds about 8 KB, and a high-resolution header approximately 32 KB. These sizes apply to images whose shape is more or less square. These numbers are somewhat relative; they are dependent on the shape of the drawing. Some can have headers that exceed 64 KB. Some applications such as Ventura Publisher can have problems importing files with large image headers. For drawings that are much larger in one direction than the other, be careful about using high-resolution headers.

Some applications do not read EPS files exported from Corel Draw unless ExportToTiff42= is set to 1 in [CorelTIFFExport] section of the CORELFLT.INI. The EPS filter shipped with Corel Draw 4.0A5 also caused problems in applications such as Quark Express and PageMaker. This is fixed in Corel Draw 4.0B3.

Colors

PostScript does not support PANTONE colors. Spot colors used in Corel Draw are therefore converted to CMYK values.

File Contents

EPS files exported from Corel Draw will contain the filename, the program name, and the date. Corel Draw automatically determines the size of the bounding box.

Text

- If you want to use PostScript typefaces in place of Corel Draw's typefaces, make sure all the necessary fonts have been downloaded to your printer. Choose All Fonts Resident when exporting.
- This same effect is available by modifying the PSResidentFonts section of your CORELFNT.INI file.
- Fonts that are not found in the printer will output as Courier or will not print.

Windows Metafile (.WMF)

Unsupported Corel Draw Features

- PostScript functions including PostScript texture fills and halftone screens.
- Bitmaps.
- Two-color and full-color patterns appear as gray in the WMF file.
- Texture fills are exported as solid gray fills.

WMF File Complexity

WMF files can grow very large if a drawing contains lots of curves or text. Some programs such as Ventura Publisher and PageMaker impose limits on the size of imported files and can have problems with these files.

Image Header

An image header can be included with the exported WMF file. This makes it possible to view the contents of the file in programs such as PageMaker, Ventura and Word for Windows. This can make the WMF file impossible to read by certain applications not designed to handle it.

Fountain Fills

The number of steps in fountain fills are determined by the Preview Fountain Steps setting in Preferences.

WordPerfect (.WPG)

Outline Attributes

Outline effects will be exported as polygons, provided that the CalligraphicClipboard value in CORELDRW.INI is set to 1.

Fountain Fills

Fountain fills tend to contain coarse banding.

Unsupported Corel Draw Features

- PostScript texture fills and halftone screens.
- Bitmaps.

Colors

The number of colors exported is set in the Export WPG dialog box.

16 Colors   Matches colors in the Corel Draw file to a standard set of 16 colors. Choosing this option usually yields acceptable results on a VGA display.

256 Colors   Provides a truer representation of your Corel Draw file although the results will vary depending on the video adapter and driver used in WordPerfect. The colors may appear as shades of gray. In this case, export the file again with 16 colors selected.

Text

Text will be automatically converted to curves when it is exported to maintain its appearance. This text will not be editable. The text can be exported as text by checking the Export Text As Text check box when exporting.

Output Workshop

Printing

Printing is probably the most important function of Corel Draw, because it is not feasible to haul a computer around everywhere to show off a drawing. Printing is also one of the most difficult topics to fully understand, especially with all the new functionality added to Corel Draw 4 in the prepress area.

Print Dialog Box

The Print dialog box (see Figure 42.1) has changed dramatically in appearance from Corel Draw 3. The biggest difference is the addition of the preview portion on the left side of the dialog box.

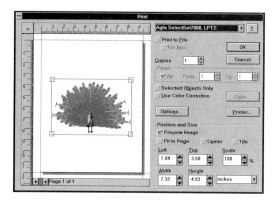

Figure 42.1. The Print dialog box.

The preview portion of the dialog box is bounded on the top and the left by rulers. Red guidelines criss-cross the page to indicate the printable area of the page, which is indicated by a page border with a drop shadow. The objects on the page are bounded by a box with squares at each of the corners. These boundaries, combined with the guidelines to show the printable area of the page, can indicate before printing if all the objects will appear on the printout. Just below the preview are left and right arrows to manipulate the view on multi-page documents.

The top right of the dialog box has a drop-down list box that lists each of the printers installed on the system. It displays both the name of the device and the port to which it is connected. To get more information about that particular device, click on the question mark button just to the left of the list box, and several windows full of information on that device will be displayed. Figure 42.2 shows the Printer Information dialog box.

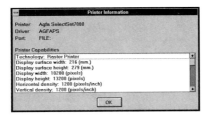

Figure 42.2. The Printer Information dialog box.

Just below the list of printers is the Print to File check box. This allows you to print a drawing to disk. The main use for this checkbox is to prepare a file for outputting at a service bureau. The For Mac checkbox will strip the Ctrl-D characters from the files being printed to disk. Since Ctrl-D is the Macintosh end-of-file character, these files will not output properly from a Macintosh unless this box is checked. Always check For Mac, because the lack of the Ctrl-D characters has no effect whatsoever on files output from a PC. The Copies text box indicates how many copies of the current drawing will be sent to the printer.

Corel *NOTE!*

> Due to a bug in Corel Draw 4.0A5, the Copies text box will send full copies of the drawing to the printer rather than sending one copy and having the printer print multiple copies. The workaround is to leave this at one and set the number of copies in the printer setup dialog box. This has been fixed in Corel Draw 4.0B3.

The next section down in the Print dialog box contains the control for multi-page documents. The choice can be made between printing all pages or just those within a selected range. On single-page documents, this whole section is grayed out.

The bottom right of the dialog box contains the Position and Size controls. The Preview Image check box controls whether the Preview image on the left side of the dialog box will be displayed. As this image is not always necessary, turning the Preview off can save significant time during the print cycle. Fit to Page will stretch the image to fill the printable area of the page. This will provide the largest possible size without having to manually make adjustments. The Center check box will center the printable objects on the page. This controls both horizontal and vertical centering. The Tile check box can tile an object larger than the printable area onto multiple pages so that it can be pieced back together. This can come in very handy for proofing Tabloid pages or banners.

The Left, Top, Width, and Height text boxes can be used to exactly position the objects on the page. Adjusting either the width or height will automatically adjust the other measurement automatically. The scale text box can also be used to resize the object and it will adjust both the Height and Width text boxes automatically. For those who prefer working visually rather than numerically, the preview image can be moved and resized by using the cursor just like the Pick tool. Clicking inside the object will bring up a four headed arrow that allows the object to be moved. Clicking on any of the four corner rectangles allows the object to be resized proportionally. Any changes made on the preview image will affect only the printed copy and not the original image.

Print Options

The Print Options dialog box shown in Figure 42.3 contains many settings for adjusting the quality of the image and for outputting reference marks for offset printing.

The first setting controls the flatness of the image. This is especially useful for complex images. Due to limitations in the PostScript language, files with complex fills such as gradients, textures, bitmaps, and PostScript can cause the PostScript output device to produce limitcheck errors. The flatness setting will actually flatten out the curves of the object to try and decrease this complexity. On high-resolution imagesetters, this change in flatness is not noticeable until it gets over 12–16. Laser printers are much more likely to be affected by this setting. The maximum value is 100, although this will produce a completely distorted image. The Auto Increase Flatness check box will automatically increase the flatness up to 10 over the setting in the Flatness text box until the graphic outputs properly.

Figure 42.3. The Print Options dialog box.

Corel *NOTE!*

> Increasing the flatness will also cause images to print much faster.
> Thus, it is a good way to proof draft pages very quickly.

The screen frequency text box controls the density of the line screen for outputting the image. This value is dependent on the output resolution of the device the file will be printed on. For more information on setting a proper line screen, see Skill Session 55 and/or ask your printer. The Fountain Steps control the number of levels of gray that will be printed. This value can range anywhere from 1 to 2000, but the limit of most PostScript devices is 256. This also is dependent on the output resolution of the printer and the Screen Frequency. Skill Session 55 discusses the relationship between these numbers.

Corel *NOTE!*

> Increasing the number of Fountain Steps will increase the complexity of
> a file. This can cause problems in outputting complex files to a high-
> resolution device and can also significantly increase print times.

The Print Negative check box will create a negative version of the file, which is very useful when outputting film for color separations. Emulsion Down will make sure that the image prints with the emulsion side of the film down when checked and the emulsion side up when unchecked. This is a value that your offset printer should provide when asking for film. All Fonts Resident will send the file to the printer expecting that all the fonts used in the file will already be resident in the printer or have previously been downloaded. The fonts must be properly registered in the CORELFNT.INI file as described in Skill Session 61. Check Print As Separations to create a separate page for each color used in the file. More information on color separations is provided in "Separations," later in this Skill Session.

The References section controls the printing of many marks that are useful when outputting to imagesetters and/or color separations. It is a good idea to turn all of these attributes on even when only one of them is necessary. All of these marks will appear outside the document page and therefore will not interfere with the drawing.

Crop marks are used to indicate the edges of the document page. They are especially useful when printing to imagesetters which use continuous rolls of paper. Without crop marks, it can be very difficult to tell where the page falls. Registration marks are used to align the various sheets of color separations so that the colors will properly align. The calibration bar will print the six colors Red, Green, Blue, Cyan, Magenta, and Yellow for calibrating the color output with actual color swatches. This can be used to make sure that the quality of color is being produced properly on a particular output device. The densitometer scale prints a scale of each color from 0 to 100 percent so that the consistency of output can be checked from one sheet of film to another. The file information will print the name of the file, date and time, and color separation information. It normally prints outside the document page, but if you check Within Page, it can print within the page.

Corel NOTE!

It is common for users to suspect a bug in the print function when the reference marks don't show on the printed page. This is normally because they will only show when the printable area of a page is larger than the size of the document page. There is a bug in 4.0A5 of Corel Draw that, when in facing pages view, the reference marks only print on the last page of the document. This can only be avoided by turning off facing pages view. Corel Draw 4.0B3 corrects this bug when printing multiple-page documents.

Separations

The Separations dialog box, shown in Figure 42.4, contains all the controls that deal with printing color separations. In the upper left, the Print Separations in Color checkbox will allow the printing of each separation in the appropriate color rather than grayscale. This can be useful if outputting to a transparency. This option is available only when printing to a color device, otherwise it is grayed out. Convert Spot Colors to CMYK will automatically break a spot color into the four process colors when printing. This is very useful when printing a piece that has previously been specified in spot colors. Changing the drawing may take several hours, whereas this checkbox can do the work on-the-fly without affecting the original drawing.

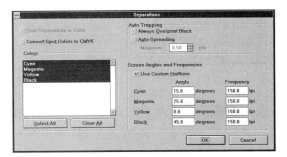

Figure 42.4. The Print Separations dialog box.

The Colors list box lists all the colors used in the drawing. When process colors are used, all four colors will automatically be listed even if some of them are not used. Individual colors can be selected by clicking on their name and multiple colors can be added by either Shift-clicking or Ctrl-clicking.

Auto Trapping in the upper right is a new feature in Corel Draw 4, and it provides the capability of automatically creating spread traps. Always

Overprint Black controls whether the color black will always be over-printed on top of other colors. This can be useful for overlapping black outlines. Auto-Spreading will automatically create spread traps where the inside object is enlarged slightly to overlap the outside object. When this option is activated, the Maximum parameters box will become enabled. The maximum specifies how much the objects will be allowed to spread. The default value is set to .5 points.

The Screen Angles and Frequencies section controls the screen angles of each of the process colors and the screen frequency at which they will print. These numbers are usually loaded from the CORELPRN.INI file to optimize the angles and frequencies for the screen frequency specified in the options dialog box. Many imagesetters will automatically substitute their preferred angles for whatever is included in the file.

Color Circuits

The Color dialog box shown in Figure 42.5 provides control over the calibration of colors between the screen and the printed page. It is accessed through the Color button in the main Print dialog box.

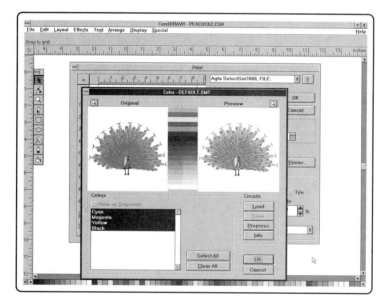

Figure 42.5. The Color dialog box.

The dialog box shows two previews of the image. The left image is the original colors that are specified in the drawing, and the right image simulates the colors that will appear on the printer. Between the two images is a color bar that compares Cyan, Magenta, Yellow, Red, Green, Blue, and several grayscales. Either of the two images can be zoomed by clicking on the magnifying glass button above the image. Figure 42.6 shows a zoomed image.

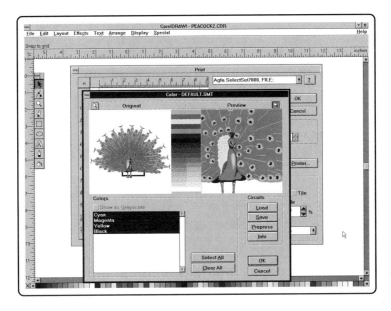

Figure 42.6. Zoomed view in the color preview window.

The colors section of the dialog box allows individual colors to be turned on and off to see how they will affect the printout. Turning the colors off in this dialog box has no control over the actual printout.

Other color circuits can be loaded by using the Load button in the Circuits section of the dialog box. Several circuits are included with Corel Draw, and others can be created by saving a circuit after adjustments have been made in the PrePress controls. The Info button invokes a dialog box with a list of information that is contained in the current color circuit. The Color Circuit Info dialog box is shown in Figure 42.7.

The Prepress button brings up the Prepress Tools dialog box shown in Figure 42.8. It controls the attributes contained within a particular color circuit.

Figure 42.7. The Color Circuit Info dialog box.

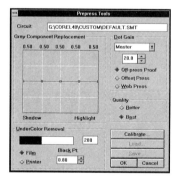

Figure 42.8. The PrePress Tools dialog box.

The top of the dialog box lists the name of the file in which the color circuit is saved. If you plan to make changes to the circuit, it would be a good idea to change the name of the file so that the current file isn't overwritten.

The Gray Component Replacement (GCR) section at the right of the dialog box controls the amount of black added to replace the cyan, magenta, and yellow that are unnecessary. This will increase the sharpness, contrast, and detail, and provide for better color fidelity. The GCR graph allows for the amount of gray replacement to be adjusted at five different levels from the extreme shadows to highlights. High values of GCR will decrease the amount of ink used, but shadowed areas will appear less glossy. Adjust the amounts by clicking on any of the five points and dragging up or down. The numbers at the top of the graph will adjust themselves automatically.

The Undercolor Removal section controls the amount of total ink density. When 100 percent of all colors is used, the amount of ink density is 400 percent. This is usually too high for most printing presses as the ink will tend to dry incorrectly and cause trapping problems. Most printers will indicate the total amount of ink density that their press can work with. Therefore, ask your printer what the total ink density should be and set the Undercolor Removal to that amount. The Black Pt is a number between 0 and 1. A 0 indicates the black produced by using 100 percent of cyan, magenta, and yellow, whereas 1 indicates the black produced by 100 percent of all four colors.

Dot Gain is the effect where halftone dots will tend to enlarge in the printing process. This usually happens because of ink absorption on the paper. The premise behind setting the dot gain is to shrink the dots ahead of time so that when they enlarge, they will be the desired size. Again, this is a number that your printer should be able to supply to you. Corel Draw includes commonly used numbers for several popular types of presses.

The quality settings of Better and Best control the quality of the color separations created. While the Better setting will not create the best possible separations, it will take a significantly shorter period of time to generate the separations. Therefore, it should be used for proofing purposes. The Best setting obviously produces superior separations.

The Load and Save buttons will allow you to load predefined color circuits and save circuits that you have modified. The Calibrate button is used to calibrate the screen to the printer being used. It will bring up the Calibrate dialog box shown in Figure 42.9.

Output Workshop

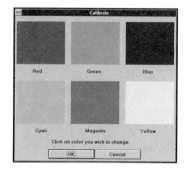

Figure 42.9. The Calibrate dialog box.

The Calibrate dialog box presents the colors red, green, blue, cyan, magenta, and yellow. It is used for calibrating each of these colors to match a printer sample from the desired output device. If your printer has calibration features, these should be used before calibrating to your screen. Before the calibration process, print a swatch from the printer with each of these six colors for reference. Each color can be adjusted by clicking on the on-screen sample. This will bring up the dialog box shown in Figure 42.10.

The colors are adjusted by either dragging the crosshair cursor around the color grid or by manipulating the hue, saturation, and luminance values. Continue modifying the color until the on-screen color matches the printed sample exactly.

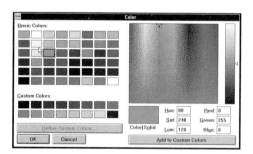

Figure 42.10. The Color adjustment dialog box.

Printer Setup

The Printer Setup dialog box is reached either through the Print Dialog box's Setup button or through the File Print Setup command. This dialog box is different for each type of printer. The dialog box shown in Figure 42.11 is that of a PostScript printer.

This initial dialog box allows for setting the paper size, including the extra page sizes necessary for printing reference marks. The orientation can be adjusted between portrait and landscape, although these can be adjusted automatically by Corel Draw. One of the most important dialog boxes is the About box. This will tell what version of the print driver is being used. The companion CD included with this book contains the newest versions of many of the popular printer drivers. It would be a good idea to check to see that you are using the latest drivers, as this can make a big difference in the performance and quality of printed output.

Figure 42.11. The Print Setup dialog box for a PostScript printer.

Output Workshop

Cross-Platform Support

Many users don't realize that Corel Draw is available on more than just the Windows platform. Currently there are versions of Corel Draw running on OS/2, UNIX, and CTOS. In the near future, a Macintosh version will be released. Unfortunately, each of these programs requires special treatment to work with files created in Corel Draw 4.0 running under Windows.

OS/2

The latest version of Corel Draw for OS/2 is 2.5. It is basically a 32-bit version of Corel Draw 2.01 for Windows. Therefore, the OS/2 version can only read Corel Draw 2.0 files. These cannot be directly created from Corel Draw 4.0 for Windows. They can be created in Corel Draw 3.0 for Windows by using the Save As 2.x option in the Save As dialog box. Corel Draw 4.0 files can be saved as Corel Draw 3.0 files in the same manner.

The files created in the OS/2 version can be read by Corel Draw 4.0 for Windows if they have been saved as version 2.x 16-bit files. While the cross-platform compatibility is not perfect, it can be done with a little work.

UNIX

The current version of Corel Draw for UNIX works exactly like the OS/2 version. It can only read 2.x files saved from either 2.0 or 3.0 of Corel Draw for Windows. There will soon be a new version of the UNIX product that will be able to directly read the Corel Draw for Windows 4.0 files. This new UNIX version should be available by the time this book is in print. Check with Corel Corporation for more information.

CTOS

The current version of Corel Draw for CTOS works exactly like the OS/2 and UNIX versions. It can only read 2.x files saved from either 2.0 or 3.0 of Corel Draw for Windows.

Macintosh

In the near future, a Macintosh version of Corel Draw will be released. It will be able to transparently read Corel Draw 4.0 for Windows files. The biggest hurdle in transporting files between a Macintosh and a PC is the actual format of the disks.

Macintosh's can read PC-formatted disks with the aid of utilities such as Insignia Solutions AccessPC, Dayna Communications DOS Mounter, and Apple's PC File Exchange. AccessPC is probably the most flexible utility as it can also read removable media such as SyQuest cartridges, Bernoulli cartridges and many of the optical cartridges. This can be very handy when working with large files.

There are utilities that allow PCs to read Macintosh diskettes, but they are not always seamless. It is much easier to have the Macintosh read and write to a PC disk.

General

Another way to share files between platforms is to convert them to another format such as WMF or Adobe Illustrator files. These files won't retain all of the features that a CDR file can retain (see Skill Sessions 40 and 41 on Import and Export filters), but will most likely give very good results in most cases.

Graphics Toolkit Workshop

Workshops

44

Graphics Toolkit Workshop

CorelPHOTO-PAINT! 1

Graphics Toolkit Workshop

Corel Photo-Paint was first introduced with Corel Draw 3.0. The program was purchased from Z-Soft and was essentially Z-Soft's own PhotoFinish program. Version 4 of Corel Photo-Paint has been updated and refined by Corel's programming team to look and feel more like Corel's Draw program. The difference is that Photo-Paint is a bitmap-drawing program and Corel Draw is a vector-drawing program.

Having two types of drawing programs to work with can be very useful. It allows the user to convert vector drawings into bitmaps and to import bitmaps into vector drawings. This cross-format concept can produce some unusual image effects.

Figure 44.1 is a good example of combining bitmaps and vectors. First a painting of the Grand Canyon was scanned into Corel Photo-Paint. The sky was enhanced with Corel Photo-Paint's Airbrush tool and various parts of the foreground rock formation were created in Corel Photo-Paint as well.

Figure 44.1. A scanned image modified in Corel Photo-Paint.

Figure 44.2 shows the completed image with the bitmaps and vectors combined. The middle ground canyon formations were manually traced and filled with vector shapes and fills. The mountain lion and deer were added for depth effect. This particular image, created by Peter McCormick, was given an Award of Excellence in Corel's 1993 World Design Contest.

Figure 44.2. The final image using bitmaps and vectors.

Corel Photo-Paint is a very powerful image-editing program. It also provides many painting tools for creating paintings from scratch. An entire book could be written on Corel Photo-Paint with all of its features. Therefore, instead of trying to cover Corel Photo-Paint the way we have covered Corel Draw, we will cover only a few of the methods of editing images to give them different appearances and looks.

Corel Photo-Paint's Color Replacer

The Color Replacer tool in Corel Photo-Paint is not found in most painting programs. It is a unique and very useful tool. The Color Replacer replaces one color within a painting with another. The possibilities are many. Consider changing the color of green summertime trees to autumn shades of reds and golds. Figure 44.3 shows a scanned-in image with lots of green trees.

Graphics Toolkit Workshop

Figure 44.3. The original scanned image.

Figure 44.4 shows the changes taking place with the use of the Color Replacer tool.

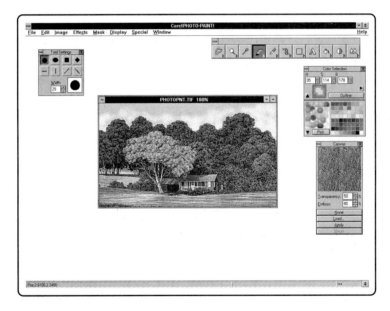

Figure 44.4. Changing colors with the Color Replacer tool.

Follow these steps to learn how to use the Color Replacer tool to change the color of trees. You, of course, can use this effect on any image that you want to change colors in.

1. Open an image in Corel Photo-Paint that has trees in the image.

2. Click and hold the Local Undo tool in the tool box until the fly-out menu appears. With your primary mouse button still held down, move to the last icon in the fly-out menu. This icon is the Color Replacer tool. While on the Color Replacer icon, release the primary mouse button. The Color Replacer tool will now show in the main tool box in place of the Local Undo tool. (To make sure you have selected the right tool, always look at the bottom left corner of the screen. A message will tell you which tool you have selected.)

3. Click the button in the Color Selection roll-up that says either Outline, Fill, or Background. Click on this button until Outline appears.

4. Select the Eye Dropper tool in the tool box.

5. Click with the Eye Dropper tool somewhere on the trees you want to change. (Do not select the darkest color, as this color will be saved in order to show shadows.)

6. Click the button in the Color Selection roll-up, as you did in Step 3, and change to Fill.

7. With the Eye Dropper tool still selected, choose a new color from the Color Palette (this is your replacement color).

8. Change the width of your brush to a high number in the Width parameters box located in the Tool Settings roll-up.

9. Select the Color Replacer tool from the tool box.

10. Begin dragging the Color Replacer tool over the entire area of your trees. Dragging over the area will change the color you selected in Step 5 to the color you selected in Step 7.

11. Repeat Steps 3 through 10 (leaving out Step 8) until you have changed enough of the green parts of the trees to the new colors you select.

Figure 44.4 shows the results of using the color replacement method.

Figure 44.5 shows the original image above the new autumnized image. The Hue and Saturation was increased in the new image in order to enhance the colors of the second image. The Hue and Saturation dialog box is accessed from the Color cascading menu in the Image menu.

Graphics Toolkit Workshop

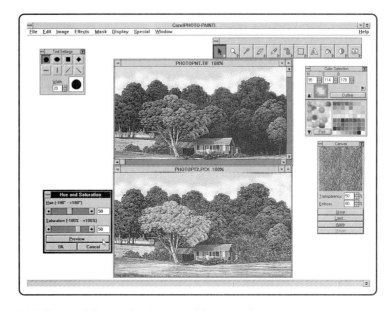

Figure 44.5. Hue and Saturation increased in a new image.

Figure 44.6 shows the image further enhanced by changing the values in the Histogram Equalization dialog box accessed from the Tone cascading menu in the Image menu. This last enhancement brought out the shadows and strengthened the autumn colors for a more pleasing look.

Filters

There are many filters in Corel Photo-Paint, many of which will be covered in Skill Session 45. Embossing is a common filter to many paint programs, but Corel Photo-Paint adds a new twist. You can emboss using three choices of gray tones and any color in the palette. When you choose colors to emboss with, you can select whether to use the outline color, fill color, or background color. The effects of embossing are shown in Figure 44.7 as it is applied to our landscape.

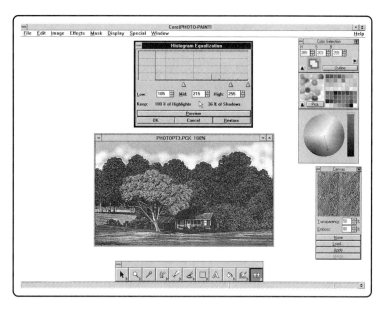

Figure 44.6. The image modified with the histogram.

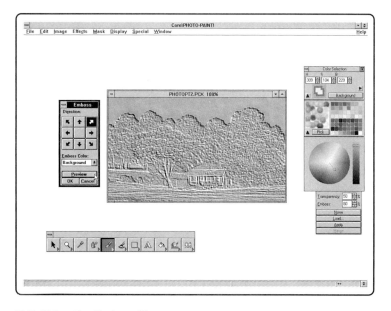

Figure 44.7. Using the Emboss filter.

Graphics Toolkit Workshop

To access the Emboss filter, select Emboss from the Effects menu.

Figure 44.8. shows the effect the Psychedelic filter has on the landscape.

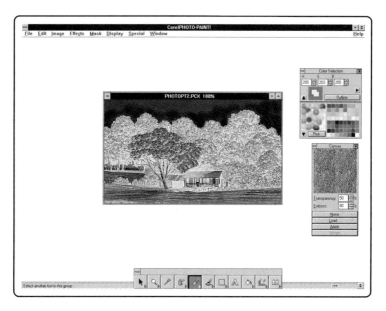

Figure 44.8. Using the Psychedelic filter.

The Psychedelic filter is accessed from the Effects menu as well.

Graphics Toolkit Workshop

CorelPHOTO-PAINT! 2

Graphics Toolkit Workshop

Corel Photo-Paint is a complete program in and of itself. To fully cover this program would require a book devoted entirely to Photo-Paint. But to write a synopsis of the program would not be fair either. We felt it important to show some of the practical uses of Corel Photo-Paint to apply to your everyday work. Chapter 44 showed some of those applications and we will continue in this chapter. This second chapter will cover the many filtering effects that can be applied to one image. The purpose of this exercise is to show how a simple photograph can be transformed in multiple ways to represent different moods. Figure 45.1 shows the original image.

The first effect applied to our photo is overlaying a transparent canvas on the image. Each effect assumes you have the original file opened on-screen. Follow these steps to apply the transparent canvas:

1. Click Canvas Roll-Up in the Display menu.
2. Click the Load button in the roll-up.
3. Select Basket 1 from the selection window.
4. Type or scroll to the number 80 in the Transparency parameters box.
5. Type or scroll to the number 50 in the Emboss parameters box.
6. Click Apply (see Figure 45.2).

Notice how the transparency of the canvas allows the original image to show through. Try experimenting with different Transparency and Emboss settings.

Figure 45.3 has had two effects applied to the image. The first effect was to invert the colors of the image. This is accomplished quickly by selected Invert from the Effects menu. Try using this on other images. You will often be pleasantly surprised.

Figure 45.1. The original scanned image.

Graphics Toolkit Workshop

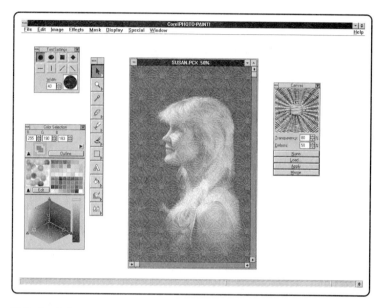

Figure 45.2. Applying a transparent overlay.

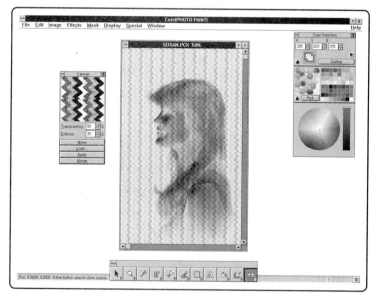

Figure 45.3. Inverting image colors and adding overlay.

With the image colors inverted, apply a new transparent canvas of Cloth 1 using a setting of 90 percent Transparency and 30 percent Emboss. This effect gives an unusual silhouette appearance.

Figure 45.4 uses the Posterize filter. Click on this filter in the Effects menu.

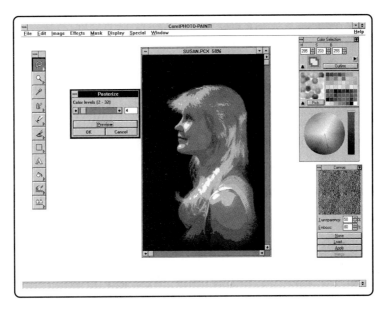

Figure 45.4. Using the Posterizing filter.

Posterizing lets you determine how many colors from the original image you want to use. Type or scroll to a number in the Posterize parameters box. Figure 45.4 used only four colors to produce the effect. Generally four to eight colors will produce the most dramatic results. You might recognize this effect being used a lot in television.

Figure 45.5 was altered using the filter Psychedelicize. This filter is found in the Effects menu and has a parameters box that lets you enter numbers from 0 to 255. This is another filter to do lots of experimenting with.

413

Graphics Toolkit Workshop

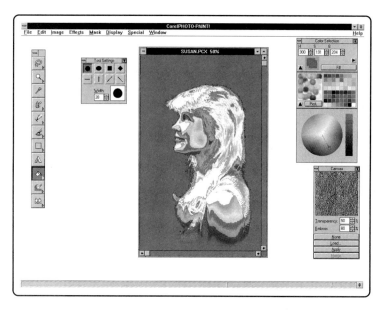

Figure 45.5. Using the Psychedelicizing filter.

Figure 45.6 uses the Solarize filter and produces a very beautiful effect by changing the colors to pastels. This effect is accessed again from the Effects menu. It is similar in a softer way to the Invert command.

Figure 45.7 has been changed dramatically with the Threshold effect. To access this filter, click and hold on Color in the Effects menu until the fly-out appears, and then click on Threshold. The Threshold dialog box allows you to enter numbers from 0 to 255. The image in Figure 45.7 uses the number 216. This effect produces some very powerful images.

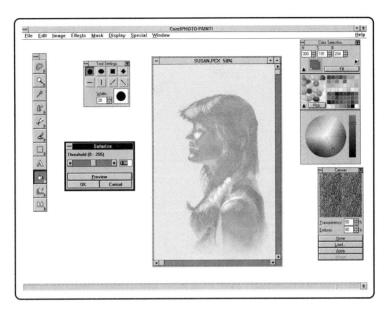

Figure 45.6. Using the Solarize filter.

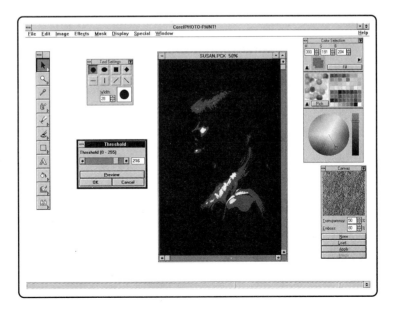

Figure 45.7. Using the Threshold effect.

415

Graphics Toolkit Workshop

CorelMOVE!

Graphics Toolkit Workshop

If you wish to experiment with creating animated files, Corel Move has the functions to allow you to create complex as well as simple animations. Tools are provided for the creation of props, actors, sound effects, and various sounds or image layers. Corel Move allows you to create various cells to form the illusion of movement, which eliminates redrawing each scene showing slight differences to create movement. For more information about Corel Move, see Section 3, "CorelMOVE!" in your CorelDRAW! 4.0 manual.

Corel *NOTE!*

Corel's CD Disk 2 contains over 200 animated flics plus hundreds of CorelMOVE actors and still cartoons to help get you started.

Animations are composed of the following components:

Props   A prop is an object that will remain stationary through the entire animation or a portion of the animation.

Actors   An actor may be composed of a single cel or multiple cels. Viewing the multiple cels in quick succession creates the illusion of movement.

Path   Movement of an actor is created on the screen by applying a path to the actor.

Sounds   Soundtracks and sound effects can be included in your animation. You can use Corel Move's Sound Recorder to create .WAV (sound) files.

TimeLines   TimeLines allow you to view the animation and modify the entrance and exit of objects during the animation.

Cues   A Cue in the animation allows the viewer to cause an action to be performed. Cues establish a condition that must be met, then set an action to take place when this condition is met.

Corel Move Screen

Double-click on the Corel Move icon brings up the Corel Move menu bar. You must first open or create an animation cell before the menu bar options are made available. Available menu options are File, Edit, View, Arrange, and Display. The tool box for Corel Move consists of the Pick tool, Path tool, Actor tool, Prop tool, Sound tool, and Cue tool. The Control Panel is located at the bottom of your screen. The various options under this panel are TimeLines, Sound icon, Playback Controls, Library icon, Loop icon, Frame Counter, and Status Line (see Figure 46.1).

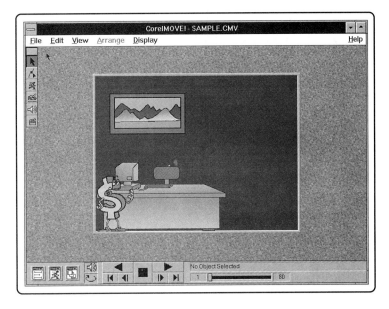

Figure 46.1. The Corel Move screen.

Corel *NOTE!*

The TimeLines roll-up displays the elements that are part of an animation. You can also edit these elements in this roll-up. Expanding the roll-up allows you to see the entry and exit frames as well as the length of the element's play in the animation sequence. For more information about the TimeLines roll-up, see Section 3, "CorelMOVE!," in Chapter 7 in your Corel Draw 4.0 manual.

Paint Window and Tools Box

The Paint Window will be displayed only when you edit or create an actor or prop. When you edit a prop or actor, the object will be displayed on-screen along with the three pull-down menus containing Paint functions. Paint functions can only be selected when editing or creating a prop or actor. The tools found in the Tools box are as follows: Marquee, Pencil, Paint Brush, Line, Rectangle, Polygon, Ellipse, Lasso, Eraser, Pattern selector, Foreground and Background color selector, and the Line Width selector (see Figure 46.2).

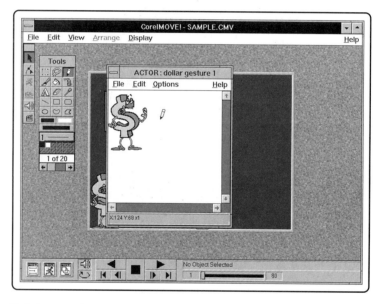

Figure 46.2. The Paint window and Tools box.

Animation Information Dialog Box

Select Animation Information from the Display menu to invoke the Animation Information dialog box (see Figure 46.3). This will allow you to set the amount of props, sounds, actors, and cues. You can change the number of frames needed, the speed of the animation, your window size, and grid spacing in this box.

Figure 46.3. The Animation Information dialog box.

Cel Sequencer

The Cel Sequencer roll-up is enabled from the Display menu. Combining animation cels with actor cels is controlled in the Cel Sequencer roll-up. When you create an actor, a number of cels are also designed. These cels help to create the illusion of movement. A path is created for the actor to follow through the frames of the animation.

The Cel Sequencer roll-up lets you rearrange the order of the cels. It also lets you choose which cel appears in a given frame. Changing the size of the object in the cel can also be done. You can use this feature to create special efffects; for example, the closer an object gets to you, the larger it appears (see Figure 46.4). For more information on Cel Sequencer, see Section 3, Chapter 7 in your Corel Draw 4.0 manual.

Figure 46.4. The Cel Sequencer roll-up.

Playback Options Dialog Box

To invoke the Playback Options dialog box, select Playback Options from the Display menu. The Playback Options dialog box allows you to select various control combinations, such as stopping points in the animation, sound playback, or automatic replay (see Figure 46.5).

Figure 46.5. The Playback Options dialog box.

Using the Animation with Corel Show

After you have created an animation, you may want to include it in a presentation using Corel Show. To add an animation to a Corel Show presentation, you will first need to select which slide follows the animation. From the Insert menu choose Animation. Type the name of the animation you want to insert in the File Name box.

After you select the file you want, the first frame of the animation is displayed. You can use the scroll bar to view the animation one frame at a time. To display the options for controlling the animation, choose Option and click on OK. For more information about Corel Show, see Skill Session 50 or Section 6 in the Corel Draw 4.0 manual.

Graphics Toolkit Workshop

CorelTRACE!

Corel Trace is a program that lets you convert bitmap images into vector format for use in Corel Draw. The new version of Corel Trace includes OCR (Optical Character Recognition). The OCR capabilities allow you to scan text from books, newsletters, and so on, and convert the text to editable text for use in Corel Draw and word processing programs like Microsoft Word.

Overall, using Corel Trace is fairly straightforward. There are a few settings which can be used to control the accuracy of the trace. These settings will be described in detail in "Settings Menu," later in this skill session.

Corel Trace is Twain-compliant, which means you can scan images directly into the program. One thing to keep in mind is to clean up the scanned image as much as possible in the scanning software before letting Corel Trace take over. A good example of cleaning up a scanned image is in the case of text. The better the scan, the better the OCR feature of Corel Trace will work.

The Basic Trace

To trace a bitmap image, start by either scanning an image into Corel Trace or choosing Open from the File menu and selecting an existing file. Double-click on the filename you want to open or highlight the filename and click on OK. Your image will appear in the left-hand window of Corel Trace.

1. Choose Default Settings from the Settings menu.
2. Click on the Outline trace button.
3. The new traced image will appear in the right-hand window.
4. Save the new trace by clicking the Save command in the File menu. From the cascading menu, click on the Trace As option. A dialog box appears, letting you name the file and choose the directory to save the file in. The file will be saved by default as an .EPS file, which can be imported into Corel Draw.
5. If you choose Image from the Save cascading menu, the source image will be saved as a .BMP bitmap file. You might use this option to save the scanned image for future use. Choosing to save the source image as a .BMP also allows you to save the traced image.

Figure 47.1 shows the Corel Trace screen with a scanned gray-scale image on the left and the traced image on the right .

Figure 47.1. The original image is on the left; the trace is on the right.

Figure 47.2 shows the traced image after it was imported into Corel Draw. The image can now be modified by changing gray-scale values or even changing to color.

Figure 47.3 shows the traced image in wireframe mode. This is a good time to remove any unwanted portions of the image and to reduce the number of nodes in the overall image. When images like this one are traced, there will be a large number of nodes for each separate object making up the image. With Corel Draw 4, you can take advantage of the Auto-Reduce feature in the Node Edit roll-up (see Skill Session 5).

Figure 47.4 shows a color photo that has been scanned into Corel Trace and the resulting trace on the right of the screen.

Graphics Toolkit Workshop

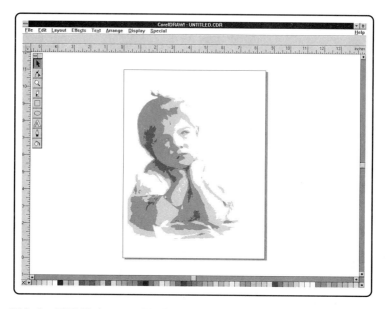

Figure 47.2. An .EPS file imported in Corel Draw.

Figure 47.3. The EPS image in wireframe mode.

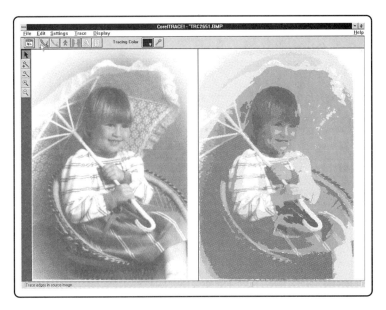

Figure 47.4. Tracing color images.

Settings Menu

The default settings will give very good results in most cases. If you're not satisfied, you can change the way that Corel Trace traces the source image by changing the settings using the Modify command in the Settings menu (see Figure 47.5).

When you select Modify, a cascading menu appears listing seven categories that can be modified:

Image Filtering   This dialog box (see Figure 47.6) lets you make adjustments to the color scheme of the source image prior to tracing. The Threshold adjustments are only available when converting to monochrome.

Color Matching   This adjustment is for controlling the number of colors the magic wand will pick up (see "Tool Box" later in this skill session). Use the slider or click on the Page button on the top right of the dialog box (see Figure 47.7) to set colors manually.

427

Graphics Toolkit Workshop

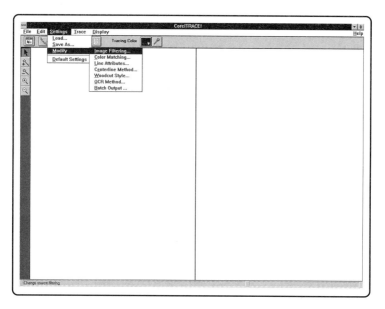

Figure 47.5. The Modify menu.

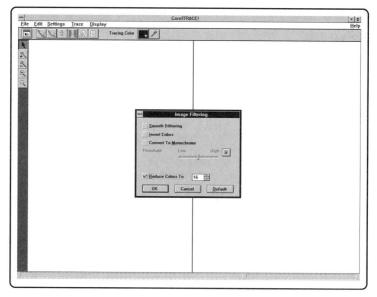

Figure 47.6. The Image Filtering dialog box.

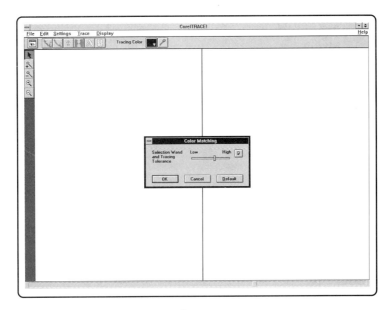

Figure 47.7. The Color Matching dialog box.

Line Attributes This dialog box (see Figure 47.8) controls how accurate the trace will be. Experimenting with different settings is about the only way to work with this dialog box.

Centerline Method The Centerline tracing method traces the line itself and not the outline of objects. Changing the maximum line width in this dialog box (see Figure 47.9) will determine the line width of the traced lines. Only images that are black and white can be traced with the centerline method. If the image is not black and white, use the Convert to Monochrome option in the Image Filtering dialog box.

Woodcut Style The Woodcut tracing method gives the trace the look of a carved out image. You can change the angle of cut and the width as well as whether you want tapered ends or not (see Figure 47.10). If you choose Continuous Cut, the cut will be made without breaks. If Continuous Cut is not selected, the cut will fade out in bright areas. The minimum width is 5 pixels.

Graphics Toolkit Workshop

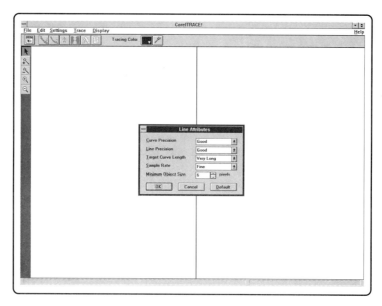

Figure 47.8. The Line Attributes dialog box.

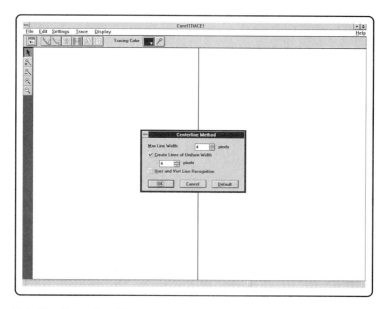

Figure 47.9. The Centerline Method dialog box.

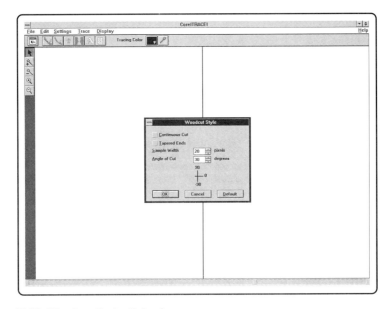

Figure 47.10. Woodcut Style dialog box.

OCR Method   The OCR Method dialog box (see Figure 47.11) lets you choose a text source before scanning. (See "Optical Character Recognition," below.)

Batch Output   The Batch Output setting lets you choose the directory into which to put files that have been batch traced. There are three additional options as to how the file is to be saved in this dialog box (see Figure 47.12).

Optical Character Recognition

To use the OCR tracing method, follow these steps:

1. Before scanning, click Settings in the menu bar. From the Settings drop-down menu, select Modify. From the Modify cascading menu, select OCR Method. Choose either Normal (for normal scanning), From Dot Matrix, or Fax Fine depending on the source of the original. Do not put a check mark in the Check Spelling box.

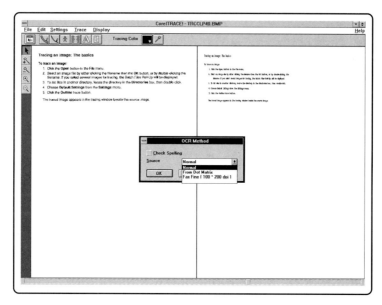

Figure 47.11. The OCR Method dialog box.

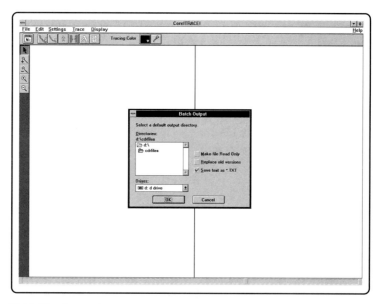

Figure 47.12. The Batch Output dialog box.

Corel *NOTE!*

> If you put a check mark in the Check Spelling box and the program does not recognize a word, it will leave the word out completely. This is a bug and should be fixed in later releases.

2. Scan in a page of text using the Acquire command in the File menu. The page can include graphics as well as text.

3. To trace text only, select the A icon on the icon bar.

4. To trace both text and graphic, select the Page icon.

5. When the trace is completed, select Save from the File menu.

6. From the Save cascading menu, select Trace As if there are graphics included in the traced file. Select Text As if there is only text in the traced file.

7. A dialog box appears. Give your trace a filename and choose a directory to save your file in. If you are saving with Trace As, you will be saving as an .EPS file. If you are saving as Text As, you will be saving as a .TXT file.

8. Import your new file into Corel Draw with the Import command in Corel Draw's File menu.

9. If your file is an .EPS file it will come in as a group of objects. Choose the Un-Group command from the Arrange menu so that you can edit the text and graphics separately.

10. If your file is a .TXT file it will come in as Paragraph text. It can be edited using the Edit Text command in the Text menu or by clicking on the Text tool in the tool box and using the cursor.

Corel *NOTE!*

> If you use the Save Trace command in the File menu instead of the Save command, Corel Trace will automatically save your trace as a TRCCLP40.EPS file in the Corel40/Programs directory. This file is no different from the .EPS file saved with the Save/Trace As method used in Step 7. Using this method to save your new trace doesn't allow you to choose the directory where you want the file to be saved.

Tool Box

The first tool in the tool box is the Pick tool. The Pick tool is used to marquee-select a portion of the image to trace. Whatever falls within the selection box will be traced.

The next two tools are the Magic Wand tools. The first Magic Wand has a plus sign. It is used to select a color range that has been specified in the Color Matching dialog box. The second Magic Wand tool has a Minus sign. It is used to deselect a color range that is specified in the Color Matching dialog box.

The fourth tool is used to magnify a selected area of the source image. The last tool is used to zoom out from a selected area.

Edit Image

When you click on the Edit menu, Edit Image is available in addition to the standard commands. When you click on Edit Image, the Source image is opened in Corel Photo-Paint. The image is Linked to Corel Trace, so any changes you make to the source image in Corel Photo-Paint will be made in the Corel Trace source image as well. This is a convenient way to make changes or clean up an image before you trace it.

Graphics Toolkit Workshop

CorelCHART!

Corel Chart has two major screen views: the Chart View and the Data Manager. You change between these views by clicking the chart/data icon in the upper left of either of these views. The Data Manager is very similar in functionality to a spreadsheet and has the ability to import spreadsheet files from the popular file formats. Chart View provides many different ways to graphically manipulate the view of the data contained in the Data Manager.

Data Manager

The Data Manager is in essence a mini-spreadsheet for entering the data that makes up a chart. While its raison d'etre is for creating charts, according to Corel it can also be used as a spreadsheet for those who don't have a separate program. The Data Manager view is shown in Figure 48.1.

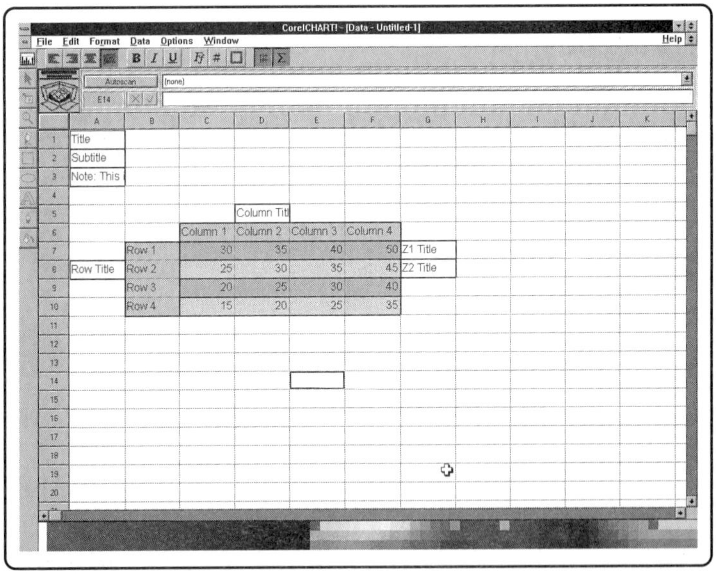

Figure 48.1. The Data Manager screen.

Just below the menu bar in the Data Manager is a formatting ribbon. Icons are included for changing the alignment, text style, font, numeric format, border format, grid, and automatic recalculation.

Data entered in the data manager is expected to follow a particular layout. Cells must be tagged with a cell type, such as Title, Column Header, Data Range, and so on. By tagging the cells, the chart view can automatically place the data into assigned positions. The Autoscan button will try to guess which cells are what type by where a group of numbers is located. One of the best ways to learn the expected cell types is to load one of the sample charts provided on Corel's second CD-ROM.

Data can also be imported from popular spreadsheets such as Excel, Lotus 1-2-3, Microsoft Works, and others. Data can also be pasted across the clipboard using DDE so that the data can be hot-linked to an external spreadsheet.

Formulas for manipulating the data can be typed directly in the formula bar just above the spreadsheet or they can be entered through the Enter Formula dialog box shown in Figure 48.2. The Enter Formula dialog box is accessed by choosing Enter Formula from the Data menu.

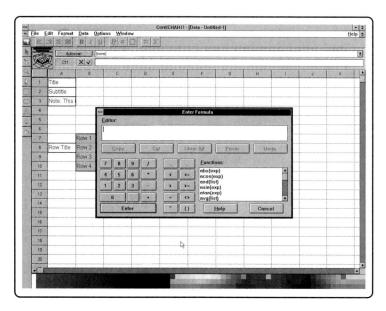

Figure 48.2. The Enter Formula dialog box.

The height and width of cells can be changed interactively by first selecting either a row or a column. The selected row or column does not have to be the one that is to be changed. As the cursor passes over the line between rows or columns, it will change its shape. At this point, click and drag the height or width to the desired size. If more than one column or row is selected when the resizing is performed, the change will apply to all the rows or columns selected.

Once all the data for the chart has been entered, it is time to move back to the chart view to make the data look good.

Chart View

The chart view is shown in Figure 48.3. On the left side is a tool box similar to the tool box found in Corel Draw. The Pick, Rectangle, Ellipse, Text, Outline, and Fill tools work almost exactly like their counterparts in Corel Draw.

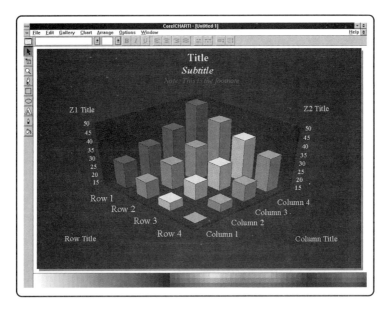

Figure 48.3. Chart view.

The second tool down (the Context tool) will bring up context-sensitive menus on any object by clicking on it while the tool is active. This same effect is available by clicking the secondary mouse button on the object when any other tool is selected. These menus contain the same commands that are available in the normal Corel Chart menus, but having them immediately available can save time.

While the Zoom tool works much like its counterpart in Corel Draw, its fly-out menu (shown in Figure 48.4) looks very different. Instead of the variable zoom levels allowed within Corel Draw, the Zoom tool in Corel Chart zooms to exact percentage levels.

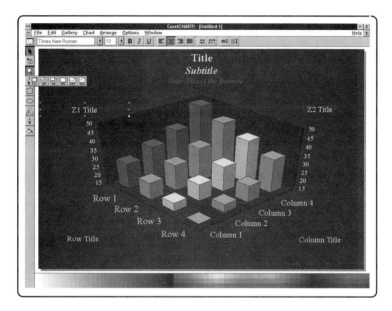

Figure 48.4. The Zoom tool fly-out.

The Pencil tool fly-out shown in Figure 48.5 is quite different from the one found in Corel Draw. The leftmost tool is for drawing straight lines. The next tool is used for drawing polygons, and works much like Corel Draw's Bézier tool except all of the lines are straight lines and the nodes cannot be manipulated. The third tool is very similar to the Freehand drawing tool in Corel Draw. Again the inability to edit the individual nodes is a definite drawback. On the far right is the arrow tool. Arrows are drawn by clicking at the starting point and then the ending point of the line. The arrowhead will appear at the ending point of the line. The arrow style can be changed by bringing up the arrow menu with the secondary mouse button.

Graphics Toolkit Workshop

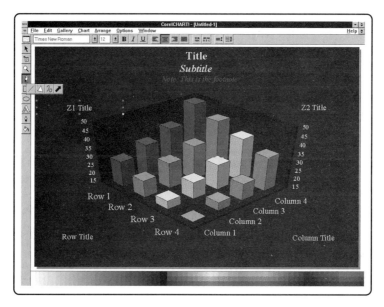

Figure 48.5. The Pencil tool fly-out.

One addition to the Fill tool is the Pictograph Roll-Up icon (⬚) found at the top right of the fly-out. It will bring up the Pictograph roll-up shown in Figure 48.6. This allows any graphic object to be imported and used as a fill to create *USA Today*-type charts. These can either be stretched to fill the area or stacked.

Just below the menu bar is the text ribbon. The various controls on the ribbon control many of the same functions found in Corel Draw's Text roll-up, such as font, type size, type style, alignment, letter spacing, and line spacing.

Along the bottom of the screen is a color pallette. The primary mouse button will assign a fill color to an object while the secondary mouse button assigns an outline color. Changing the color of one element of a chart will automatically change all other related elements. The color palette is very similar to the one found in Corel Draw, but there should be no difference. This difference applies to many of the tools and is frustrating when all the programs come from the same vendor.

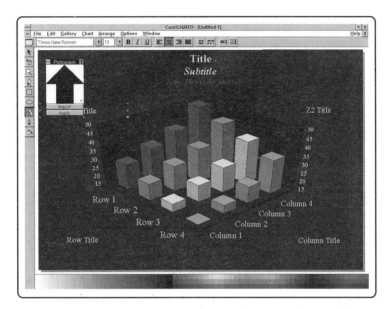

Figure 48.6. The Pictograph roll-up.

Creating a Chart

Corel Chart offers over 80 different chart styles from which to choose.
These can be selected from the Gallery menu. After choosing a particular
chart type, a fly-out will appear with several subtypes and a thumbnail
view of what a chart might look like. The Gallery menu with the subtype
fly-out is shown in Figure 48.7.

When a 3D chart type has been chosen, the whole chart can be manipulated in all three dimensions through the use of the 3D roll-up, shown in
Figures 48.8, 48.9, 48.10, and 48.11.

Each of the four groups of tools can control the manipulation of the chart
by moving, stretching the axes, thickening walls, or rotating the chart in
3D space.

Graphics Toolkit Workshop

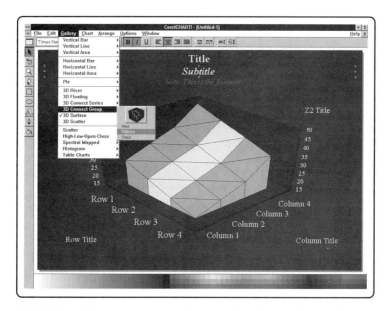

Figure 48.7. Gallery Menu with subtype fly-out and a thumbnail sample.

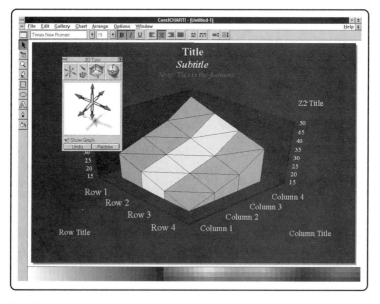

Figure 48.8. The 3D Tool roll-up with movement tools selected.

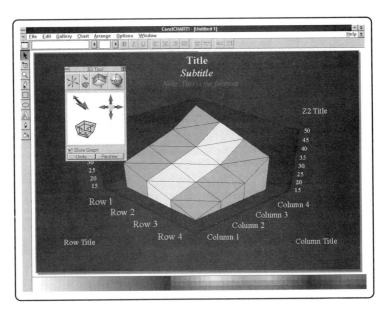

Figure 48.9. The 3D Tool roll-up with scaling tools selected.

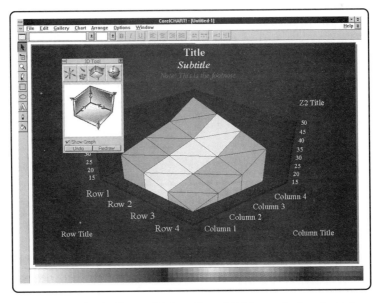

Figure 48.10. The 3D Tool roll-up with length and thickness tools selected.

Graphics Toolkit Workshop

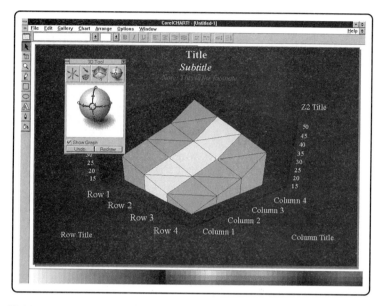

Figure 48.11. The 3D Tool roll-up with rotation tools selected.

Other chart attributes can be changed by bringing up the context-sensitive menus with the secondary mouse button. The best way to learn about all the changes that can be applied is to switch between the many different chart types and then bring up the menus on the various chart elements. Many of the functions in the context-sensitive menus are also found on the Chart menu. To get full use out of Corel Chart, it is necessary to understand each of these options and the results they produce.

Graphics Toolkit Workshop

CorelMOSAIC!

Corel Mosaic lets you manage your files by viewing them graphically as well as by name. Graphics are previewed as an Image Header with the thumbnail version of the file displayed. This helps you find your file if you can't remember or identify a file by its name.

You can start Corel Mosaic from within, as well as independently of, Corel Draw. Select Open from the File menu. Press the Options button in the Open Drawing dialog box. When it expands, press the Mosaic button to start Corel Mosaic (see Figure 49.1).

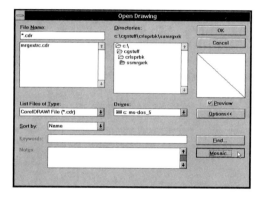

Figure 49.1. The expanded Open Drawing dialog box with the Mosaic button pressed.

Corel Mosaic Window

Corel Mosaic can let you view numerous types of file extensions. Some of these include AI, PCX, EPS, and CDR. The example shows 24 Corel Draw clip art files. Double-clicking on a file will open the file and the application it was created in (see Figure 49.2).

Corel Mosaic File Menu

The File menu allows you to open new catalogs and libraries, existing catalogs and libraries, view directories and change the ones you're in as well as deleting a catalog or library. All print options can be executed only after selecting a catalog file or library (compressed) file. Printing your files can be done by selecting a file and then selecting Print Files from the File menu. Printing thumbnails and changing the Print Setup and the Page Setup can also be done in this menu. Selecting Preferences allows you to change the font, background color, the way the files are viewed, and other options. Exit shuts down Corel Mosaic (see Figure 49.3).

Figure 49.2. Corel Mosaic displaying 24 Corel Draw clip art files.

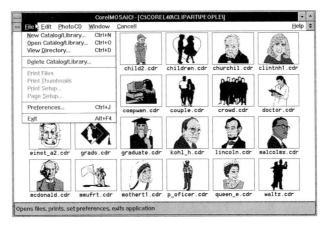

Figure 49.3. Corel Mosaic with the File menu selected.

Corel Mosaic Edit Menu

In the Edit menu, you can select your files by a keyword—a keyword may be a word that helps you remember what a file is and can also be used for searching for the file. This menu also allows you to select all files or clear all files on-screen. Once you have a file selected, you can insert files into the catalog, expand files that are compressed, or update the catalog's information in file.

The next group of options and their function follow:

- Edit takes you into an application where you can edit the selected file (A .PCX file will open Corel Photo-Paint, a .CDR file will open Corel Draw, and so on).
- Convert From CorelDRAW! takes you to your open Corel file with the Export File dialog box open.
- Import From CorelDRAW! takes you to your open Corel file with the Import File dialog box open.
- Delete is used for deleting the selected file.

The Edit menu also has options for extracting and merging from one Corel file to another.

This menu also allows you to add or delete keywords associated with the file by selecting Keywords. You may edit the description of your file or get more information on the selected images on-screen.

Figure 49.4. Corel Mosaic with the Edit menu selected.

Corel Mosaic PhotoCD Menu

The PhotoCD menu can only be used if you have a Kodak Photo CD. Inserting the CD and then selecting Photo CD will allow you to perform Kodak Photo CD operations. Once you have selected View Kodak Photo CD, you will be able to view thumbnails of what files exist. If you want to export selected groups of photos to bitmap file formats, you will need to select Convert Images (see Figure 49.5).

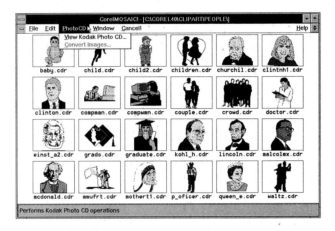

Figure 49.5. Corel Mosaic with the PhotoCD menu selected.

Corel Mosaic Window Menu

The Window menu is used for positioning the screen view of the open Catalog or Library. The selections under this file are as follows:

- Cascade allows you to view the open windows stacked one under the other.
- Tile Horizontally arranges the open windows stacked or placed side by side for viewing.
- Arrange Icons is used to arrange the iconized windows.

You will see that a list of the files in the currently selected Catalog or Library appears at the bottom of this menu (see Figure 49.6).

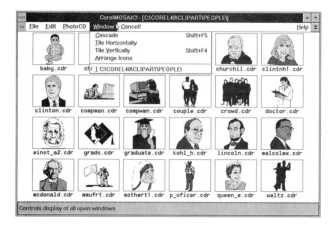

Figure 49.6. Corel Mosaic with the Window menu selected.

Corel Mosaic Cancel Menu

The Cancel menu is only available when Corel Mosaic is invoked from another application such as Corel Draw. This menu will exit Corel Mosaic (see Figure 49.7).

Figure 49.7. Corel Mosaic with the Cancel menu selected.

Corel*NOTE!*

Corel Mosaic can also be invoked when importing a file from Corel Draw.

Corel Mosaic Help Menu

The Help menu (see Figure 49.8) will allow you to review the table of contents for Corel Mosaic, explain how to use help, search for help on certain functions of Corel Mosaic, and review a detailed explanation of how they work. The selection About Corel Mosaic provides current information on the version of Corel Mosaic that is being used, as well as the amount of free space on your disk. You can double-click on the Corel Mosaic icon to see a neat little animation!

Figure 49.8. Corel Mosaic with the Help menu selected.

451

Graphics Toolkit Workshop

CorelSHOW!

Graphics Toolkit Workshop

The Corel Show window shown in Figure 50.1 has many similarities to
Corel Draw. Its tool box is located on the left side of the screen. The top
icon is the Pick tool and works very much like the Pick tool found in
Corel Draw. Context-sensitive menus are controlled by the second icon.
They can be brought up by selecting the icon and then clicking on the
object on which the context-sensitive menu is desired. This can also be
accomplished by clicking the secondary mouse button with any tool
selected. Zooming is controlled by the third icon down and works
exactly like zooming in Corel Draw. The fourth icon brings up a dialog
box like that shown in Figure 50.2 for accessing background libraries.

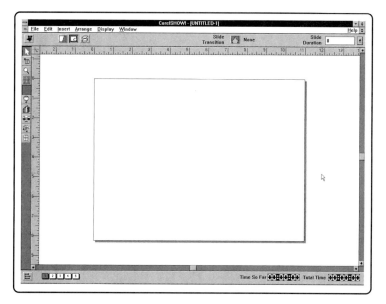

Figure 50.1. The Corel Show screen.

From the background libraries, a background can be chosen which is
used throughout a presentation as a base to place all other objects on.
A limitation of Corel Show is the fact that only one background can be
used in a presentation. Therefore, in order to use different backgrounds,
it is necessary to import each one of them as a graphic and place it on
the appropriate pages. Backgrounds can be turned off on pages where
they are not desired by choosing Edit Omit Background.

Figure 50.2. The Background Library dialog box.

The bottom half of the tool box contains icons for OLE linking and embedding to Corel Draw, Corel Chart, Corel Photo-Paint, and Corel Move. The last icon will OLE-link or embed to any other OLE-compliant application installed on your system.

Across the top of the screen are several icons for working with the slides. The far left icon will generate the screen show from the slides that have been created. The next group of three icons control the viewing of backgrounds, viewing individual slides, and the slide sorter view. A sample of each of these views is shown in Figures 50.3, 50.4, and 50.5.

The next icon to the right controls the transitions that occur as the slide first comes on screen and when it leaves the screen. Clicking on the icon will bring up the dialog box shown in Figure 50.6. The chosen transitions can be previewed by clicking on the Preview button.

On the right side of the screen is a text box for entering the amount of time in seconds that the current slide will be displayed on-screen. Default times are given in the drop-down list box ranging from 0 to 60 seconds although much longer times can be entered by typing the number of seconds.

Along the bottom of the screen are yet more controls. On the left side is an icon that brings up the Timelines dialog box shown in Figure 50.7. The three buttons at the top of the dialog box control what is shown. The far left button controls the slide names in the left half of the dialog box, the middle button controls sound names shown in the left half of the dialog box and the right button controls the timelines at the right half of the dialog box.

Graphics Toolkit Workshop

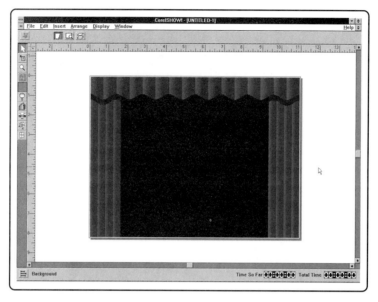

Figure 50.3. Background view.

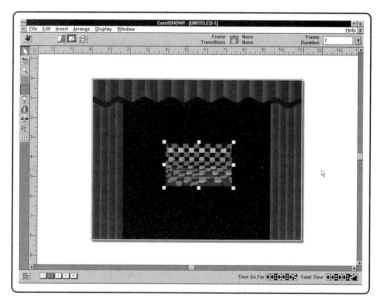

Figure 50.4. Slide view.

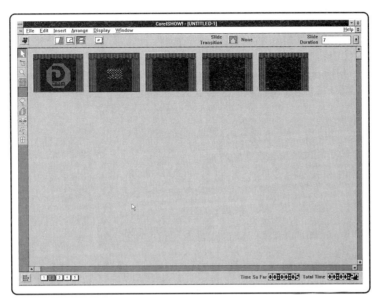

Figure 50.5. Slide sorter view.

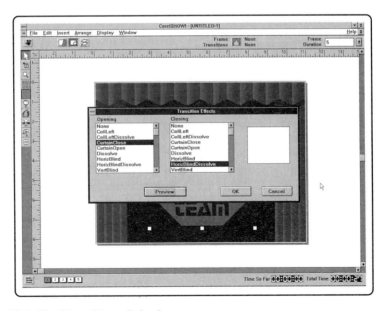

Figure 50.6. The Transitions dialog box.

Graphics Toolkit Workshop

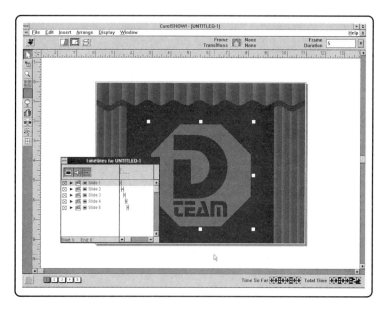

Figure 50.7. The Timelines dialog box.

Individual slides can be turned off by unchecking the check box next to
their name in the Timelines dialog box. Cues (see Figure 50.8) can be
edited by clicking on the clapboard icon. The main slide view can be
changed to a particular slide by double-clicking on its name. Duration
times of slides can be altered by adjusting the timelines shown (assum-
ing that they are activated) in the right half of the dialog box. This can be
very helpful for synchronizing sounds with pictures.

Cues allow branching within a presentation depending upon whether a
particular condition is met. Objects can be used much like buttons
allowing the user to interact with the screen show.

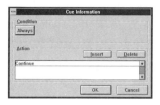

Figure 50.8. The Cues dialog box.

Buttons along the bottom of the screen represent the slides. Each slide has a button with each number on it. Changing to a different slide is as easy as clicking on the appropriately numbered button.

At the bottom right of the screen are two digital clocks that indicate the current position in a presentation and the total time of the presentation. This can be handy for making sure that a 10-minute presentation fits within that time frame.

Linking versus Embedding

Corel Show relies upon Object Linking and Embedding (OLE) to create its files. Corel Show itself has little functionality of its own for creating graphics, but rather relies upon other OLE applications to supply it with data.

This external data can be brought into Corel Show in two different ways. It can either be embedded or linked to the original data file. Embedding will increase the size of the Corel Show file dramatically, as all the included data will be saved within that file. When linking is used, the Corel Show file will remain fairly small, as much of the data is stored in external files. This can cause problems in trying to manage all the files used within a presentation. The dialog box that controls linking and embedding is shown in Figure 50.9.

Figure 50.9. The Insert Object dialog box.

Corel*NOTE!*

> Animations and sounds do not have the same choices as other objects.
> Animations are linked and sounds can be embedded by checking the
> Embed check box.

The Insert Object dialog box is accessed by selecting the Insert Object
command. When the Create New option is chosen, the new object will
be embedded. Choosing Create from File will change the dialog box to
that shown in Figure 50.10 which gives the option of linking the file. The
object will still be embedded unless the Link check box is checked.

Figure 50.10. The Insert Object dialog box with Create from File chosen.

After the correct file is chosen or created, a cursor will appear which
allows a marquee box to be drawn representing the area that the new
object will cover. Again, animations and sounds are handled differently.
Sounds will be shown only in the Timelines dialog box. Animations can
either be brought in at their created size or full screen. This option is
chosen in the Insert Animation dialog box with the Options button
selected.

Linked objects have the option of having the link updated automatically
each time the Corel Show file is opened or by manually choosing the
update option. These choices are made within the Edit Links dialog box
shown in Figure 50.11.

The Edit Links dialog box provides information on every linked object by listing its file name, creator, and its update method. The creator
cannot be changed, but the source file and update method can easily
be changed from within the dialog box. Any object can have its link

updated by choosing the Update Now button. The link can also be broken, thus embedding the object by selecting the object name and clicking on the Break Link button.

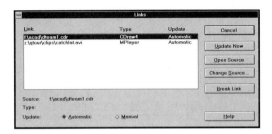

Figure 50.11. The Edit Links dialog box.

Creating a Presentation

Creating a presentation is simply a matter of bringing in various elements and combining them using the methods previously described. A good way to get an idea of what types of presentations can be created is to look at the sample files located on Corel Draw's second CD-ROM.

New presentations are always created with five slides. Adding slides is done by choosing the Insert New Page command. You can delete selected slides by pressing the Delete key.

When bringing in animations, it is important to assign a duration very close to the length of the animation itself. If the time assigned is too short, the animation will be cut off. Times longer than the animation will leave a blank screen for a few seconds.

Cautions

Because of the fact that Corel Show relies upon OLE to bring in all graphics, it requires a large amount of system resources. Using Corel Show with less than 8 MB of RAM is nearly impossible. Regardless of the amount of memory in the system, it is beneficial to create a very large swap file. Shows of more than 50 slides can bring a system to a screeching halt and therefore should be broken into separate slide shows if possible.

Graphics Toolkit Workshop

Because the version of OLE that shipped with the original release of
Corel Show (4.0A6) was still in prerelease form, the speed of Corel Show
is quite slow. If you are still using this version of Corel Show, give Corel a
call and request that the latest version be sent. This should bring both a
speed increase and improved stability.

Advanced Topics Workshop

Workshops

Advanced Topics Workshop

Styles and Templates

The Styles feature allows objects that have similar features such as fill, outline, font, and various effects to be easily modified by simply redefining the style association with the objects. Many users may already be familiar with the concept of styles from using a word processor or page layout program. Corel Draw takes that one furthur by having styles that may be applied to graphic objects as well. The style definitions are saved in a template file, which is also commonly referred to as a style sheet. This way the styles can be applied to other projects as well.

The most important thing to remember about styles is where to find the functionality for creating, modifying, and applying styles. All of the functions are found in two different places, the Styles roll-up and the Object menu. Figure 51.1 shows the Styles roll-up and Figure 51.2 shows the Object menu.

Figure 51.1. The Styles roll-up.

Figure 51.2. The Object menu.

Styles are created by first applying the desired style attributes to Artistic text, Paragraph text, or a Graphic object. Once all the appropriate attributes have been selected, bring up the Object menu. The Object menu can either be defined to be the function that the secondary mouse button automatically brings up, or if something else is selected, it will be activated by holding the secondary mouse button down for a second or two. For more information about setting these options, see Skill Session 60, "Setting Preferences."

Once the object menu appears, select the Save Style As command if this is the first time this style has been used or Update Style if changes are being made to an existing style. The Save Style As dialog box shown in Figure 51.3 will appear with each of the style options to be saved checked. Enter a name for the style in the text box at the top of the dialog box. If some of the attributes are not to be saved, uncheck them before clicking OK. The available style options will depend on what type of object is being defined and the modifications that have been made to the object.

Figure 51.3. The Save Style As dialog box.

Once a style has been created, it will automatically be shown in the Styles roll-up. Styles of each type can be viewed individually, or by clicking on the styles types at the top of the roll-up, they can all be turned on or off. Styles can be easily applied to a new object by first selecting the object and then clicking on the desired style in the Styles roll-up and clicking on Apply. Styles can also be applied through the Apply Styles command in the Object menu. A third way to apply styles is through keyboard shortcuts, which can be assigned for various styles.

Corel *NOTE!*

Only one style may be applied to a paragraph. Paragraph styles can be applied by selecting any part of the paragraph and clicking on the appropriate style.

467

Keyboard shortcuts can be defined by bringing up the Set Hotkeys dialog box shown in Figure 51.4. This dialog box is accessed by selecting the fly-out menu at the top of the Styles roll-up and choosing the Set Hotkeys command.

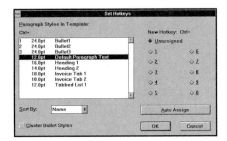

Figure 51.4. The Set Hotkeys dialog box.

The Hotkeys can be defined automatically by clicking on the Auto Assign button or they can be manually assigned by selecting a style and then clicking on the radio button for the hotkey. Sorting of the hotkeys can be done either by Name or by Font Size. The styles containing bullets can be grouped together by choosing the Cluster Bullet Styles check box. Hotkeys are then used by selecting an object and using the Ctrl key with the hotkey number.

Templates

Templates hold a collection of styles. They can be loaded using the Style roll-up menu command Load Template. This can be helpful if someone else has created a template. A good example would be the templates that were included on Corel Draw CD. Through this same menu, templates can be saved using the Save Template command. This should be done anytime that an element of the template will be changed. The reason for this change is that the template may be attached to other drawings and any changes made will also affect that drawing.

The Style roll-up also allows styles to be deleted using the Delete Style command. Therefore, any excess styles can be removed so that they do not cause confusion. Styles can also be searched on to find objects that are tagged with that style. Select the style to be found and choose the Find command. The first object of that particular style will be selected.

The menu command will now change to Find Next and additional objects of the style can be searched.

The Object menu can also be used to set either the fill or the outline to Overprint when printed to a PostScript printer. This is much quicker than wading through several levels of the Fill or Outline dialog boxes, as with previous versions of Corel Draw. The Object Data roll-up described in Skill Session 52 can also be accessed through the Object menu.

Advanced Topics Workshop

Object
Database

Corel Object Database lets you create a database that contains information about the objects within a file. You can enter different types of information about objects or grouped objects. The information can be dates, prices, times, text, and so on. The database will be set up containing various categories, with the information organized into columns. This can assist you with a drawing by assigning parts numbers, prices, and different information for the components of your objects.

After you create a database, you can access information by clicking on the object with the secondary mouse button. Hold the button down for a second to activate the Object menu. Choose the Data Roll-Up command from the bottom of the Object menu (see Figure 52.1). You can access one or more objects through the Object Data Manager. There are basic functions such as printing, editing, copying, deleting columns, and summarizing information for the objects with databases.

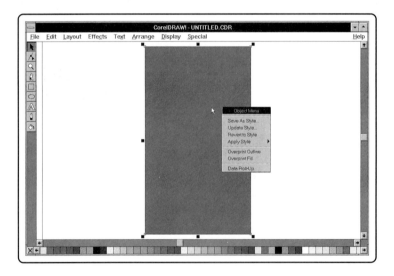

Figure 52.1. The Object menu with object selected on-screen.

Object Data Roll-Up

The Object Data roll-up lets you view the data that pertains to selected objects. You can edit the data of any selected object. You can resize the area of display field, value, or name to fit your requirements. The box will display fields and their associated values for the current object. If there aren't any objects selected, the Data roll-up will be empty. There is a fly-out menu that gives you access to the Object Data Field Editor as well as copying information from and deleting single or all fields (see Figure 52.2).

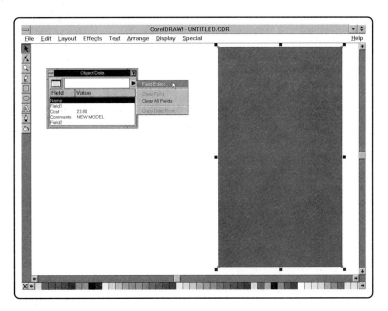

Figure 52.2. The Object Data roll-up with the fly-out menu.

Object Data Field Editor

In the Object Data Field Editor, you can delete, create, and assign categories to your objects before entering the data. You can also change the format by accessing the Format Definition dialog box. Summarizing the totals of the group as well as creating a new field and adding selected fields can be done in this dialog box (see Figure 52.3).

Figure 52.3. The Object Data Field Editor dialog box.

Object Data Format Definition

Pressing the Change button in the Field Editor invokes the Format Definition dialog box (see Figure 52.4). You can select a format type for the display of the data, as well as create your own format. In the Create Field, you can type in the new format you require. The Sample box displays the appearance of how the data will look in the Object Data roll-up.

Figure 52.4. The Format Definition dialog box.

Object Data Manager

In this dialog box (see Figure 52.5), you can change the page setup and enable the Print Guidelines so that lines will print between the cells in your data sheet, as well as printing columns, rows, filenames, and page numbers. You also have basic editing functions such as Cut, Copy, Paste, and so on.

Figure 52.5. The Object Data Manager dialog box.

The Field Options let you change Data Format, Display Totals, access the
Field Editor, and so on. The Preferences have settings for displaying the
information in different formats, showing the details of a field or group of
fields, as well as showing the type of data that exists.

Advanced Topics Workshop

Contour

Contour is a new feature added to Corel Draw 4. To access the Contour roll-up, select it from the Effects menu.

Contouring is very straightforward. When you add contouring to an object, duplicate shapes of the original are created either toward the center and smaller than the original or away from and larger than the original.

The Contour roll-up, shown in Figure 53.1, provides seven methods of controlling the look of a contour. The first option is To Center. Clicking on this check box will force the added contour shapes toward the center of the original object. When you click To Center, the Steps parameters box is grayed out because the To Center option determines the number of steps needed for equal spacing from the number entered in the Offset Parameters box.

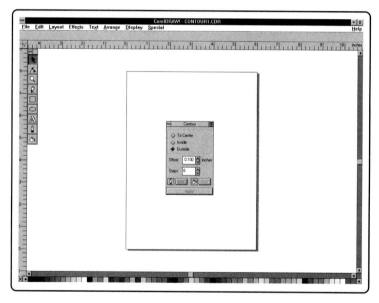

Figure 53.1. The Contour roll-up.

Corel *NOTE!*

Important! When you use the To Center option the number of new shapes created will get extremely large if the number in the Offset Parameters box is set smaller than .01 inches.

The Offset Parameters box sets the spacing between the shapes that are added in the contouring process. The amount of Offset is equal on all sides. (Think of it as the amount of spacing rather than Offset.)

Figure 53.2 illustrates how using the To Center option affects the look of a contour. The top left contoured object had a width of just over 2 inches. Therefore, it was limited to two steps because the Offset was set to 0.5 inches. Remember the 0.5 offset applies to both sides of the object so you are decreasing the size of the first duplicate by 1 inch. This limits how many 1-inch objects will fit into a space of just over 2 inches. If the original object were enlarged and the offset left the same, you would see more steps.

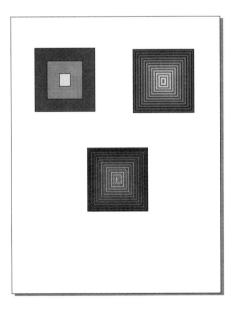

Figure 53.2. Contours using the To Center option.

Advanced Topics Workshop

The top right contour in Figure 53.2 has 12 steps in the same size square as the first because the offset was reduced to 0.1 inches. The bottom Contour has 24 steps in it with an offset of 0.05.

The second option, Inside, also forces the added shapes toward the center of the original object, but it allows you to predetermine the number of steps you want in the contour. (You are still limited to the total number of steps you can use, depending on the size of the original object and the size of the Offset.) There is a limit of 999 steps. The distance between each step is always determined by the number you enter in the Offset parameters box. Using different Offset settings will dramatically change the look of the contour.

Figure 53.3 illustrates two different looks using the Inside method. The contour on the left was set at six steps and 0.1 inches was used for the Offset. Notice the difference between it and the top right contour in Figure 53.2. The reason for the obvious difference is that in Figure 53.3, the center object is larger because only six steps were designated. When the To Center option was used in Figure 53.2 using the same Offset of 0.1, it used as many steps as were possible to reach the center.

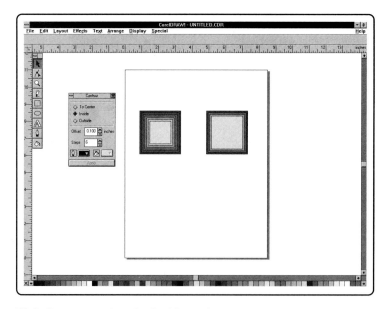

Figure 53.3. Contours using the Inside option.

The Contour on the right in Figure 53.3 used the same offset but with only three steps. Notice the center object of the contour is even larger.

The third option is Outside. Choosing this option forces the new contour shapes outward away from the original. You do not have the same limitations to be concerned about when it comes to figuring out how many shapes will fit inside a given area. This is because you are expanding shapes, not contracting shapes. As with the Inside option the number of steps is limited to 999 and as before keep in mind the number you enter in the Offset parameters box will have a great deal to do with the final results. Figure 53.4 illustrates some Outside variations.

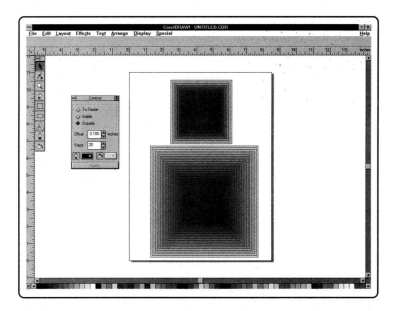

Figure 53.4. Contours using the Outside option.

The top Contour in Figure 53.4 has the Offset set to 0.1 and six steps. The bottom Contour has the Offset set to 0.1 and twenty steps. The only thing to keep in mind when increasing the number of steps is that your contour does not expand out beyond the printable page.

Advanced Topics Workshop

The last options you have to consider are the outline and fill colors. Clicking on the Outline and Fill buttons brings up a palette to select a color from.

When you create a contour, the original object's color blends with the colors selected in the Contour roll-up. It is best illustrated by contouring an object filled with Yellow, with the color Red selected from the Fill palette in the roll-up. If you were to blend two objects together with the Blend effect, using the same colors, you could not tell the difference. Figure 53.5 illustrates this using a square object. Quite often you will want to use a different color for the outline to show more of a contour look. The color palette accessed from the outline button lets you choose the color you need. The size of the outline is determined by the setting in the regular Outline dialog box accessed from the Outline tool in the tool box.

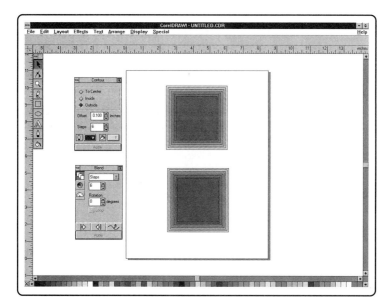

Figure 53.5. Comparing a contoured object to a blended object.

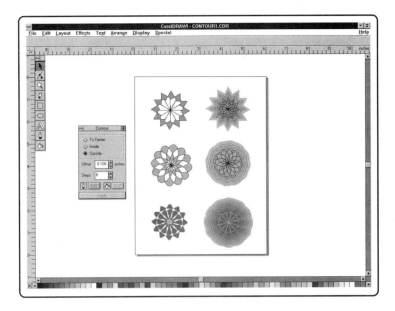

Figure 53.6. Contouring fancy shapes.

Figure 53.6 shows how fancy shapes can be changed with the Contour effect. These shapes were created in Skill Session 16.

Advanced Topics Workshop

PowerLines

Advanced Topics Workshop

Power Lines are new to Corel Draw 4. The manual tells us they are to be used to create lines with variable weights to give your illustrations a hand-drawn look. Perhaps this exciting new feature should be named Power Shapes. Semantics not withstanding, the Power Line feature provides a method for those who thought they couldn't draw a straight line to become artists.

At first glance, the previews of the preset shapes offered in the selection list box appear fairly boring, and for most users they are. The real power of Power Lines is being able to edit these preset shapes into something you will find exciting and new. Figure 54.1 shows the Power Line roll-up accessed from the Effects menu.

Figure 54.1. The Power Line roll-up.

Figure 54.2 shows what effect certain *presets* have on a straight line drawn horizontally across the screen. The first six lines have respectively, the presets Wedge 1, Wedge 2, Woodcut 1, Woodcut 4, Trumpet 1, and Bullet 2, applied to them. The two bottom shapes are formed with the presets Tear Drop and Nib. With the exception of the last two there is not much exciting to say about the rest, correct? If you agree, you'll be missing out on the magic of Power Lines.

Beginning with Figure 54.3, you will be taken through the steps which will create a beautiful vase. You will do this with only three basic edits to one of the standard presets. You will also learn that Power Lines are created as separate parts, similar to an extruded object (see Skill Session 21).

Corel NOTE!

In order to apply other effects to a Power Line, you must first separate it with the Separate command in the Arrange menu.

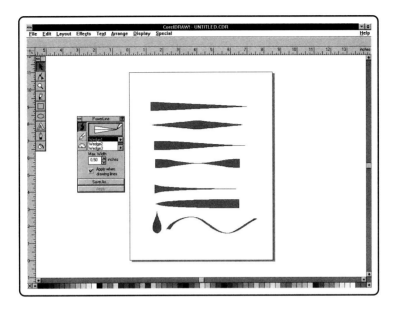

Figure 54.2. The basic preset shapes.

To begin drawing the vase, follow these steps:

1. Open the Power Lines roll-up from the Effects menu.
2. Draw a straight line vertically down the center of the page. Make sure that Apply When Drawing Lines is not checked.
3. Click the down arrow in the Preset list box.
4. Scroll down to Max Width and make it your selection.
5. Enter the number 2.0 in the parameters box. Figure 54.3 shows the shape you should have at this point.
6. With your vertical line selected, click on Apply.

   Remove the fill from your new shape. If you don't have an outline, add a thin outline.
7. Click the ⚼ tool.
8. Double-click the top node of your original line.
9. The Node Edit roll-up will appear on-screen (see Figure 54.4).
10. Check the Pressure Edit box.

487

Advanced Topics Workshop

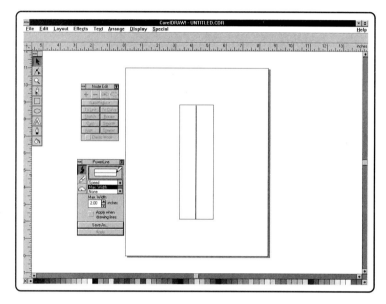

Figure 54.3. Beginning a PowerLine shape.

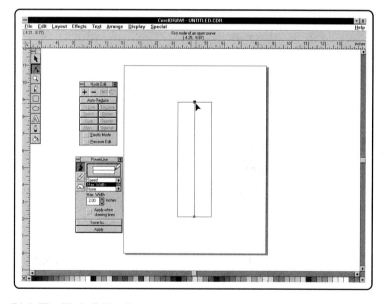

Figure 54.4. The Node Edit roll-up.

11. With the Shape tool still selected, click partway down the center line. This will place a small circle on the line (see Figure 54.5).

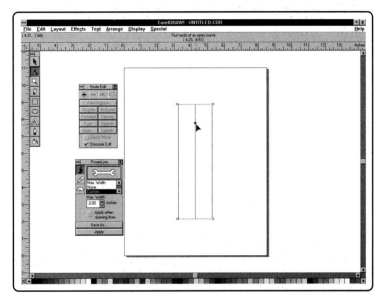

Figure 54.5. Adding a circle node.

12. Click the + (plus sign) button in the Node Edit roll-up.

13. A new horizontal line appears with Pressure Edit handles in place of the small circle (see Figure 54.6).

Corel *NOTE!*

If you do not follow these steps exactly, you will not be able to edit the shape.

14. With the Shape tool still selected, drag toward the center line until you reach the desired position (see Figure 54.7).

Advanced Topics Workshop

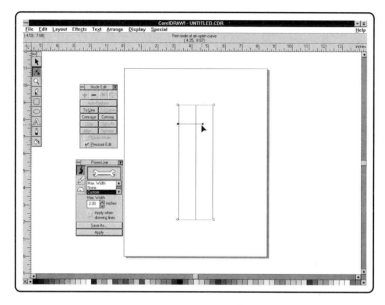

Figure 54.6. Pressure edit line and handles.

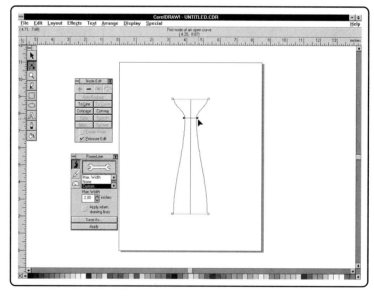

Figure 54.7. Beginning the shape of the vase.

Corel *NOTE!*

The first time you drag, the handles will move together. If you later want to adjust the handles, they will move independently.

15. Click farther down on the center line to add a new circle.

16. Click the + (plus sign) button again in the Node Edit roll-up.

17. A new set of Pressure handles appears. Drag outward with one of the handles to the desired position (see Figure 54.8).

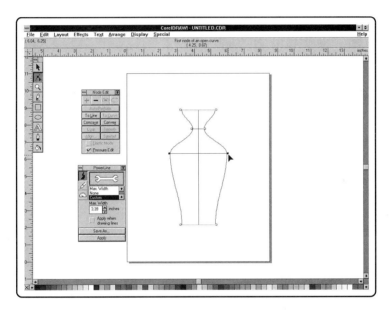

Figure 54.8. Looking more like a vase.

18. Click the center line a short distance from the bottom.

19. Click the + (plus sign) button again and drag inward with one of the handles to the desired position (see Figure 54.9).

20. Select the ▸ tool and fill your shape with a texture from the Textures Fill icon in the Fill roll-up or fly-out menu (see Figure 54.10). In this project, the texture Cosmic Minerals was used.

Advanced Topics Workshop

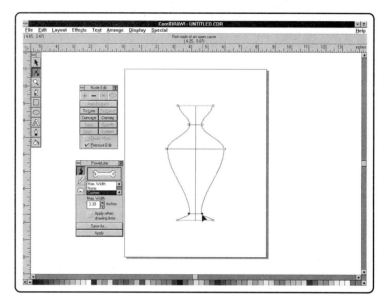

Figure 54.9. The finished shape.

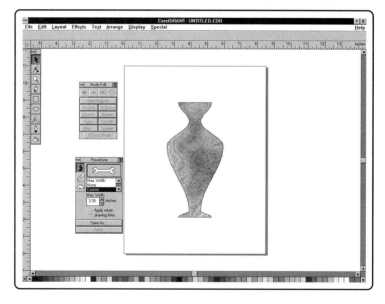

Figure 54.10. The completed vase.

Congratulate yourself—you just created a beautiful vase!

When you create something you like and want to use it again in other projects, you can save your new creation by clicking on the Save As button at the bottom of the Power Line roll-up. A dialog box will appear allowing you to give your shape a name. The next time you want to create your custom shape, it will be available in the Preset list box.

Figure 54.11 shows the original vase and a new one drawn with a simple straight line the same length as the original, and with Vase selected in the Preset selection box. The second vase was filled with a different texture.

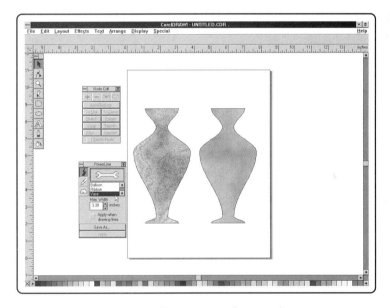

Figure 54.11. The original vase, and a new vase drawn using presets.

Corel *NOTE!*

When you use your new shape, be sure you enter the same numbers in the Max Width parameters box as you had for the original. If you forgot what the numbers were, simply experiment with a few different

Advanced Topics Workshop

> settings. If your shape still does not look like it should, do one or both of the following: Close and then reopen the Power Line roll-up, or exit and reopen Corel Draw itself. At the present time, Power Lines is somewhat unstable, so don't think your new creation was not saved correctly. If you don't draw the beginning line the same length as the original the shape will either be squatty or skinny. You can adjust for this by stretching up or down with the ⬚ tool to the proper dimensions. You cannot stretch horizontally.

Let's dissect a Power Line to see what it contains:

1. First, select the vase shape. The status line tells you that it is a Power Line on Layer 1.

2. Click the Separate command in the Arrange menu.

3. The status line now tells you it is a group of two objects (see Figure 54.12). There are actually three objects on-screen, if you include the original line you drew to create Power Line.

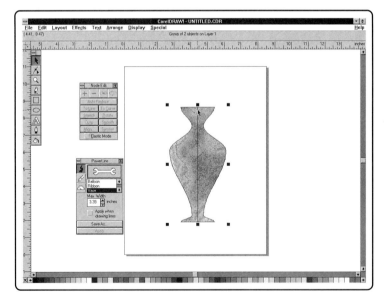

Figure 54.12. A separated Power Line.

4. Click Un-Group in the Arrange menu.

5. Select each object and move them apart (see Figure 54.13).

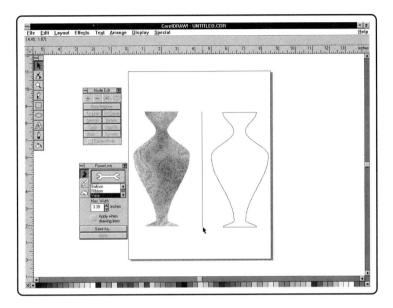

Figure 54.13. The individual parts of a Power Line.

6. The first object is your new vase. The second object is the original line. The third object is an outline of the vase.

7. Leave the vase and delete the second and third objects.

8. Click the vase with the ↰ tool.

9. Marquee-select the entire shape. Notice the number of nodes that make up your vase. The status line indicates 194 nodes (see Figure 54.14).

10. Click the Auto-Reduce button in the Node Edit roll-up. Notice the number of nodes has been reduced to 15 (see Figure 54.15).

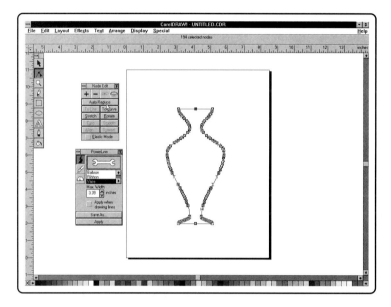

Figure 54.14. A Power Line with nodes selected.

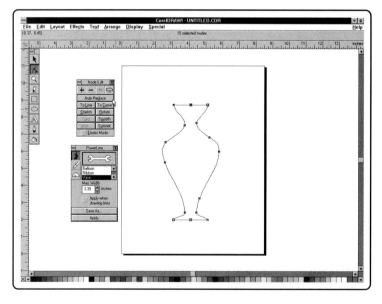

Figure 54.15. Reducing the number of nodes with the Auto-Reduce button.

When working with Power Lines, it is very important to know that the number of nodes created in each object can reach very large numbers. The vase in this project was quite small in comparison to the default presets. Experiment by drawing a freehand curved line using the preset Wedge 1. Separate the shape and ungroup the objects. You will probably come up with 10 objects. With the Shape tool, click on the separate objects. Now start adding up the number of nodes in each object. The number will amount to close to a thousand nodes. This large number of nodes can crash a lot of printers and, of course, the file size is increased by the numbers of nodes. Get in the habit of separating and ungrouping your Power Lines and then using the Auto-Reduce function in the Node Edit roll-up on each object when you are sure you will not be making any more changes.

If you want to apply any additional effects to your Power Line shapes you must first separate the Power Line before you apply any new effects.

Figure 54.16 shows what adding additional effects to the vase can do to make it look more three dimensional. The following are the added steps needed to complete the picture, beginning with the shape in Figure 54.15.

1. Fill the vase with the texture Cosmic Minerals.
2. Apply an extrusion to the vase.
3. Separate the extrusion and add Brightness to the left side parts of the extrusion. Add Darkness to the right side parts of the extrusion.
4. Make a duplicate of the original vase and fill it with Deep Navy Blue.
5. Resize the duplicate and put it behind and to the side of the vase to create a shadow.
6. Add a floor and wall, and put them to the back for a background. Fill both the floor and wall with a gradient fill of Deep Navy Blue to Powder Blue.
7. Draw a freehand shape behind the vase and at the base of the vase running to the bottom of the wall. Fill this shape with Deep Navy Blue.

That's all there is to it!

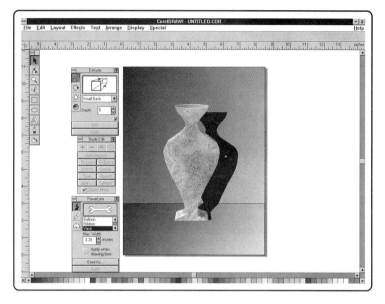

Figure 54.16. Adding effects to show dimension.

Other Uses for PowerLines

There are many more effects you can create with Power Lines. For example, you can apply a Power Line to shapes you have already drawn. This method can produce some painterly effects to your drawings.

Probably the most used preset after creating custom shapes will be the Nib preset. Using the Nib allows you to draw shapes with a calligraphy style. Figure 54.17 shows four different effects using the Nib preset.

To access the Nib controls, click on the Pen Nib icon in the roll-up. When you click this icon, the roll-up shows a round nib shape and a intensity setting slider.

The intensity slider defaults to 50. Just below the slider is a small Page icon. Click this icon to change the dialog box again. This time you have three adjustments you can make to the shape of the nib: Angle, Nib Ratio, and Intensity (this is the same intensity setting that you had access to in the previous roll-up). When you are working with nibs you should go directly to this configuration.

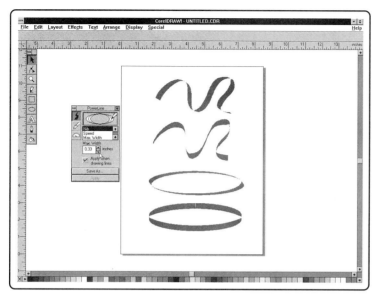

Figure 54.17. Using the Nib preset effect.

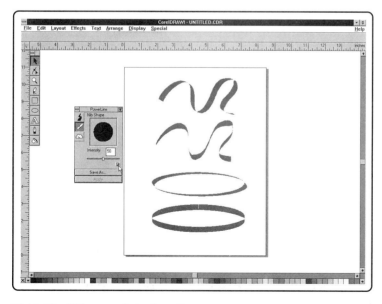

Figure 54.18. The Nib controls in the roll-up.

Advanced Topics Workshop

When you change the settings in the different parameter boxes, a different calligraphic effect will be applied to your lines. Figure 54.19 shows the effect on the wavy lines with different settings:

- The top line was created with the following settings: Angle 50, Nib Ratio 100, and Intensity 75.

- In the second wavy line, Angle was set to 15, Nib Ratio to 100, and Intensity to 75.

- The settings for the first ellipse were: Angle 50, Nib Ratio 100, and Intensity 75.

- The bottom ellipse had the following settings: Angle 0, Nib Ratio 100, and Intensity 100.

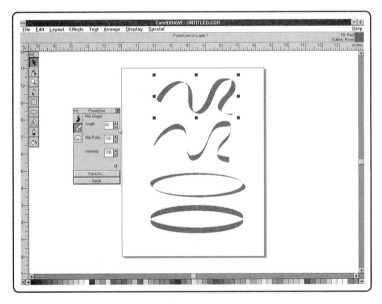

Figure 54.19. Using various settings for different effects.

Power Lines are something completely different to vector drawing programs, and there are many more effects that can be accomplished with this amazing new tool. Experiment and practice using Power Lines, because the more you use them the more effects you will discover.

55

Advanced Topics Workshop

Halftone Dots, Process Color Theory, and Moiré Patterns

The last few years have brought about a great leap in technology that makes working with full color documents much easier and less expensive. While color is still not affordable (or necessary) for every job, it can be used more often to get just the right effect. Color can get very expensive when mistakes are made. Most of these mistakes can easily be avoided by understanding how color works and what pitfalls to avoid. Hopefully this book can pay for itself many times over, just in the money this skill session can save in ruined film.

Halftone Dots

It is a common misconception when dealing with printing grayscales that they are controlled solely by the resolution of the output device. This is not completely true. While higher resolution plays a large part in the quality of the output, it is equally dependent on the line screen chosen.

The line screen determines how many lines of printer dots will be used to create halftone dots. So, it is a combination of line screen and output resolution that produces quality output. These two in combination determine the number of grayscales that can be simulated. This can be expressed in a simple mathematical formula:

Number of grayscales = (*Output resolution* (dpi) / *Line screen* (lpi))^2

Thus, a 300 dpi laser printer with Corel Draw's default 60 lpi line screen can produce 25 levels of gray. This is hardly continuous tone—the output is grainy and not very attractive. On the other hand, a 2400 dpi imagesetter printing at a 133 lpi line screen can produce approximately 325 levels of gray. This is much higher than the PostScript maximum of 256 and therefore is more than adequate for continuous grays.

The reason behind this is that the output resolution divided by the line screen tells how many dots will make up the grid used to simulate gray levels. So on a 300 dpi laser printer, you have a grid of pixels that is 5 pixels wide by 5 pixels high. Using all the possible combinations, there are only 25 different "halftone" dots that can be created. Figure 55.1 shows this halftone dot grid for the laser printer and the grid for the imagesetter mentioned with a 133 line screen. Notice the large difference in the halftone dots.

 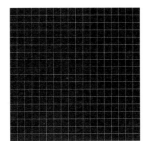

Figure 55.1. Two different halftone dots.

There are several line screens that are fairly popular for printed publications. This is determined by the type of paper used, printing press, and the necessary quality. Newspapers commonly use a line screen of approximately 85 lines per inch, magazines typically use either 110 or 133 lines per inch, and high-quality color may have line screens of 150 lines per inch or higher. Therefore the optimum output device should be able to produce at least 256 levels of gray at the necessary line screen.

Process Color

Process color uses halftone dots of the four colors cyan, magenta, yellow, and black to simulate the full range of visible color. While these colors in combination cannot simulate every color, they can get most of them. This is accomplished by mixing percentages of each of the four colors and aligning them at just the right angles to fool the eye into seeing the desired color.

Traditional shops could work only with percentages in five percent increments, while the computer allows one percent increments. This allows for much more accurate color due to the additional shades available. Figure 55.2 shows a grayscale legend that ranges from 10 to 30 percent of black. The top sample changes in five percent increments, while the bottom sample changes in one percent increments.

As shown by Figure 55.2, the extra grays can make quite a difference. When that is multiplied by the four different colors, the results can be radically different using the two different models.

Figure 55.2. Gray scale models.

The biggest problem is that while the computer can accurately hit the exact percentages every time, imagesetters must be calibrated on a regular basis to be consistent. Therefore, even the same file can look different if printed at different times. This can be quite frustrating, but a good imagesetter operator can keep this problem to a minimum by making all the proper adjustments.

Now if all the colors were printed at exactly the same position, the dots would just end up on top of each other and the color would be extremely muddy. Therefore, each color is rotated a certain amount to create a rosette which simulates a color. The commonly used angles are 15 degrees for cyan, 75 degrees for magenta, 0 degrees for yellow, and 45 degrees for black. In actuality, these angles are usually optimized and the angles are not whole numbers. Corel Draw or your service bureau will handle these optimized angles for you. Figure 55.3 shows a grid of dots in each of the four colors that are rotated to the proper angles to show the "rosettes" of color. A color version of this figure is shown in the color insert in this book.

Moiré Patterns

At times, the angles of the screen patterns will not mesh properly and produce what are called moiré patterns. The best way to demonstrate this is to improperly rotate the cyan and magenta colors only. Notice in Figure 55.4 how a recurring unwanted pattern shows up. Again, a color version is shown in the color insert.

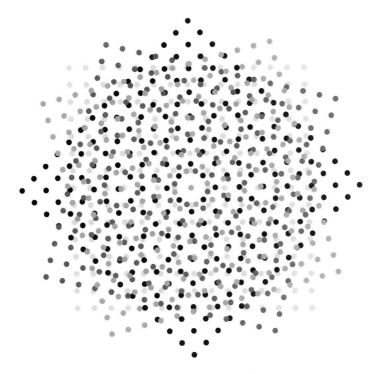

Figure 55.3. Halftone dots in each of four colors rotated to produce rosettes.

Moiré problems can also be quite troublesome when something in the photograph contains a recurring pattern, such as a striped shirt or a chain-link fence.

The best way to avoid moiré patterns is to output at a resolution of 2400 dpi or above. Producing a color proof before the project hits a printing press is an absolute must so that any moires can be corrected before a piece is printed. It is much cheaper to reproduce some film than to have to reprint a whole piece.

Another step to take for avoiding moire patterns is to make sure that the four pieces of film are in perfect register. This means that each piece of film is placed in the exact same position so that the halftone dots will properly align themselves. For proper registration, it is absolutely necessary to output all color work on film from an imagesetter that was made for color work. Older imagesetters tend to stretch or shift the film ever so

505

slightly, which causes the output to misregister. The newer imagesetters feed the film in a different method to avoid these problems. If in doubt, ask your service bureau.

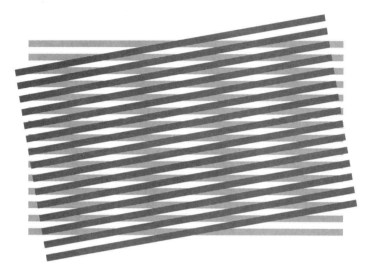

Figure 55.4. A demonstration of moiré problems.

Advanced Topics Workshop

Scanning

There are three types of scanners: hand-held, flat-bed, and drum. They all work on the same principle of capturing images. The most common scanners are the hand-held and flat-bed type. Drum scanners are reserved for the high-end user and service bureaus.

Scanning an image is similar to taking a picture with a camera. Instead of using natural light or flash bulbs, a scanner uses a light bar and lens to illuminate and record the subject. In the case of flat-bed scanners, the object to be scanned is placed on the scanner glass and exposed by a traveling light bar. (If you are familiar with office copy machines, it is the same process). Instead of film in the case of cameras, or selenium-coated drums in the case of copy machines, the scanned image is stored electronically by the scanner's software in the computer's memory and then stored on the hard drive or removable drive.

Photographers can choose between color or black-and-white film and then rely on the proper exposure and lighting conditions to make that perfect picture. They also can change the contrast and brightness and tones in the dark room, but this can be very costly and time-consuming. The computer scanning process also gives you a choice of black-and-white or color when scanning images. The scanner's software lets you automatically expose the image with a click of a button and choose between different settings to allow the scanner to pick up particular information from the image.

Using the scanning software is similar to the photographer's dark room but much faster. It allows you to alter the information from the image before it is stored in the computer or placed in an application. You can change just about everything relating to the image: image size, contrast and brightness, color hues and saturation, and light and shadows.

A photographer plans beforehand before pressing the shutter on the camera. The photographer has to decide what the final picture should look like and how it will be used. Similarly, you will be more successful if, before you scan an image, you know the requirements of the applications and printer you will be using.

Scanning Basics

The image that you scan can be just about anything you want to capture: drawings, original photos, previously printed images, or small three-dimensional objects, if you're using a flat-bed scanner.

It is important to know prior to scanning the image how the image will be used. For example, will the image be used in a flyer or saved on disk for multiple uses? If your original is a color image but you will be using it for the first time as a grayscale, you might consider scanning in color in case you may need it in color at a later time. You can then convert the color image to grayscale in another application for the first use.

Each scanner manufacturer provides its own software with its scanners, and third-party software is also available. It therefore would not be productive to discuss how to adjust for different types of originals like halftones in this chapter. For information about the the Hewlett-Packard IIC and the Agfa Arcus Plus, see Part III, "Companion Hardware Work-shops."

Printing can be done either by using a desktop black-and-white or color printer, or by using a phototypesetting service bureau. The limitations of your desktop printer need to be considered when you scan an image, along with the requirements of the service bureau you use.

Advanced Topics Workshop

Service Bureaus

Corel Draw provides the ability to create many different kinds of art-work. But, this artwork cannot always be shown to others on a computer screen. The final media type varies widely depending on the reason for the project. Many projects are only needed for black-and-white output, and a laser printer will suffice. Others require color, high-resolution, film, vinyl, or many other materials.

This is the reason that service bureaus exist. They buy all that expensive equipment that you can't afford or don't need on a regular basis. Service bureaus then "rent" that equipment and their expertise to you so that the project can be output on the desired media.

This process can lead to a great business relationship if handled prop-erly. Unfortunately, it doesn't always work out perfectly. The key is a clear line of communication in both directions. This will help to prevent problems and alleviate those that can occur in preparing and outputting the project.

When to Start Looking

Just as you wouldn't look for an obstetrician a week before your due date, you shouldn't look for a service bureau on the eve of an important project. Create a simple project ahead of time and use it to test all as-pects of the service-bureau experience. You may even want to run the same project through several service bureaus and compare the quality of service and output. While this may cost a little in the beginning, it will definitely be worth it in the long run.

This project can also give you a good sample to show to clients. Clients want to see that you've done a project similar to that which you will do for them. Show them that you've not only done something similar, but also done research to provide the best quality product for them.

Where to Start Looking

The best way to find a good service bureau for outputting the project at hand is to ask fellow Corel Draw users who have produced similar jobs. These users may have already tried several service bureaus and found a good one. Or they may not have found a good one, but they might be able to steer you away from the bad ones. So, before you look through ads, contact the users who have already been there. If you can't find another user with a good reference, ask the service bureau for a reference from Corel Draw users. If they don't have a good Corel Draw reference, they may not be used to working with that type of file. Remember that service is what is being provided, and if they aren't willing to give references, they may not be worth working with.

Another thing to consider is what type of output is required. Some service bureaus offer many types of output, but more than likely they specialize in a certain output media. Therefore, a service bureau that produces great film negatives may only do so-so 35mm slides. It is not uncommon to use several different service bureaus depending on your needs.

Service bureaus have traditionally been dominated by Mac-centric shops. While they might be able to output your project, they aren't always interested in working with PC files. If they aren't interested in helping you, why should you help them?

The output media is one of two things that your service bureau must properly support. They also must be able to support your input media. For many users this is a floppy disk. When the files get too big for a diskette, a compression program such as PKZIP can make the files fit onto that same floppy. But, can the service bureau unzip the files? If they run on a Mac, the answer is "Maybe." If they run on a PC, they will more than likely support it. Now what if that file is much larger? The answer really varies at this point. In Companion Hardware 8, the Syquest line of removable drives are covered. These are by far the most popular device at service bureaus. It may be worth considering what type of media the service bureau supports before you look into purchasing something for your system. If the service bureau considers you an important enough client, they may purchase the device you have.

What to Provide

Now that you've chosen a service bureau, you must decide what type of file to send. Service bureaus will prefer one of two types of files. The first is the native application file, in this case a Corel Draw file. But you also must consider what all is contained in that Corel Draw file. Are there any nonstandard fonts? Which fonts are standard? Just because you can pull one of those 750 fonts off Corel's CD doesn't mean that your service bureau has a particular font loaded or even has a CD drive to load from.

That doesn't even approach the problems which could occur if there are fonts from a third-party vendor.

For these reasons, the best way to send a file to the service bureau is to send a Print To Disk file. With this approach, the only worry is the type of media the service bureau can accept and what type of output device for which the file should be created. It is not necessary for the service bureau to have any special files, fonts, or applications. All they will need to do is send the Print To Disk file directly to their output device.

Unfortunately, service bureaus don't always like to work with this type of file because the file must be created a certain way for it to output without error. Many times a mistake is made in creating the file and then the service bureau is held accountable by the customer. While the service bureau could make a mistake, it is most likely the customer's fault. In Skill Session 42, the steps necessary to produce a file that should be acceptable to almost any service bureau are discussed.

Checklist:
Things to Include in a Print to Disk File

Paper Size   Should it be larger than the final page size to accomodate crop and registration marks?

Paper Orientation   Is the page landscape or portrait?

Scaling   This should realistically be set to 100 percent for anything sent to a service bureau as other settings could cause problems.

Tiling   Again this could be very problematic for a service bureau. Look into whether a larger paper size is available that could accomodate the full image.

All Fonts Resident   This should almost always be set to No (not checked). Unless you are absolutely sure that the service bureau has included all fonts and that they are all downloadable, it is much easier to just include them in the file, although the file can be significantly larger.

Film Negative   This is usually necessary only for film. Ask the printer who will be printing the piece what is desired.

Emulsion   Again, check with the printer. The emulsion side of film is the side that has been developed.

Reading   Again, check with the printer. This specifies whether the image is right reading (looks normal) or wrong reading (everything is backwards) when holding up the film.

Color Separations   Does the project contain more than one color? If so, should it be color separated or just output as a composite? Color printers would want a composite, where film negatives want the separation.

Crop & Registration Marks, Calibration Bar, Densitometer Scale   An absolute must for color separations. This is the only way to make sure the pieces line up correctly and to verify accuracy.

Image Information   A must for color separations. It contains the name of the color output on each piece. The printer will scream trying to figure out what is yellow and what is cyan when this step is forgotten.

Fountain Steps   Resolutions over 2,400 dpi should always use 256 for the best results, although higher levels will cause jobs to become more complex and thus take longer and increase the risk of crashing. See Skill Session 55 for more information on the correct setting.

Screen Frequency   This is a number that should be supplied by the printer. See Skill Session 55 for more information on the correct setting.

Print To File   Always turned on for a Print To File file.

For Macintosh   Should always be checked even if the file is to be output from a PC. This changes the first character of the file from a Ctrl-D (Mac end-of-file) character to a space. Removing this character will not affect the file in any way other than to make it more compatible with service bureaus.

Turnaround Time

It always seems that the project must be finished right now, but by planning ahead just a little bit, you can save quite a bit of money. Normally, service bureaus have various rates depending on whether they

515

must immediately drop everything for your job or run it late at night when the machines aren't as busy. The rates for rush jobs are significantly higher, and by finishing a day or more early you can save a notable amount of money.

Advanced Topics Workshop

Sheet-Fed Offset Lithography

Advanced Topics Workshop

So you're done with your project and it's now time to print it. Many lucky people either hand off the project to a service bureau or their creative director. Here the process of outputting the project is handled.

What if you alone handle the project from beginning to end? Your client doesn't want to hear about extra expenses incurred because you did something wrong and weren't notified of it until after printing it. What this means is that someone has to pay to find out if their project is okay or not. Not a happy thought.

A good way to avoid this problem is to speak to your printer or call your service bureau and familiarize yourself with the equipment that they will use to output or print your project on. Then you can build your project to meet their specifications. Always include the printer or service bureau at the beginning of your project to save you and your client time and money.

The graphic arts industry requires mass production printing. Distinguishable qualities and appearances set printing processes apart from each other. *Letterpress* is characterized by sharp printing. However, images may appear grainy or speckled. Gradient tints such as blends, linear fills, vignettes, and airbrush type effects may have distinct breaks. *Lithography* is distinguished by smooth transition of color. *Gravure printing* is saturated with color. The main considerations in selecting a printing process are:

- Secure and accurate mounting of the image transfer (blanket in Lithography).
- Precise positioning of the paper during printing process.
- Conveyance of paper through the press.
- Storage and application of the ink to the plate (dampening solution in Lithography).
- Correct printing pressure for transfering the inked image to paper.
- Options for hand-fed printing on preprinted letterhead.

Sheet-fed or roll-fed (web-fed) presses are used for printing magazines and newspapers. Extensive print jobs such as books are done on web-fed presses. A perfecting press prints on both sides of paper in one pass through the press. Presses can possess the capability to use single or multiple colors. The two types of color printing are two-color and four-color.

Web Offset Presses

This is lithographic printing where the printing is done on large rolls of printing stock. These large rolls as well as the paper on them are commonly referred to as a *web* in the printing industry. The web press is primarily used in the printing of newspapers. Some web presses feed the web between a blanket cylinder and an impression cylinder. Other web presses are constructed with two blanket cylinders; this may be called a *blanket-to-blanket* arrangement.

Letterpress Printing

This relief-printing method transfers images or impressions by direct contact of the paper with raised inked surfaces. The three basic letterpress presses are *rotary, platen,* and *flat-bed cylinder.* For letterpress printing, magnetic cylinders and steel-backed polymer plates are the preferred combination.

Rotary Letterpress

If you want speed and efficiency, the rotary letterpress should be your choice because these presses were built for long runs. Rotary presses have cylindrical impression and printing surfaces. The plates are held by the plate cylinder, the impression cylinder adds the pressure, and with each revolution of the impression cylinder, the sheet is printed. Specialized locking devices will hold curved plates with the same circumference as the plate cylinder onto the cylinder.

Platen Letterpress

If you need short-run printing, the Platen Letterpress should be your choice because of its extreme versatility for embossing, scoring, and die-cutting. This method uses platen and bed surfaces that open and close like an oyster to carry the paper and type form on flat surfaces. Most platen letterpresses allow impression lever control.

Flat-Bed Cylinder Letterpress

The flat-bed cylinder letterpress uses a moving flat bed that holds the form while the pressure is provided by a stationary rotating impression cylinder. In the vertical version of this press, the cylinder and the form move up and down in the same manner as a car engine cylinder would, which allows one revolution for a printed impression where the horizontal press would need to make two revolutions.

Silk-Screen Printing

Silk-screen printing is stencil printing with a metal, silk, or nylon screen. Ink is forced through the screen with a rubber roller called a squeegee, transferring the image onto paper, T-shirts, and so on. This method can be done by hand with a screen frame or on two different types of presses.

One press uses flat screens requiring motion at different intervals. The second press uses rotary screens with a mounted rubber roller and automatic disbursement of the ink. These presses run quickly and continuously. This method of printing uses a much greater quantity of ink than other printing methods, and that produces unusual effects. Because of the amount of ink used the sheets must be placed separately for drying or passed through heated tunnels or driers to expedite drying and the elimination of smudging. You can make a design appear as suede, leather, or felt by printing a sticky side and then sprinkle with silk, rayon, or cotton flock. This printing process is used for various products such as posters, greeting cards, menus, wallpaper, draperies, and so on.

Varnish

Varnish is the application of a permanent substance onto the printed sheet for protection or appearance purposes.

Advanced Topics Workshop

Tweaking Windows

Corel Draw asks a lot from a computer, and many times its slow performance is directly related to the computer being improperly prepared to run Corel Draw. Most of these tips will be directly applicable to other Windows programs as well.

Which Windows?

If your system is still running Windows 3, you must upgrade to Windows 3.1 to run Corel Draw 4. But, Windows 3.1 may not be the best Windows to run. Because Corel Draw 4 relies upon OLE2, the DOS utility SHARE must be loaded for everything to work right. Windows for Workgroups includes a virtual share that is not loaded from DOS and therefore is more efficient. For this reason, loading Windows for Workgroups may be a good idea even on a machine that is not networked.

Windows NT is now available, and many people feel that it will be the answer to the problems with Windows 3.1. That may be the case, but the performance of Corel Draw 4 may actually decline under Windows NT, if it works at all. Windows NT will not be supported by Corel until 5.0 of Corel Draw is released as a Windows NT-specific version.

Hard Drive or CD

Corel Draw's footprint on a hard drive can be quite large, and many users with CD-ROM drives choose to run Corel Draw directly from the CD. This will cause a general slowdown in all the applications, as the CD-ROM drive is more than ten times slower than a hard drive. Not only the performance issues should be considered, because accessing other CDs while Corel Draw is running will be a major problem. If you don't have enough space to install Corel Draw on the hard drive, it's time to shop for a new hard drive.

Memory

While the Corel Draw box states that the program will run with 4 MB of memory, realistically it will "walk." In reality, 8 MB of memory is an absolute minimum to run Corel Draw. This will almost double the performance over a machine with only 4 MB of RAM. The more memory available, the fewer times that applications and documents will need to be swapped out to the hard drive. Therefore, it must be stressed that you should buy as much memory as possible and that no amount is ever too much. Many power users complain that they "only" have 32 MB of memory. Photo-Paint is especially in need of large amounts of memory. It will typically need at least five times the size of a file to work with it. Therefore to work with a 4 MB file, you'll need 20 MB of memory.

Virtual Memory

For users that don't have the actual memory chips, it should be simulated with virtual memory. This is accomplished by creating a permanent swap file. The swap file should be at least big enough to bring the total memory size up to 16 MB by combining real RAM and the virtual RAM. Therefore, a system with 8 MB of RAM should also have an 8 MB swap file. For more information on how to create a swap file, see Chapter 14 of the *Microsoft Windows User's Guide*.

Processor

Obviously a 486 will provide better performance than a 386, and a faster clock speed is better than a slower one. Unfortunately though, the math coprocessor built into 486 chips is not used at all by Corel Draw. Corel Draw relies entirely upon integer math and thus does not use the floating-point capabilities of the math chip.

The new Pentium chip will undoubtedly bring an increase in speed to Corel Draw, but its influence won't really be felt until a new operating system (Windows NT, OS/2, UNIX, etc.) takes advantage of its power and an optimized version of Corel Draw is released to work with the Pentium. So, the power of the Pentium will be underutilized by the current version of Corel Draw.

Video Cards

Video cards have increased their power dramatically in the past two years. Not only has their power increased, but also their resolution and color depth. If video performance seems to be lacking, it might be worth looking into a new card. The video card makers also issue new drivers quite regularly that will usually increase the performance of Windows. So, before shopping for a new card, it might be worth looking into whether a new driver is available.

Running Multiple Applications

One of the biggest benefits of Windows is the ability to run multiple applications at the same time. Unfortunately, this can hinder the performance of larger applications such as Corel Draw. Therefore, for the best performance, try to keep the number of running applications to a minimum.

System Resources

Corel Draw will take approximately 31 percent of system resources with nothing displayed and all the Roll-Up windows active. This can put a system dangerously close to the point of instability. A system normally has 75–80 percent of its resources free when first loaded. Many things can contribute to the use of resources, and each program run will take some share depending on the complexity of the program. Systems tend to become unstable when the percentage of resources dips below 20–25 percent. The easiest way to check this number is in Program Manager's Help About Program Manager dialog box. The free memory and free system resources will be displayed. Another quick way is to use the QwikDRAW utility included on the CD which has icons for both numbers.

Fonts

Inside the Corel Draw 4 box are more than 750 fonts, and many users are tempted to install them all. This will usually render Windows totally useless as it won't run at all. Even if it does run, it will slow to a crawl in managing all those fonts. If at all possible, it is best to keep the total number of fonts installed under 100. This will save memory and keep applications running at near their top speed. If deciding between all those fonts is a daunting choice, then it might be worth looking into a font-management utility such as FontMinder from Ares Software, FontHandler from Qualitype, or the shareware FontMonster found on the enclosed CD.

Wallpaper, Screen Savers, and So On

Windows provides many ways to customize a system by installing bitmapped wallpaper, screen savers, patterns, and many other cute utilities. All of these things take time to load and use up memory that could be put to better use. So, weed out those extra utilities that aren't needed.

Printing

Printing can be one of the most frustrating tasks under Windows and especially with Corel Draw. The computer system can literally be tied up for hours while waiting for a file to print. The best way to speed up this process is to use a print spooler other than Print Manager. The best utility for speeding up printing is Lasertools PrintCache. It sets up an area of memory or hard drive and all applications will print to that space instead of directly to the printer. PrintCache then pumps the data to the printer at a speed higher than normal. The best part is that the application can be free to work on something else while the file is printing in the background.

Disk Access

Corel Draw really puts a hard drive through its paces, and if a hard drive is not taken care of, Corel Draw will slow dramatically. Hard drives should be optimized at least once a week to pack data into contiguous clusters. Utilities that provide this capability are included with the Norton Utilities, PC Tools, WinMaster, and even MS-DOS 6.0.

A disk cache should also be used. Windows included the SmartDrive cache that provides very good performance. Other disk cache utilities are available that can provide better performance, although the difference can be minimal. For more information on how to set up SmartDrive properly, see the *Microsoft Windows User's Guide,* Chapter 14.

Phone Numbers

For more information about PrintCache, contact Lasertools at (800) 767-8004.

For more information about FontMinder, contact Ares Software at (415) 578-9090.

For more information about FontHandler, contact Qualitype at (800) 950-2921.

Advanced Topics Workshop

Setting
Preferences

The Preference command in Corel Draw lets you customize certain Corel Draw functions to suit your particular drawing style. There are six additional dialog boxes available from within the Preferences dialog box. Click on the Special menu and then click on Preferences to bring up the Preferences dialog box, shown in Figure 60.1.

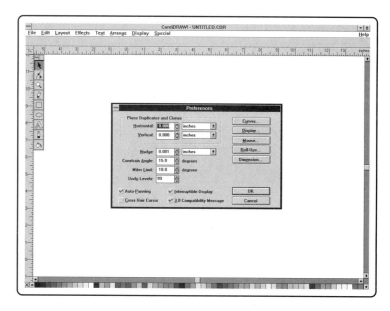

Figure 60.1. The main Preferences dialog box.

Place Duplicates and Clones

This command is used to determine how far away the duplicated or cloned object will be placed from the original. If you enter a positive value—for example, 0.50 inches—in both the horizontal and vertical boxes, the duplicate or clone copy would be offset 1/2 inch above and 1/2 inch to the right of the original.

Some users prefer to use a setting of 0.0 inches. This setting places the duplicate or clone directly on top of the original. An example of using this method would be in creating a Neon effect (see Skill Session 32).

In addition to inches, you can use millimeters, picas, and points.

Nudge

The arrow keys on your keyboard are the keys to this function. The value you put in the Nudge parameters box is the distance the selected object or objects and curved node or nodes will move when you press an arrow key. For example, when you press and release the ↑ key, the object will move upward the distance of your setting in the Nudge parameters box. If you hold down the arrow key, the object will move in continuous steps until you release the key. The object or curved node will always move in the direction of the arrow keys.

For an interesting example, marquee-select several nodes in a curve and use the arrow keys to move them. This could come in handy for certain applications.

Constrain Angle

When you hold down the Ctrl key while performing the following functions, the degree of angle is constrained by the number you put in the parameters box.

- Skewing and rotating objects.
- Adjusting control points and handles when drawing curves in Bézier mode.
- Drawing straight lines in freehand mode.

Miter Limit

This option determines the lower limit for creating miter joints at the corners of objects. If an object is drawn with angles below the limit entered in the parameters box, the joints will be beveled. This option is available to eliminate the problem of corner joints extending far beyond the actual corners at small angles.

Undo Levels

The number entered in this parameters box sets the number of times an action or operation can be reversed (undone) using the Undo command in the Edit menu. This setting also applies to the Redo command in the Edit menu. The maximum number is 99.

Corel *NOTE!*

The Corel Draw manual tells you that there is no limit, but this was changed to 99 after the manual was printed.

Important! The higher the number you set for Undo, the more memory is required by your system. The reason is that your system has to keep in memory everything you did during a session up to the number you set. For example, if you set the Undo level to 99, your system's memory would have to store the last 99 actions you did in memory. This can slow down the system greatly and even cause you to run out of memory. The default setting for Undo Levels is 4.

Auto-Panning

When you click Auto-Panning, you are enabling the Auto-Panning feature. This feature allows you to drag an object beyond the visible portion of the working area of your screen. When you drag an object outside the working area, the screen will scroll so that you can still see your object. To disable this feature, click on the check box again.

Cross Hair Cursor

Clicking the Cross Hair cursor changes your normal cursor to cross hairs extending the full length and width of the drawing area. When you move to the menus and tool box, the cross hairs change back to an arrow.

Interruptible Display

When you enable Interruptible Display you can stop the redrawing of complex drawings by clicking anywhere on the screen while the screen is redrawing. This can be useful to isolate a particular object or to select a different tool or menu without having to wait for the screen to redraw.

One thing to be careful about using Interruptible Display: Even though you cannot see an object on-screen, you can still select it. This means all the objects are there, but they have not been redrawn. This can lead to problems with complex drawings with lots of objects. You may have stopped the redraw to select an object just after it has been redrawn and find when you try to select it, a different object is selected. This happens because all objects are drawn from back to front. This problem can be lessened by using wireframe mode instead of preview mode.

3.0 Compatibility Message

When this option is enabled, a message appears on-screen when opening a Corel Draw 3.0 file in version 4. The purpose of this message is to give you the option of using the text spacing that was used in your version 3.0 file or have it converted to version 4 text spacing. If all the text in the version 3.0 file had the same typeface, you probably would not see any difference in the text spacing. If you used several typefaces or used Paragraph text, converting to version 4 could have adverse effects. If the 3.0 compatibility message is disabled, Corel Draw 3.0 files will be automatically converted to version 4.

Setting Curve Preferences

When you click the Curves button in the Preferences dialog box, the Preferences - Curves dialog box appears (see Figure 60.2).

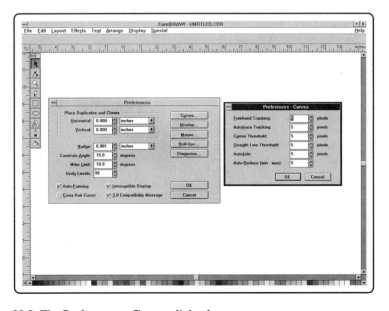

Figure 60.2. The Preferences - Curves dialog box.

Advanced Topics Workshop

Freehand Tracking

The number entered in the parameters box determines how closely Corel Draw tracks your freehand drawing when it calculates the Bézier nodes that will be used in the object you draw. The lower the number entered, the greater number of nodes Corel Draw will use as it tries to create your freehand line as close as it can to your intended shape. Using a higher number will cause the shape to be drawn more loosely with fewer nodes.

Autotrace Tracking

This setting follows the same logic as freehand tracking except it applies to Autotracing Bitmaps.

Corner Threshold

The number entered here determines whether smooth nodes or cusps will be used when drawing freehand or autotracing. If the number is lower, more Cusp nodes will be used. If the number is higher, more smooth nodes will be used. Those users who are doing a lot of freehand drawing should use 10 as the setting.

Straight Line Threshold

This setting follows the same logic as Corner Threshold. When drawing a freehand straight line, the lower the number, the more curve nodes will represent the line. The higher the number, the more straight line nodes will represent the line.

AutoJoin

The AutoJoin setting determines how close you have to be to the beginning node of a line you have drawn to join it with the end node to complete a closed object. An example of this is drawing a freehand circle. To draw the circle you would start with the Pencil tool and begin to draw a circle. When you reach the beginning point of your circle, you want the last node to join with the first node to form a closed object, the circle. If your last node does not join with the first node, you will have an open path. An open path cannot be filled with a color, so your circle will only have an outline of a circle.

The lower the number you enter in the AutoJoin parameters box, the more precise you need to be in getting your last node close to the beginning node. A higher number allows you to be less precise.

Auto-Reduce

The Auto-Reduce setting determines to what degree the Auto-Reduce function found in the Node Edit roll-up will reduce the number of nodes in an object. The lower the number, the fewer nodes in an object. The higher the number, the more nodes there will be in an object. The minimum setting is 1 and the maximum is 10.

Setting Display Preferences

When you click on the Display button in the Preferences dialog box the Preferences - Display dialog box appears (see Figure 60.3).

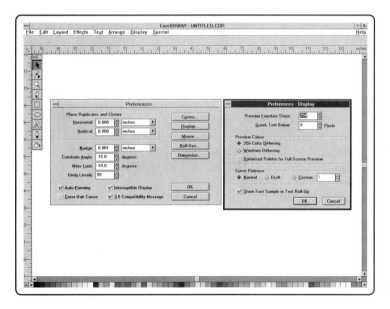

Figure 60.3. The Preferences - Display dialog box.

Preview Fountain Steps

The number entered in the Preview Fountain Steps parameters box sets the number of steps used when displaying fountain fills on the drawing screen when in preview mode. The lower the number, the faster the screen redraw time. If the number is set too low, you will not see a true representation of what the final fountain fill will look like when printed or made into slides. Also, if you are exporting a SCODL file, the number of fountain stripes set here will also be exported with the same number of stripes. As a rule of thumb, leave the setting at the default setting of 20.

The number set here in Preferences - Display does not affect any custom settings you have set in the Fountain Steps Option box in the Fountain Fill roll-up accessed from the tool box. This number also does not affect the number of fountain stripes used when printing. The number of fountain steps used for printing is set in the Print Options dialog box.

Greek Text Below

The settings you use in Greek Text Below only affect the display of text on-screen. Small text takes longer to redraw, particularly when using Paragraph text. To help this situation, you can make any text that is smaller than the number you specify display on-screen as small rectangles. You can still read the text by zooming in on it.

When you have a lot of Paragraph text entered on-screen and you are working on a graphic that might take a while to redraw, try entering a number larger than the largest typeface in your text. This will cause the screen redraws to represent all the text in small rectangles, speeding up redraw time considerably.

The default setting for Greek text is 9 pixels.

Preview Colors

The three options listed under Preview Colors affect only how the colors are displayed on-screen; they do not affect the printed output. Which option you use depends on your display driver. If your system has a display driver that supports 256 colors, the 256 Dithering option will automatically be selected. If you only have a 16-color, standard VGA display, the Windows Dithering option will be selected. If you have a 24-bit true-color display, the Windows Dithering option will be automatically selected as well.

If you select the Optimized Palette for Full Screen Display option, Corel Draw will change the colors it normally uses and display up to 256 pure colors when displaying a full screen preview. This option does not work with all display drivers.

Curve Flatness

When you have large numbers of complex curves in a drawing, the screen redraw time increases, and more importantly the printing time on non-PostScript printers also increases. The settings effects made here can improve these problems. The normal setting displays the most accurate representation of curves. It has a value of 1. Draft displays the least accurate representation and has a value of 10. If you are having problems, especially when printing, use the Custom setting and type a value between 1 and 10 until your problem is solved.

Show Font Sample

Enabling the Show Font Sample in Text roll-up will force a fly-out box to appear, showing a sample of the font you choose in the Text roll-up.

Mouse Options

When you click on the Mouse button in the Preferences dialog box, the Preferences - Mouse dialog box appears (see Figure 60.4).

This dialog box is expressly for assigning a separate function to the secondary mouse button. The dialog box refers to setting the right mouse button, but in deference to left handers, we refer to it as the secondary mouse button.

The default setting in this dialog box is Object Menu. The Object menu is new to Corel Draw 4 and is a fantastic new feature. You do not have to select Object Menu to still be able to access it with the secondary mouse button. If you assign a different function to the secondary mouse button, you bring up the Object Menu by clicking and holding the secondary mouse button until the Object menu appears.

When you do assign a new function to the secondary mouse button, you must perform a fast click to activate the function. Clicking too slowly could bring up the Object menu.

Advanced Topics Workshop

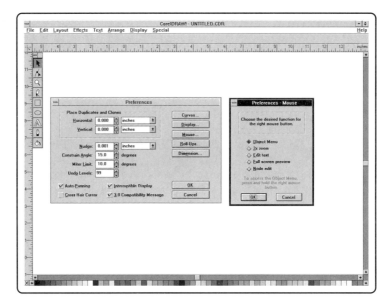

Figure 60.4. The Preferences - Mouse dialog box.

The Options that are available for assignment to the secondary mouse button are: 2X Zoom, Edit Text, Full Screen Preview, and Node Edit.

Setting Roll-Up Preferences

When you click on the Roll-Up button in the Preferences dialog box, the Preferences - Roll-Ups dialog box appears (see Figure 60.5).

The purpose of this dialog box is to let you specify how you want roll-ups to display the next time you open Corel Draw. These are default settings, so whatever options you choose will remain in effect until you change them.

No Roll-Ups

This option closes all roll-ups that are currently open when you exit Corel Draw. When you restart Corel Draw no roll-ups will appear on-screen.

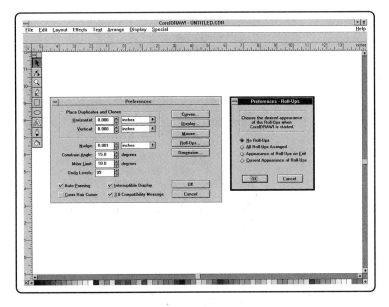

Figure 60.5. The Preferences - Roll-Ups dialog box.

All Roll-Ups Arranged

This option displays all the roll-ups in a rolled-up configuration and stacks them along the upper left and right corners of the drawing window.

Appearance of Roll-Ups on Exit

This option displays the roll-ups as they appeared on-screen when you exited Corel Draw.

Current Appearance of Roll-Ups

This option displays the roll-ups that are currently displayed on-screen at the time you select the option.

This could sound somewhat confusing until you try using the different options; then you will understand them more fully.

Setting Dimension Line Preferences

When you click on the Dimension button in the Preferences dialog box, the Preferences - Dimension dialog box appears (see Figure 60.6).

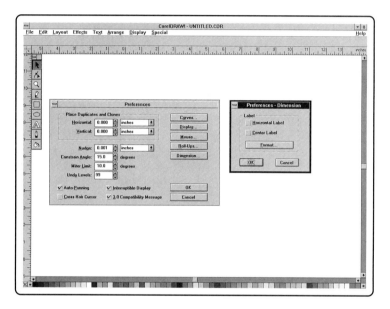

Figure 60.6. The Preferences - Dimension dialog box.

The first two options in this dialog box are Horizontal Label and Center Label. These options effect where and how the actual text is placed on the dimension lines. You can select one or both options. If you select both of the options they work together (that is, the dimension text will appear in the center of the dimension line in a horizontal position).

Choosing Horizontal places the text in a horizontal position regardless of the angle of the line.

Choosing Center places the text in the center of the dimension line. If the dimension line is on an angle, the text will be on an angle as well.

Corel *NOTE!*

> Some of the Corel Draw manuals are incorrect in describing how
> dimension text is applied.

The correct way to apply dimension text is to click once where you want
your line to start. Click a second time where you want the line to end.
Move the crossed line cursor to the point on the line where you want the
text to appear and click a third time. If you want the text to appear
outside the line, click the third time in a location where you want the
text to appear. An extra line will be drawn connecting the dimension
line to your text. If you have selected Center in the options box, the text
will appear in the center of the line as long as your third click is somewhere on the dimension line.

The last option in the Preferences - Dimension dialog box is Format.
When you click on the Format button, the Format Definition dialog box
appears (see Figure 60.7).

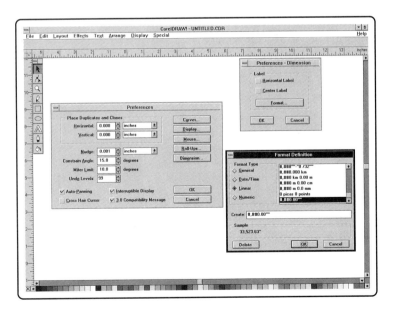

Figure 60.7. The Format Definition dialog box for dimension lines.

Choose from the format parameters box the form you want to use. The form you choose is the form the dimension text will use. For example, if you choose Linear from the list of format types, you will have 10 choices for displaying dimensions. The default setting is feet and inches, represented in the dialog box as (#,### FT 0 IN).

If your rulers are set to inches, all your measuring under 12 inches will be displayed in inches. In many cases, you will want to use the dimension line feature to measure drawings represented in feet and inches, as you would in drawing the plans of a a house. To do this, you must change the rulers to feet and inches in the Grid Setup dialog box.

Corel*NOTE!*

Before you add dimension lines to your drawings, make sure the drawing is completely done because the dimension lines are not linked to the drawing. This means that if you were to resize a part of the drawing, the dimension line measurement will not change accordingly. If you do resize part of a drawing, you will need to delete the old line and draw a new dimension line.

Advanced Topics Workshop

Understanding INI Files

This section provides a general understanding of the numerous settings contained in the initialization files. Before you make any changes to the files manually, it is a very good idea to make a backup copy in case you make a mistake. Incorrect settings can cause Corel Draw to fail to load at all. Additional settings may appear in your .INI files that are not documented as this book goes to press. If you do not understand them, you might want to check in the help files for additional information or contact Corel.

CORELAPP.INI

[Config] Section

3DLook=

This specifies whether the gray, custom-looking controls that provide a 3D appearance will be used. When disabled, the Windows Control Panel can be used to select a color scheme. A *0* indicates that the 3D look is disabled. A *1* indicates that the 3D look is enabled. The default value is 1. Figure 61.1 shows Corel Draw with the 3D look and Figure 61.2 shows Corel Draw without a 3D look.

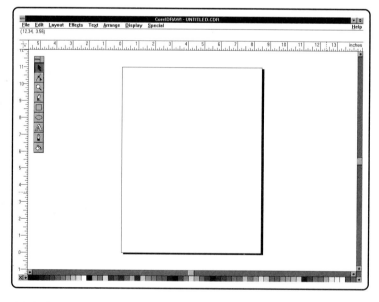

Figure 61.1. Corel Draw without a 3D look, with the standard pallete and standard toolbox.

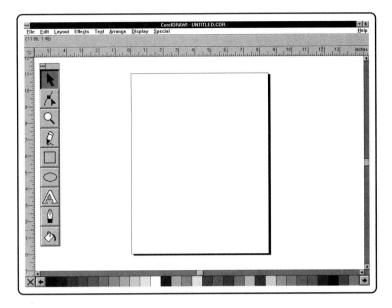

Figure 61.2. Corel Draw with a 3D look, the big palette, and the big toolbox.

BigPalette=

This specifies the size of the color palette at the bottom of the screen. A *0* indicates the standard-sized color palette and a *1* indicates a larger-sized color palette which can be useful for users with large, high-resolution monitors. The default value is 0. Figure 61.1 shows Corel Draw with the standard-sized color palette and Figure 61.2 shows Corel Draw with the big color palette.

BigToolbox=

This specifies the size of the toolbox. A *0* indicates the standard-sized toolbox and a *1* indicates a larger-sized toolbox which can be useful for users with large, high-resolution monitors. The default value is 0. Figure 61.1 shows Corel Draw with the standard-sized toolbox and Figure 61.2 shows Corel Draw with the big toolbox.

Advanced Topics Workshop

ChartDir=

This shows the full path to the directory where Corel Chart-specific files are stored. This is usually *drive*:\COREL40\CHART.

CustomDir=

This shows the full path to the directory where all custom files are stored. This is usually *drive*:\COREL40\CUSTOM.

DataDir=

This shows the full path to the directory where all data files are stored. This is usually *drive*:\COREL40\PROGRAMS\DATA.

DrawDir=

This shows the full path to the directory where Corel Draw-specific files are stored. This is usually *drive*:\COREL40\DRAW.

FiltersDir=

This shows the full path to the directory where filters are stored. This is usually *drive*:\COREL40\PROGRAMS.

FontRasterizer=

This specifies whether the internal font rasterizer is enabled or disabled. The rasterizer improves the appearance of fonts printed at small sizes. A *0* indicates that the rasterizer is disabled, which may be necessary for printer drives that conflict with the rasterizer. This is symptomized by text which prints incorrectly. A *1* indicates that the rasterizer is enabled. The default value is 1.

FontsDir=

This shows the full path to the directory where .WFN fonts are stored. This is usually *drive*:\COREL40\SYMBOLS.

FountainPresets=

This specifies the name of the file used to store fountain fill presets for radial, conical, and linear fills. It is created when Corel Draw is loaded for the first time. The default value is CORELDRW.FFP.

HyphenateDict=

This specifies which file is used as the hyphenation dictionary file. It should not be changed. The default value is HECRP301.DAT.

MosaicDir=

This shows the full path to the directory where Corel Mosaic-specific files are stored. This is usually *drive*:\COREL40\PROGRAMS.

MoveDir=

This shows the full path to the directory where Corel Move-specific files are stored. This is usually *drive*:\COREL40\MOVE.

PhotoPaintDir=

This shows the full path to the directory where Corel Photo-Paint-specific files are stored. This is usually *drive*:\COREL40\PHOTOPNT.

ProgramsDir=

This shows the full path to the directory where all program files are stored. This is usually *drive*:\COREL40\PROGRAMS.

ShowDir=

This shows the full path to the directory where Corel Show-specific files are stored. This is usually *drive*:\COREL40\SHOW.

SpellDict=

This specifies which file is used as the spelling dictionary file. It should not be changed. The default value is IENM9150.DAT.

SpellLanguage=

This specifies which dictionary will be used by the spell checker. Choices include English, French, German, Swedish, Spanish, Italian, Danish, Dutch, and Finnish. The default value is English.

Advanced Topics Workshop

TextureMaxSize=

This specifies the maximum width (in device pixels) that an object being filled with a texture may be before the resolution of the bitmap is reduced. The default resolution of the bitmap is 120 dpi. The texture generator is optimized for thresholds that are a power of 2 plus 1 (for example, 257, 513, 1025, and so on). The default value is 257.

ThesaurusDict=

This specifies which file is used as the thesaurus dictionary file. It should not be changed. The default value is COM_THES.DIS.

TraceDir=

This shows the full path to the directory where Corel Trace-specific files are stored. This is usually *drive*:\COREL40\TRACE.

TTFOptimization=

This specifies whether Corel Draw will use its own internal TrueType rasterizer or the one provided with Windows. A *0* indicates that the Windows rasterizer will be used which is slower than Corel Draw's own rasterizer. Some printers and screen drivers have problems with Corel Draw's rasterizer and therefore should use this setting. A *1* indicates that Corel Draw's internal TrueType driver will be used. The default value is 1.

[Registration] Section

SerialNumber=

This specifies the Serial Number entered during the installation of Corel Draw. It is of the format CD4-*xxx-xxx-xxx* where each *x* is replaced by a digit.

UserName=

This specifies the user name entered during the installation of Corel Draw.

CORELDRW.INI
[Config] Section
AutoBackupDir=

This specifies the full path to the directory where auto backup files are stored. Auto backup files have the extension .ABK and can be renamed to .CDR files in case of a computer crash before saving the file. It is usually drive:\COREL40\AUTOBACK. If no directory is specified, auto backup files will be placed in the same directory as CORELDRW.INI. Note that auto backup files will only be present in this directory if the computer crashed before saving a file.

AutoBackupMins=

This specifies the number of minutes between auto backups. A *0* indicates that no auto backups will be created. Any other whole number between 1 and 99 indicates the number of minutes between backups. The default value is 10.

AutoReduceOnImport=

This specifies whether imported vector files will use auto-reduction algorithms when converting the vector paths into Bézier curves. A *0* indicates that auto-reduction will not be used, while a *1* indicates that it will be used. The default value is 0.

CalligraphicClipboard=

This specifies whether the calligraphic pen outlines are retained when a drawing is copied to the clipboard or exported using one of the vector export filters. Ignoring them will decrease the size of the file and the time required to transfer it either to file or the clipboard. Certain export filters will ignore this setting altogether and always retain calligraphic outlines. A *0* indicates that calligraphic outlines are ignored and a *1* indicates that they will be retained. The default value is 1.

ClipboardFountains=

This specifies whether high-quality fountain fills can be copied to the clipboard. When enabled, fountain fills pasted into another application and printed on a PostScript printer will have better results. Enabling this

Advanced Topics Workshop

function can increase the time taken to copy and paste objects significantly. You may want to export the file as an EPS file and import it into the other application instead. A *0* indicates that clipboard fountains are disabled, while a *1* indicates that they are enabled. The default value is 0.

CMYKPalette=

This specifies the file name of the last process color palette used by Corel Draw. This value is automatically updated every time Corel Draw is exited and read every time Corel Draw is started. The default value is CORELDRW.PAL, which is the same as PURE99.PAL.

DelayToDrawWhileMoving=

This specifies the amount of time in milliseconds that you must pause when moving an object before it will begin to redraw. This setting only takes effect when ShowObjectWhenMoving is set to 1 and MaxCharsToDrawDuringKern is set to 10 or higher. The default value is 500 milliseconds and can range anywhere from 1 to 32,000 milliseconds.

EditTextOnscreen=

This specifies whether text will be edited on-screen when using the Text tool or the Edit Text dialog box will automatically be brought up. A *0* indicates that the Edit Text dialog box will automatically come up, while a *1* indicates that text will be edited on-screen. The default value is 1. Users with slower computers may want to use the Edit Text dialog box as it will be much quicker.

ExportToTiff42=

This specifies whether Corel Draw will export TIFF format files and whether headers will use TIFF 4.2 or 5.0. Some applications cannot use 5.0 files; and therefore, it may be useful to export TIFF files as 4.2. A *0* indicates that TIFF files will be exported as 5.0, while a *1* indicates that they will be exported as 4.2. The default value is 0.

FullScreenBmpThumbnail=

This specifies whether rotated bitmaps will be displayed in full-screen preview. A *0* indicates that a thumbnail preview will be used for faster redraws, while a *1* indicates that the full bitmap will be used. The default value is 0.

INKPalette=

This specifies the filename of the last spot color palette used by Corel Draw. This value is automatically updated every time Corel Draw is exited and read every time Corel Draw is started. The default value is CORELDRW.IPL which is the file containing the Pantone spot color reference.

MakeBackupWhenSave=

This setting specifies whether a .BAK file is created each time a file is saved. A *1* indicates that a .BAK will be created and a *0* indicates that no backups will be created. The default value is 1.

MaxCharsToDrawDuringKern=

This specifies a threshold value to determine if character outlines will be shown when a text block is being kerned. If the number of characters selected is less than this value, then the outlines will be shown; otherwise, they will not be displayed. The default value is 25. Note that this must be set higher than 10 for DelayToDrawWhileMoving to be activated.

MaximizeCDraw=

This specifies whether Corel Draw will be maximized when it is started. A *0* indicates that Corel Draw will be started at the default size while a *1* will maximize Corel Draw. The default value is 0.

MinCharsToBreak=

This specifies the number of characters that must appear on a line for Paragraph text that has been enveloped. If fewer than this number of characters exists, then the text will not appear on a particular line. The default value is 3.

ShowObjectsWhenMoving=

This specifies whether an object's outline will be redrawn as it is being moved. Complex objects can take some time to redraw and thus a redraw may not always be desirable. A *0* indicates that objects will not be shown when moving while a *1* indicates that they will be shown. The default value is 0. Note that this must be set to 1 for DelayToDrawWhileMoving to be activated.

Advanced Topics Workshop

TemplateDir=

This specifies the full path to the directory where templates will be stored. It is usually *drive*:\COREL40\DRAW\TEMPLATE. This entry is required.

TextOnClpMetafile=

This specifies whether text cut or copies to the clipboard is output as text or converted to curves. A *0* indicates that the text is output as text and a *1* specifies that the text will be converted to curves when output. The default value is 0.

UseClippingForFills=

This specifies whether Windows clip regions will be enabled or disabled. Video drivers for some accelerator boards do not work well when clipping regions are enabled. Disabling Windows clip regions will result in slower redraw speeds, but provide better compatibility. A *0* indicates that Windows clip regions will never be used, a *1* indicates that they are used in preview only, a *2* indicates that they are used for Printing only and a *3* indicates that they are always used. The default value is 3.

[bmpExport] Section

BitsPerPixel=

This specifies the pixel color depth of the last .BMP file exported from Corel Draw. The default value is 24, representing full color. An 8 would indicate 256 colors.

Compress=

This specifies whether or not the last .BMP file exported from Corel Draw was compressed. A *0* indicates that no compression was used, while a *1* indicates that compression was used. The default value is 0.

DotsPerInch=

This specifies the resolution in dots per inch that was used for the last .BMP file exported from Corel Draw. The default value is 150.

RenderFlags=

This specifies flags that are set by the image rasterizer when a bitmap file is exported.

[epsExport] Section

ConvColorToGray=

This specifies the status of the Convert Color Bitmaps to Grayscale check box the last time an EPS file was exported. A *0* indicates that color bitmaps will not be converted to grayscale, while a *1* indicates that color bitmaps will be converted to grayscale. The default value is 0.

FontResident=

This specifies the status of the All Fonts Resident check box the last time an EPS file was exported. A *0* indicates that the check box was disabled, while a *1* indicates that the check box was enabled. The default value is 0.

FountainSteps=

This specifies the value of the Fountain Steps field the last time an EPS file was exported. The default value is 30. Values can range from 2 to 256.

HeaderRes=

This specifies the value of Header Resolution for the TIFF header in an EPS file the last time an EPS file was exported. The default value is 300. Possible values are 0, 30, 75, and 300.

TextAsCurve=

This specifies whether text exported in an EPS file will be exported as text or curves. It is automatically saved each time an EPS file is exported. A *0* indicates that the text is exported as text, while a *1* indicates that the text will be exported as curves. The default value is 1.

[wmfExport] Section

DlgIncludeHeader=

This specifies the value of the Include Placeable Header check box the last time a WMF file was exported. A *0* indicates that a placeable header will not be included, while a *1* indicates that one will be included. The default value is 0.

DlgTextAsText=

This specifies the value of the Export Text As field the last time a WMF was exported. A *0* indicates that text will be imported as text, while a *1* indicates that text will be exported as curves. The default value is 0.

[ObjectDataPreferences] Section

HighlightTopLevelObjects=

This specifies whether or not the cells in the Object Data Manager representing top-level objects are highlighted. A *0* indicates that the top level object cells are not highlighted, while a *1* indicates that they will be highlighted. The default value is 1.

ItalicizeReadOnlyCells=

This specifies whether or not the cells in the Object Data Manager that cannot be edited are italicized. A *0* indicates that noneditable cells are not italicized, while a *1* indicates that the cells will be italicized. The default value is 1.

ShowGroupDetails=

This specifies the number of objects within a group that can be displayed in the Object Data Manager. The default value is 10. The value can range from 0 to 10.

[LastUsed] Section

1=, 2=, 3=, 4=

This specifies up to the last four files used. These files will be listed at the bottom of the File Menu.

[DimensLabelFormat] Section

Linear=

This specifies the last variable used for the Auto Dimension feature. It is in the format of Linear=*last unit used^last format used*. This should not be changed in the .INI file.

[ObjectDataFieldNames] Section

Comments=

This specifies variable information for the format selection most recently used for Comments. The default value is 1,0,0,0,2,1,0^General.

Cost=

This specifies variable information for the format selection most recently used for Cost. The default value is 1,1,1,0,1,4,0^$"$"#,##0.00.

Name=

This specifies variable information for the format selection most recently used for Name. The default value is 1,0,0,1,0,1,0^General.

CORELFNT.DOC.

[Fonts] Section

This section is used to provide the use of .WFN fonts from Corel Draw 2.x and earlier. The easiest way to add these fonts is to copy the appropriate lines from the CORELDRW.INI file for fonts from 2.x or the WIN.INI file for fonts from 1.x. The lines follow the syntax:

FontName=xx fontname.wfn

FontName is the name of the font shown in menus and it is case sensitive. *xx* is a number representing the font weights contained in the .WFN file. *fontname*.wfn is the name of the file containing the fonts. An example is shown below.

Avalon=15 avalon.wfn

[Symbols] Section

This section contains information about the symbols that are contained in .WFN files. Its syntax is *Symbol=symbol*.wfn. An example is shown below.

> Arrows1=arrows1.wfn

[FontMapV20] Section

This section contains information for translating the font information contained in 2.x files into that used in 3.x and higher files. It follows the syntax:

> *fontname*.wfn=*FontName x,x,x,x*

fontname.wfn is the name of the file containing the old .WFN font. *FontName* is the screen font name of the TrueType or PostScript version of the font. *x,x,x,x* are numbers generated by the WFNMap program that provide compatibility with the spacing of the old .WFN font. Fonts provided by Corel will already be listed in the section. Only non-Corel fonts will need to be added. An example is shown below.

> aardvark.wfn=Aardvark 0,606,0,0

[FontMapV30] Section

This section provides compatability between the font names used in Corel Draw 3.0 and 4.0. The 3.0 name is on the left side of the equal sign and the 4.0 name is on the right side. Anytime a Corel Draw file references a name found on the left side of the equation, it will automatically substitute the name found on the right side of the equation. While this section is meant for providing compatibility between versions of Corel Draw, it can also be used for custom font substitution if you know the names of the font you wish to substitute for and the name you want substituted. Two examples are shown below.

> Arabia-Normal=Arabia-Normal
> Aardvark-Bold=Aachen BT-Bold

[PSResidentFonts] Section

This section lists the screen font names of all available fonts and their equivalent Adobe PostScript name as recognized by Adobe-licensed

PostScript devices. It is broken up by comments into three different sections.

The first section lists the standard 35 fonts found in most PostScript printers. Those names followed by a 1 are resident in all PostScript printers, while those followed by a 3 are resident only on some printers. The first version of Corel Draw 4.0 had numerous errors in this section, although none of them as harmful as a 1 and a 3 having the same meaning.

The next grouping lists the TrueType fonts that come standard with Windows 3.1. The third grouping lists all the other fonts that came on the Corel Draw 4.0 CD. Two remaining groupings have the names for Corel Draw 3.0 fonts and their equivalents. These fonts are all followed by a 0, indicating that they are not resident on a PostScript printer. Changing this number to a 3 will indicate that the font is resident; and therefore, the font must be downloaded before you attempt to print a document using one of these fonts. Pre-downloading fonts can be very useful when printing long documents so that the real font is used and not converted to curves or bitmapped. This same functionality is available by choosing All Fonts Resident in the Print Options dialog box. Several examples are shown below.

> AvantGarde Bk BT-Italic=AvantGarde-BookOblique 3
> Arial-Normal=Helvetica 1
> Aachen BT-Bold=AachenBT-Bold 0

CORELPRN.INI
[Config] Section
DumpEntireBitmap=

This setting specifies how bitmaps will be printed to Hewlett-Packard LaserJet Series IV printers. If this is set to 0, the bitmap will be sent one raster line at a time to ensure that the bitmap will print correctly. Incorrect printing can occur if the printer driver's graphics mode is set to print raster images as transparent. A 1 will send the whole bitmap at once, which is faster, but less reliable. The default value is 0.

Advanced Topics Workshop

PSBitmapFontLimit=

This specifies the size at which a font will be printed as a bitmap on a PostScript printer. The benefits to printing fonts as bitmaps are that they will look better at small sizes and print faster than when the font is converted to curves. Bitmap fonts tend to use quite a bit of memory and should be used sparingly in order to avoid PostScript errors when printing. Only certain fonts qualify to be converted to bitmaps, and must meet the following criteria:.

- The font is not a resident font as specified in the CORELFNT.INI file's [PSResidentFonts] section described above.
- The size of the printed character in pixels is no more than that specified by PSBitmapFontSizeThreshold (normally 75 pixels). On a 300 dpi device that is 18 points; at 600 dpi it is 9 points, and so on.
- The text has not been scaled or skewed.
- The text has no outline and its fill is a uniform fill.
- The text has not been enveloped or non-linearly transformed in any way.
- The document is not being printed by using either the Scale or the Fit To Page options in the Print dialog box.

The value of PSBitmapFontLimit can range from 0 to 250 with its default value set to 8. If you are having trouble printing PostScript fonts, change the value to 0 and the problem may go away.

PSBitmapFontSizeThreshold=

This specifies the maximum height in pixels of text that will be printed as bitmaps on a PostScript printer. Larger values indicate that bigger bitmaps can be created, which can take a longer a time to print. Any text larger than this value will be converted to curves if the font is not a resident font as specified in CORELFNT.INI's [PSResidentFonts] section described above. The value of PSBitmapFontSizeThreshold can range from 0 to 32767 with its default value being 75.

PSComplexityThreshold=

This specifies the threshold at which a filled path is deemed too complex by Corel Draw and is therefore broken into less complex paths. When a path is broken into more than one path, the appearance of the object will not change. Paths that are particularly complex are those which contain fountain fills, vector fills, bitmap fills and PostScript fills. This setting only has an effect when printing to a PostScript device. The common symptom of overly complex paths are Limitcheck Errors. PSComplexityThreshold can range from 20 to 20000 with a default of 1500. A more reliable default is 200. This will cause print times to be slightly longer, but it will help to decrease the possibilities of Limitcheck Errors. In the long run this will save both time and money at the service bureau.

Corel *NOTE!*

Due to bugs in Corel Draw versions 4.0A5 and 4.0B3, objects may not print correctly when PSComplexityThreshold is lowered.

PSOverprintBlackLimit=

This specifies the percentage of black trap that will be added when printing color separations. It only has an effect when Always Overprint Black is checked in the Print Separations dialog box. The default value is 95 percent and can range from 0 to 100 percent. Anything less than 95 percent will allow white space to appear on separation layers.

WarnBadOrientation=

This specifies whether Corel Draw will issue a warning message when the page orientation of the printer does not match that of the page being printed. A *0* indicates that the message will be disabled while a *1* enables the message. The default value is 1.

[PSDrivers] Section

This section is used to list PostScript drivers that may be used with Corel Draw. A *1* indicates that the driver is a PostScript driver, while a *0* indicates a non-PostScript device. Three drivers are listed in a standard configuration: MGXPS for the Micrografx PostScript driver, PSCRIPT for the standard Windows PostScript driver and AGFAPS for the Agfa PostScript driver. To add additional drivers, use the filename preceding the period followed by an equals sign and a 1 (for example, USPC.DRV would be shown as USPC=1).

MGXPS=1
PSCRIPT=1
AGFAPS=1

[ColorPath] Section

CircuitPath=

This specifies the full path name to the location where color calibration files are stored. The default path name is *drive*:\COREL40\CUSTOM. None of the settings in this section should be changed in the .INI file. They will be automatically updated when certain selections are made within Corel Draw.

cmyk2rgb=

This specifies the file used to convert CMYK files to RGB. The default value is default.rgb.

CurrentTemplate=

This specifies the most recently used color template. The default value is default.smt.

rgb2cmyk=

This specifies the file used to convert RGB files to CMYK. The default value is default.cmy.

The next several sections are the various line screen values and separation angles to be used according to the resolution of the output device.

[*XXX*dpi].

The section name will have the value in dots per inch (indicated here as *XXX*) followed by dpi.

Default=

This lists the default screen frequency in lines per inch. The default value varies according to the resolution of the output device.

*XX*lpi=

This specifies the values of the screen angles that Corel Draw will use in order to prevent the appearance of moire patterns. These values are optimized for each specific resolution and screen frequency and should never be changed. Many times these values will be overridden by the RIP (raster image processor) used to image the file on an imagesetter. Contact the service bureau that will be printing the files for more information.

WIN.INI

[CorelGraphics4] Section

Dir=

This specifies the full path to the directory where the initialization files for all Corel programs are located. The default value is *drive*:\COREL40\CONFIG, where *drive* is the hard drive where the programs are located.

Part

Companion Software Workshops

CorelDRAW!

Part II

1

Adobe
Type
Manager

Adobe Type Manager (ATM) is an essential utility for professional users of Corel Draw. Because it can work with Type 1 fonts, it is almost mandatory for users of PostScript printers, as the fonts can be directly downloaded to the printer. Service bureaus are also very reluctant to work with anything except PostScript fonts; PostScript is the standard output format for most high-end devices. Adobe Type Manager provides users with the ability to use PostScript Type 1 fonts in most Windows applications, including Corel Draw. The benefits of Type 1 fonts are described in depth in Skill Session 35. It is essential that you use Adobe Type Manager 2.0 or higher in order to work correctly with Draw. The current version as of this writing is 2.5. You may already have a copy of ATM that was bundled with another application, such as WordPerfect, Ventura Publisher, PageMaker, FrameMaker, and most Lotus applications. Therefore, before you buy a copy, check your other software to see if you already have one.

Many users confuse the ATM Control Panel (see icon in Figure CSW1.1) with Window's Control Panel Fonts (see icon in Figure CSW1.2). ATM Control Panel is the way that PostScript Type 1 fonts are installed into Windows. Information is copied into both the ATM.INI file and WIN.INI file so that the fonts can be used on both the screen and the printer. After the fonts are installed, Windows will have to be restarted if you are using ATM 2.0. Newer versions do not require Windows to restart. Figures CSW1.3 and CSW1.4 shows the ATM screens for installing fonts. Note that fonts installed through the ATM Control Panel are not visible in the Windows Control Panel.

Figure CSW1.1. The Adobe Type Manager Control Panel icon.

Figure CSW1.2. The Windows Control Panel Fonts icon.

Figure CSW1.3. The initial Adobe Type Manager Control Panel screen.

Figure CSW1.4. The Add Fonts screen.

Corel Draw 4 supports dynamic updating of the font list, so it is possible to minimize Corel Draw and install fonts that will be immediately available. This can be very beneficial should you find that you need a font in the middle of working on a project.

The fonts that come with Corel Draw are all provided in PostScript Type 1 format, so exactly the same fonts are available as the TrueType fonts that the default install adds. The spacing and kerning should be identical for both formats, so there should be no compatibility problems should you decide to switch from one format to another.

2

Adobe Photoshop

Adobe's Photoshop program has long been the top image-editing program on the Macintosh. It is now available to the PC user running under Windows. It has outstanding color separation capabilities along with PostScript compatibility. It is the same version as the new Mac 2.5 version and the files of both are compatible.

Photoshop includes all the standard painting and editing tools and adds some unique filters and effects not found in other programs.

A new feature is called Variations. This is a great new feature that allows you to view and edit multiple images of the original all at the same time. Figure CSW2.1 shows the Variation editing screen with eight different variations applied to the original.

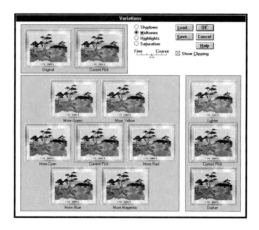

Figure CSW2.1. The Variation editing screen.

Another new feature is Dodge and Burn. Photographers have long used these techniques photographically. Dodging lightens the area when the tool is dragged over an area and Burning darkens the area.

One of the most interesting features is the ability to paint with custom brush tips made from other images or parts of images. An example of this is a silhouette of a deer (one of the sample brush tips). When you paint with this tip, each time you click with the mouse an image of the deer appears. If you drag in a painting motion, the deer becomes part of the stroke which can produce some interesting results.

Photoshop also introduces a new patented Duotone feature that lets you use a color overlay effect allowing you to apply sepia tones to gray-scale images. You can even create Tritones and Quadtones. This new effect can make a mundane gray-scale into a powerful and touching image.

Another feature that you should try is the Quick Mask feature. This feature lets you mask small areas of an image so that you can work on it without disturbing adjacent areas.

As with all high-end, image-editing programs, Photoshop has an array of special effects. The Solarize filter will give a surrealistic look to your photos or paintings. Figure CSW2.2 is an example of this effect.

Figure CSW2.2. Applying the Solarize effect.

The program is Twain-compliant, allowing you to scan directly into Photoshop. It supports the standard formats including .JPG and .IFF from the Amiga.

Adobe Photoshop is a welcome addition to the PC platform, further adding to the burgeoning graphics field.

Above: A scanned picture of a painting done by co-author Peter McCormick and modified in CorelPHOTO-PAINT!.

Right: Created in CorelDRAW! by co-author Peter McCormick by importing the image above, and covering the interior formations of the canyon with fountain fills, and completing the picture with imported clip art. Won award of excellence in Corel's Fourth Annual World Design Contest.

MARTIN

Above: Created entirely in CorelDRAW! by Brett Martin.

These photos were created entirely in CorelDRAW! by co-author Peter McCormick with extensive use of blending fountain fills.

Desert Dreams

Desert   Dreams   II

Desert Dreams   III

BUMPER TO BUMPER

Above: Logo created by co-author Carlos Gonzalez using techniques from Project 2.

Right: Logo created by co-author Foster Coburn.

Below: Logo created by Candace Wade of The Image Makers, Scottsdale, AZ.

VALLEY OF THE SUN

VSSF

SCHOLARSHIP FOUNDATION

Above: Logo created by co-author Foster Coburn.

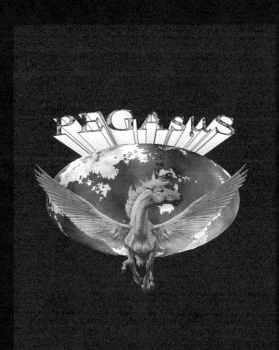

Left: Logo created for a T-shirt by David J. Adducci, 3441 West Kings Ave., Phoenix, AZ 85023, (602) 993-8718 in CorelDRAW! and CorelPHOTO-PAINT!.

Below: Created in CorelDRAW! by co-author Peter McCormick. Won Bonus prize in November 1991 in Corel's Third Annual World Design Contest.

Above: CorelDRAW! image modified in Fractal Design Painter by co-author Peter McCormick.

Below: Created entirely in CorelDRAW! by co-author Peter McCormick.

Above: Created entirely in Fractal Design Painter by co-author Peter McCormick.

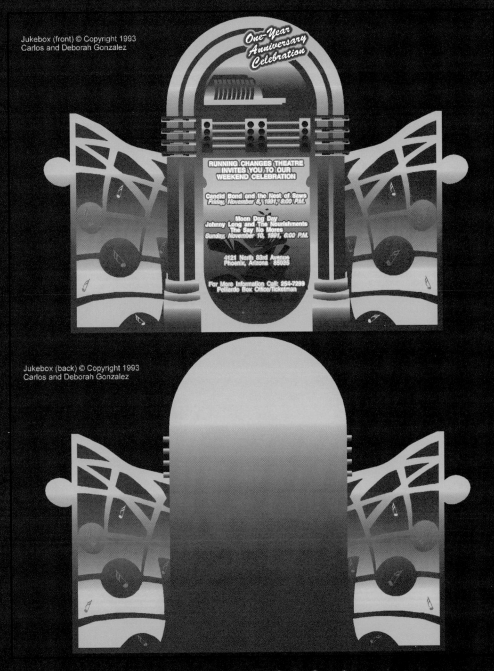

Jukebox (front) © Copyright 1993
Carlos and Deborah Gonzalez

One-Year
Anniversary
Celebration

RUNNING CHANGES THEATRE
INVITES YOU TO OUR
WEEKEND CELEBRATION

Candid Bond and the Nest of Saws
Friday, November 8, 1991, 8:00 P.M.

Moon Dog Day
Johnny Long and The Nourishments
The Say No Mores
Sunday, November 10, 1991, 6:00 P.M.

4121 North 83rd Avenue
Phoenix, Arizona 85035

For More Information Call: 254-7299
Polliardo Box Office/Ticketman

Jukebox (back) © Copyright 1993
Carlos and Deborah Gonzalez

Above: Created entirely in CorelDRAW! by co-author Carlos Gonzalez.

Left: Created by co-author Peter McCormick by exporting Corel images of the dolphin and shell and modifying them extensively in Fractal Design Painter X2.

Golden Gate

Above: Created entirely in CorelDRAW! by co-author Peter McCormick.

Above: Created in Pixar's Typestry by co-author Peter McCormick.

Right: Logo for co-author Foster Coburn's company, Smart Typesetting. Created in CorelDRAW! 2.0. Won Award of Excellence in Corel's 1993 World Design Contest.

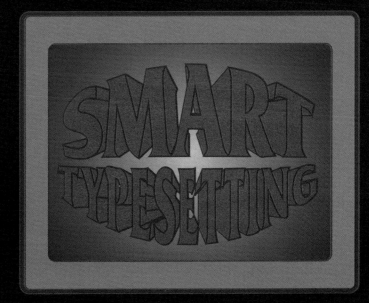

Top: Image scanned into CorelPHOTO-PAINT! as described in Skill Session 44.

Left: Figures from Skill Session 45.

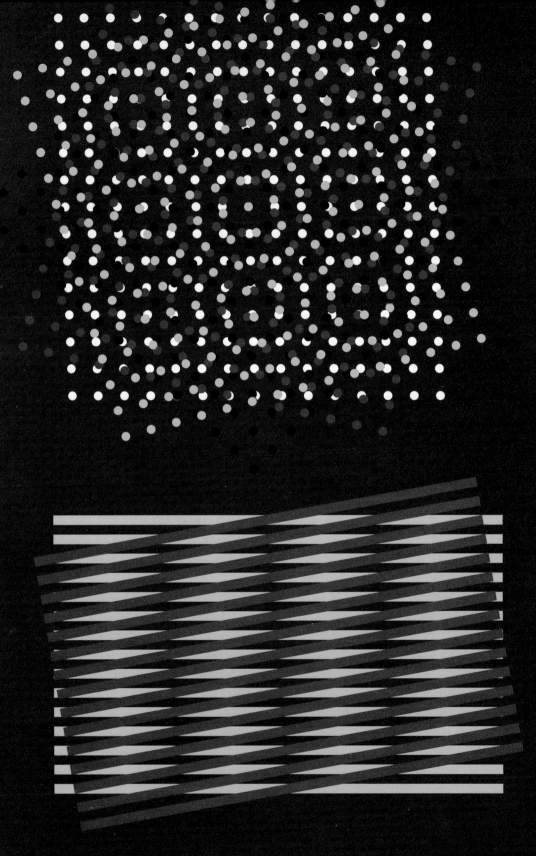

Above: Figures from Skill Session 55.

3

Altsys
Fontographer

Altsys Fontographer is a fantastic tool for the creation and modification of typefaces in both TrueType and PostScript format. While Corel Draw is capable of creating both formats itself, it has severe limitations as a type design tool. These limitations include the inability to provide kerning information and the lack of hinting for the best output at small sizes. Fontographer overcomes those limitations, and then some.

One of the best ways to use the two products together is to create the characters or symbols in Corel Draw and export them in either PostScript or TrueType format. Once the font has been created, it can then be imported into Fontographer for tuning. Fontographer can also be used to create the characters directly, although some Corel Draw users may prefer to create things in Corel Draw. Figure CSW3.1 shows Fontographer's character-editing window and its many tools for creating lines and curves. One of the most interesting tools is the pressure-sensitive tool, which can be used with tablets such as the Kurta XGT (see Companion Hardware Workshop 3, "Kurta XGT Tablet").

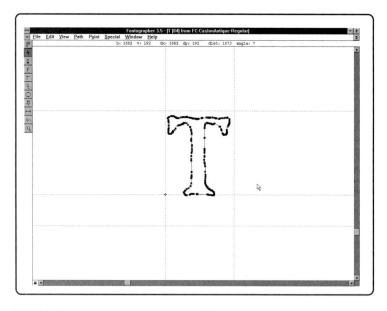

Figure CSW3.1. Fontographer's character-editing window.

A great benefit of using Fontographer over Corel Draw for type design is the fact that the whole character set is available at any time, as shown in Figure CSW3.2. You can easily access any character for editing by double-clicking on its bitmap representation in the grid. This can be very helpful for copying characters from one position to another or combining certain aspects of different characters together.

Figure CSW3.2. A complete character set.

The biggest benefit that Fontographer provides is its ability to adjust the spacing and kerning information easily. In the character window shown in Figure CSW3.1, the sidebearings are easily adjustable to change the space surrounding the character. (Sidebearings are two imaginary lines that provide a right and left boundary to a type character.) The left sidebearing cannot be moved, but the character itself can easily be moved so that it is positioned correctly. The right sidebearing is fully adjustable.

Figure CSW3.3 shows the metrics window, in which the kerning information is adjusted. If you don't want to start from scratch, kerning information can be imported from either a .PFM or an .AFM file. A sample .AFM file with over 2,600 kerning pairs is provided on the *CorelDRAW! Unleashed* companion CD to help get you started. Once the kerning pairs are imported, each of the pairs can easily be adjusted to provide the best fit.

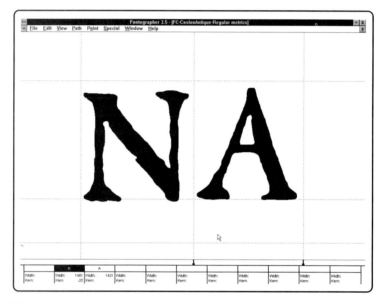

Figure CSW3.3. The metrics window.

Other advanced tools are provided for increasing or decreasing the weight of the font, creating condensed and extended weights, resizing characters, changing the font's attributes, and adjusting hinting parameters. While some of these functions are available in Corel Draw, it would be very tedious to adjust each character individually. Fontographer allows the whole font to be adjusted at once.

For more information, contact Altsys Corporation, 269 Renner Road, Richardson, TX 75080, (214) 680-2060.

4

Fractal Design's Painter

Fractal Design's Painter is a phenomenal paint program. While it provides many tools for editing images, its real strength is in the creation of images. Painter was the first paint program that successfully mimicked the tools of natural media. Other programs, including Corel's Photo-Paint, have tried to imitate Fractal's technology to no avail.

Painter provides brushes that simulate oil paint, watercolors, chalk, charcoal, pencil, and numerous other media. While each of the brushes in itself is quite ingenious, the real power lies in the nearly infinite modifications that can be made to them. There are literally thousands of adjustments that can be made to each brush that will produce a different stroke effect. Don't let the vast array of possibilities scare you from this program, as it is a very intuitive program to work with.

Some of the brushes give you the capability to easily mimic the painting styles of famous artists such as Van Gogh and Seurat. By using the Auto Clone feature it is extremely easy to turn a scanned photograph into a painting. And again, if you don't like the styles provided, it is easy to create your own custom brushes.

The artistic realism is only heightened by the ability to choose the texture of the canvas that will be painted upon. These textures range from simple paper grains to some outrageous types such as the nubs on a basketball. The textures can also be applied to a painting after it has been created to add a finishing touch. In fact, several textures can be added to the same painting. By using Painter's friskets, the textures (or any other effect for that matter) can be applied to only certain selected areas of a painting.

You can draw friskets freehand using Painter's Knife tool or import them from one of Painter's frisket palettes. You can also create Friskets from an imported Encapsulated PostScript file, including files exported from Corel Draw as Adobe Illustrator EPS files. Painter can also use both TrueType and PostScript Type 1 fonts to create a frisket. This can lead to some really interesting type effects.

Some of Painter's more interesting image-editing features are glass distortions and custom lighting. Glass distortions give a painting the appearance of being viewed through some form of glass. The glass takes on the texture of the paper texture you choose from a whole library of glass types that are available. The custom lighting features allow for a scene to be easily relit to give it an entirely different look. Probably the best examples of this are the two images shown in Figure CSW4.1 and Figure CSW4.2. You may recognize Figure CSW4.1 as the award-winning Venice drawing done in Corel Draw. It was exported from Draw to TIF format and imported into Painter. By applying some custom lighting and some touch-up work, Venice is transformed from day to night. To view these pictures in color, refer to the color insert in this book.

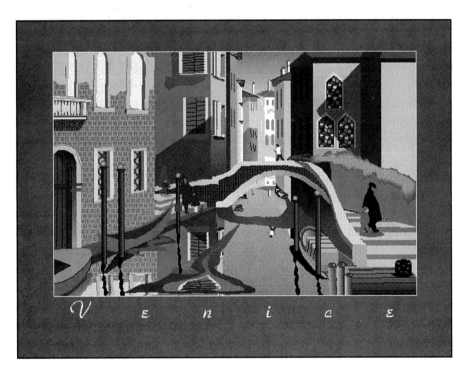

Figure CSW4.1. Venice by day.

Figure CSW4.2. Venice by night.

Fractal Design has recently introduced an expert extension called Painter X2 which allows you to use layering with Painter. This new extension has created an entirely new way of working with bitmaps similar to layering in Vectors. You are able to make a layer transparent so that you can see through it to the layer beneath. The layering method is accomplished with the use of floating friskets. All the effects used in Painter can be applied to these friskets.

For more information about Painter, contact Fractal Design Corporation, P.O. Box 2380, Aptos, CA 95001, (408) 688-8800.

5

Typestry

Pixar of Richmond, California has created a text-rendering program that allows you to create text effects with a real 3D look. Light and dark, shadows, perspective, and texture are the elements that give the illusion of three dimensions. Typestry allows you to do all these things easily.

Pixar began as a division of Lucas Films, for which they won an Academy Award for technical achievement. Typestry uses its own RenderMan renderer, a state-of-the-art design capable of producing photorealistic images. This is the same renderer used to create some of the scenes in the movies *Terminator 2* and *Beauty and the Beast.*

Typestry's manual is a work of art in itself. Full-color illustrations of what effects will look like fill the 64 page manual. You don't have to read for hours before you can create a rendering.

The authors of *CorelDRAW! Unleashed* are amazed at how incredibly beautiful objects can be made to look with this program. We say objects because you're really not limited to text *per se.* You can use any Type 1 or TrueType font for your text. What this really means is that you can use programs like Fontographer, FontMonger, and Corel Draw to take objects you create and make them into Fonts. Remember, Corel Draw allows you to export objects like symbols and small drawings as TrueType fonts. Once they are fonts, Typestry will render them like any other Type 1 or TrueType font.

You can fill text with such textures (called *looks*) as Brushed Copper, Silver, and Gold. Other looks include Wood Grain, Marble, Dragon Hide, and many more. Lighting effects are easily applied, as well as shadows.

The examples of different effects in Figure CSW5.1 are just a few of the hundreds of effects that can be created.

Using Typestry to enhance your Corel Draw images will give your illustrations a look that your competitors will envy. This may sound like an ad for typestry, but the results speak for themselves.

Typestry also comes with a great animation program that will allow you to create animations of your renderings.

Figure CSW5.1. Text rendered in Typestry using the Lizard texture.

There is one caveat in recommending Typestry. The more powerful the system the better, and a math coprocessor is a must. Putting aside sometimes hours for completion of a complicated rendering is also a consideration. All things considered, the results are worth the time. Isn't it better to have one outstanding image than ten mediocre ones for that special project?

For more information about Typestry, contact Pixar, 1001 West Cutting Boulevard, Richmond, CA 94804, (510) 236-4000.

Part

Companion Hardware Workshops

Part III

1

Agfa Arcus Plus

The Arcus Plus scanner provides very high quality scans without the price of the high-end drum scanners. It is a flatbed CCD scanner like many of the lower-priced scanners. But where the Arcus Plus really excels is in its ability to get quality color scans by scanning 10 bits of data for each color rather than the 8 bits that most scanners scan.

This extra data may seem like it is just wasted, since color files can save only 8 bits per color. The advantage to having this extra data is that the best 8 bits are taken from the 10 bits gathered during the scan and saved to disk. Sometimes during scanning, a bit can be dropped or rounding errors can occur. By having the extra 2 bits, this problem can be all but eliminated, helping to keep color as accurate as possible.

In order to help get the best scan possible, Agfa bundles their FotoLook software driver. Color tags are provided that map the RGB data scanned by the scanner into calibrated CMYK data. The user can set the white/ black point, Dmax and Dmin, automatic exposure control, and the tonal curve for gamma corrections. Descreening is available, so halftones can be scanned without picking up moire patterns. All of these features help to ensure that a scan can be done correctly the first time. A TWAIN driver is available so that the Arcus Plus can be used with CorelPHOTO-PAINT!, CorelTRACE!, and other TWAIN-compliant applications.

The Arcus Plus also provides higher input resolution than most scanners in its price range. The optical resolution is 600 dpi horizontal by 1,200 dpi vertical. This can be interpolated in software to 1,200 dpi in both directions for color files and 2,400 dpi for black and white lineart. The extra resolution can be very useful when needing to enlarge a picture.

Reflective materials up to 8 inches by 11.8 inches can be scanned. With the add-on transparency module, tranparencies up to 6 inches by 8.7 inches can also be scanned.

Hooking up the Arcus Plus is a breeze in that it can be connected to any Adaptec ASPI-compliant SCSI card. In theory it should be able to hook to other ASPI compliant cards, but Agfa recommends only the Adaptec. Many scanners require their own proprietary card, which takes a slot away from something else. The ability to hook the Arcus Plus to a standard SCSI card alleviates this problem, as the Adaptec card can also be hooked to a CD-ROM, hard drive, removable cartridge drive, and many other devices.

For more information, contact Miles Inc., 200 Ballardvale Street, Wilmington, MA 01887-1011, (508) 658-5600.

2

Hewlett-Packard IIC Scanner

If you have put off purchasing a scanner because you don't know how a scanner could help you in your projects or you feel you can't justify the cost, you're missing out on a big asset to desktop publishing. The capability of capturing all or part of an image you have created in another medium, or from someone else's work (that is copyright-free, of course), can greatly speed up the completion of a project. The process of scanning an image into a image-editing application is more than just making a duplicate of the original. When you scan an image, you can

- Crop certain portions.
- Change the tonal values (brightness and contrast).
- Resize the image.

Color scanners allow you to change the intensities of colors and hues before you bring the image into your applications. The top scanners on the market today are Twain-compliant, which allow you to scan directly into the software application that you will use for the finished project. Corel's Photo-Paint is one of the applications that supports Twain.

There are three basic types of scanners: handheld, flatbed, and drum. The handheld scanners are the least expensive. They are also more difficult to operate because they are limited to a specific scanning width, usually four inches. These are referred to as *halfsheet scanners*. Halfsheet scanners require software that will *stitch* the two halves of a scanned sheet together.

Flatbed scanners don't require stitching, and they come in different sizes, usually 8 1/2×11 inches or 8 1/2×14 inches.

Drum scanners are the best, but they are also the most expensive and are usually reserved for high-end users and service bureaus.

A scanner operates much like a camera. The *light bar* illuminates the image so that the image can be captured by the lens. The image is then converted to an electronically digitized image with the software supplied by the scanner's manufacturer. Finally, the image is saved to disk.

The HP IIc is a high-quality color scanner with an 8 1/2×14-inch copy board. It comes with Deskscan II software, which gives the user control over the operation of the scanner and the scanned image—type, size, contrast and brightness, intensity and hues of colors, and shadows. It is Twain-compliant, so each application you use that also supports Twain will interface with it. If your software does not support Twain, you still can use the HP IIc. Use the software supplied, store the scanned image to a directory, and then open it in your application for editing.

The HP IIc has a street price of around $1,500 and is considered the top scanner on the market in its price range. Many users feel it is better than some in even higher price ranges.

This author has used the HP IIc for over a year and it has superior quality and reliability. The scanner is capable of scanning images in black-and-white, halftone, and color. Color can be scanned in at 24-bit color (millions of colors). Its Deskscan II software is very intuitive, so you can make adjustments to the image easily.

The one drawback is that Hewlett-Packard uses a proprietary SCSI card that does not allow you to daisy-chain other SCSI hardware with it. This means that you have to give up an extra slot in your system for the HP card. Corel's new EZ SCSI is supposed to eliminate this problem.

3

Kurta XGT Tablet

A Word About Tablets in General

More and more graphic artists are discovering the benefits of using a digitized tablet in place of the old-fashioned mouse.

There are two significant reasons for using tablets. To begin with, they provide a completely natural way of drawing—using a pen instead of a mouse. Everyone, regardless of whether they consider themselves artists, drew their first line with a pencil or pen. When computers were introduced, we were suddenly told to draw with a brick attached to a string. To make matters worse the string had to be constantly "pulled on" to give you more room to continue drawing. Tablets and pens have removed these restrictions and allow users to draw the way they were originally taught. Many first-time users of tablets find they have a great deal more talent than they had given themselves credit for.

The second reason for using a tablet is for the relief of stress pain in the hand and wrist. The old-fashioned mouse is a carrier of Carpal Tunnel Syndrome. States all over the country are spending millions of dollars in workman's compensation claims due to Carpal Tunnel Syndrome induced by the use of the mouse. This sounds like a statement made by a lobbyist for the tablet industry, but the statement is true. If you are experiencing hand or wrist pain using the mouse, you will eliminate or greatly reduce your problems if you switch to a tablet.

The Kurta Tablet

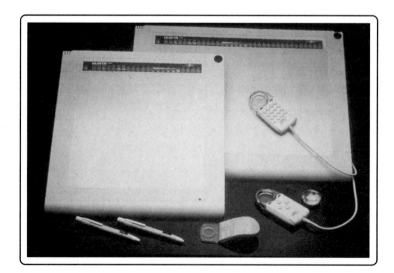

The Kurta XGT tablet is a high-performance, graphics digitizing tablet that combines sophisticated software and programmable functions. The XGT features new pointing devices that include second-generation cordless technology and pressure output. New with the XGT digitizing tablet is a pressure-sensitive drawing pen and an ergonomically designed cursor. Both corded and cordless pens are available, as well as four- or sixteen-button cursors.

The XGT interfaces to virtually any computer system that supports an RS232 serial interface. The XGT works with almost any software that supports a mouse or digitizing tablet. This of course includes CorelDraw.

The XGT can even emulate other competitor tablets including Summagraphics, Wacom, Seiko, Graphtec, Hitachi, and even a Microsoft serial mouse. You might wonder why they would design a tablet to emulate a competitor. The answer lies in the fact that some older software applications may have a driver only for one of the tablets listed, and the publishers are no longer producing the software. If you use one of these older applications, you can switch to the other tablet mode with a press of a button.

Most Kurta tablets, including the XGT, support templates. Templates are surface menus (an actual piece of paper or plastic), that have macros printed on them to provide shortcut commands in place of using shortcut keys on the keyboard. The template is placed under the protective overleaf on the tablet for positive positioning. Most templates on the market today are for CAD applications; however, there is a template for CorelDraw available through Kurta's BBS.

The programmable features of the XGT are outstanding. You can scale the tablet to the screen for tracing in artwork at its proper dimensions. You can scale the tablet so that you have less hand movement in relation to the screen. And you can even set up multiple scaled areas on the tablet for different uses by using Personalities keys. It also has a function button and scale for a pressure pen.

All Kurta tablets come with a lifetime limited warranty. And they are manufactured in the United States.

The Kurta XGT tablet recently won *PC Magazine*'s Editor's Choice Award as the number-one tablet over its competitors.

Corel*NOTE!*

If you've ever wondered why other graphic artists seem to have that certain something that makes their work more finished than yours, it may be that they are using a digitized tablet and you are using a mouse.

For more information on the Kurta XGT, contact Kurta Corporation, 3007 E. Chambers Street, Phoenix, Arizona, 85040-3796, (602) 276-5533

4

Matrox
MGA Card

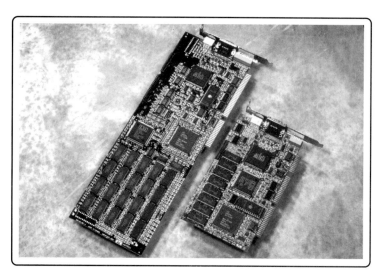

Video cards are probably the most important add-in card for improving the working conditions of Corel Draw. Corel Draw demands all the available screen real estate and number of colors that its user can afford. Also, because of its high dependency on graphics, the speed of the video card can have a great impact on the performance of Corel Draw itself. Matrox's MGA Ultima and Impression cards deliver on all counts.

Both of the cards are based on Matrox's own MGA chip. This chip offers an internal 64-bit architecture to provide workstation-level video performance. This, combined with up to 3MB of video RAM, allows resolutions as high at 1600×1200 with 256 colors and full color at 1024×768. All this power shines with a 486 processor and really screams when dropped into a Pentium box.

Since it does provide workstation-level performance, its driver suite reflects that. Drivers are provided for Windows 3.1, Windows NT, OS/2 2.1, UNIX operating systems, and DOS applications such as GEM, Lotus 1-2-3, WordPerfect, FrameWork, Ventura Publisher, and AutoCAD 11 and 12.

Included utilities allow the automatic switching of display modes on the fly without restarting Windows. The ConsistentColor utility helps to match the screen colors to those on the printed page. WinSqueeze offers transparent JPEG compression, and ClearType anti-aliases TrueType to enhance its display quality.

The MGA cards also provide for the future with the daughtercards it supports. The Marvel video graphics controller allows the use of live video. This makes it very easy to create Video for Windows files for use in CorelSHOW! and to capture video stills for placing as bitmaps. The VideoPro board allows the creation of broadcast-quality video recording in either NTSC or PAL formats. The LaserPro board increases printing speed to LaserJet II, IID, III, and IIID printers by up to 600 percent and double their resolution from 300 dpi to 600 dpi.

The Ultima board is available for the ISA bus and its price starts at $599. The Impression boards are available for ISA, EISA, VL-Bus, PCI, and MicroChannel versions. The price for the Impression line begins at $1299 and ranges to $1,699 for the full-blown Micro Channel version. Boosting the maximum resolution from 1280×1024 to 1600×1200 will cost an additional $149 for any of the Impression boards. The LaserPro addition costs $299, and the Marvel live-video attachment is $999. A price has not yet been set for the VideoPro board.

For more information, contact Matrox Electronic Systems, Ltd., 1055 St. Regis Blvd., Dorval, Quebec, Canada H9P 2T4, (800) 361-1408.

5

SyQuest Removable Drives

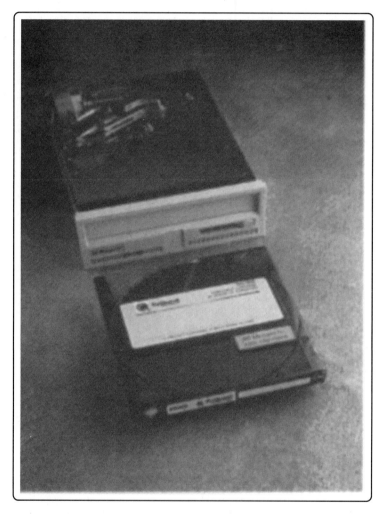

Removable hard drives come in many sizes and shapes. Some of these drives use optical mechanisms, and some work much like internal hard drives. Syquest drives are of the latter. They all work much alike, but come in four different types. Each of the drives offers a self-calibrating servo system for full interchangability and data integrity. Automatic error detection and correction schemes are also provided for defect management.

Three of the four types use cartridges that are virtually identical in that they have a 5 1/4-inch size. The most popular of the three (and the first available) is the 44MB (SQ555) cartridge. This is a standard in over 90 percent of service bureaus throughout the country. This drive gained its popularity on the Macintosh platform and began to make inroads into the PC market about two years ago. Soon after that an 88MB (SQ5110) drive was introduced. It is able to read the 44MB cartridges, but it cannot write to them. Due to the fact that it can't write to the older cartridges, it has not been as popular. Within the last year, a new

603

88 MB (SQ5110C) drive was introduced that can both read and write the 44 MB cartridges. All of these drives have an access speed of approximately
20 ms.

The newest drive comes in a 3 1/2-inch form factor, and it has a capacity of 105 MB (SQ3105). Not only does it provide more storage in a smaller cartridge, it also is a much faster mechanism with an access speed of 14.5 ms.

All of the drives are SCSI devices and as such can share the same adapter card as most CD-ROM drives. The SQ3105 is also available with an IDE interface. The drives can be mounted either internally or externally depending on what best suits the system to which they will be attached.

The street price of the drives ranges from a low of about $350 for the 44 MB drives to $600 for the 105MB drives. Cartridges range from $65 to $100 depending on their capacity. There are many manufacturers who use the SyQuest drives and repackage them under their own label. Be careful though about using non-SyQuest cartridges because they have been shown to damage the drives. This allows for a fairly inexpensive way to store large chunks of data, keep software that is rarely used, or to take large files to a service bureau.

For more information, contact SyQuest Corporation, 47071 Bayside Parkway, Fremont, CA 94538, (800) 245-2278.

6

Toshiba TXM3401B CD-ROM

When my Toshiba TXM3401B external drive first arrived, I could hardly wait to install it. But too many times before I had been burned by poor documentation and installation procedures that had left me frustrated and weary. However, the Toshiba CD-ROM installation proved to be so easy that I was left wondering, *Is that all?* This is the closest I've come to the proverbial "plug-and-play" procedure. I believe that Toshiba has set a benchmark for ease of installation.

The documentation was clear and concise. It told me exactly what I needed to do and how to do it in a step-by-step procedure   just the thing for someone who really doesn't like to install hardware or has little, if any, experience under the "hood" of the computer. There is a "Quick Start" that really is quick. If you require any other information, the rest of the chapters in the installation manual should cover anything that might come up. The total installation time was only 25 minutes, and the longest part of the installation was removing and replacing the cover of the computer.

Better yet, the equipment performed as advertised. Other CD drives I've seen do not perform as quickly, or even possess the capability of reading Photo CDs. With the TXM3401B, I had no problems reading Photo CDs, multimedia CDs, or any of the Corel Draw CDs I have from older versions of the program.

The Toshiba TXM3401B external CD-ROM is a double speed drive. It features 2.2 times the rotational speed, and provides a 330KB/sec data transfer rate. This helps to achieve an industry-first 200 ms random access time. An internal drive is also available. It has a very desirable 256 KB of onboard cache. This great feature helps in the fast delivery of information from the CD drive to your computer's CPU. The onboard cache determines the amount of data that the disc can have ready and waiting for you at a specific time, so the more onboard cache you have, the better. Most single-speed CD drives offer only 64 KB of onboard cache.

This Toshiba unit uses caddies; just place the CD into the caddy and place it into the CD drive. The CD-ROM is quite compact, considering all the new options made available to me. The CD-ROM uses a SCSI-2 host interface.

A welcome feature of the Toshiba CD-ROM is its contamination-free design. It combines a sealed enclosure with a closable front-facing door. Another feature is the automatic lens cleaning capability. This feature helps to prevent drive contamination as well as extends the time required between maintenance for cleaning.

Adding a CD-ROM drive has opened up a whole new world for me. I have access to clip art, fonts, and other applications. Books of all types, as well as encyclopedias, libraries, games, educational materials, utilities, upgrades, and tools, are also expanding the CD-ROM market. The CD drive even allows me to listen to music while I work at my computer!

Part

Project Workshops

Part IV

1

Creating a Map Using the Layers Option

Remember, when using Layers in Corel Draw your available memory resources are the only limit to the number of layers in your drawing.

This lesson will guide you with the use of Layers. You will learn how to create and view individual layers or a combination of layers at once. This workshop is based on the majority of existing maps, so feel free to alter it to fit your needs.

Follow these steps to create the map used in the following examples.

1. Draw a rectangle using the Pencil tool, making sure that the ends of the lines cross over each other (see Figure P1.1).

Corel*NOTE!*

In the Layers roll-up, Guides are listed first. When you draw a line and place it directly on the guide, it will be difficult to select the line.

You could marquee-select the line or select any item in your Corel document and tab around until you find it. If the line is the only object on the page, you can always choose Select All from the Edit menu.

Also, by moving the Guides layer to a lower position in the order inside the Layers roll-up, you can select objects that are on different layers a little easier.

2. Select the two vertical lines and blend them with eight steps (see Figure P1.2). Then select the two horizontal lines and blend them with 11 steps.

3. The vertical and horizontal blends have been applied and the blended objects are now separated (see Figure P1.3). For more information about separating objects, see Skill Session 23 and Command Reference 6.

4. Draw a line that runs diagonally from the top left of the map to the bottom right (see Figure P1.4).

5. Select all objects and combine them. Switch to the 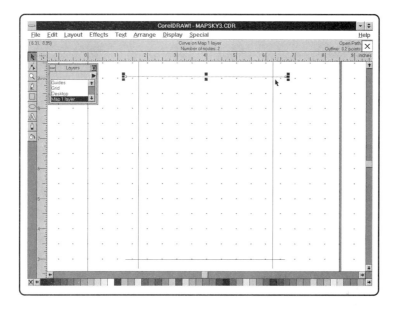 tool. Double-click the first line down from the top and add four nodes.

You double-click the line with the tool to bring up the Node Edit roll-up.

Figure P1.1. The rectangle made up of lines that cross over each other at the ends.

6. Pull the two middle nodes downward approximately 1/4 inch from their initial position (see Figure P1.5).

7. Add four nodes to the sixth vertical line from the left and pull the two middle nodes toward the right approximately 1/4 inch (see Figure P1.6).

8. Using the tool, select the third line in from the left where it intersects the ninth line down from the top. Double-click the line to invoke the Node Edit roll-up and break the line at this intersection.

9. Slide the node that belongs to the top half of the broken line up to meet the first horizontal line above it. Slide the node belonging to the bottom half of the broken line down to meet the horizontal line below it (see Figure P1.7).

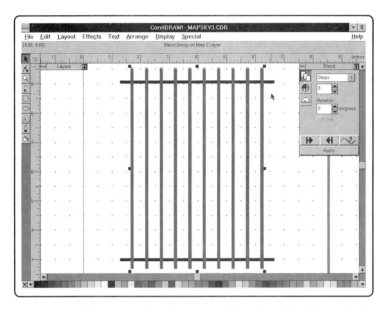

Figue P1.2. The Blend Roll-Up with eight steps selected and the blended objects.

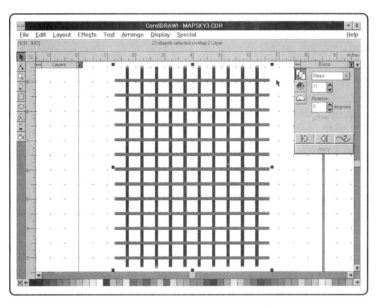

Figure P1.3. The objects used to create the map after vertical and horizontal lines were blended and their blend groups separated.

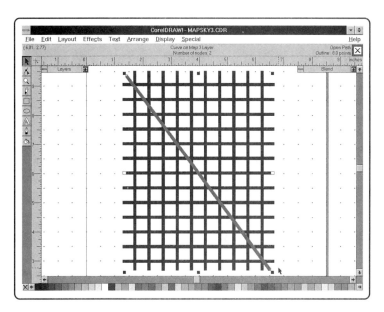

Figure P1.4. The map with a diagonal line added.

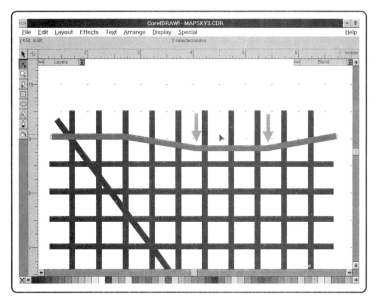

Figure P1.5. The map with the top line edited, nodes added, and reshaped.

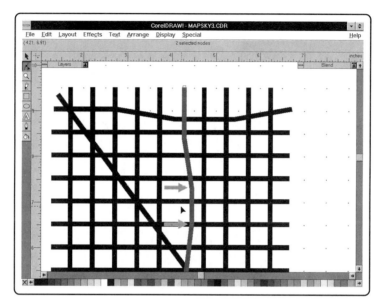

Figure P1.6. The map with the sixth vertical line edited, nodes added, and reshaped.

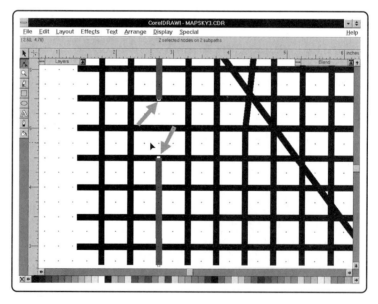

Figure P1.7. The broken line with the nodes repositioned.

10. Select the ninth line down from the top. Using the ⚲ tool, break the line where it intersects the third line in from the left. Slide one of the nodes to the left to meet the first vertical line to the left and then slide the other one to meet the first vertical line to the right (see Figure P1.8).

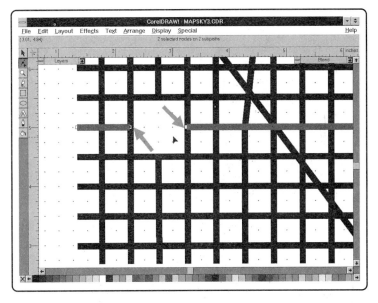

Figure P1.8. The second broken line with the nodes repositioned.

11. Now select the map and press the + (plus) key on your keypad to make a copy of the map. By using the + (plus) key, you leave a copy of the selected object(s) where the original object is positioned.

Corel*NOTE!*

Any new object that is drawn, created, imported or pasted will automatically be placed on the layer that is currently selected in the Layers roll-up. These objects can be moved to different layers if needed.

12. Create a layer called Blackline Layer, place the copy there, and give it the outline attributes of 12 points, Black. Rename the layer the map was created on to Whiteline Layer, and give it the outline attributes 8 points, White. In the Layers roll-up, select Whiteline Layer and move it above Blackline Layer (see Figure P1.9).

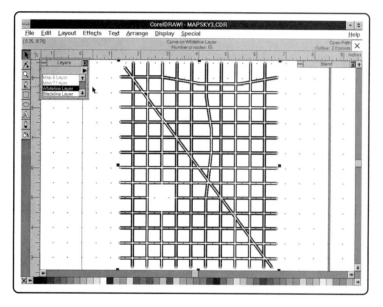

Figure P1.9. Arrangement of Blackline and Whiteline layers.

13. Create a new layer called County Layer to be used as a background and then draw the outlines of the counties on that layer. Color-coded counties are used in many maps. The shapes for the counties used for this example were created using the main roads on the map as guides. Your counties can be whatever shape you want them to be (see Figure P1.10).

14. Create another layer called Text Layer. On this layer you can place all the street names, callouts, and other necessary verbiage. Go through all other existing layers in the Layers roll-up (except for the Whiteline Layer, Blackline Layer, and the Text Layer) and make them invisible by selecting those options in the Layers pop-up menu (see Figure P1.11).

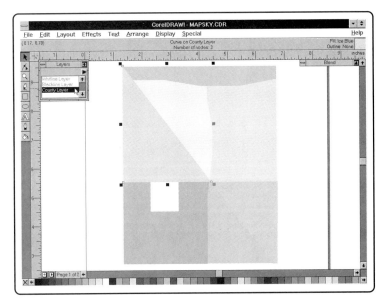

Figure P1.10. The County Layer showing the different shapes and colors of the counties.

Figure P1.11. The Layers roll-up showing that the Whiteline, Blackline and Text layers are the only current active layers.

15. Uncombine the map lines on the Whiteline Layer so that you can select each line individually. Select a street name or word from the Text Layer and then select a line from the Whiteline Layer; align that word to the selected line of the map using the Align command from the Arrange menu (see Figure P1.12).

Corel *NOTE!*

You may have to manually adjust some of the text to align with the odd-shaped lines on the map.

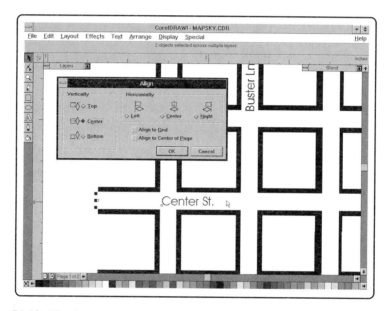

Figure P1.12. Aligning street names to lines on the map.

16. Create icons or use the icons in the Symbols roll-up to designate buildings, parks, fuel areas, and landmarks. You can place these icons on one layer or place all similar icons on individual layers. For this example, each icon was placed on its own separate layer and given an appropriate name. For example, fuel icons were placed on a layer called Fuel Layer. The icons used are also color-coded (see Figure P1.13).

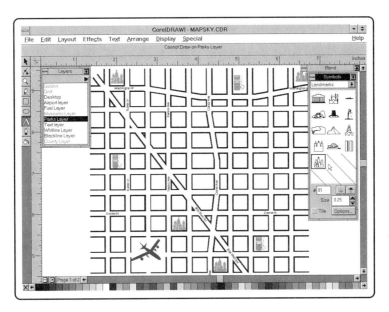

Figure P1.13. The Symbols roll-up and several layers displaying icons.

17. Now you are ready to view the entire map and to check for hidden objects. Start with the default settings for guides, grids, and desktop layers. The next layers should fall in descending order as follows: Airport Layer, Parks Layer, Museum Layer, Fuel Layer, Text Layer, Whiteline Layer, Blackline Layer, and County Layer (see Figure P1.14).

18. Create a legend for the map using the icons from the separate layers and circles filled with the same colors as the counties (see Figure P1.15). Place these objects on a new layer called Legend Layer (see Figure P1.16).

The completed legend can also be seen in the color page section of this book.

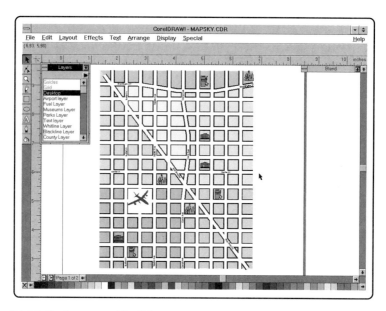

Figure P1.14. Entire map with all layers on and in order.

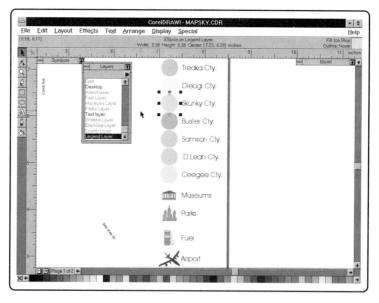

Figure P1.15. The map legend created by using icons from the separate layers and colored circles.

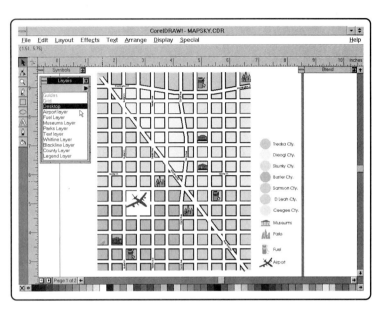

Figure P1.16. The map and the legend.

2

Creating a Chrome Effect

The following procedures are to be used with a scanned-in image as a template. However, the same effects can be applied to existing clip art, freehand drawings, and text. This method of creating chrome in Corel is one of many ways to achieve this effect.

To add a chrome effect to a standard black ink on white background logo, you first enlarge the original logo by 200 percent on a copy machine. This size is large enough to allow you to clean up the logo. To return the logo to its original size all you have to do is reduce it by 50 percent.

When you clean up, make sure that all the edges on the logo are as straight as possible and that any curved areas have no excess toner hanging from them. Use Pro-white or your favorite correction fluid to help with the cleanup.

Start with as sharp and clean an object as possible to make your finished piece much better. You could clean up the object in a scanning/paint program, which may involve a bit of pixel editing. Scan in the logo to use as a guide in Corel Draw. See Skill Session 56, "Scanning," for more information.

You can save the scanned image as a TIF file at a resolution of 300 dpi. Save the file as CHROME.TIF. However, any format that allows you to trace and view your image in Corel will be fine. Select the format that works best for you.

In Corel Draw, open a new file and select Import from the File menu. In the Import dialog box (see Figure P2.1), select TIF from the List Files of Type list and press Enter. Find the scanned logo in the directory you saved it to and import that file. You can trace the image with the AutoTrace feature provided with Corel instead of using Corel Trace. See Skill Session 47, "CorelTRACE!," for more information.

Corel*NOTE!*

To help you make a more accurate trace, you may want to select the For Tracing option in the Import dialog box.

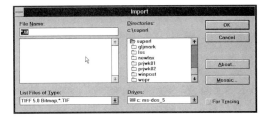

Figure P2.1. The Import dialog box.

Select the imported TIFF image. The status line indicates that you have a bitmap selected. Select the 𝓁 tool (F5). This activates the AutoTrace feature (see Figure P2.2). For more information, see Skill Session 39, "Manually Tracing versus AutoTracing."

Trace the entire outline of the image. After saving the current changes, zoom in (F2) to all vertical areas and make sure that these lines are straight.

If the lines appear crooked, use the Shape Node Edit tool (F10) to select the top and bottom nodes of that line and double-click any of the selected nodes to call up the Node Edit roll-up (see Figure P2.3). From the list, select Align.

In the Node Align dialog box, select Align Vertical and click OK (see Figure P2.4). This ensures a straight line, even if the line appears to be crooked on-screen. You can also use the Snap to Grid or Snap to Guidelines options if you know the object's width and height.

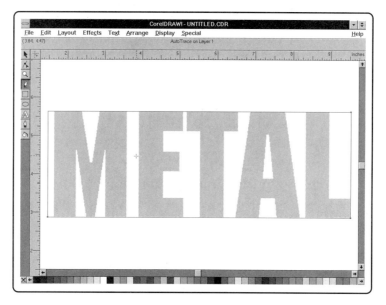

Figure P2.2. The Pencil tool's AutoTrace feature.

Figure P2.3. The Node Edit roll-up.

Figure P2.4. The Node Align dialog box.

628

Once you trace the logo, move the individual letters away from each other to allow you to apply the contour effect to each letter without overlapping contour outlines. To activate the Contour roll-up, select Contour Roll-Up from the Effects menu or press Ctrl-F9 (see Figure P2.5).

Next, select all of the traced "letters" and combine them into one object by selecting Combine from the Arrange menu or by pressing Ctrl-L (see Figure P2.6). Now select the combined object and activate the Contour roll-up. Select Outside, enter 0.10 inches in the Offset field and 2 in the Steps field, and click on Apply.

From the Arrange menu, select Separate to separate your contoured logo (see Figure P2.7). Select the original traced logo's outline and apply a new contour to it. In the Contour roll-up, select Inside, enter an offset of 0.10 inches, and change the number of steps to 1. Click Apply.

Separate and ungroup this contour group, and then select the traced logo and use the Break Apart command to turn it back into individual letters. You should recombine any letterforms that have "holes" in them, such as the uppercase *A* in the example.

Figure P2.5. The Contour roll-up.

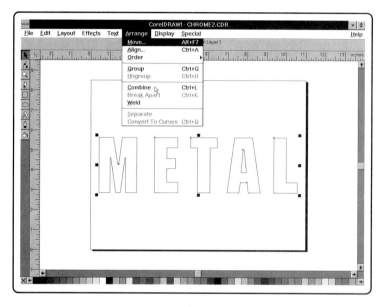

Figure P2.6. Selecting Combine from the Arrange menu.

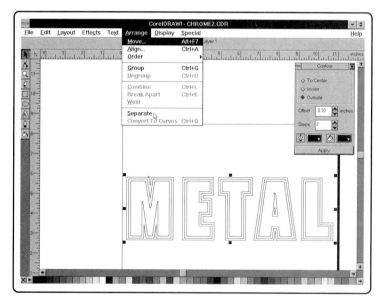

Figure P2.7. Separating the contoured logo.

When you select all of the Contour outlines, the status line reads "Curve on Layer 1," unless you are working in multiple layers (see Figure P2.8). Break apart all of the contour lines and group the outlines of the letters with the letter they belong to.

Make a duplicate of the original logo and nudge it away from the rest of the objects in your file so that you can work on it easier. Draw a horizontal line wider than the duplicate logo and center it to the duplicate. This will provide a guide for what I call a "waterline."

Now either move, delete, or break apart and rejoin nodes from the duplicate logo nearer to the waterline. Convert the horizontal lines close to the waterline to curves using the Node Edit roll-up. To invoke the Node Edit roll-up, use the ↗ tool to double-click the object's outline (see Figure P2.9). This makes it possible to curve these lines into more interesting paths. After you've done that, put the reworked logo outline back in place. (See Skill Session 5, "The Shape Tool," for more information about the Node Edit roll-up.)

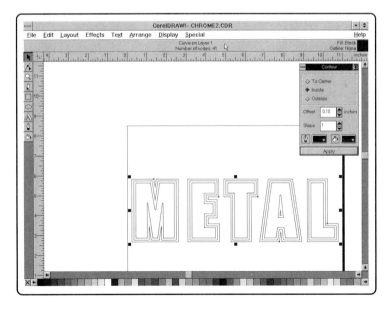

Figure P2.8. The status line reads "Curve on Layer 1."

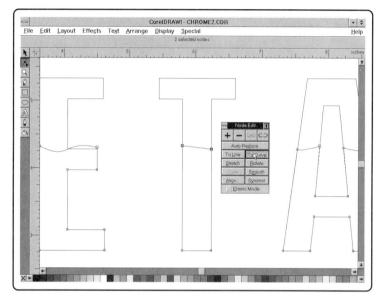

Figure P2.9. Changing a line to a curve with the Node Edit roll-up.

Make a duplicate of this waterline version of the logo. With the Node Edit tool, marquee-select the top nodes on the logo and move them upward 0.25 inches. Then bring the smaller height waterline logo to the front.

Find a star shape to use as a highlight on the logo. Select the $\mathbb{A}$ tool (F8). Hold down the primary mouse button and a fly-out menu appears (see Figure P2.10). Select the star-shaped icon to bring up the Symbols roll-up (see Figure P2.11). Under the category Stars 1, enter symbol 33. You can see the selected star. You can now drag and drop it onto the work area.

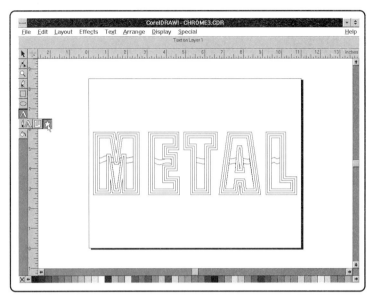

Figure P2.10. The Text tool fly-out menu.

All the hard work is done, so have some fun and fill all the objects that you've created (see Skill Session 12 for more information about fills). Remember to stack these objects on top of one another in the following order:

1. Fill Object 1 of the traced object with 100 percent black and no outline.

2. Fill Object 2 with a linear fill from 100 percent black to 0 percent black, at an angle of 90 degrees, and no outline.

3. Fill Object 3 with 100 percent white, with a black outline of 0.2 points.

4. Select Object 4 and fill it with linear fill of 55 percent black to 100 percent white.

5. Select the waterline version of Object 5 and fill it with a linear fill of 100 percent white to 80 percent black and no outline.

6. Select the smaller image of your waterline version of Object 6. Use a linear fill of 100 percent white to 50 percent black with an angle of 90 degrees and no outline (see Figure P2.12).

633

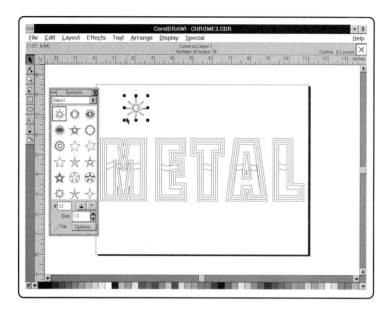

Figure P2.11. The Symbols roll-up.

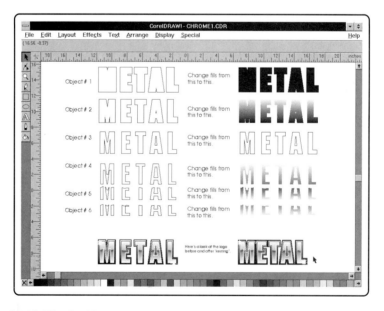

Figure P2.12. The final logo.

You now can select the star symbol and fill it with 100 percent white with no outline (see Skill Session 11 for more information about the Outline tool). Place it wherever you like. Now move the grouped letter/ outlines closer to each other as if you were adjusting the kerning. See Skill Session 29, "Spacing, Kerning, and Changing Character Attributes," for more information.

You can achieve some interesting effects just by changing the color scheme of any or all the objects. Figure P2.13 shows one example. (See the color section of this book.)

All that's left is to preview and print. Find someone who can output your file at a high resolution and you're all done.

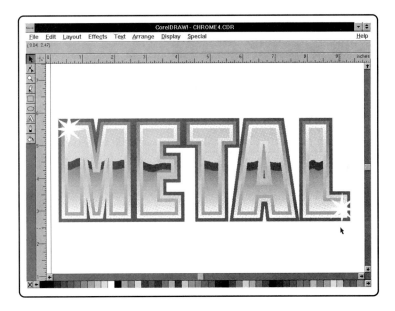

Figure P2.13. The color logo.

635

3

Creating a Gem Box Package Design

To create the gem box, use an octagon and a hexagon. The hexagon forms the lid of the gem box and the octagon forms a cone-shaped bottom. Use the symbols that Corel supplies: numbers 216 and 37 respectively. Find them in the Symbols roll-up under the Geographic Symbols category (see Figures P3.1 and P3.2).

Figure P3.1. The Geographic Symbols category in the Symbols roll-up.

Use two hexagons, a small one sized at 2.35 inches and a larger one sized at 5.74 inches (see Figure P3.3). Align the small hexagon to the center of the large one. See Skill Session 17, "Aligning Objects," for more information about aligning.

The sides of one of the panels in the octagon and hexagon should be the same length. For example, if one side of the octagon is one inch long, the side of the hexagon must the same. Enlarge and/or reduce the symbols until the sides are equal in length (see Figures P3.4 and P3.5). After you resize the hexagon, break it apart and delete the smaller outline.

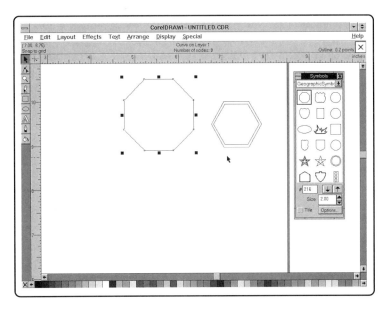

Figure P3.2. The octagon and hexagon symbols.

Figure P3.3. Typing a new measurement in the Symbols roll-up.

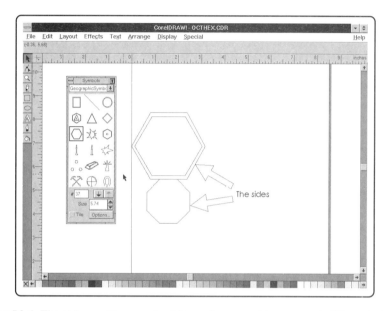

Figure P3.4. The sides on the panels of the octagon and hexagon at different sizes.

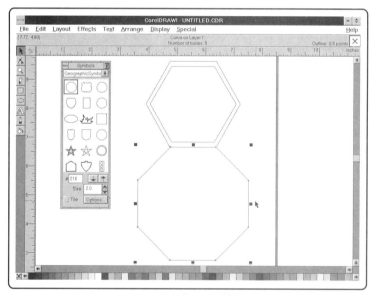

Figure P3.5. The sides on the panels of the octagon and hexagon with the same length after enlarging the octagon.

Draw a trapezoid using a rectangle converted to curves (use Ctrl-Q for a keyboard shortcut). Place it between the large and small hexagons. The bottom width of the trapezoid should be as wide as the top side of the small hexagon (see Figure P3.6). The top of the trapezoid should not be as wide as the top of the large hexagon. Stay back .43 inch from the top left and top right of the large hexagon (see Figure P3.7).

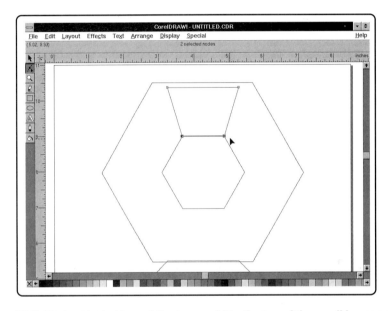

Figure P3.6. Fitting the bottom of the trapezoid to the top of the small hexagon.

Create a center cross hair using a vertical line and a horizontal line. Align it to the small hexagon (see Figure P3.8). Double-click on the trapezoid to invoke its center of rotation and move it to the center of the cross hair. In the Rotate dialog box, enter 60 degrees, click on the Leave Original check box, and then click on OK (see Figure P3.9).

Use the Repeat command to rotate the trapezoid five more times (see Figure P3.10). Reshape the hexagon from a "tie" shape to a triangular shape by adding a straight line where two of the trapezoids meet the hexagon's outline (see Figure P3.11). Place a slot in the top panel of the hexagon 1/4 inch from the top and center it.

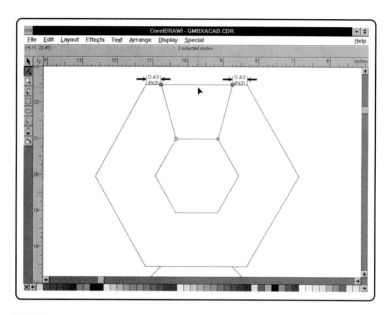

Figure P3.7. Fitting the top of the trapezoid to the top of the large hexagon.

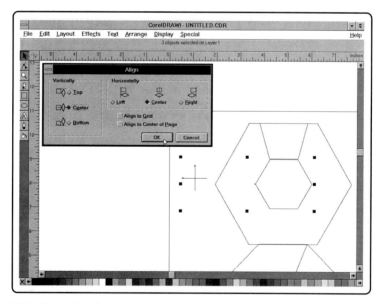

Figure P3.8. Centering the cross hair to the small hexagon.

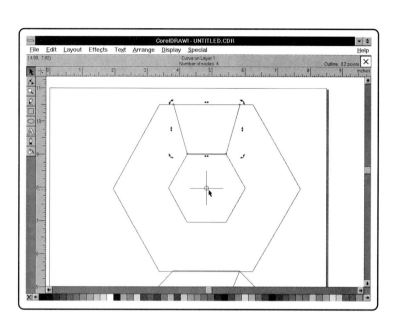

Figure P3.9. Moving the trapezoid's center of rotation.

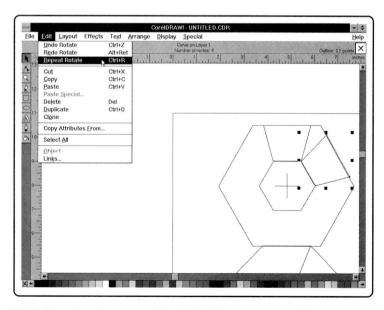

Figure P3.10. Rotating the trapezoid with the Repeat command.

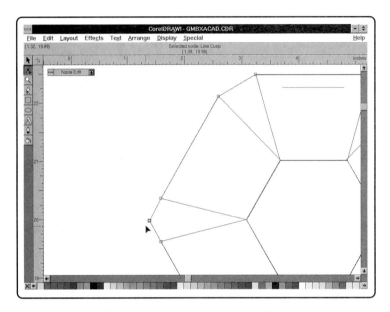

Figure P3.11. Reshaping from a "tie" shape to a triangular shape.

Draw a line from one corner of the octagon to the other (see Figure P3.12). Rotate the line 45 degrees and click on the Leave Original check box. Repeat three more times. The octagon will lose two of its panels so that it can match up with the hexagon lid. Cut the panels away and rejoin the existing lines to form the new shape. (see Figures P3.13 and P3.14).

Combine and join a glue flap and the insert tab corresponding to the slot on the hexagon to the new shape. To create the glue flap use a thin rectangle, 3 inches long and 0.25 inch wide, and then convert it to curves (see Figures P3.15 and P3.16). Edit the two nodes closest to the shape to form a thin trapezoid (see Figures P3.17 and P3.18).

Next create the insert tab. Draw a rectangle and rotate it 45 degrees. Select it with the ⚲ tool and turn it into a rounded corner rectangle (see Figures P3.19 and P3.20). See Skill Session 5, "The Shape Tool," for more information about rounded corner rectangles.

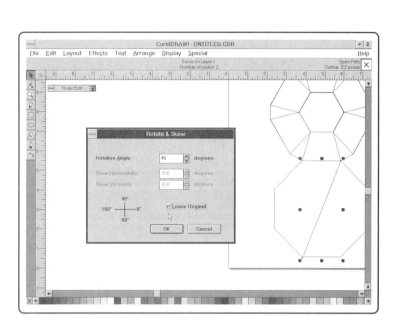

Figure P3.12. Rotating the line on the octagon.

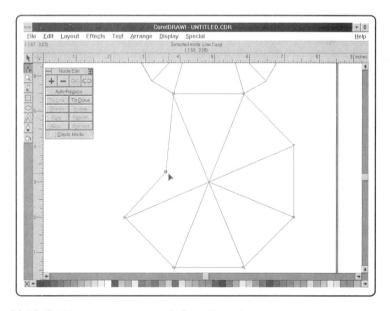

Figure P3.13. Cutting away two panels from the octagon.

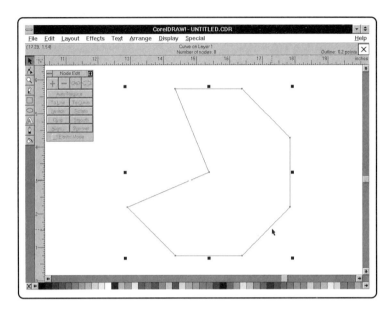

Figure P3.14. The newly formed shape.

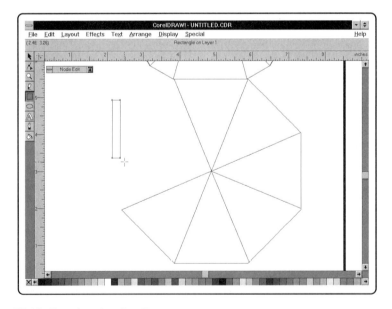

Figure P3.15. Creating the glue flap.

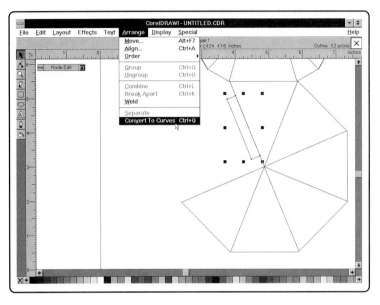

Figure P3.16. Converting the glue flap to curves.

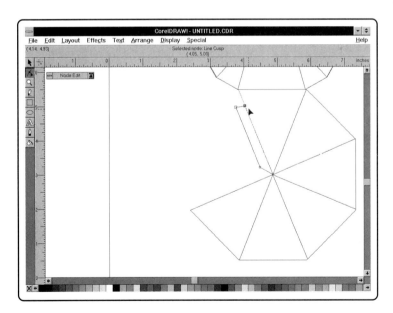

Figure P3.17. Editing the glue flap into another trapezoidal shape.

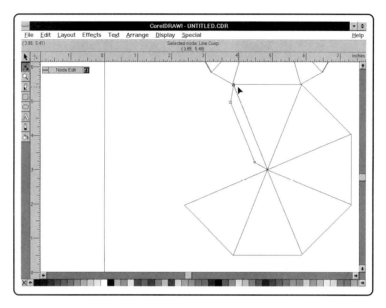

Figure P3.18. Editing and moving the nodes on the glue flap closer to the shape.

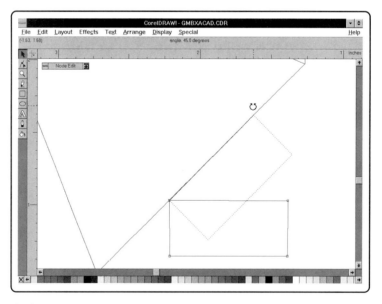

Figure P3.19. Rectangle rotated 45 degrees.

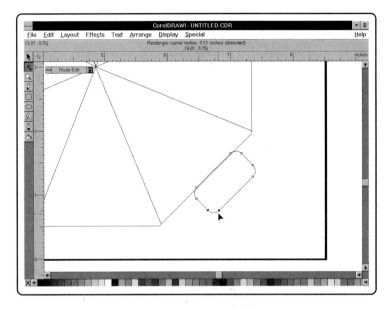

Figure P3.20. Rounded corners added to rectangle.

Then convert it to curves. Select the two nodes on the left side and delete them. Double-click on the curved line and select To Line in the Node Edit roll-up. Move the nodes back so they align with the octagon (see Figures P3.21 and P3.22).

Select the altered hexagon, octagon, glue flap, insert tab and slot, and combine them (use Ctrl-C for a keyboard shortcut). Break apart and rejoin specific nodes to end up with a shape similar to a question mark (see Figure P3.23). This is the die-cut for the gem box.

Use the Layers roll-up to make a new layer called "Die-cut." Move all necessary elements to this layer (see Figure P3.24). For more information about layers, see Skill Session 28, "Layers."

Next, lay out the type, diamond logo, and company name. Place them on the top of the gem box and on every other panel of the cone-shaped bottom. You can indicate the type of jewelry for display in the box on the top of the lid. Create a layer called "Text" and move these elements there (see Figure P3.25).

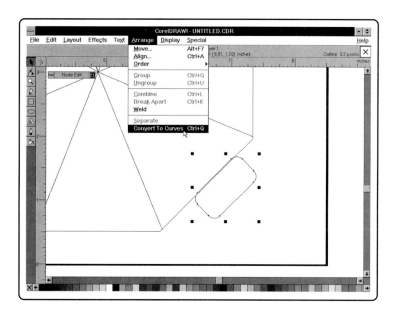

Figure P3.21. Convert rectangle to curves.

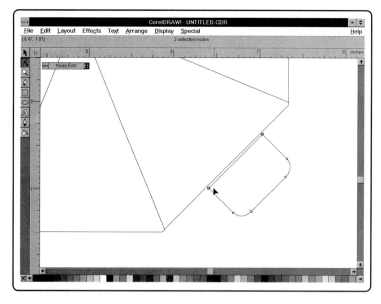

Figure P3.22. Realigning the nodes with the octagon.

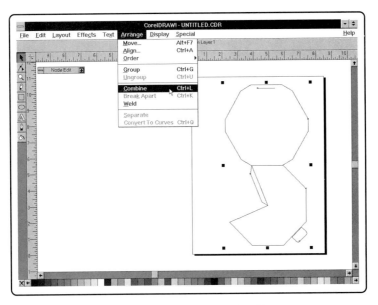

Figure P3.23. Selected elements combined to form the die-cut.

Figure P3.24. The Layers roll-up.

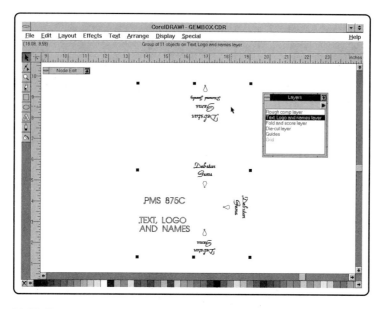

Figure P3.25. Type, logos, and names for the Text layer.

By using various elements, you can create the separate layers a printer or service bureau may require to produce the gem box. Here are the gem box's required layers:

- The Die-cut (see Figure P3.26).
- The Fold and Score (see Figure P3.27).
- The Text (see Figure P3.28).
- The Rough comp (see Figure P3.29). The rough comp serves as a guideline so you know what to expect the finished gem box to look like.

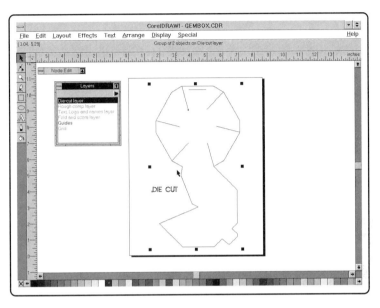

Figure P3.26. The Die-cut layer.

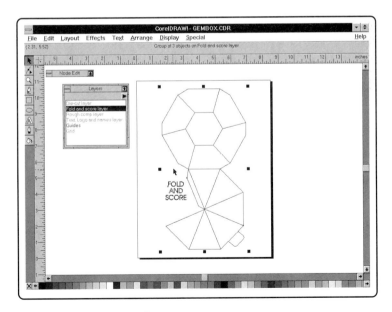

Figure P3.27. The Fold and score layer.

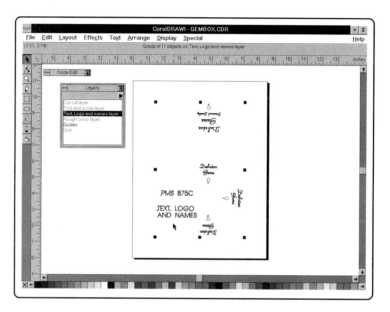

Figure P3.28. The Text layer.

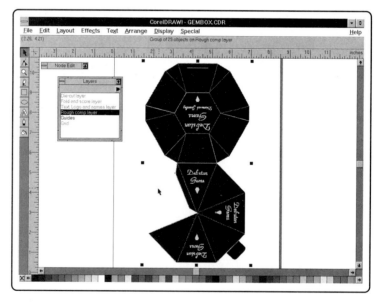

Figure P3.29. The Rough comp layer.

Project

4

Polygons and Stars

One of Corel Draw's missing features is the ability to easily create polygons and stars that are perfectly sized and shaped. This project will show you how to easily create them by using carefully created guidelines in conjunction with multiple layers.

The first step in creating these shapes is to drag horizontal and vertical guidelines onto the page that intersect somewhere near the center as shown in Figure P4.1.

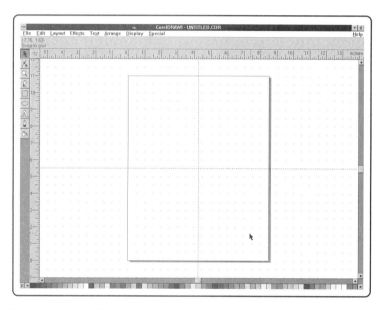

Figure P4.1. Initial guidelines.

The next step is to choose the ⌁ tool so that lines may be drawn easily by dropping points at the appropriate locations. Using this tool, draw a horizontal line with three nodes. The first node should be at the intersection of the two initial guidelines, the next node should be approximately two inches to the right and the last node an additional one inch to the right. Of course, these measurements are purely arbitrary for the purposes of this project. In the future, feel free to adjust these numbers to get just the right shape. Figure P4.2 shows the line just created.

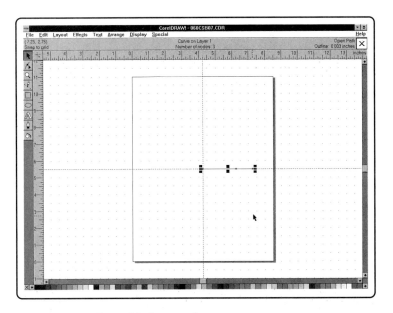

Figure P4.2. Beginning line with three nodes.

Click on the line twice so that the Rotate and Skew handles are showing. The center of the line will be its center of rotation. Drag the center of rotation so that it sits on the left end of the line. Now with the line selected, choose Effects Rotate & Skew. Enter a value of 30 for the Rotation Angle and select the Leave Original check box. This will create a second copy of the line that is rotated 30 degrees from the original. Now use Edit Repeat (Ctrl-R) to repeat this process 10 more times. There should now be 12 lines showing on the page at perfectly spaced 30-degree angles, as shown in Figure P4.3.

Marquee-select all the lines. The status bar should read "12 objects selected." Move them to the Guides layer by choosing Move To in the Layers roll-up and then selecting the Guides layer. They should all have changed to the Guides color (normally blue) and become dotted lines.

Choose the $\mathcal{P}$ tool and use it to draw a line with nodes at the end of each guideline. After drawing the lines, there should be a 12-sided polygon, as shown in Figure P4.4.

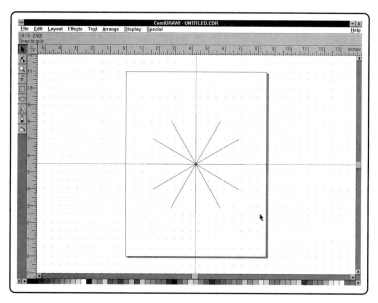

Figure P4.3. Twelve perfectly spaced lines.

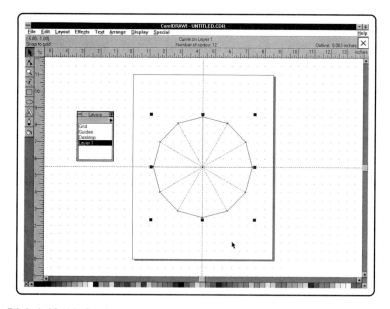

Figure P4.4. A 12-sided polygon.

Move the polygon aside or delete it completely. Choose the ℓ tool again and alternate putting nodes at the end node and then the middle node of the guidelines. When all nodes have been drawn, there should be a six-pointed star, as shown in Figure P4.5.

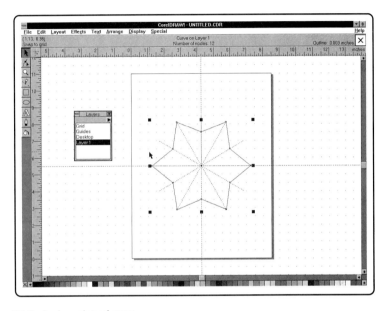

Figure P4.5. A six-pointed star.

By changing the location of the middle node on the original line drawn, the "pointiness" of the star can be controlled. Try creating the original guidelines from scratch, but this time make the first node one inch from the left end and the third node an additional two inches to the right. The resulting star should look like the one in Figure P4.6.

The number of sides on the polygon and/or number of points on the star can be controlled easily by changing the initial amount of rotation. The formulas for figuring the angle of rotation are as follows:

Angle of Rotation = 360 / Number of Sides

or

Angle of Rotation = 360 / (Number of Points × 2)

659

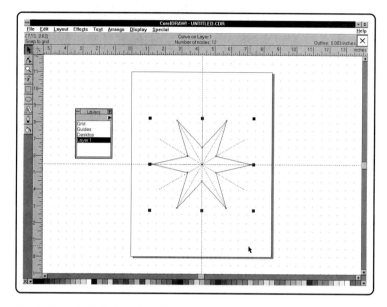

Figure P4.6. The modified six-pointed star

Do some experimenting with these techniques to create more objects like those shown in Figure P4.7.

Figure P4.7. More polygons and stars.

Ortho To Iso

Many times it is necessary to create a realistic three-dimensional drawing, yet Corel Draw does not provide any way to automatically do this as in CAD packages. This does not mean that it cannot be done. Unfortunately, it means a little more work.

The following instructions explain how to take the front, side, and top views of an object and combine them into a three-dimensional object. The instructions for views of both 30 and 45 degrees are included.

The first step in this process is to create the three orthographic views which are going to be combined into the three-dimensional object. That is, the views should all be drawn as a flat view. For the purposes of this illustration, three squares will be created with the letters *F, S,* and *T* on them to indicate front, side, and top. These rectangles will be combined to form a cube. While this is a fairly simple illustration, the same techniques can be used to create a very complicated drawing. Figure P5.1 shows the three objects before any transformations.

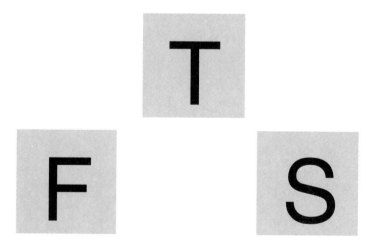

Figure P5.1. The three orthographic views of the object.

Stretch the front and side views horizontally by the cosine of the angle of rotation (86.6 percent for a 30-degree view or 70.7 percent for a 45-degree view). Figure P5.2 shows an example of the 30-degree view.

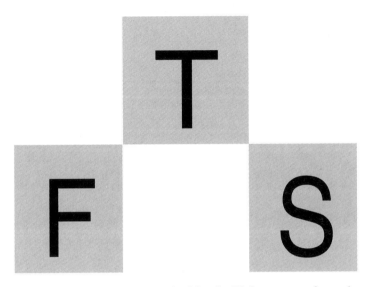

Figure P5.2. Side and front views stretched for the 30-degree transformation.

Now rotate the top view by 45 degrees. This step remains the same regardless of the view chosen. Figure P5.3 shows the objects after having rotated the top view.

Now skew the front view by the negative amount of the view chosen (either −30 or −45 degrees). Skew the side view by the amount of the view chosen (either 30 or 45 degrees). Figure P5.4 shows the objects after being skewed by −30 and 30 degrees respectively.

The top side should be left alone if this is the 45-degree view. For the 30-degree view, it should be stretched 123 percent horizontally and 71 percent vertically. Figure P5.5 shows the view after the transformations for the 30-degree view.

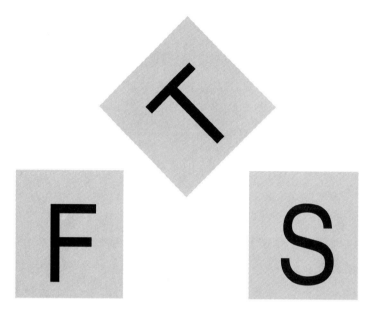

Figure P5.3. Top view rotated by 45 degrees.

Figure P5.4. Front and side views skewed.

Figure P5.5. Top view after having been transformed.

Now, assemble all the pieces and the object is complete. Figure P5.6 shows the object after assembling the pieces.

While these instructions are great for objects that have no thickness, they need to be slightly altered for objects whose sides have a thickness. A clone of that side after transformation would need to be created and moved an appropriate distance along the side to create the appropriate compound object. Figure P5.7 shows an example of a more complicated object created using this method.

Figure P5.6. The completed cube.

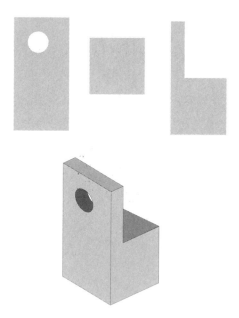

Figure P5.7. A more advanced three-dimensional object.

6

Landscape

Creating a painting in Corel Draw is no different in many ways than painting on canvas with traditional painting tools. You begin with the background and continue painting to the foreground. The nice thing about using Corel Draw is that if you forgot to put something in the background after you have already started painting the foreground, you can put something new in the background by using the Order command in the Arrange menu.

This lesson in painting a landscape takes you step by step until the painting is completed—right down to the frame.

1. Click Page Setup in the Layout menu and select Letter paper size and Landscape orientation.

2. Draw a rectangle across the top half of the page and fill with a fountain fill, using White at the bottom and Baby Blue at the top (see Figure P6.1).

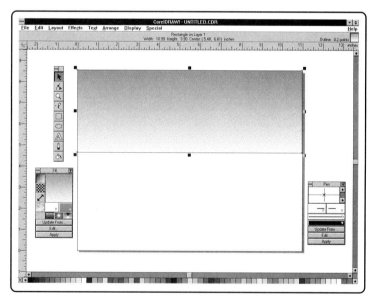

Figure P6.1. Using a fountain fill to create the sky.

You use White because you want to show a natural sky effect. The lighter color at the bottom represents the atmosphere that is present in nature. You will be using this technique when you draw the mountains as well.

3. With your sky rectangle still selected, click the top-center handle and drag a mirror image of the sky until you reach the bottom of the page. Hold down the secondary mouse button and release the primary mouse button to leave the original behind. You can accomplish this duplicate action by hitting the plus (+) key before releasing the primary mouse button (see Figure P6.2). Remove the outlines from both objects.

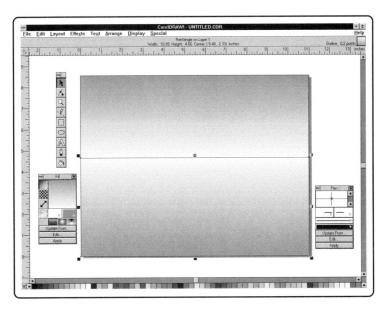

Figure P6.2. Mirroring the sky.

4. With the ℓ tool, draw a freehand shape of the background mountains. Your shape will be made up of curves so that you can reshape your mountain with the Shape tool if you are not satisfied with your first effort.

Corel*NOTE!*

Don't worry about getting your lines to line up exactly with the sides of
the paper. They will be covered up when you add the frame.

Fill your mountains with a fountain fill, with White at the bottom
and Deep Navy Blue at the top. Again, you are creating atmosphere
at the bottom of your mountains by using White at the bottom of
the fill (see Figure P6.3).

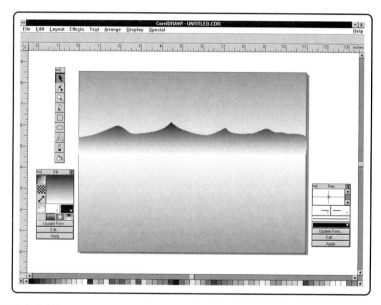

Figure P6.3. Adding mountains.

5. Make a duplicate of your mountains by selecting them and dragging the center of the mountains downward so that they overlap
   the original mountains (do not click a selection handle). Hold down
   the secondary mouse button before you release the primary mouse
   button as you did in Step 3 to leave the original. Use the ↙ tool and
   reshape your second range of mountains so that they look different
   from the first.

Fill your second range of mountains with a fountain fill of White to Twilight Blue as you did in Step 4.

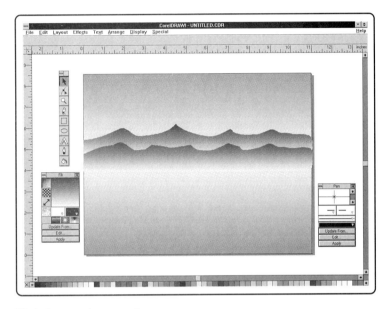

Figure P6.4. A second mountain range.

6. Repeat Step 5 and change the look of the third range of mountains with the ⋏ tool.

    Fill the third range of mountains with a fountain fill of Banana Yellow at the top and Ghost Green at the bottom (see Figure P6.5).

7. Repeat Step 5 again and shrink this fourth range of mountains down to the size indicated in Figure P6.6. Use the Stretch and Mirror command in the Effects menu. Select the object, click on a corner handle, and drag inward until you reach the size you want. Click on a side handle and hold down the Shift key. Drag to the side until you reach the desired shape. Fill this small range with a fountain fill of Banana Yellow at the top and Dark Green at the bottom.

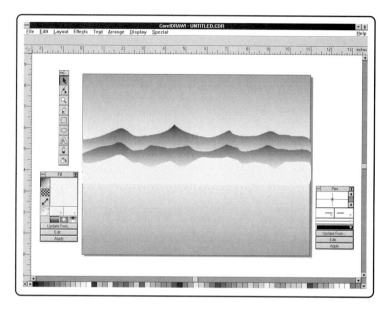

Figure P6.5. A third mountain range.

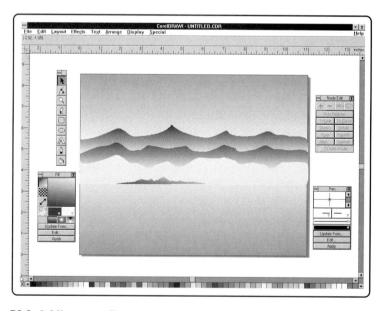

Figure P6.6. Adding a small mountain range.

8. Using the ✏ tool again, draw a freehand shape of a peninsula of trees jutting out from the right side of the page.

Fill this shape with a fountain fill of Banana Yellow at the top and Dark Green at the bottom (see Figure P6.7).

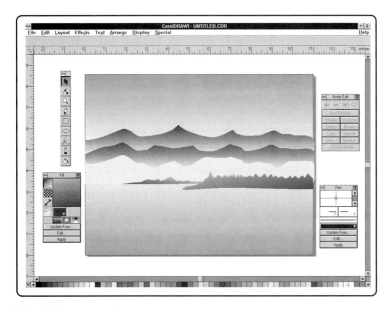

Figure P6.7. Adding some trees.

9. Either draw a new peninsula of trees on the left side of the page or make a duplicate mirror image of the first trees you did in Step 8. Place this second peninsula lower on the page than the first to add more depth to the painting.

Fill this second peninsula with the same colors as Step 8 (see Figure P6.8).

10. Using the ✏ tool, draw a freehand shape indicating a land mass starting at the base of the left peninsula and ending at the bottom of the page.

Fill this object with a fountain fill of Dark Green at the top and Banana Yellow at the bottom (see Figure P6.9).

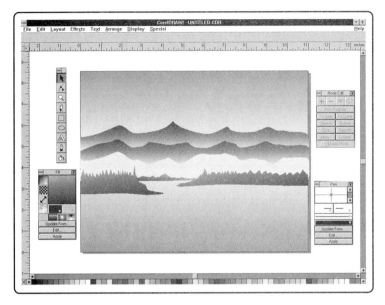

Figure P6.8. More trees.

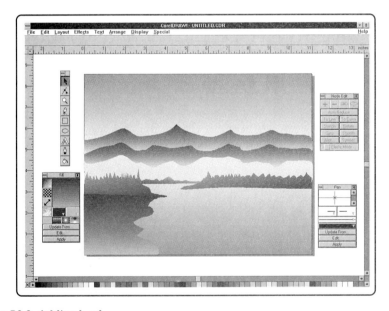

Figure P6.9. Adding land.

11. Draw another freehand shape on the right side of your painting, indicating a foreground hillside.

   Fill this shape with a fountain fill of Light Yellow at the top and Sea Green at the bottom. Click in the middle of the fountain fill preview box and change the angle of the fountain fill a slight bit to the left (see Figure P6.10).

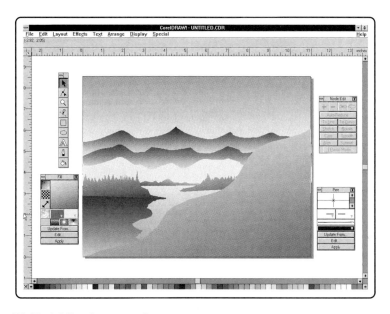

Figure P6.10. Adding foreground.

12. Import an animal or another object of choice from your Clip Art directory, using the Import command in the File menu.

   When the imported object appears, shrink it to an appropriate size by dragging on one of the corner handles, or resize it by using the Stretch & Mirror command in the Effects menu. Place the object to the left of the center on the hillside (see Figure P6.11).

13. You are now ready to put the finishing touch to your painting by adding a frame.

   Using the rulers as a guide, draw a rectangle that fills the page area within 1/2 inch of the sides and top and 1 inch from the bottom.

Draw another rectangle that fills the entire page. Select the two rectangles and combine them using the Combine command in the Arrange menu. You have just created a mask that allows the underlying painting to show through. Color the mask with a fill of Baby Blue.

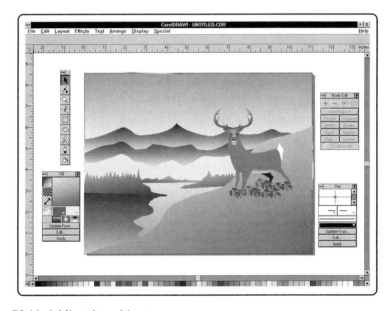

Figure P6.11. Adding the subject.

Congratulations! you have just completed a painting in Corel Draw. The completed painting is shown in Figure P6.12.

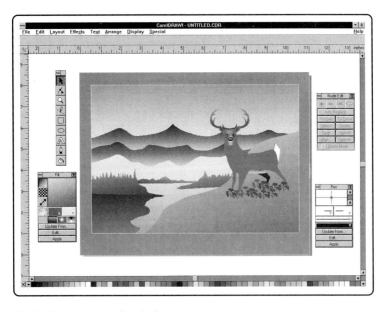

Figure P6.12. The completed painting.

7

Gallery

Creating perspective drawings is easy to do using just a few of the effects in Corel Draw. Achieving the appearance of three dimensions and form requires creating the illusion of space through the use of light, shadow, size, and perspective. As always, a painting or drawing begins with the background and continues to the foreground. The nice thing about using Corel Draw is that you can put something in the background as an afterthought without starting all over.

Figure P7.1 depicts a scene in an art gallery. This lesson will help you create the scene step by step until the drawing is completed right down to the frame. Refer to the finished drawing as you go through the steps to help you understand the creative process. The first two steps will be creating the floor and the back wall. The third step is to create the second wall group. From there you will create the right side wall and give it perspective. The next step is to draw the third wall on the left. The final wall is created in the sixth step.

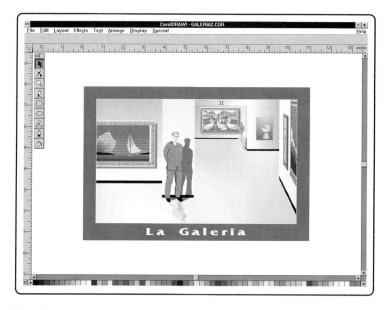

Figure P7.1. The original drawing.

Before beginning the drawing set your page size as Horizontal Letter (8 1/2×11).

1. With the ☐ tool, draw a rectangle across the full length of the page starting at the bottom to approximently three quarters of the way up.

2. Fill the rectangle with the texture fill Swirls from the Styles texture library in the Fill roll-up. With the rectangle still selected, click on the Edit button in the roll-up and change the color of the Swirls texture to White and 20-percent Gray. This color scheme will represent a marble floor (see Figure P7.2).

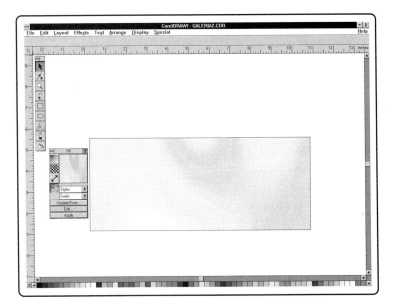

Figure P7.2. Creating the floor.

3. Draw another rectangle across the full length of the page starting at the top and ending just beyond the top of the first rectangle. Fill this rectangle with a horizontal fountain fill of 30-percent Gray to White running from left to right. This will be the back wall (see Figure P7.3). The shading will change later.

4. Draw a narrow rectangle to form a header wall on the top, beginning approximately at the center and finishing on the right side. Shade this rectangle with a horizontal fountain fill of 20-percent Gray to White. This shape will be shortened on the right later to adjust the lighting (see Figure P7.4).

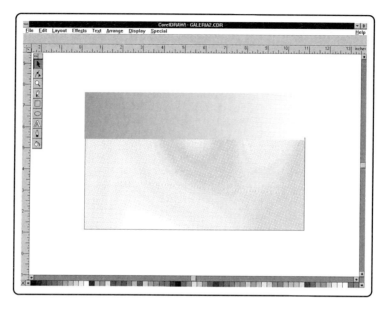

Figure P7.3. Creating the back wall.

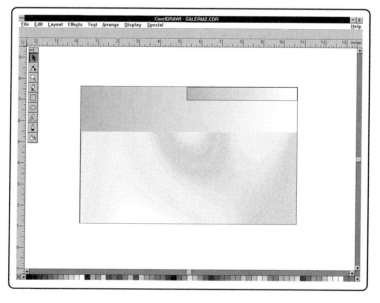

Figure P7.4. Creating the header wall.

5. Draw another rectangle to form a second wall. Bring the bottom down below the junction of the back wall and floor enough so that it creates the illusion of space between it and the back wall. Shade the wall with a horizontal fountain fill of White to 20-percent Gray (see Figure P7.5).

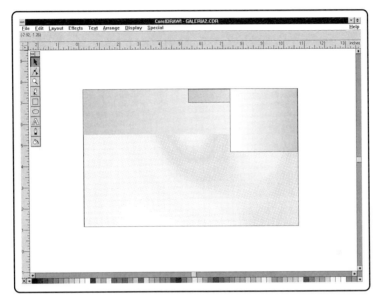

Figure P7.5. Creating a second wall.

6. Draw a small vertical rectangle at the end of the wall you just cre-ated. Start at the bottom of the wall and end at the bottom of the header wall you created in Step 4. Using the Perspective effect, drag upward with the ⚲ tool on the lower left node to give per-spective to the end wall. Shade the wall with a vertical fountain fill of 20-percent Gray to 10-percent Gray at the top (see Figure P7.6).

7. Draw a long rectangle from top to bottom on the right side. Using the Perspective effect again, drag upward on the lower-left node to a point on the page that gives the illusion of space between it and the second wall in Step 5. You may have to use the selection handles to shorten the width of the wall depending on how wide you draw this wall. Shade the wall with a horizontal fountain fill of White to 10-percent Gray (see Figure P7.7).

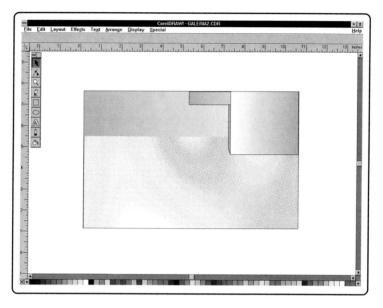

Figure P7.6. Creating a side wall using Perspective.

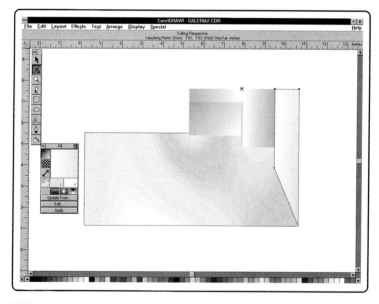

Figure P7.7. Adding the right end wall using Perspective.

8. Now let's draw the wall on the front left. Draw a wide rectangle beginning at the top and ending approximently three quarters of the way down. Fill this wall with a horizontal fountain fill of 20-percent Gray and White (see Figure P7.8).

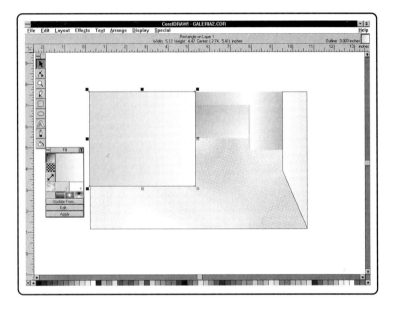

Figure P7.8. Creating the front wall.

9. The last wall to draw is the end wall in the foreground. Draw another long rectangle beginning at the top and ending below the front wall in Step 8. This will create another illusion of depth to the drawing. Fill this wall with a vertical fountain fill of White to 10-percent Gray (see Figure P7.9).

At this point, select all the objects on the screen and remove the outlines by clicking the X icon in the Outline dialog box, accessed through the Outline tool in the Tool Box.

Before going on to Step 10, you need to shorten and change the lighting on the back wall and also shorten the header wall.

First, click on the back wall and drag the left middle selection handle to the right until the left side lines up with the right edge of the front wall in

Step 6. With the wall still selected, edit the fountain fill and reverse the direction of the fill so that it runs from White on the left to 20-percent Gray on the right.

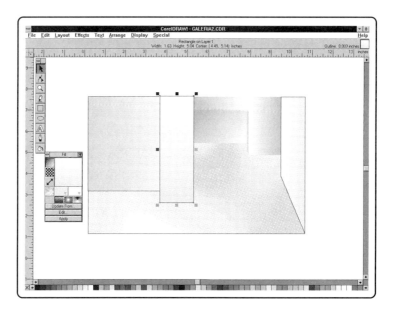

Figure P7.9. Creating the foreground end wall.

Next, click on the header wall and drag the middle right selection handle to the left until the right side lines up with the left side of the second wall you created in Step 5. You do not need to change the direction of the fountain fill in the header.

10. Add the paintings on the walls. Use drawings and paintings you have created in the past, or use clip art for your paintings.

   Using the Import Command in the File menu, import your paintings one at a time. Resize each painting to fit each wall. The paintings you place on the right-hand wall will need to have the Perspective effect applied to them just as you did with the wall. One additional effect to add is the baseboards on each wall. These are drawn with basic rectangles and filled with Black (see Figure P7.10).

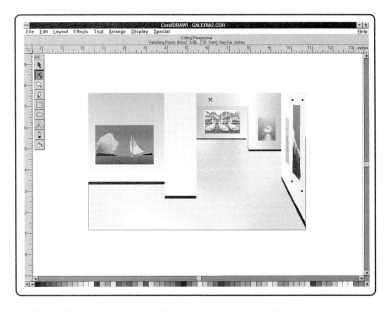

Figure P7.10. Adding pictures, baseboards, and perspective.

11. Figure P7.11 shows an enlarged view of a vase on a pedestal. The vase was created using Power Lines in Skill Session 54. The pedestal was created using two rectangles filled with the same texture as the floor. Create your own vase or suitable object for a pedestal and place it next to the back end wall of your drawing. This use of a free-standing object provides a further illusion of depth in your drawing. Create small shadows at the base of the pedestal and against the end wall using rectangles again. Fill the shadow shapes with 50-percent Black.

12. Put picture frames around the paintings on the wall. Create your own or use clip art. The frames used in this drawing were taken from Image by McCormick's Potpourri Clip Art found on the companion CD included with this book. Import the clip art just as you did the paintings and resize them for each painting. Don't forget to use perspective again on the paintings on the right. Instead of putting a frame on the seashell painting, two shaded rectangles were used to give the illusion of a recessed aquarium (see Figure P7.12).

Figure P7.11. Adding a freestanding object to create depth.

Figure P7.12. Adding picture frames.

690

13. It's time to add a gallery guard. The guard is again imported clip art. In order not to have the guard look pasted on, make a duplicate of the guard and fill the entire shape with a fill of 60-percent Black to create a shadow on the wall behind him. Using the Order command in the Arrange menu, move the shadow Back One so that it is behind the guard. Offset the shadow to the right. Using the ⬀ tool, draw the small shadows on the floor at the guard's feet.

    Next, make a mirror image of the guard to create the illusion of a reflection on the floor. Adding reflections, when the situation calls for it, adds a greater appearance of depth to your drawings. To create the reflected image, make another duplicate of the guard using the Stretch and Mirror command in the Effects menu. Choose Vertical mirror and click on the Leave Original check box before you click OK. With the ⬀ tool, drag your new mirrored shape downward to line up the feet with the feet of the original guard. Using the Order command in the Arrange menu, move the reflection Back One. With the reflected object still selected, drag on the bottom center handle of the highlight box and shorten the reflection as shown in Figure P7.13. With the reflection still selected click again on a handle to change the handles to arrows. Use the bottom center arrow and drag to the right so the reflection is pointing toward the center of the entire scene (reflections always come to the viewers eye, sort of a reverse perspective). Fill this reflected image of the guard with a fill of approximently 15-percent Black. You will probably need to adjust this percentage until it looks correct in relationship to the contrasting floor.

14. Add a frame. Creating the frame involves using the Masking technique. Draw a rectangle covering an entire image area. Using the rulers, draw another rectangle 1/2 inch in on all sides of the first rectangle. Select both rectangles and combine them using the Combine command in the Arrange menu. You have now created a frame around the scene. Fill the frame with a color of choice and add a title at the bottom (see Figure P7.14).

Figure P7.13. Creating the gaurd with shadows and reflection.

Figure P7.14. Creating a frame for the drawing.

8

Layout for Business Cards, Letterheads, and Envelopes

Corel Draw has a few different ways to ease the setup of business card, letterhead, and envelope layout. The four examples we will be discussing are: Grid Setup, Guidelines, Freehand Drawing, and Page Setup.

Grid Setup

Go to the Layout Menu and select Grid Setup (see Figure P8.1). In the Grid Setup dialog box (see Figure P8.2) set the Grid Frequency at 4 inches horizontal and 4 inches vertical, enable the Show Grid and Snap To Grid options, and then press the OK button.

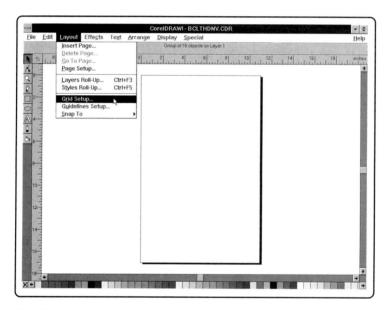

Figure P8.1. The Layout menu with Grid Setup highlighted.

With the grid on (see Figure P8.3), select the Rectangle tool and draw a rectangle that is 3.5 inches wide and 2 inches high (see Figure P8.4). You can draw the envelope and letterhead shapes using the same method.

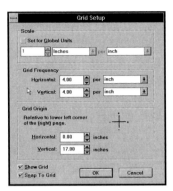

Figure P8.2. The Grid Setup dialog box.

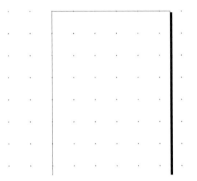

Figure P8.3. The Show Grid enabled.

Guidelines

Pull two vertical guidelines onto the screen from your rulers.
Place them 3.5 inches apart. Pull down two horizontal guidelines
and place them 2 inches apart. With Snap To Guidelines enabled,
use the Rectangle tool to draw a business-card-sized rectangle in
the area between the guidelines (see Figure P8.5).

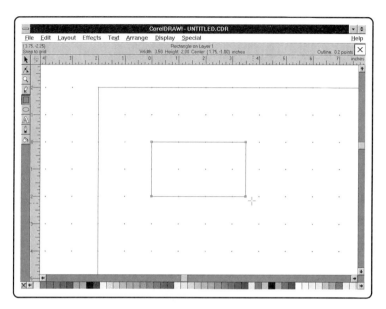

Figure P8.4. A business-card-sized rectangle drawn by snapping to grid.

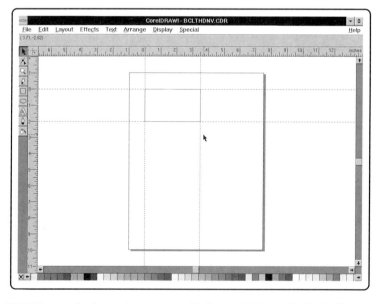

Figure P8.5. Rectangle drawn between guidelines with Snap To Guidelines enabled.

Freehand Drawing

Select the ☐ tool. Watch the status line as it tells you the width and height of the rectangle being drawn. When you arrive at 3.5 inches in height and 2 inches in width, stop drawing the rectangle. You can also use the rulers to guide you when you are drawing freehand (see Figure P8.6).

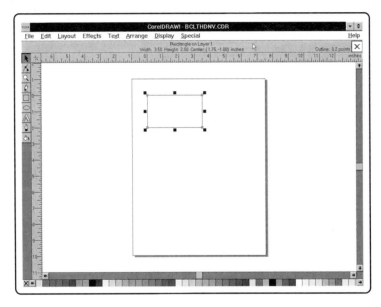

Figure P8.6. Rectangle drawn freehand.

Page Setup

Invoke the Page Setup dialog box from the Layout menu or by double-clicking the page border on your screen. In the Page Setup dialog box, under Paper Size, select Letter. Press the Add Page Frame button (see Figure P8.7). Change the Page Size and select Envelope #10. Press the Add Page Frame button (see Figure P8.8). Once again, in the Paper Size list, select Custom. In the Width and Height section, type 3.5 and 2 respectively. Press the Add Page Frame Button (see Figure P8.9). You now have the three necessary shapes for your letterhead, envelope, or business card layout.

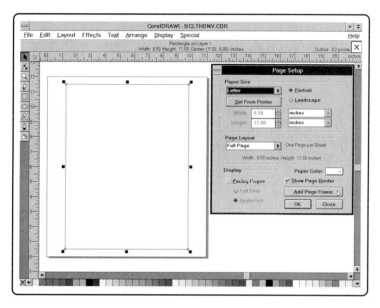

Figure P8.7. Grid Setup dialog box with Letter size frame added to the document.

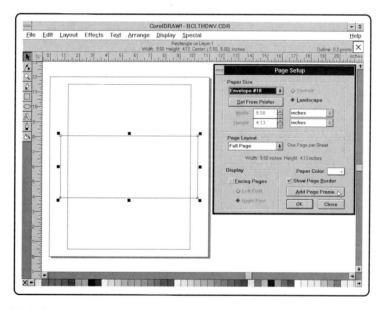

Figure P8.8. Grid Setup dialog box with Envelope #10 size frame added to the document.

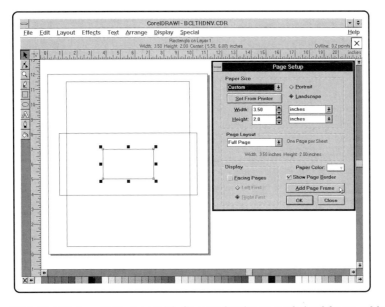

Figure P8.9. Grid Setup dialog box with Custom business-card-sized frame added to the document.

Corel NOTE!

Check with your local post office regarding the minimum postcard or envelope sizes and graphic element placement before finalizing your design.

Creating a Quick Border

To create borders for your letterhead you will want to select graphic elements from your existing logo or design. Select your graphic element, press and hold down the Ctrl key, pull the selected elements down, and click the secondary mouse button to leave the original. You can repeat this step by selecting Ctrl+R as often as you need for the area you wish to cover (see Figure P8.10).

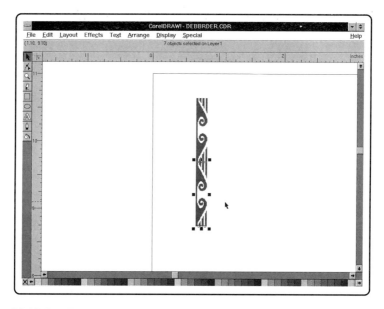

Figure P8.10. Duplicating elements to create a quick border.

Corel*NOTE!*

You can also pull the selected object to the left, right, or diagonally before you click the secondary mouse button to leave the original.

Business Card, Letterhead, and Envelope Samples

As shown in Figures P8.11 and P8.12, borders and logos can be used in various layout setups. See the color insert in this book.

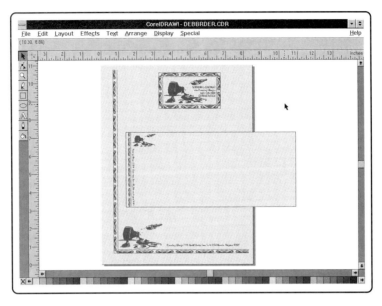

Figure P8.11. Running Changes' business card, letterhead, and envelope.

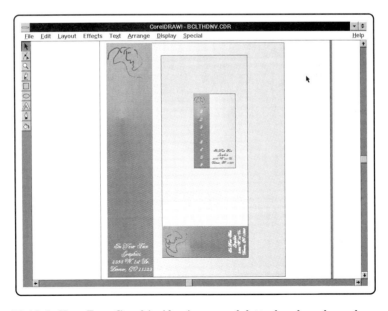

Figure P8.12. In Your Face Graphics' business card, letterhead, and envelope.

Part

Command References

Part V

1

File Menu Commands

The File menu includes commands for opening new documents and new documents from templates, as well as existing files. Saving, importing, exporting, and inserting objects are found in this menu, too. Printing and exiting the current Corel Draw session is also done here (see Figure CR1.1).

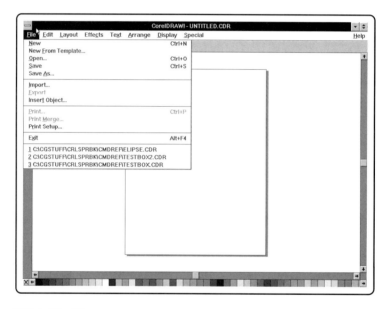

Figure CR1.1. The File menu.

New

Select this option to create a new file using the default settings.

Selection

Keyboard shortcut: Alt+F, N

Pointing device: **F**ile, **N**ew

706

Usage

Select various commands from this menu.

1. Select New from the File menu to start a new document (see Figure CR1.2).

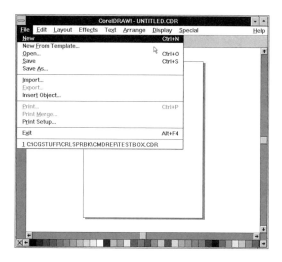

Figure CR1.2. Selecting New from the File menu.

New From Template

Select this option for the Load Template dialog box.

Selection

Keyboard shortcut: Alt+F, F

Pointing device: File, New From Template

Usage

1. Select New From Template from the File menu.
2. Select the template you want (see Figure CR1.3). For more information about templates, see "Layout Menu Commands" in the Command References.

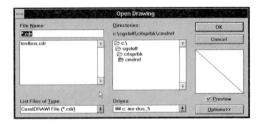

Figure CR1.3. The Load Template dialog box. Select File, New From Template to change to a different template.

Open

This command opens an existing file.

Selection

Keyboard shortcut: Alt+F, O or Ctrl+O

Pointing device: **F**ile, **O**pen

Usage

1. Select Open from the File menu.
2. Choose the directory to open a file from and the type of file you want to open (see Figure CR1.4).
3. Select the file to open.

Figure CR1.4. The Open Drawing dialog box. Select File Open to select a different file.

Save

Select this option to save the current drawing to the hard drive or a drive of your choice.

Selection

Keyboard shortcut: Alt+F, S or Ctrl+S

Pointing device: **F**ile, **S**ave

Usage

1. Open a new Corel Draw file.
2. Create elements that are needed in the file.
3. To save current placement and settings, select Save from the File menu.
4. In the Save Drawing dialog box, give the file a name and directory (see Figure CR1.5).
5. Under the Image Header section, select the Image Header Type. This allows you to later preview a file before you open it.
6. Click the OK button.

You can save Corel Draw 4 files as Corel Draw 3.0 files. Typefaces not supplied in Corel 3.0 should be converted to curves. Some affects, such as conical fill, do not work in Corel 3.0.

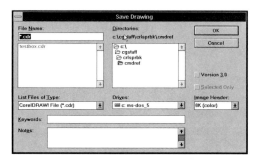

Figure CR1.5. The Save Drawing dialog box. Selecting File, Save lets you save the file in which you are working.

Save As

To save an existing file under a new name, choose Save As from the File menu.

Selection

Keyboard shortcut: Alt+F, A

Pointing device: **F**ile, Save **As**

Usage

1. Open an existing file.
2. To create a new version of the same file for editing, select Save As from the File menu.
3. In the Save Drawing dialog box, give the file a new name and/or directory. This allows you to make minor or major changes to the new file while still retaining the original file intact.
4. Click the OK button.

Import

Select this option from the File menu for a selection of files to import. Corel can import over 31 kinds of file formats, including .EPS, .CDR, and .PCX.

Selection

Keyboard shortcut: Alt+F, I

Pointing device: **F**ile, **I**mport

Usage

1. Select Import from the File menu.
2. In the Import dialog box, select the type of file you wish to import from the List File of Type pull-down menu (see Figure CR1.6).
3. Change directories if necessary.
4. Locate the file you wish to import.
5. Click the OK button.

Figure CR1.6. The File Import dialog box. Select File Import to bring up the Import dialog box where you can select the type of file you want to import.

About Import Filter

Select this option from the Import dialog box for information about the current type of filter or file extension that you have selected to import. For more information about Import filters, see Skill Session 40.

Selection

Keyboard shortcut: Alt+F, I, A

Pointing device: **F**ile, **I**mport, **A**bout

Usage

1. Select Import from the File menu.
2. In the Import dialog box, select the type of file you wish to import from the List File of Type pull-down menu.
3. Click on the About button.
4. The About Import Filter dialog box appears, displaying current information on the selected file import filter (see Figure CR1.7).
5. Click OK.

Figure CR1.7. The About Import Filter dialog box displays current filter information.

711

Import, Mosaic

Select this option to invoke CorelMOSAIC!, a file-viewing module provided with Corel Draw. CorelMOSAIC! is a visual file selector. It lets you
see the files you are looking at before you open them. This helps if you
have forgotten the name of the file and can only recognize it visually.
For more information about CorelMOSAIC!, see Skill Session 49.

Selection

Keyboard shortcut: Alt+F, I, Alt+M

Pointing device: File, Import, Mosaic

Usage

1. Select Import from the File menu.
2. In the Import dialog box, press the Mosaic button. This brings up
   the CorelMOSAIC! application (see Figure CR1.8).
3. Search through various directories and file formats to view files.
4. Select the desired file and double-click it to bring it up. Mosaic
   serves as a visual file locator.

*Figure CR1.8. The CorelMOSAIC! application. Select CorelMOSAIC! to view files
before opening them.*

Export

Select this option from the File menu for a selection of files to export.
Corel Draw can export over 21 kinds of file formats, including .PCX,
.BMP, and .DXF.

Selection

Keyboard shortcut: Alt+F, E

Pointing device: **F**ile, **E**xport

Usage

1. Select Export from the File menu.
2. In the Export dialog box, select how you want your file or selected
   object to be exported from the List Files of Type pull-down menu
   (see Figure CR1.9).
3. Select a new directory if necessary.
4. Click OK.

*Figure CR1.9. The File Export dialog box. Selecting File Export brings up the Export
dialog box where you can convert your file to the new format you have selected.*

Different file export filters give you different options from which to
select. These options include color, black and white, grayscale, and so
on. For more information about export filters, see Skill Session 41.

About Export Filter

Select this option from the Export dialog box for information about the current type of filter or file extension that you have selected to export.

Selection

Keyboard shortcut: Alt+F, E, Alt+A

Pointing device: **F**ile, **E**xport, **A**bout

Usage

1. Select Export from the File menu.
2. In the Export dialog box, select the type of filter you wish to export to from the List Files of Type pull-down menu.
3. Click the About button. The About Export Filter dialog box appears, displaying current information on the selected file export filter (see Figure CR1.10).
4. Click OK.

Figure CR1.10. The About Export Filter dialog box displays current filter information.

Insert Object, Create New

Select this function to insert objects from various other applications. The Insert Object dialog box displays a list of object types from which you can select the object to insert into your document. The Create New setting is selected by default.

Selection

Keyboard shortcut: Alt+F, T

Pointing device: **F**ile, Inser**t** Object

Usage

1. Select Insert Object from the File menu.

2. In the Insert Object dialog box, choose the Object Type from the list. This will insert the selected object type into your Corel document (see Figure CR1.11).

3. Click OK.

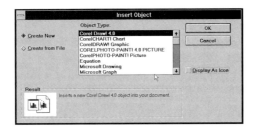

Figure CR1.11. The Insert Object dialog box showing the default Create New setting. Use the List Object Type for inserting the object you select into your document.

Insert Object, Create from File

Select this option to insert a file into your Corel Draw document.

Selection

Keyboard shortcut: Alt+F, T, F

Pointing device: **F**ile, Inser**t** Object, Create from **F**ile

Usage

1. Select Insert Object from the File menu. This will insert the contents of a file as an object into your document (see Figure CR1.12).

   You can later activate the application in which it was created by double-clicking the object.

2. Click OK.

Figure CR1.12. The Insert Object dialog box showing Create from File selected.

Insert Object, Create from File, Link

Select this function to insert the file's contents into your document and create a link to the source file.

Selection

Keyboard shortcut: Alt+F, T, Alt+F, L

Pointing device: **F**ile, Inser**t** Object, Create from **F**ile, **L**ink

Usage

1. Select Insert Object from the File menu. This will insert the contents of a file as an object into your document.

   You can later activate the application in which it was created by double-clicking the object.

   With Link enabled, you can edit the file in its original application, and it will automatically update itself in your document (see Figure CR1.13).

2. Click OK.

Figure CR1.13. The Insert Object dialog box with the Link option enabled.

Insert Object, Create from File, Browse

Select the Browse option to invoke the Browse dialog box. Here you can select the files and their types, as well as drives and directories.

Selection

Keyboard shortcut: Alt+F, T, Alt+F, B

Pointing device: **F**ile, Inser**t** Object, Create from **F**ile, **B**rowse

Usage

1. Select Insert Object from the File menu. This will insert the contents of a file as an object into your document.

   You can later activate the application in which it was created by double-clicking the object.

2. Click the Browse button. The Browse dialog box will appear (see Figure CR1.14). You can select filenames, directories, types of files, and drives in this dialog box.

3. Once you find the file for which you are looking, press OK.

Figure CR1.14. The Browse dialog box with files displayed.

Print

Select Print to invoke the Print dialog box. This command lets you print the current document as well as select which printer to use. You have several options for printing your document. The selections shown in Figure CR1.15 are for the IBM Proprinter X24. Different printers have their own specific dialog boxes. See Skill Session 42 for more information about printing.

Selection

Keyboard shortcut: Alt+F, P or Ctrl+P

Pointing device: File, Print

Usage

1. Select Print from the File menu.
2. In the Print dialog box, select from various options.
3. Once you have selected your options, press OK.

Different printers have different options available.

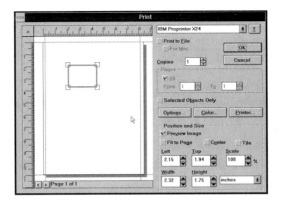

Figure CR1.15. The Print dialog box with options for the IBM ProPrinter X24.

Print Merge

Select the Print Merge command to bring up the Print Merge dialog box (see Figure CR1.16). This merges your drawing with a text file and sends it to print.

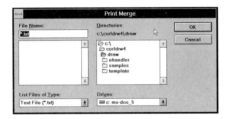

Figure CR1.16. The Print Merge dialog box.

Selection

Keyboard shortcut: Alt+F, M

Pointing device: **F**ile, Print **M**erge

Usage

1. Select Print Merge from the File menu.
2. In the Print Merge dialog box, select your text file.
3. Click OK.
4. The merged text file and your drawing will be sent to the printer.

Print Setup

The Print Setup dialog box (see Figure CR1.17) lets you select the default printer or a specific printer from a pull-down list. You can change the orientation of your paper from portrait to landscape or vice versa. You can change the size of the paper you are printing on as well as the source. The Options option varies with different printing devices.

Selection

Keyboard shortcut: Alt+F, R

Pointing device: File, Print Setup

Usage

1. Select Print Setup from the File menu.
2. Select either the Default Printer or a Specific Printer.
3. Change the orientation of your page.
4. Change your paper size and source.
5. Different options are available for different printers.
6. Click OK.

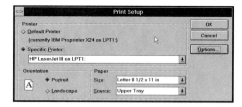

Figure CR1.17. The Print Setup dialog box.

Print Setup, Options

The Options dialog box shown in Figure CR1.18 is for HP LaserJet III on LPT1. This is the dialog box that allows you to change the default options.

Selection

Keyboard shortcut: Alt+F, R,O

Pointing device: File, Print Setup, Options

Usage

1. Select Print Setup from the File menu.
2. In the Print Setup dialog box, press the Options button.
3. In the Options dialog box, make the necessary changes required.
4. Click OK.
5. Different printers will have different options available.

Usage varies with different printers. Select this command to see what options are available to you.

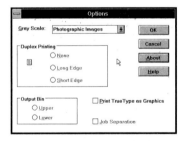

Figure CR1.18. The Options dialog box for the HP LaserJet III.

Print Setup, Options, About

This dialog box (see Figure CR1.19) contains information about the printer driver you are using. It includes the version of the driver that is currently in use.

Selection

Keyboard shortcut: Alt+F, R, O, A

Pointing device: File, Print Setup, Options, About

Usage

1. Select Print Setup from the File menu.
2. In the Print Setup dialog box, press the About button. In the About dialog box, information about the current printer driver is displayed.
3. Press OK.

Figure CR1.19. The About dialog box.

Exit

This command shuts down your current file and application (see Figure CR1.20).

Selection

Keyboard shortcut: Alt+F, X or Alt+F4

Pointing device: **F**ile, **E**xit

Usage

1. Select Exit from the File menu to exit the current Corel Draw session.

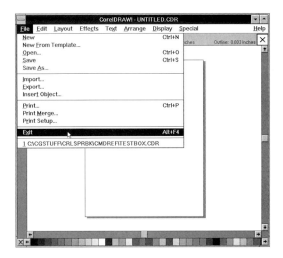

Figure CR1.20. The Exit selection of the File menu.

1, 2, 3, 4

Selecting 1, 2, 3, or 4 opens up previous Corel Draw documents in the order that you last worked on them. This function lists only four previous files at a time (see Figure CR1.21).

Selection

Keyboard shortcut: Alt+F; 1, 2, 3, or 4

Pointing device: File; 1, 2, 3, 4

Usage

1. In the File menu, select from any of up to 4 previous open documents.
2. Press on the number next to the document you wish to open.
3. This will open that document.

This opens previous CorelDRAW! files and bypasses the File Open command in the menu. This only works with previously opened files.

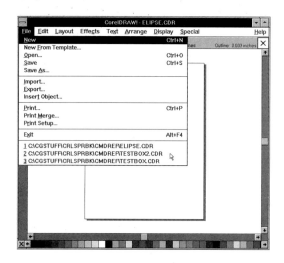

Figure CR1.21. The File menu's previous open file selection.

2

Edit Menu Commands

The Edit menu (see Figure CR2.1) provides selections for undoing, redoing, and repeating the last change you made. You can also cut, copy, paste, delete, duplicate, and clone. The commands Copy Attributes From, Select All, Object, and Links are also found here.

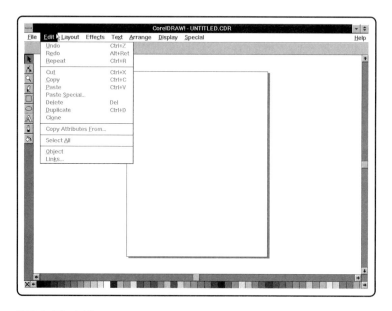

Figure CR2.1. The Edit menu.

Undo

Select this option to undo the last change you have made (see Figure CR2.2). You can have up to 99 levels of undo, but setting the levels of undo at 99 will cause Corel to use up more memory. If the application seems to be reacting slowly, change the undo levels to a smaller setting. See the "Special Menu Commands," "Preferences" in the Command References for more information.

You cannot Undo the following operations: any change of view (Zoom In, Zoom Out, and so on), any file operations (Open, Save, Import, and so on), and any selection operation (marquee-select, node select, and so on).

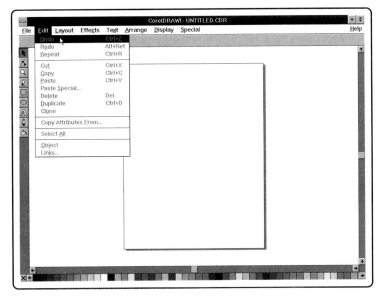

Figure CR2.2. Use the Edit Undo command to undo your last change.

Selection

Keyboard shortcut: Alt+E, U or Ctrl+Z, or Alt+Backspace

Pointing device: **E**dit, **U**ndo

Usage

1. Select Undo from the Edit menu. Objects do not need to be selected.

The object is now returned to its previous state before the last change.

2. Undo can be repeated up to 99 times. Levels are set in Preferences under the Special menu.

Edit Undo works only during the current session. Undo works with all object manipulations such as skew, fill, rotate, and so on.

If you select an object and change its fill, you can select Edit Undo to revert to the previous fill. The current fill of an object is shown in the upper right corner of the status line (see Figures CR2.3 through CR2.5).

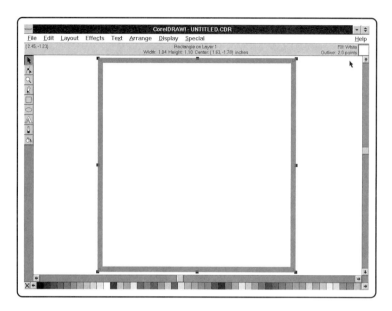

Figure CR2.3. A rectangle that has had its fill changed to White.

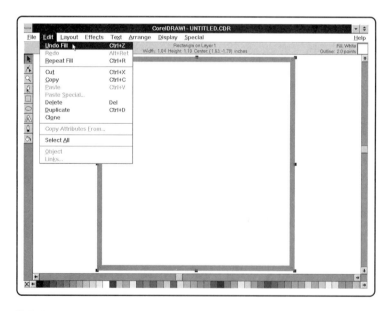

Figure CR2.4. The rectangle selected with the Edit menu showing Undo Fill (the Undo command undoes the last change made, in this case a fill).

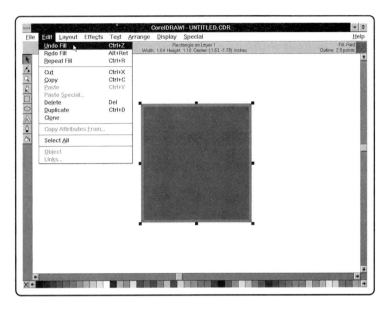

Figure CR2.5. The rectangle with its old fill of Red, shown after undoing the fill of White.

Redo

The Redo command (see Figure CR2.6) lets you redo the last changes you have made to your file, up to 99 levels. This command is available after selection of the Undo command. The Redo command changes according to the last affect applied (Redo Delete, Redo Fill, and so on).

Selection

Keyboard shortcut: Alt+E, E or Alt+Ret

Pointing device: Edit, Redo

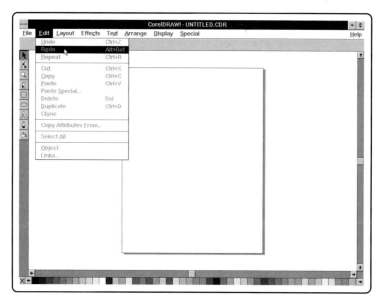

Figure CR2.6. Use the Edit Redo command to redo your last change.

Usage

1. Select Redo from the Edit menu.

2. The object(s) will change back to their previous position or attributes.

In Figures CR2.7 through CR2.9, a symbol has been manipulated by moving it from its initial position. Using the Redo command allows you to revert the symbol back to its initial position. This command is helpful when comparing various positions or attributes that are applied to an object.

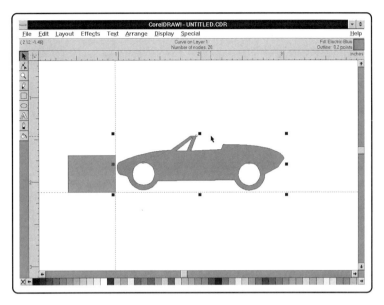

Figure CR2.7. A car from the Symbols roll-up that has been moved from below and to the right of the rectangle and is now placed above one of the grid lines.

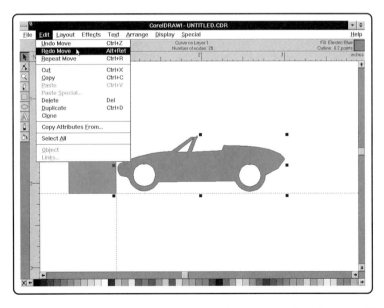

Figure CR2.8. The car symbol selected with the Edit menu pulled down and Redo highlighted.

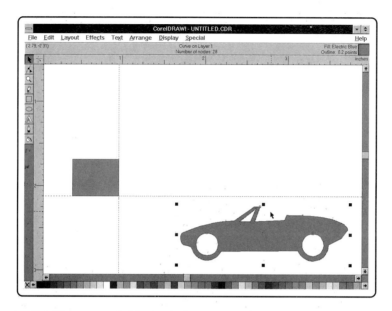

Figure CR2.9. The car symbol has now been moved back to its original position, below the grid line to the right of the rectangle. This command allows you to see if the new position is what you like and lets you revert to the old position and then back to the new position.

Repeat

Select this option (see Figure CR2.10) to repeat the last change you have made to your document. Use this command when repeating a change that you want to repeat exactly, such as moving an object several times the same distance. You can repeat as many times as you want.

Selection

Keyboard shortcut: Alt+E, R or Ctrl+R

Pointing device: **E**dit, **R**epeat

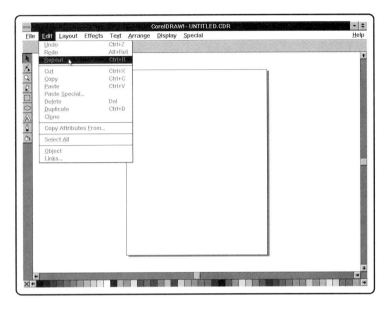

Figure CR2.10. The Edit Repeat command. To repeat the last change to an object, use this command.

Usage

1. Manipulate object(s) using fill, move, and so on.
2. Select the object(s) you wish to repeat attributes to.
3. Choose Repeat from the Edit menu.
4. The selected object(s) will now reflect the most recent command or action.

When using the Repeat command you can apply the last action to the current selected object(s) or other object(s) in your file.

You can use the Repeat command to create a simple border. The example shown is a letterhead created using this method. The dinosaur was selected and moved to the right while using the Leave Original option. This left the original dinosaur in position and created a duplicate in the new position. Repeating this step creates the border (see Figures CR2.11 through CR2.13).

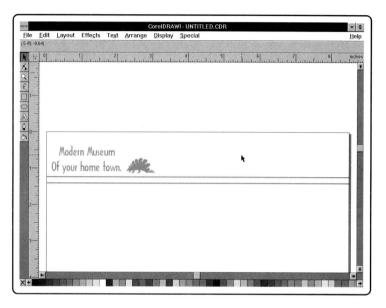

Figure CR2.11. A sample of letterhead for a museum.

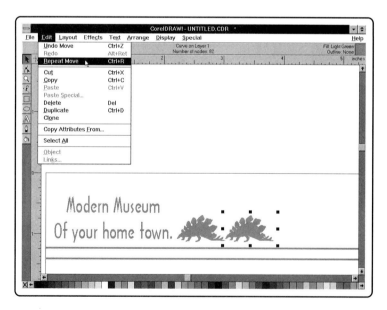

Figure CR2.12. The dinosaur on the letterhead is moved and the original is left behind.

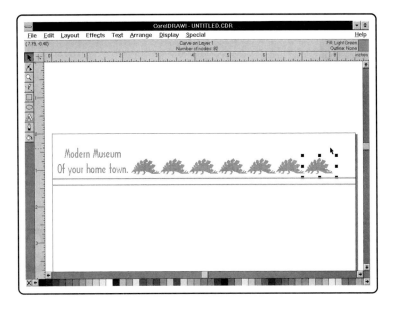

Figure CR2.13. The dinosaur is repeated to form a border on the letterhead.

Cut

Use this command (see Figure CR2.14) to cut an object from your document to the clipboard. This will remove the object from your document.

Selection

Keyboard shortcut: Alt+E, T or Ctrl+X

Pointing device: **E**dit, **C**ut

Usage

1. Select the object(s) you want to cut from your document.
2. Select Cut from the Edit menu.

3. The "CorelDRAW is Cutting" prompt appears on-screen.

4. The cut object is now placed onto the Windows clipboard.

The clipboard is a temporary area used to transfer information between Windows applications.

Figure CR2.14. Use the Edit Cut command to cut one or more objects from your file.

The example shown in Figures CR2.15 through CR2.17 displays two gems. One of them is selected and cut from the file. The CorelDRAW! is Cutting prompt box appears on-screen. The selected gem is then placed onto the Windows clipboard and the file reflects only one gem remaining.

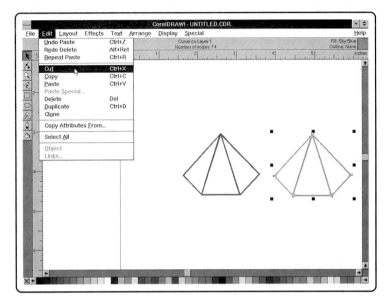

Figure CR2.15. A blue gem and red gem. The blue diamond shape is selected and the Edit menu with Cut highlighted is displayed.

Figure CR2.16. The Cut dialog box appears on-screen after you select Cut.

Copy

This command (see Figure CR2.18) allows you to temporarily copy objects to the clipboard without removing the originals from your document.

737

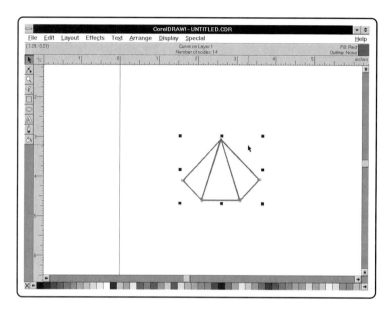

Figure CR2.17. Where there were two gems there is now only one. The preselected blue gem is now cut to the Windows clipboard and the red one is all that is left in your file.

Selection

Keyboard shortcut: Alt+E, C or Ctrl+C

Pointing device: **E**dit, **C**opy

Usage

1. Select the object(s) you want to copy from your document.
2. Select Copy from the Edit menu.
3. The CorelDRAW! is Copying prompt appears on-screen.
4. A copy of the object is now placed onto the Windows clipboard. The original object is left in your file.

The Copy command is similar to the Cut command except that it does not remove your original from your file. Figure CR2.19 shows a geometric pattern selected and copied to the clipboard.

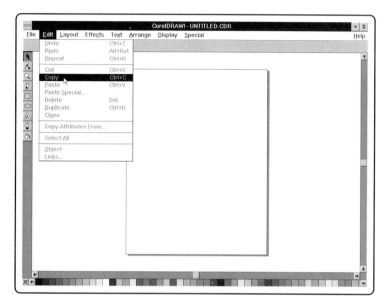

Figure CR2.18. Use the Edit Copy command to copy one or more objects to the clipboard.

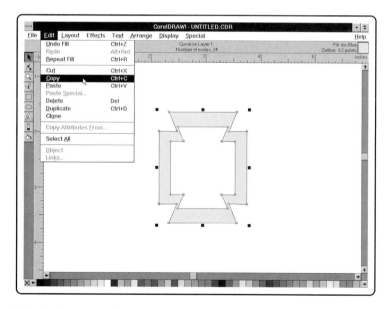

Figure CR2.19. A pattern that is selected and copied. A dialog box similar to the one in Figure CR2.16 appears on-screen, informing you that Corel Draw is copying to the Windows clipboard.

Paste

Select this command (see Figure CR2.20) to paste the last object(s) you have cut or copied to the clipboard. This command is available after cutting or copying object(s). See Corel's online Help menu for general pasting limitations.

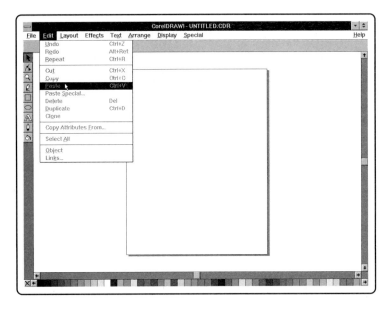

Figure CR2.20. Use the Edit Paste command to paste cut or copied objects.

Selection

Keyboard shortcut: Alt+E, P or Ctrl+V

Pointing device: **E**dit, **P**aste

Usage

1. Cut or copy the object(s) you wish to paste.
2. Select Paste from the Edit menu to insert the object(s) from the clipboard into your file.

Figures CR2.21 and CR2.22 show a previously copied geometric pattern pasted from the clipboard into file. When you paste copied or cut object(s), they will position themselves where the original object(s) were positioned.

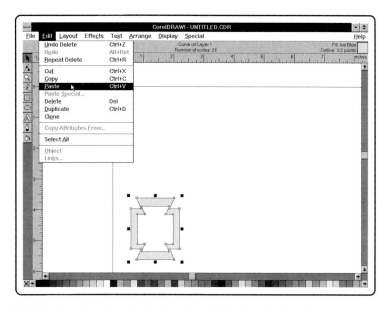

Figure CR2.21. A pattern is selected and copied to the clipboard.

Paste Special

This command (see Figure CR2.23) lets you paste objects that have been copied or cut to the Windows clipboard from other applications. See Chapter 17 of the CorelDRAW! 4 manual, "Working with Other Applications."

Selection

Keyboard shortcut: Alt+E, S

Pointing device: **E**dit, Paste **S**pecial

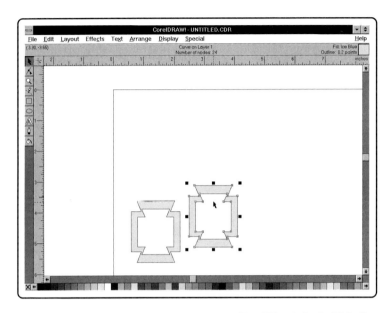

Figure CR2.22. The pattern will be pasted on top of itself by default. This figure shows a pasted pattern after it has been moved to the right.

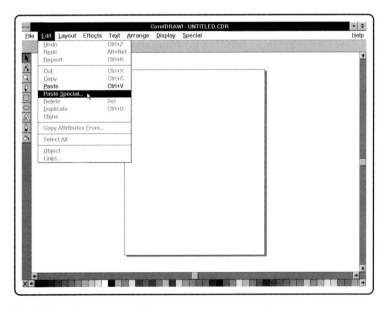

Figure CR2.23. The Edit menu with Paste Special selected.

Usage

1. After you've copied or cut object(s) from another application, select Paste Special from the Edit Menu.

   This allows you to paste such information as charts or text documents into your Corel file.

2. The Paste Dialog box appears on-screen. Select how you want the information to be pasted in.

3. Click OK.

Corel *NOTE!*

First open a file in another application, such as CorelPHOTOPAINT!; then cut or copy an object and minimize that application. Return to Corel Draw, and you can now activate Paste Special.

The Paste Special dialog box offers two options: Paste allows you to insert information from the clipboard into your file without creating a link to the source file, and Paste Link inserts the contents of the clipboard and creates a link to the source application from which the information was cut or copied (see Figures CR2.24 and CR2.25).

Figure CR2.24. After selecting Paste Special, this dialog box will appear.

Figure CR2.25. The Paste Special dialog box with Paste Link enabled. This option inserts the copied or cut object from the clipboard into your Corel Draw document. It also establishes a link to the original source file.

Paste Link can only be enabled if the contents on the clipboard were taken from an application that has the capability to link information to your Corel Draw file.

Delete

Edit Delete allows you to delete selected objects from your current document. It is similar to using the Cut command. When you delete, you can use Undo to bring back what you have deleted (see Figure CR2.26). After selecting Paste Special this dialog box will appear.

Selection

Keyboard shortcut: Alt+E, L or Delete

Pointing device: **E**dit, Delete

Usage

1. Select the object(s) that you want to delete.
2. Select Delete from the Edit menu.

Use this option only when you are sure you will no longer need the object(s) being deleted.

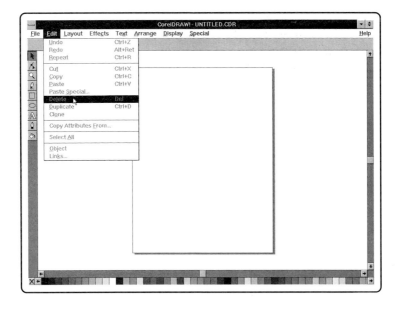

Figure CR2.26. The Edit menu with the Delete command highlighted.

Duplicate

The Duplicate command (see Figure CR2.27) allows you to select an object (or objects) and duplicate it directly to the screen. The positioning of the duplicate defaults to 0.25 inch horizontally and vertically. See "Special Menu Commands," "Preferences" in the Command References for more information.

Using the Duplicate command does not erase the contents of the Windows clipboard.

Selection

Keyboard shortcut: Alt+E, D or Ctrl+D

Pointing device: **E**dit, **D**uplicate

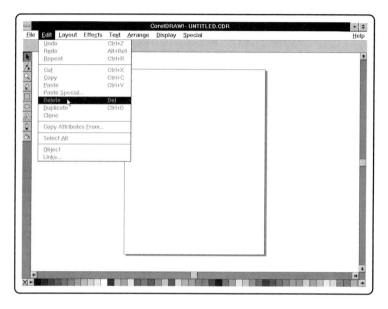

Figure CR2.27. The Edit menu with the Duplicate command highlighted.

Usage

1. Select the object(s) you wish to duplicate.
2. Select Duplicate from the Edit menu.
3. The duplicate will be placed according to the setup in Preferences.

The hammer icon is selected and then duplicated. The duplicate was positioned 0.25 inch horizontally and 0.25 inch vertically away from the original (see Figures CR2.28 and CR2.29).

Clone

The Clone command (see Figure CR2.30) works differently than the Duplicate command. The difference is that the object you clone from becomes the *master object*. Most attributes you give it will be applied to the clones automatically.

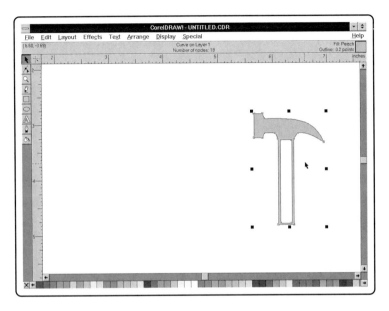

Figure CR2.28. An object selected on-screen.

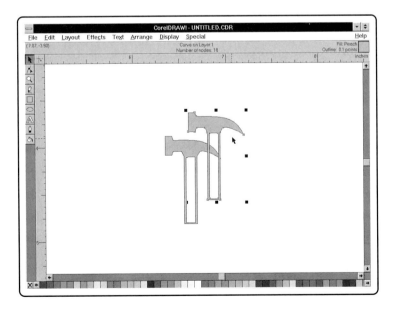

Figure CR2.29. The object after duplication.

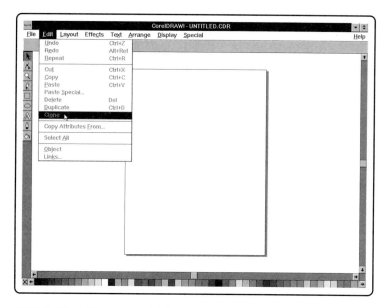

Figure CR2.30. The Edit menu with Clone highlighted.

Selection

Keyboard shortcut: Alt+E, O

Pointing device: **E**dit, Cl**o**ne

Usage

1. Select the object(s) you want to clone.
2. Select Clone from the Edit menu.
3. After cloning, most attributes you apply to the master object(s) will be applied to the clones automatically.

The Scissors icon was placed in the Corel Draw file. The icon was cloned twice. You can select the original and clone it twice, or you can clone once and then duplicate the clone and repeat the duplicate to create more clones. The master object is called the *Control Object*. The cloned objects are called *clones*. The status line will reflect this information when these objects are selected individually. When attributes are applied to the master they will automatically be applied to the clones (see Figures CR2.31 through CR2.33).

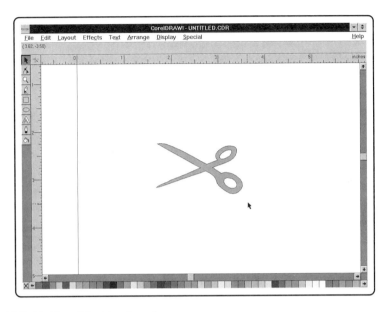

Figure CR2.31. The object to clone from.

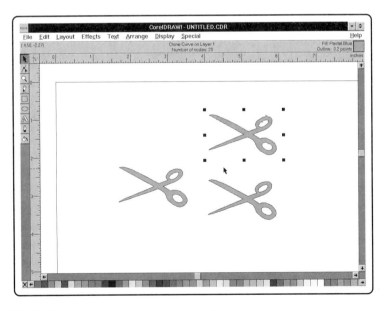

Figure CR2.32. Clones made from the master object.

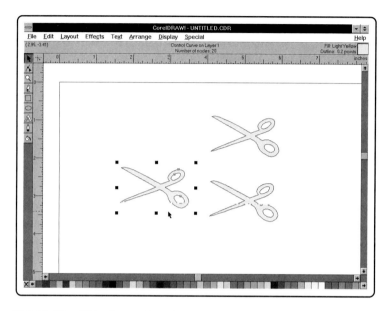

Figure CR2.33. The fill is changed on the master and the clones change automatically.

Copy Attributes From

This command (see Figure CR2.34) lets you copy PowerLines, fills, outlines, pen colors, and text attributes to other objects. This is an easy way to make other objects appear the same way a final object you have selected does.

Selection

Keyboard shortcut: Alt+E, F

Pointing device: **E**dit, Copy Attributes **F**rom

Usage

1. Select the object(s) you want to change.
2. Select Copy Attributes From in the Edit menu.
3. The Copy Attributes dialog box will appear.

4. Select the desired options (see Figure 2.35).

5. Click the OK button.

6. A From? arrow will appear on-screen. Use it to select the object you wish to copy attributes from (see Figure 2.36).

7. Your object(s) will now reflect the options chosen in the Copy Attributes dialog box (see Figure 2.37).

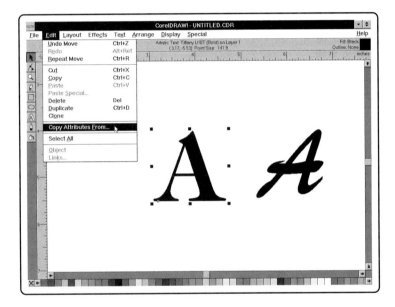

Figure CR2.34. The Edit menu with Copy Attributes From selected and a text object on the screen.

Figure CR2.35. The Copy Attributes dialog box with Outline Pen, Outline Color, Fill, and Text Attributes selected.

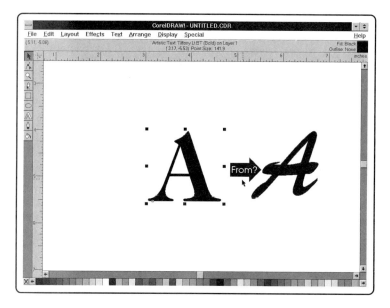

Figure CR2.36. The From? arrow appears on-screen. It lets you select the object that the attributes are copied from.

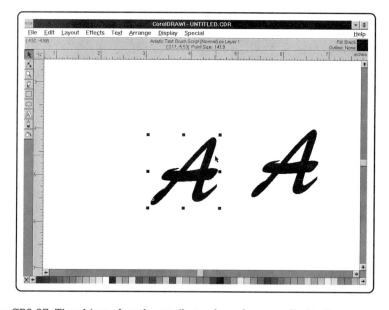

Figure CR2.37. The object after the attributes have been applied to it.

Select All

Choose this option (see Figure CR2.38) to select everything in your document. This allows you to select even objects that you cannot see. It includes objects that are not on your drawing page as well as items that are on top of each other.

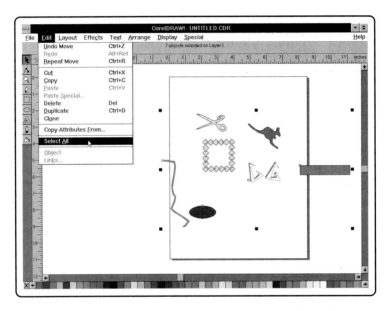

Figure CR2.38. The Edit menu with Select All highlighted, and all objects on-screen selected.

Selection

Keyboard shortcut: Alt+E, A

Pointing device: **E**dit, Select **A**ll

Usage

1. Create or place various objects in your document.
2. Select Select All from the Edit menu. All objects in your document are now selected.

Object

After cutting or copying an object from another application, choose Paste Special to put it into your Corel Draw document. The status line tells you what type of object it is. The Edit menu will change from Object to Edit Word Document Object (or whatever application the object was brought in from).

This works with objects that have been brought into the Corel file through the Paste Special command.

Selection

Keyboard shortcut: Alt+E, O

Pointing device: **E**dit, **O**bject

Usage

1. Select Object from the Edit menu (it will display where this object originated from).
2. The source application will open up.
3. Make any edits required and save.
4. Exit the application to return to your Corel file.

Links

Choose the Paste Special command and enable the Links command. With Links enabled, any changes made to the object in its original source application will be reflected in your Corel Draw document. This is handy in that you do not have to worry about updating your Corel Draw file when changes are made in the linked object's source application. Figure CR2.39 shows the Links dialog box. For more information about editing links, see Corel Draw's online help and Chapter 17 of the Corel Draw 4 manual, "Working with Other Applications."

Selection

Keyboard shortcut: Alt+E, K

Pointing device: **E**dit, Lin**k**s

Usage

1. Select Links from the Edit menu.

2. The Links dialog box will appear, displaying all links in the current file.

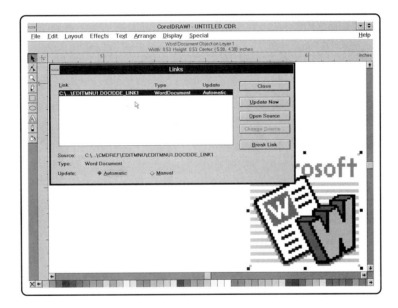

Figure CR2.39. The object selected and the Links dialog box displayed.

3

Layout Menu Commands

In the Layout menu, there are selections provided for multipage documents. The selections are Insert Page, Delete Page, Go To page and Page Setup. You can also select Layers Roll-Up and Styles Roll-Up. The Grid Setup, Guidelines Setup, and the Snap To options are also enabled from this menu (see Figure CR3.1).

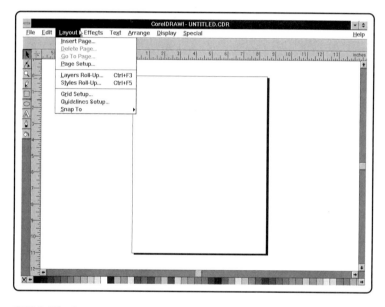

Figure CR3.1. The Layout menu.

Insert Page

Selecting this command invokes the Insert Page dialog box. You can insert up to 999 pages in your Corel Draw file. The pages can be inserted before or after the page number specified in the lower right corner of the Insert Page dialog box (see Figure CR3.2).

Corel*NOTE!*

When you have more than a one-page document, arrows for selecting the pages appear at the lower left of the screen next to the horizontal scroll bar. Double-click the arrows to invoke the Insert Page dialog box.

Figure CR3.2. The Insert Page dialog box and its available options.

Selection

Keyboard shortcut: Alt+L, I, Alt+I

Pointing device: **L**ayout, **I**nsert Page, **I**nsert

Usage

1. Move to the page where you wish to insert a new page(s).
2. Select Insert Page from the Layout menu.
3. In the Insert Page dialog box, select Insert.
4. If you wish to insert more than one page, type in a new value. You also can use the arrows to increase or decrease the number of pages to insert.

Selection

Keyboard shortcut: Alt+L, I, Alt+B

Pointing device: **L**ayout, **I**nsert Page, **B**efore

Usage

1. Move to the page where you wish to insert a new page(s).
2. Select Insert Page from the Layout menu.
3. In the Insert Page dialog box, select Before. This puts the number of pages you select before the currently selected page.

Selection

Keyboard shortcut: Alt+L, I, Alt+A

Pointing device: **L**ayout, **I**nsert Page, **A**fter

Usage

1. Move to the page where you wish to insert a new page(s).
2. Select Insert Page from the Layout menu.
3. In the Insert Page dialog box, select After. This puts the number of pages you select after the currently selected page.

Selection

Keyboard shortcut: Alt+L, I, Alt+P

Pointing device: **L**ayout, **I**nsert Page, **P**age

Usage

1. Select Insert Page from the Layout menu.
2. In the Insert Page dialog box, select Page. This lets you change the currently selected page.

Delete Page

Selecting the Delete Page option brings up the Delete Page dialog box. This allows you to delete one or several pages from a multipage document.

Selection

Keyboard shortcut: Alt+L, D

Pointing device: **L**ayout, **D**elete Page

Usage

This command brings up the Delete Page dialog box, which has two options. You either can delete the selected page or type a new page number to delete. You also can delete several pages at one time (see Figure CR3.3).

Figure CR3.3. The Delete Page dialog box and its available options.

Selection

Keyboard shortcut: Alt+L, D, Alt+D

Pointing device: **L**ayout, **D**elete Page, **D**elete Page

Usage

1. Select Delete Page from the Layout menu.
2. In the Delete Page dialog box, select Delete Page. This lets you delete the currently selected page.

Selection

Keyboard shortcut: Alt+L, D, Alt+D, Alt+T

Pointing device: **L**ayout, **D**elete Page, **D**elete Page, **T**hru Page

Usage

1. Select Delete Page from the Layout menu.
2. In the Delete Page dialog box, select Delete Page.
3. Select Thru Page. This lets you delete several pages at a time.

Go To Page

Selecting the Layout Go To Page option brings up the Go To Page dialog box. This command allows you to move from one page to another, in any order you wish in a multipage document (see Figure CR3.4).

Figure CR3.4. The Go To Page dialog box.

Corel *NOTE!*

> At the lower left area of the screen, next to the horizontal scroll bar, there is a status bar which indicates the current page (for example, "page 2 of 3"). You can double-click this section to invoke the Go To Page dialog box.

Selection

Keyboard shortcut: Alt+L, G

Pointing device: **L**ayout, **G**o To Page

Usage

1. Select Go To Page to bring up the dialog box.
2. Type the page number that you want to go to.
3. Click OK.

Page Setup

Selecting Page Setup from the Layout menu brings up the Page setup dialog box. Various settings are available.

Selection

Keyboard shortcut: Alt+L, P

Pointing device: **L**ayout, **P**age Setup

Usage

This command brings up the Page Setup dialog box. Some of the options can be selected through the keyboard. These options have the letter that you select from the keyboard underlined, for example, the letter P in Portrait (see Figure CR3.5).

Figure CR3.5. The Page Setup dialog box and its options.

Corel *NOTE!*

> To bring up the Page Setup dialog box you also can double-click the page border of the printable area of the screen.

Selection

Keyboard shortcut: Alt+L, P, Alt+P

Pointing device: **L**ayout, **P**age Setup, **P**ortrait

Usage

Selecting Portrait in the Page Setup dialog box changes the orientation of your page from Landscape.

Selection

Keyboard shortcut: Alt+L, P, Alt+L

Pointing device: **L**ayout, **P**age Setup, **L**andscape

Usage

Selecting Landscape in the Page Setup dialog box changes the orientation of your page from Portrait.

Selection

Keyboard shortcut: Alt+L, P, Alt+S

Pointing device: **L**ayout, **P**age Setup, **S**et From Printer

Usage

1. Invoke the Page Setup command.
2. Select the Set From Printer option in the dialog box.
3. Print your drawing.
4. You will receive a prompt if the page orientation of your drawing doesn't match your printer page.
5. Select whether you want Corel Draw to adjust the orientation to match automatically.
6. Click OK.

Selection

Keyboard shortcut: Alt+L, P, Alt+B

Pointing device: **L**ayout, **P**age Setup, Show Page **B**order

Usage

Selecting Show Page Border in the Page Setup dialog box toggles this option on or off (the printable page's border disappears or reappears on your screen).

Selection

Keyboard shortcut: Alt+L, P, Alt+A

Pointing device: **L**ayout, **P**age Setup, **A**dd Page Frame

Usage

Select Add Page Frame in the Page Setup dialog box. This places a frame the same size as the current page size in your document.

Selection

Keyboard shortcut: Alt+L, P, Alt+F

Pointing device: **L**ayout, **P**age Setup, **F**acing Pages

Usage

Selecting Facing Pages in the Page Setup dialog box lets you select whether the right or left pages are first.

Selection

Keyboard shortcut: Alt+L, P, Alt+F, T

Pointing device: **L**ayout, **P**age Setup, **F**acing Pages, Lef**t** First

Usage

1. In the Page Setup dialog box, select the Facing Pages option.
2. Select Left First, and your document will begin with a left-hand page.

Selection

Keyboard shortcut: Alt+L, P, Alt+F, R

Pointing device: **L**ayout, **P**age Setup, **F**acing Pages, **R**ight First

Usage

1. In the Page Setup dialog box, select the Facing Pages option.
2. Select Right First, and your document will begin with a right-hand page.

To change the page size, invoke the Page Setup dialog box and tag the arrow below the Paper Size section. Select from the available options on the list. Selecting Custom allows you to type in the width and height (see Figure CR3.6).

Figure CR3.6. The Page Setup dialog box with the Paper Size pull-down menu.

Selection

Keyboard shortcut: Alt+L, P, Tab, Tab

Pointing device: **L**ayout, **P**age Setup; under Paper Size, select the down arrow

Usage

1. In the Page Setup dialog box, select the Paper Size pull-down menu by selecting the arrow.
2. Select from the available preset sizes, or select Custom and type in the sizes you require.

Selecting Page Layout from the Page Setup dialog box allows you to choose from six available layouts. Select a different option, and information about that page layout appears next to the pull-down menu (see Figure CR3.7).

Selection

Keyboard shortcut: Alt+L, P, Tab (five times)

Pointing device: **L**ayout, **P**age Setup; under Paper Layout, select the down arrow

Figure CR3.7. The Page Setup dialog box with the Page Layout pull-down menu.

Usage

1. In the Page Setup dialog box, select the Page Layout pull-down menu by selecting the arrow.
2. Select from six available preset sizes.

Selecting Paper Color from the Page Setup dialog box allows you to change the paper color. You can select new colors from several color palettes (see Figure CR3.8).

Selection

Pointing device: **L**ayout, **P**age Setup, Paper Color

Usage

1. In the Page Setup dialog box, press the Paper Color button.
2. Select a color from the fly-out palette.
3. Press the More button for other palettes.

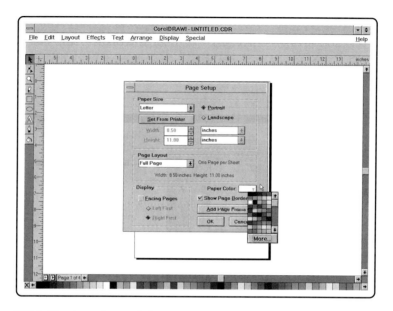

Figure CR3.8. The Page Setup dialog box with the Paper Color pull-down menu selected.

Layers Roll-Up

Selecting this command brings up the Layers roll-up. You can add additional layers as well as rename them and change the attributes of individual layers (Figure CR3.9). For more information about the Layers roll-up, see Skill Session 28.

Selection

Keyboard shortcut: Alt+L, L or Ctrl+F3

Pointing device: **L**ayout, **L**ayers Roll-Up

Usage

1. Select Layers Roll-Up from the Layout menu.
2. In the Layers roll-up, you can change the individual settings of the layers. You can also change the order of the layers.

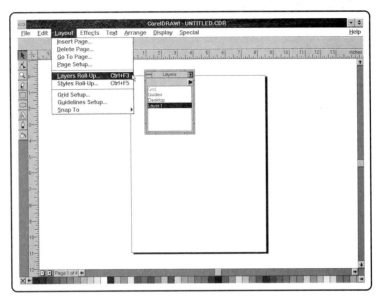

Figure CR3.9. The Layout menu with Layers Roll-Up selected and the Layers roll-up displayed.

Styles Roll-Up

Selecting this command invokes the Styles roll-up. You can save and apply styles to text (see Figure CR3.10). For more information about the Styles roll-up, see Skill Session 51.

Selection

Keyboard shortcut: Alt+L, T or Ctrl+F5

Pointing device: Layout, Styles Roll-Up

Usage

1. Select Styles Roll-Up from the Layout menu.
2. Select the styles you wish to apply to paragraphs or text, such as bullets or indents. Or create your own style by changing attributes such as boldfaced or italicized text.

769

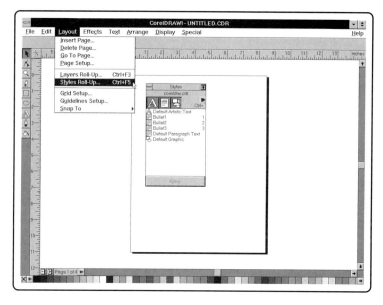

Figure CR3.10. The Layout menu with Styles Roll-Up selected and the list of styles displayed.

Grid Setup

This command brings up the Grid Setup dialog box. In this dialog box, you can change the settings of your grid, the measurement system you are using, and whether to show the grid on screen or just snap objects to it. For more information on the Grid Setup dialog box, see Skill Session 26.

Corel*NOTE!*

Double-clicking the rulers invokes the Grid Setup dialog box.

Selection

Keyboard shortcut: Alt+L, R

Pointing device: **L**ayout, **G**rid Setup

Usage

1. Select Grid Setup from the Layout menu.
2. In the Grid Setup dialog box, you can change the existing settings to accommodate your current drawing requirements.
3. Choose from various options in the Grid Setup dialog box. This allows you to create a customized grid that will assist you when you are drawing precise illustrations (see Figure CR3.11).

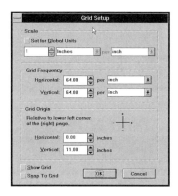

Figure CR3.11. The Grid Setup dialog box and its available options.

Guidelines Setup

This command brings up the Guidelines Setup dialog box. In this dialog box, you can change the settings of your guides as well as their positioning. You also can indicate whether to have objects snap to the guides. For more information on the Guidelines Setup dialog box, see Skill Session 27.

Corel*NOTE!*

> Double-clicking the guidelines invokes the Guidelines Setup dialog box.

Selection

Keyboard shortcut: Alt+L, U

Pointing device: **L**ayout, **Gu**idelines Setup

Usage

1. Select Guidelines Setup from the Layout menu.
2. In the Guidelines Setup dialog box, you can change the existing guides to accommodate your current drawing requirements.
3. Choose from various options that allow you to place the guides either horizontally or vertically, and delete, move, and add new guides (see Figure CR3.12).

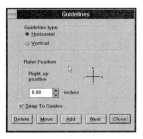

Figure CR3.12. The Guidelines Setup dialog box and its available options.

Snap To

If you want the objects on your screen to snap to grids, guidelines, or objects while you are placing them in your printable area, select Snap To from the Layout menu (see Figure CR3.13).

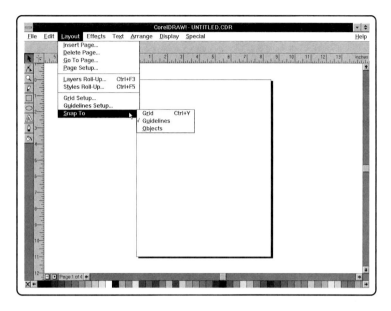

Figure CR3.13. The Layout menu with Snap To selected and the fly-out list of Grid, Guidelines, and Objects displayed.

Selection

Keyboard shortcut: Alt+L, S

Pointing device: **L**ayout, **S**nap To

Usage

1. Select Snap To from the Layout menu. This command pulls out a cascading menu.
2. Select from three options: Grid, Guidelines, or Objects.

Selection

Keyboard shortcut: Alt+L, S, R or Ctrl+Y

Pointing device: **L**ayout, **S**nap To, **G**rid

Usage

This command snaps objects to the grid.

Selection

Keyboard shortcut: Alt+L, S, U

Pointing device: **L**ayout, **S**nap To, G**ui**delines

Usage

This command snaps objects to guidelines.

Selection

Keyboard shortcut: Alt+L, S, O

Pointing device: **L**ayout, **S**nap To, **O**bjects

Usage

1. Select Layout Snap To.
2. From the cascading menu, select Snap To Objects.
3. An object will snap to the nodes of another object with this option enabled (see Figure CR3.14).

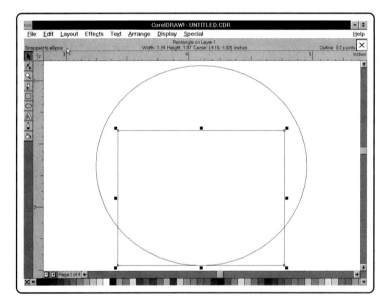

Figure CR3.14. A rectangle snapping to an ellipse.

4

Effects
Menu
Commands

The Effects menu provides commands for applying different effects that transform objects. The effects are Rotate and Skew, Stretch and Mirror, and Add Perspective. There are also five roll-ups: the Envelope roll-up, the Blend roll-up, the Extrude roll-up, the Contour roll-up, and the PowerLine roll-up. You can also return objects to their original attributes by selecting Clear Effect and Clear Transformations. The other option, Copy Effect From, copies effects from one object to another (see Figure CR4.1).

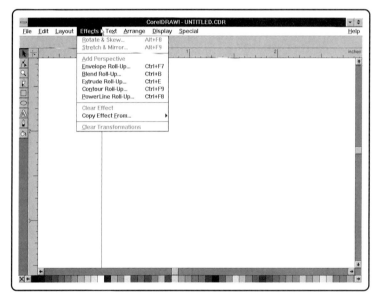

Figure CR4.1. The Effects menu.

Rotate & Skew

Select this option to invoke the Rotate & Skew dialog box (see Figure CR4.2). You must have an object selected to invoke this dialog box. If an object is not selected, this option is grayed out in the Effects menu. For more information about Rotate & Skew, see Skill Session 16.

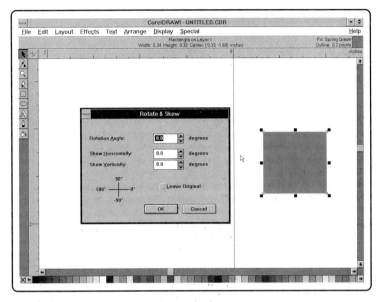

Figure CR4.2. An object selected and the Rotate & Skew dialog box.

Corel*NOTE!*

When you skew, you make your object oblique or give it a slant. Your object can run at an angle. This allows you to make text italic even if you do not have the italic version of the text. However, true italic is always preferable. See "True Italic versus Skewing," in Skill Session 36, "Basic Typography."

Selection

Keyboard shortcut: Alt+C, R or Alt+F8

Pointing device: Effe**c**ts, **R**otate & Skew

Usage

1. Select an object in your file and invoke the Rotate & Skew dialog box.
2. In the Rotation Angle box, type the number of degrees you want your object to rotate.
3. In the Skew Horizontally box, type the number of degrees to skew your object horizontally.
4. In the Skew Vertically box, type the number of degrees to skew your object vertically.
5. Enable the Leave Original option to keep the original object; the changes are applied to a duplicate of that object.

Stretch & Mirror

Select this command to invoke the Stretch & Mirror dialog box. This allows you to alter objects by entering different percentages of heights and widths. For more information about Stretch & Mirror, see Skill Session 16.

Selection

Keyboard shortcut: Alt+C, S or Alt+F9

Pointing device: Effects, Stretch & Mirror

Usage

1. Select Effects, Stretch & Mirror to invoke the Stretch & Mirror dialog box (see Figure CR4.3). This works only if you have an object selected.
2. Choose from various options.
3. Click OK.

Stretch & Mirror, Stretch Horizontally

Selection

Keyboard shortcut: Alt+C, S, Alt+H or Alt+F9, Alt+H

Pointing device: Effects, Stretch & Mirror, Stretch Horizontally

Usage

1. With an object selected, invoke Stretch & Mirror from the Effects menu.

2. In the Stretch & Mirror dialog box, select Stretch Horizontally.

3. Type a new horizontal percentage for your object.

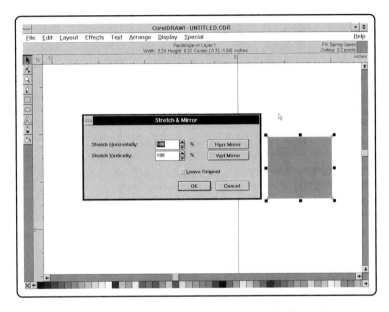

Figure CR4.3. The Stretch & Mirror dialog box and its available options.

Stretch & Mirror, Stretch Vertically

Selection

Keyboard shortcut: Alt+C, S, Alt+V or Alt+F9, Alt+V

Pointing device: Effe**c**ts, **S**tretch & Mirror, Stretch **V**ertically

Usage

1. With an object selected, invoke Stretch & Mirror from the Effects menu.

779

2. In the Stretch & Mirror dialog box, select Stretch Vertically.

3. Type a new vertical percentage for your object.

Stretch & Mirror, Horz Mirror

Selection

Keyboard shortcut: Alt+C, S, Alt+O or Alt+F9, Alt+O

Pointing device: Effects, Stretch & Mirror, Horz Mirror

Usage

1. With an object selected, invoke Stretch & Mirror from the Effects menu.

2. In the Stretch & Mirror dialog box, select Horz Mirror.

   This option mirrors your object horizontally.

Stretch & Mirror, Vert Mirror

Selection

Keyboard shortcut: Alt+C, S, Alt+E or Alt+F9, Alt+E

Pointing device: Effects, Stretch & Mirror, Vert Mirror

Usage

1. With an object selected, invoke Stretch & Mirror from the Effects menu.

2. In the Stretch & Mirror dialog box, select Vert Mirror.

   This option mirrors your object vertically.

Stretch & Mirror, Leave Original

Selection

Keyboard shortcut: Alt+C, S, Alt+L or Alt+F9, Alt+L

Pointing device: Effects, Stretch & Mirror, Leave Original

Usage

1. With an object selected, invoke Stretch & Mirror from the Effects menu.

2. In the Stretch & Mirror dialog box, select Leave Original.

   This changes a duplicate of your object without changing the original object.

Add Perspective

Select an object and select Add Perspective from the Effects menu. This allows you to change the perspective of your object, providing the illusion of distance and depth. For more information about Add Perspective, see Skill Session 20.

Select Add Perspective from the Effects menu to place nodes around the object. These nodes allow you to manipulate the object. By selecting one node, you can move it around and change the way your object appears. An × appears on-screen, which represents the object's vanishing point. Select and move the × around to change the perspective of your object (see Figure CR4.4).

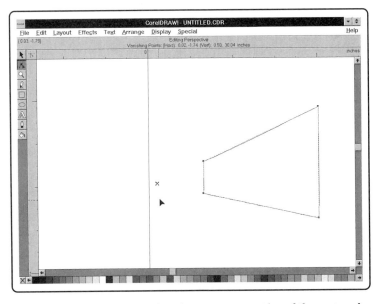

Figure CR4.4. The × on-screen showing the new perspective of the rectangle.

Selection

Keyboard shortcut: Alt+C, A

Pointing device: Effe**c**ts, **A**dd Perspective

Usage

1. Draw an object.
2. Select Add Perspective from the Effects menu.
3. Select the × that appears on-screen and move it to change the perspective of the rectangle.
4. Nodes appear around your rectangle. You can select the nodes individually to give your object a new appearance.

Envelope Roll-Up

Select Envelope Roll-Up from the Effects menu to invoke the Envelope roll-up (see Figure CR4.5). This is used to apply envelopes to objects. Envelopes can be seen as containers used to shape text or objects. For example, you can apply an ellipse to some text. The text will take on the shape of the ellipse. For more information about the Envelope roll-up, see Skill Session 22.

Selection

Keyboard shortcut: Alt+C, E or Ctrl+F7

Pointing device: Effe**c**ts, **E**nvelope Roll-Up

Usage

1. Select Envelope Roll-Up from the Effects menu to invoke the Envelope roll-up.
2. In the Envelope roll-up, you can apply existing settings. You can also edit the object's envelope manually.

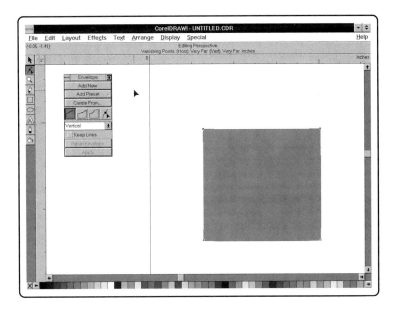

Figure CR4.5. The Envelope roll-up and its available options.

Blend Roll-Up

Select Blend Roll-Up from the Effects menu to apply blends to objects. For more information on the Blend roll-up, see Skill Session 19.

Selection

Keyboard shortcut: Alt+C, B or Ctrl+B

Pointing device: Effects, Blend Roll-Up

Usage

1. Select the objects to blend.
2. Select Blend Roll-Up from the Effects menu to invoke the Blend roll-up.
3. Specify the number of steps.
4. Specify the angle of rotation.
5. Click Apply (see Figure CR4.6).

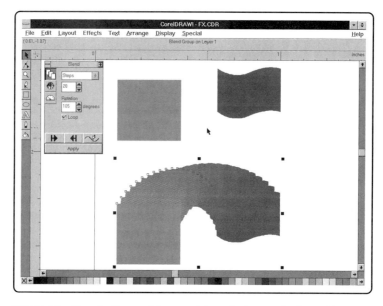

Figure CR4.6. The Blend roll-up with two objects before and after a blend is applied.

Extrude Roll-Up

To use this command, select Extrude Roll-Up from the Effects Menu. The roll-up appears on-screen. If an object is selected when you invoke the Extrude Roll-Up, you'll see a preview of your object using the settings displayed in the roll-up (see Figure CR4.7). For more information about the Extrude roll-up, see Skill Session 21.

Selection

Keyboard shortcut: Alt+C, X or Ctrl+E

Pointing device: Effects, Extrude Roll-Up

Usage

1. Select an object and invoke the Extrude roll-up.
2. Change the settings in the roll-up and preview what the extruded object will look like.

3. Click the Apply button and your object now appears three-dimensional.

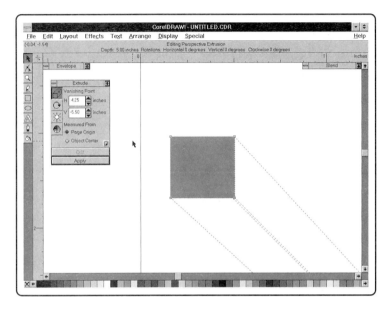

Figure CR4.7. The Extrude roll-up and preview of the extruded object.

Contour Roll-Up

To use this command, select an object and then select Contour Roll-Up from the Effects menu. The roll-up appears on-screen (see Figure CR4.8). You can select whether the contour applies itself to the center, the inside, or the outside of the object, and change the offset or number of steps of the contour. You can also change the outline as well as the fill of the contour in this roll-up. For more information about the Contour roll-up, see Skill Session 53.

Selection

Keyboard shortcut: Alt+C, N or Ctrl+F9

Pointing device: Effects, Contour Roll-Up

Usage

1. Select an object and invoke the Contour roll-up.

2. Choose whether to apply your contour to the Center, Inside, or Outside of your object.

3. Change the number in the Offset box.

4. Change the number in the Steps box.

5. Choose an outline color.

6. Choose a fill for the contour. The object color will blend toward the color of the contour fill.

7. Click the Apply button to see the contour applied to your object. This gives the illusion of a pyramid or stacking of objects viewed from overhead. A contour may appear to look like a blend.

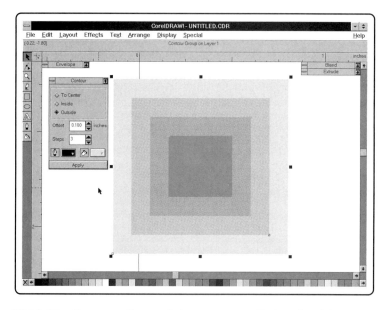

Figure CR4.8. The Contour roll-up and the contour applied to the object.

Corel*NOTE!*

> The number of steps to the contour is limited to 999. If objects are filled with bitmap texture or grouped, contours cannot be applied to them.

PowerLine Roll-Up

To use this command, select PowerLine Roll-Up from the Effects Menu. The roll-up appears on-screen (see Figure CR4.9). You can choose to draw with the Pencil tool in PowerLine mode from this roll-up. Select the object you want to apply PowerLine effects to. For more information about the PowerLine roll-up, see Skill Session 54.

Corel*NOTE!*

> You can apply PowerLine effects to objects as well as lines.

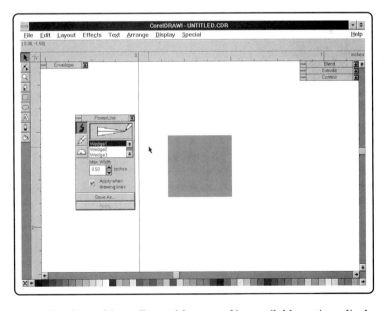

Figure CR4.9. The PowerLine roll-up with some of its available options displayed.

Selection

Keyboard shortcut: Alt+C, P, or Ctrl+F8

Pointing device: Effects, PowerLine Roll-Up

Usage

1. Select an object and invoke the PowerLine roll-up.
2. Change the settings in the roll-up and select the effect you want your object to look like.
3. Click on the Apply button and your object now has the look of the selected effect.

Clear Effect

To use this command, select Clear Effect from the Effects menu. This option clears the last effect applied to an object. For example, if the last effect applied to the object was Perspective, the Effects menu reads Clear Perspective (see Figure CR4.10).

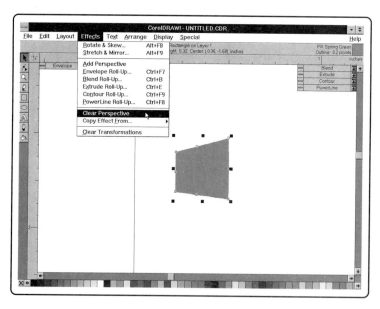

Figure CR4.10. The object selected with the Effects menu pulled down and Clear Perspective highlighted. (Perspective was the last effect applied.)

Selection

Keyboard shortcut: none

Pointing device: Effects, Clear Effect

Usage

1. Select an object that has an effect already applied to it.
2. Select Clear Effect from the Effects menu.
3. The object's last applied effect is removed.

Copy Effect From

To use this command, select Copy Effect From in the Effects Menu. A cascading menu with the choices Copy Perspective From or Copy Envelope From appears (see Figure CR4.11). Select one of these two and a From? arrow appears. With this arrow, choose the object from which you are copying the effect.

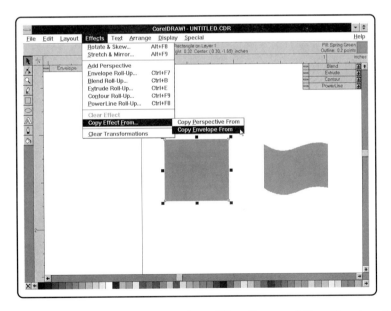

Figure CR4.11. The object selected and Copy Effect From and Copy Envelope From highlighted in the Effects menu.

Selection

Keyboard shortcut: Alt+C, F, P or Alt+C, F, E

Pointing device: Effe**c**ts, Copy Effect **F**rom, Copy **P**erspective From or Effe**c**ts, Copy Effect **F**rom, Copy **E**nvelope From

Usage

1. Select an object and select Copy Effect From.
2. Now select Copy Perspective From or Copy Envelope From.
3. Select the object you are copying the effect from with the From arrow.
4. Your object now has the effect that you copied from the other object (see Figure CR4.12).

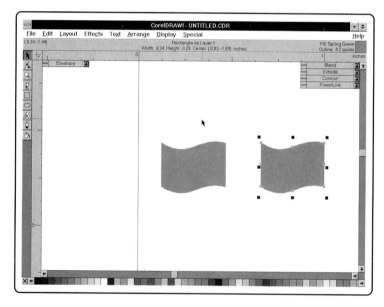

Figure CR4.12. The object after it has had an envelope effect copied to it.

Clear Transformations

To use this command, select an object and choose Clear Transformations in the Effects menu (see Figure CR4.13). This returns your object to its original condition (see Figure CR4.14).

Selection

Keyboard shortcut: Alt+C, C

Pointing device: Effects, Clear Transformations

Usage

1. Select an object and select Clear Transformations.
2. Your object returns to its original form.

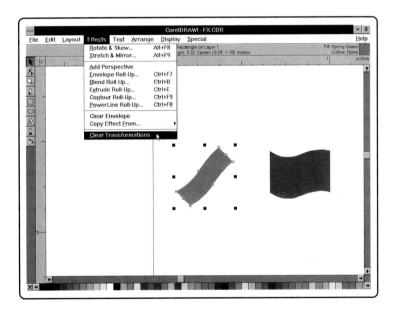

Figure CR4.13. The object selected and Clear Transformations highlighted in the Effects menu.

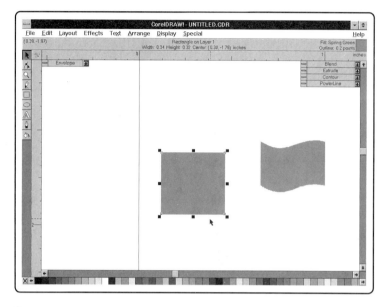

Figure CR4.14. The object after it has had Clear Transformations applied to it.

5

Text Menu Commands

The Text menu provides commands for text attributes. These are: Text Roll-Up, Character, Frame, and Paragraph. You can also select Fit Text To Path, Align To Baseline, and Straighten Text. Spell Checker, Thesaurus, Find, Replace, and Edit Text are also found on this menu (see Figure CR5.1). Many of these text options are also covered in the text workshop section of this book. See Skill Sessions 29 through 36.

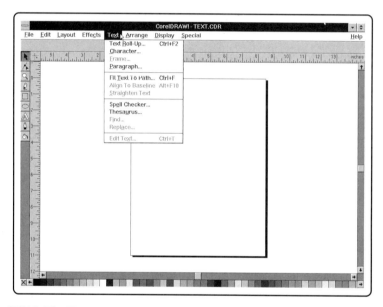

Figure CR5.1. The Text menu.

Roll-Up

Select this option (see Figure CR5.2) to invoke the Text roll-up (see Figure CR5.3). Use the Text roll-up to change the attributes of selected text. Choose an attribute, such as justification or type style, and click the Apply button.

Selection

Keyboard shortcut: Alt+X, R or Ctrl+F2

Pointing device: Te**xt**, Text **R**oll-Up

Usage

1. Select the text to which you want to apply attributes.

2. Select Text Roll-Up from the Text menu.

3. Choose the attributes you want from the Text roll-up and click the Apply button.

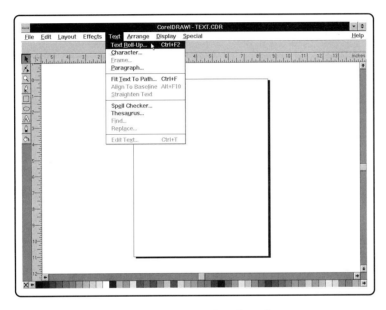

Figure CR5.2. The Text menu with Text Roll-Up selected.

Changing Fonts in the Text Roll-Up

To change a font from the Text roll-up, click on the down arrow from the font options pull-down menu. A fly-out appears, previewing the font (see Figure CR5.4). This helps when choosing a different font for your selected text. It also provides a preview of what you will get before you apply the attribute.

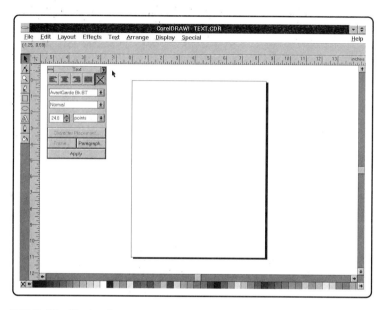

Figure CR5.3. The Text roll-up.

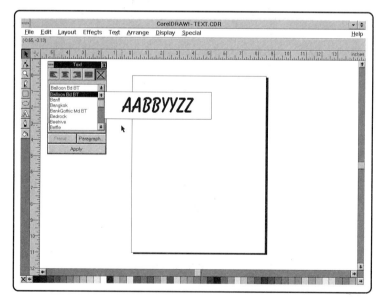

Figure CR5.4. The Text roll-up with a fly-out menu that previews how the selected font will look.

Selection

Pointing device: Click the down arrow and select the name of the font from the font options pull-down menu.

Usage

1. Select the text you want to change.
2. Choose a different font from the Text roll-up.
3. A fly-out with the preview of the font is displayed.
4. Click the Apply button to change the text to the selected font.

Changing Style in the Text Roll-Up

To change the style of selected text, choose the down arrow in the box directly below the font option box. A fly-out appears, previewing the text's style. You may have four options to choose from: Normal, Bold, Italic, and Bold-Italic (see Figure CR5.5).

Corel*NOTE!*

Not all fonts have all four options available.

Selection

Pointing device: Click the down arrow and select the style of the font from the pull-down menu.

Usage

1. Select the text you want to apply a style to.
2. Click the down arrow in the style box.
3. A pull-down menu appears with available style options for the selected font.
4. Select from Normal, Bold, Italic, or Bold-Italic.
5. Click the Apply button to change the text to the new style.

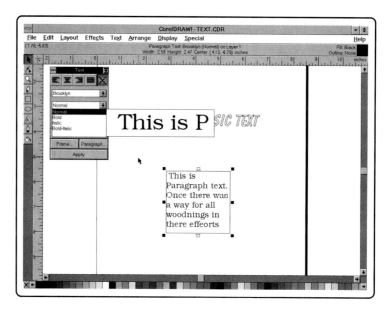

Figure CR5.5. The Text roll-up showing the style of the selected paragraph text.

Changing the Text Size and Measurement System in the Text Roll-Up

Below the Styles options there is a box on the lower left that lets you select the size of your text. The box on the lower right changes the measurement system. Changing the size of the text is done by typing a new value for size or using the up or down arrows. Change the measurement system by selecting from the options in the pull-down menu.

Corel*NOTE!*

Resizing Artistic text changes the point size of the text. Resizing Paragraph text changes the frame that the text is in and not the size of the text.

Character Placement

Click the Character Placement button to invoke the Character Placement dialog box. This box includes options for changing the spacing of your text. You can change the horizontal or vertical spacing. The angle of the selected text can also be altered. You can also superscript or subscript the selected text (see Figure CR5.6). For more information about Character Placement, see Skill Session 29.

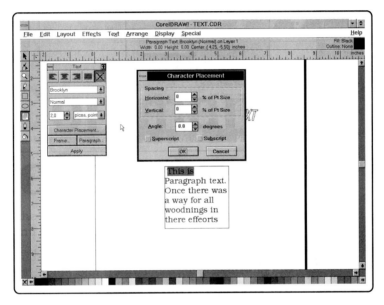

Figure CR5.6. The Text roll-up displaying the size and measurements of the text; the Character Placement dialog box with the settings of the currently selected text in the paragraph.

Selection

Pointing device: From the Text roll-up, click the Character Placement button.

Usage

1. Select the text to be changed and invoke the Text roll-up.
2. Click Character Placement.

3. Enter new values in their respective sections.

4. Click OK.

Changing Text Justification in the Text Roll-Up

To change the justification of either Artistic or Paragraph text, invoke the Text roll-up and from the very top row select from five available alignment options. These options are Left, Center, Right, Justify, and None (see Figure CR5.7).

Selection

Pointing device: In the Text roll-up, click any of the five icons for alignment options.

Usage

1. Select the text and invoke the Text roll-up.

2. Select an alignment icon.

3. Click Apply to align the text.

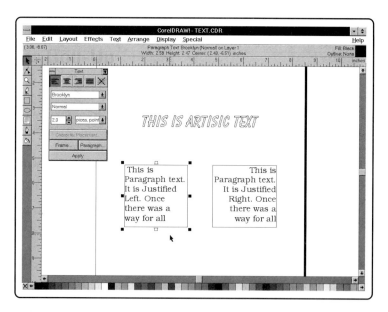

Figure CR5.7. The Text roll-up displaying the left- and right-justified Paragraph text.

Character

The next item in the Text menu is Character. Select this command to invoke the Character Attributes dialog box, which allows you to change the attributes of the selected text (see Figure CR5.8).

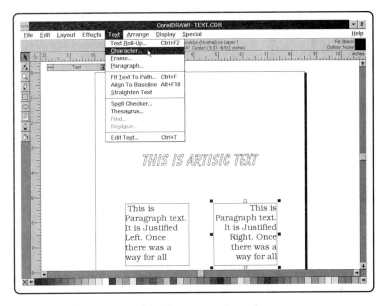

Figure CR5.8. The Text menu with Character selected.

Corel*NOTE!*

Double-clicking the node or nodes of selected text with the Shape tool also invokes the Character Attributes dialog box.

Selection

Keyboard shortcut: Alt+X, C

Pointing device: Te**x**t, **C**haracter

Usage

1. Select the text.
2. Select Character from the Text menu. This invokes the Character Attributes dialog box.

The Character Attributes dialog box (see Figure CR5.9) allows you to change various elements of your text. You can change the fonts, size, and measuring system as well as the style and the placement. These options are similar to the ones described for the Text roll-up.

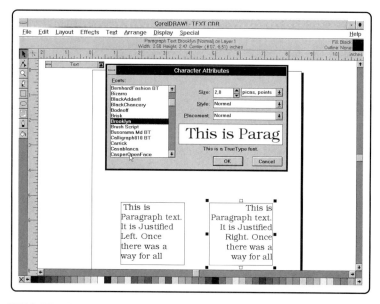

Figure CR5.9. The Character Attributes dialog box and its options.

Character Attributes, Fonts
Selection

Keyboard shortcut: Alt+X, C, first letter of name of font

Pointing device: Te**x**t, **C**haracter, Fonts

Usage

1. Select text.
2. Select Character from the Text menu.
3. Select a font from the Fonts list.
4. Click OK.

Character Attributes, Size

Selection

Keyboard shortcut: Alt+X, C, Alt+Z

Pointing device: Text, Character, Size

Usage

1. Select text.
2. Select Character from the Text menu.
3. Select Size from the Character Attributes dialog box.
4. Type a new value.
5. Click OK.

Character Attributes, Style

Selection

Keyboard shortcut: Alt+X, C, Alt+S

Pointing device: Text, Character, Style

Usage

1. Select text.
2. Select Character from the Text menu.
3. Select Style from the Character Attributes dialog box.
4. Select a style from the pull-down menu. From the keyboard, use the ↓ key to select between styles.
5. Click OK.

Frame

The next item in the Text menu is Frame. Select the Paragraph text and then select the Frame option from the Text menu. This invokes the Frame Attributes dialog box (see Figure CR5.10). For more information about frames, see Skill Sessions 10 and 30.

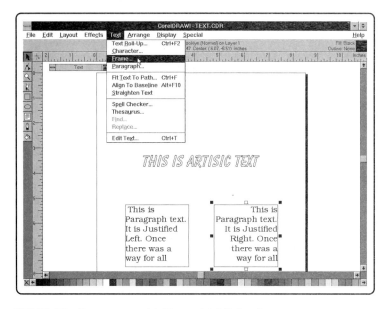

Figure CR5.10. The Text menu with Frame highlighted.

Corel*NOTE!*

The Frame option is available only for Paragraph text.

Selection

Keyboard shortcut: Alt+X, F

Pointing device: Te**x**t, **F**rame

Usage

1. Select Paragraph text.
2. Select Frame from the Text menu. This invokes the Frame Attributes dialog box.

In the Frame Attributes dialog box, you can change the number of columns, gutter width, and measurement system (see Figure CR5.11).

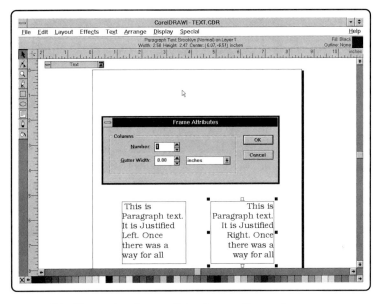

Figure CR5.11. The Frame Attributes dialog box and its options.

Frame Attributes, Number

Selection

Keyboard shortcut: Alt+X, F, Alt+N

Pointing device: Te**x**t, **F**rame, **N**umber

Usage

1. Select Paragraph text.
2. Invoke the Frame Attributes dialog box by selecting Frame from the Text menu.

3. In the Number box, type or use the up and down arrows to change the value for the number of columns.

Frame Attributes, Gutter Width

Selection

Keyboard shortcut: Alt+X, F, Alt+G

Pointing device: Text, Frame, Gutter Width

Usage

1. Select Paragraph text.
2. Invoke the Frame Attributes dialog box by selecting Frame from the Text menu.
3. In the Gutter Width box, type or use the up and down arrows to change the value for the width of the gutters.

Paragraph

Select Paragraph from the Text menu to invoke the Paragraph dialog box. In the section called Category, there are four selections: Spacing, Tabs, Indents, and Bullet. Each category has its own Paragraph dialog box (see Figures CR5.12 through CR5.15). For more information about paragraphs, see Skill Sessions 10 and 30.

Selection

Keyboard shortcut: Alt+X, P

Pointing device: Text, Paragraph

Usage

1. Select Paragraph text.
2. Select Paragraph in the Text menu. This invokes the Paragraph dialog box.
3. Select the Category for which you want to make changes.
4. Make the changes you want using the appropriate options.
5. Click OK.

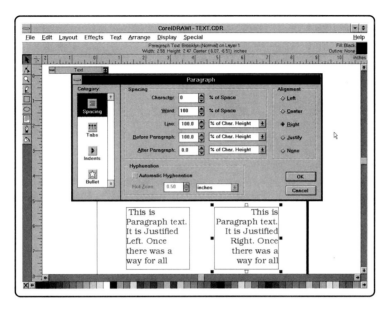

Figure CR5.12. The Paragraph dialog box displaying the Spacing Category and its available options.

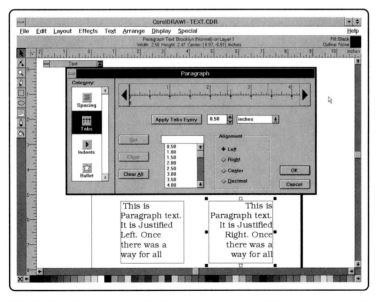

Figure CR5.13. The Paragraph dialog box displaying the Tabs Category and its available options.

807

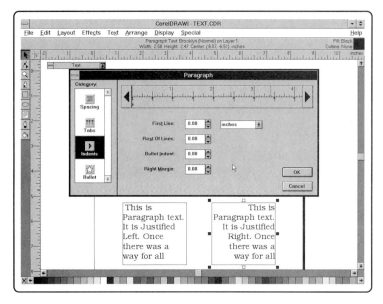

Figure CR5.14. The Paragraph dialog box displaying the Indents Category and its available options.

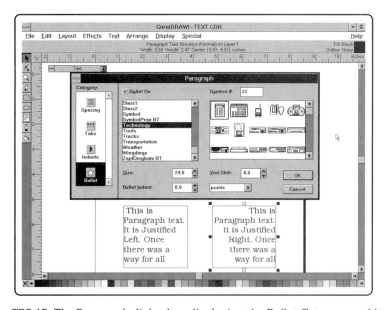

Figure CR5.15. The Paragraph dialog box displaying the Bullet Category and its available options.

Fit Text To Path

Corel Draw allows you to make your text fit to odd-shaped paths. Select your text and the object with which you want the text to flow; then select Fit Text To Path from the Text menu (Figure CR5.16).

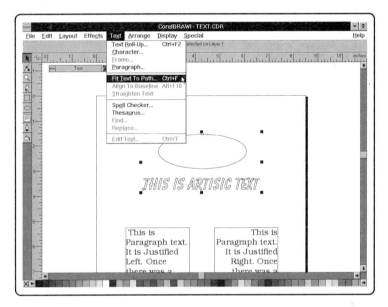

Figure CR5.16. Artistic text and an object selected and the Text menu with Fit Text To Path highlighted.

When you select Fit Text To Path from the Text menu, the Fit Text To Path roll-up appears. Select the options that you want to use and click the Apply button. The text now flows along the path of the object (see Figure CR5.17). For more information about the Fit Text To Path roll-up, see Skill Session 31.

Corel*NOTE!*

Fit Text To Path is available only for Artistic text mode.

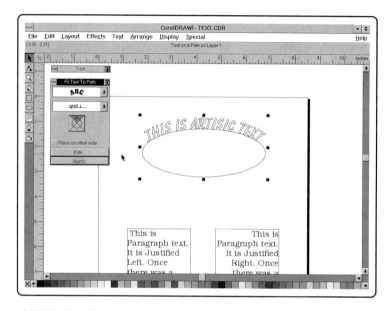

Figure CR5.17. The Fit Text To Path roll-up with the settings applied to the text and the object.

Selection

Keyboard shortcut: Alt+X, T or Ctrl+F

Pointing device: Te**xt**, Fit **T**ext To Path

Usage

1. Select Artistic text.
2. Select the object you are fitting the text to.
3. Select Fit Text To Path from the Text menu.
4. In the Text roll-up, select your options and click Apply.

Align To Baseline

Sometimes when you change the attributes of your text, the alignment may be altered. If the characters of the text do not appear to be on the baseline, you can select Align To Baseline from the Text menu. This option aligns all the nodes of your text to an imaginary baseline (see Figure CR5.18).

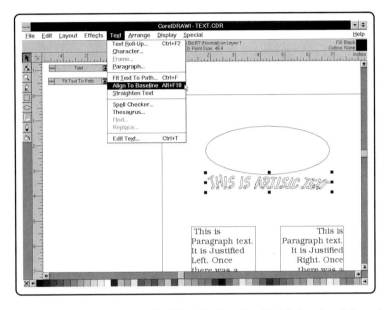

Figure CR5.18. The Text menu with Align To Baseline highlighted and the selected text aligned.

Corel *NOTE!*

> The baseline is an imaginary horizontal line. All the letters in a font will rest on this line.

Selection

Keyboard shortcut: Alt+X, L or Alt+F10

Pointing device: Te**x**t, **A**lign To Baseline

Usage

1. Select altered text.
2. Select Align To Baseline from the Text menu.
3. The text is aligned to its baseline.

Straighten Text

The Straighten Text option from the Text menu removes attributes previously applied to text. The text is returned to original form (see Figure CR5.19). These attributes include rotation and vertical or horizontal shifts, as well as angles that have been applied to the characters in the text.

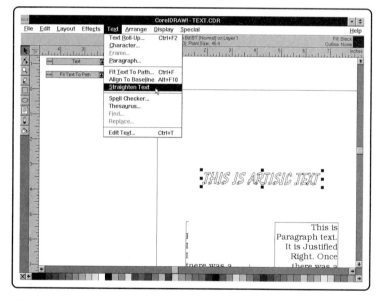

Figure CR5.19. The Text menu with Straighten Text highlighted and the straightened text selected.

Selection

Keyboard shortcut: Alt+X, S

Pointing device: Te**x**t, **S**traighten Text

Usage

1. Select altered text.
2. Select Straighten Text from the Text menu.

Spell Checker

If you want to check for any errors in your text, you can do so by selecting Spell Checker from the Text menu. Select this option to invoke the Spelling Checker dialog box (see Figure CR5.20). You can spell-check by either selecting the Artistic or Paragraph text you want to check or marqueeing a specific word with your A tool. You do not have to select text to be able to use the Spell Checker.

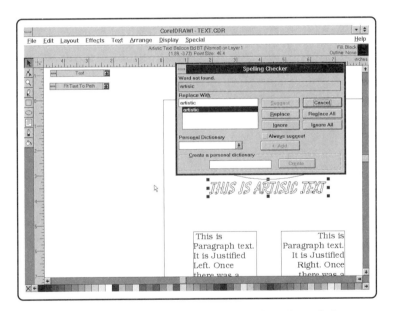

Figure CR5.20. The Spelling Checker dialog box and selected text being spell-checked.

There are many options in the Spelling Checker dialog box. It will look at your text and stop at a word that it believes is misspelled. You can ask the Spelling Checker to suggest correctly spelled words by enabling the Always suggest option. You can also ask it to replace just that word, or by selecting Replace All, replace every instance of that word with the correctly spelled word. Sometimes, you may want to leave a word unchanged. In this case you can click on the Ignore or Ignore All button.

You can create a personal dictionary; click on the Create button and then type a name for the dictionary. This will now be reflected under the Personal Dictionary section. For example, if there are specific acronyms that you consistently use, you can now add them to your personal dictionary and use it with your documents.

Selection

Keyboard shortcut: Alt+X, E

Pointing device: Text, Spell Checker

Usage

1. Select text with the Pick tool or by marqueeing a word, or you can invoke Spell Checker with nothing selected.
2. Select Spell Checker from the Text menu.
3. Select the options in the Spell Checker that you need.

Thesaurus

When you want to use words with similar meanings, you can select Thesaurus from the Text menu. The Thesaurus dialog box (see Figure CR5.21) gives you the option of checking for synonyms and definitions of words.

Corel *NOTE!*

> To look up a word that is not in your document, select Thesaurus and the dialog box will come up; type the word you want to check in the Synonym For box and then click on Lookup.

Selection

Keyboard shortcut: Alt+X, U

Pointing device: Te**x**t, Thesa**u**rus

Usage

1. Select text you want to check or just invoke the Thesaurus without text selected.
2. Select Thesaurus from the Text menu.
3. Select Lookup to check for synonyms.
4. Choose whether to replace the word or cancel.

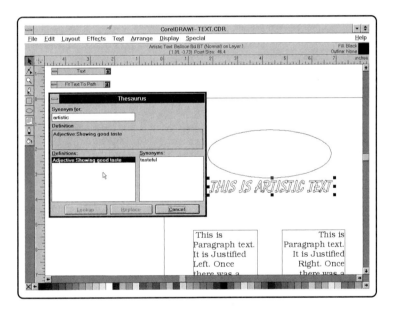

Figure CR5.21. The Thesaurus dialog box and selected text being checked.

Find

When you want to find a word, select Find in the Text menu to invoke the Find dialog box. This is helpful when you need to find a word in a large document. Under Find What, type the word you want to find and

select whether you want the search to match its case; then click on the
Find Next button (see Figure CR5.22).

Selection

Keyboard shortcut: Alt+X, I

Pointing device: **Text, Find**

Usage

1. Select Find from the Text menu.
2. Type the word you want to find in the Find What box.
3. Decide whether you want to Match Case and enable this option if
   you do.
4. Click the Find Next button to find your word.

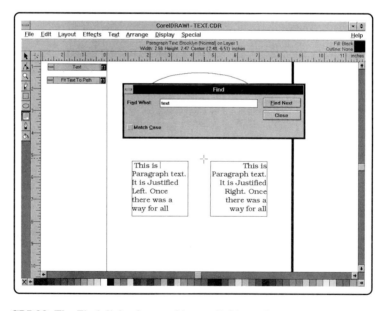

Figure CR5.22. The Find dialog box and its available options.

Replace

You can easily replace text by using the Replace command on the Text menu. Select this option to invoke the Replace dialog box. Under Find What, type the word you want to find. Under Replace With, type the word you want to use to replace it with. Other options under Replace include Find Next, Replace, Replace All, and Match Case (see Figure CR5.23).

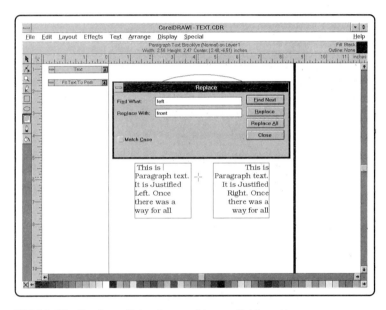

Figure CR5.23. The Replace dialog box and its available options.

Selection

Keyboard shortcut: Alt+X, A

Pointing device: Te**x**t, Repl**a**ce

Usage

1. Select Replace from the Text menu.
2. In the Find What section, type the word you want to replace.

3. In the Replace With section, type the new word.

4. Click the Replace button.

Edit Text

When you want to edit either Artistic or Paragraph text, select the text and then select Edit Text from the Text menu. This invokes the Edit Text dialog box. The title of the box will reflect whether you have Paragraph text or Artistic text selected. There are many options to use when editing text. You can change the Font, Alignment, Size, and measurement system, as well as the Style.

Three other options are Spacing, Import, and Paste. You can enter text in this dialog box as well as retype what already exists. Below the Styles section, there is a preview of the selected font (see Figure CR5.24). For more information about editing text, see Skill Session 10 and Skill Sessions 29 through 36.

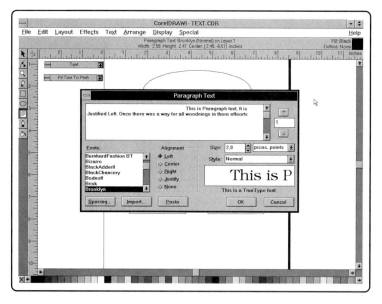

Figure CR5.24. The Edit Text dialog box with Paragraph text selected.

Selection

Keyboard shortcut: Alt+X, X or Ctrl+T

Pointing device: Te**x**t, Edit Te**x**t

Usage

1. Select text you want to edit.
2. Select Edit Text from the Text menu.
3. In the dialog box, change the options and settings to fit your needs.
4. Click OK.

6

Arrange Menu Commands

The Arrange menu (see Figure CR6.1) provides commands for arranging the objects in your document. These commands are Move, Align, and Order. You can also Group and Ungroup objects. The Combine, Break Apart, and Weld options are also selected from this menu. The Separate command allows you to separate objects that have been blended or extruded, as well as create other effects. The Convert To Curves option allows you to make text into an object.

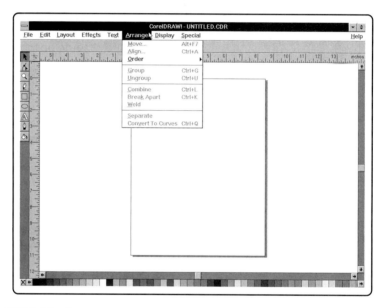

Figure CR6.1. The Arrange menu.

Move

This option is grayed out when there is no object in your file. Place an object in your file and pull down the Arrange menu, and you will see that Move is now enabled (see Figure CR6.2). For more information about moving objects see Skill Session 18.

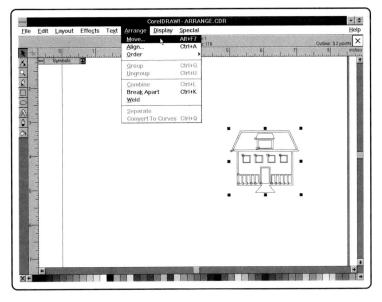

Figure CR6.2. An object selected and Move highlighted from the Arrange menu.

Selection

Keyboard shortcut: Alt+A, M or Alt+F7

Pointing device: **A**rrange, **M**ove

Usage

1. Select an object in your document.

2. Select Move from the Arrange menu. The Move dialog box appears.

In the Move dialog box (see Figure CR6.3), you can set new horizontal and vertical values. The measurement system reflects the current setting in the Grid Setup dialog box. For more information about Grid Setup, see Skill Session 26.

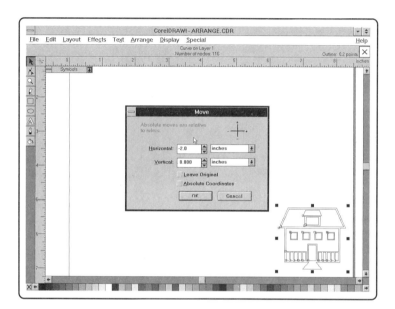

Figure CR6.3. The Move dialog box.

Move, Horizontal

Selection

Keyboard shortcut: Alt+A, M, Alt+H

Pointing device: **A**rrange, **M**ove, **H**orizontal

Usage

1. Enter a new horizontal distance to move your object.
2. Click the OK button (see Figure CR6.4).

Move, Vertical

Selection

Keyboard shortcut: Alt+A, M, Alt+V

Pointing device: **A**rrange, **M**ove, **V**ertical

Usage

1. Enter a new vertical distance to move your object.
2. Click the OK button.

There are two other options: Leave Original and Absolute Coordinates. If you select Leave Original, a duplicate of the selected object is moved to the new location; the original will stay where it is. Select Absolute Coordinates to move the object relative to the rulers.

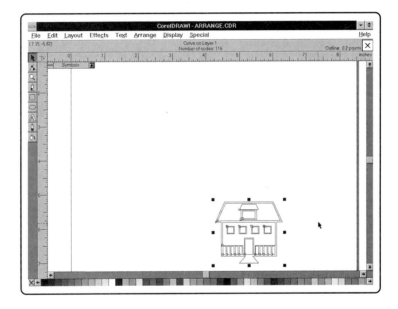

Figure CR6.4. The moved object.

Move, Leave Original

Selection

Keyboard shortcut: Alt+A, M, Alt+L

Pointing device: **A**rrange, **M**ove, **L**eave Original

Usage

1. Enable the Leave Original option.
2. Click the OK button.

Move, Absolute Coordinates

Selection

Keyboard shortcut: Alt+A, M, Alt+A

Pointing device: **A**rrange, **M**ove, **A**bsolute Coordinates

Usage

1. Enable the Absolute Coordinates option.
2. Click the OK button.

Corel*NOTE!*

All options in the Move dialog box can be enabled individually or in various combinations. For example, you can change the Vertical position and enable the Leave Original option.

Align

You can use this option to align an object to your page, or you can select more than one object and align them to each other. In Figure CR6.5, two objects are aligned. For more information about aligning objects, see Skill Session 17.

Selection

Keyboard shortcut: Alt+A, A or Ctrl+A

Pointing device: **A**rrange, **A**lign

Usage

1. Select the objects to be aligned.
2. Select Align from the Arrange menu.
3. The Align dialog box appears.

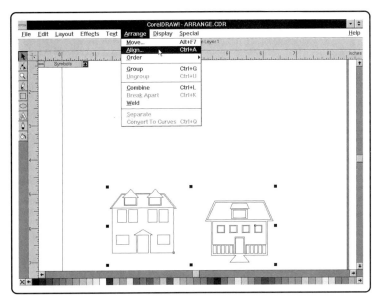

Figure CR6.5. Two objects aligned to each other and Align highlighted in the Arrange menu.

In the Align dialog box (see Figure CR6.6), you can align objects vertically and horizontally. There are three options in each section. The vertical alignment options are Top, Center, and Bottom. The horizontal alignment options are Left, Center, and Right. There are two other options: Align to Grid and Align to Center of Page.

Corel*NOTE!*

> The last object that you select is what the other objects are aligned to. After selecting your options from the Align dialog box, press the Enter key or the OK button in the dialog box.

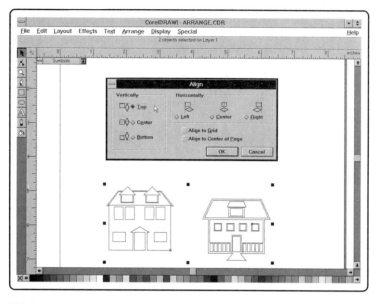

Figure CR6.6. Two objects selected and the Align dialog box with the Top selection enabled in the Vertically section.

Align, Top

Selection

Keyboard shortcut: Alt+A, A, Alt+T or Ctrl+A, Alt+T

Pointing device: **A**rrange, **A**lign, **T**op

Usage

1. Select Top from the Vertically section.
2. Click the OK button. The objects are aligned along the top (see Figure CR6.7).

Align, Center

Selection

Keyboard shortcut: Alt+A, A, Alt+E or Ctrl+A, Alt+E

Pointing device: **A**rrange, **A**lign, Center

Usage

1. Select Center from the Vertically section.

2. Click the OK button. The objects are aligned along their vertical center.

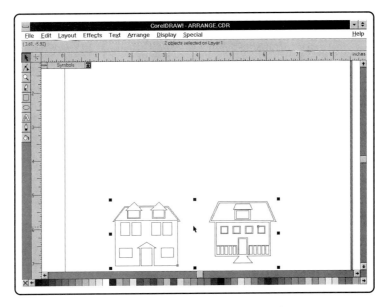

Figure CR6.7. Two objects aligned along the top of each other.

Align, Bottom

Selection

Keyboard shortcut: Alt+A, A, Alt+B or Ctrl+A, Alt+B

Pointing device: **A**rrange, **A**lign, **B**ottom

Usage

1. Select Bottom from the Vertically section.

2. Click the OK button. The objects are aligned along their bottoms.

Align, Left

Selection

Keyboard shortcut: Alt+A, A, Alt+L or Ctrl+A, Alt+L

Pointing device: **A**rrange, **A**lign, **L**eft

Usage

1. Select Left from the Horizontally section.
2. Click the OK button. The objects are aligned along their left side.

Align, Center

Selection

Keyboard shortcut: Alt+A, A, Alt+C or Ctrl+A, Alt+C

Pointing device: **A**rrange, **A**lign, **C**enter

Usage

1. Select Center from the Horizontally section.
2. Click the OK button. The objects are aligned along their horizontal center.

Align, Right

Selection

Keyboard shortcut: Alt+A, A, Alt+R or Ctrl+A, Alt+R

Pointing device: **A**rrange, **A**lign, **R**ight

Usage

1. Select Right from the Horizontally section.
2. Click the OK button. The objects are aligned along their right side.

Align, Align to Grid

Selection

Keyboard shortcut: Alt+A, A, Alt+G or Ctrl+A, Alt+G

Pointing device: **A**rrange, **A**lign, **A**lign to Grid

Usage

1. Select Align to Grid.
2. Click the OK button. The objects are aligned to the current grid setup.

Align, Align to Center of Page

Selection

Keyboard shortcut: Alt+A, A, Alt+P or Ctrl+A, Alt+P

Pointing device: **A**rrange, **A**lign, Align to Center of **P**age

Usage

1. Select Align to Center of Page.
2. Click the OK button. The objects are aligned to the center of the page.

Order

This option allows you to change the order of one or more objects. Every time you draw a new object, it is as if you are drawing that object on top of the last object drawn or placed in your document. This is a default setting.

When you select Order from the Arrange menu, a cascading menu appears. The selections are To Front, To Back, Forward One, Back One, and Reverse Order (see Figure CR6.8). For more information about ordering objects, see Skill Session 13.

Corel *NOTE!*

The Reverse Order option will only work with two or more objects selected.

Selection

Keyboard shortcut: Alt+A, O

Pointing device: **A**rrange, **O**rder

Usage

1. Select objects that you want to change the order of.
2. Select Order from the Arrange menu.
3. From the cascading menu, select the option you want.

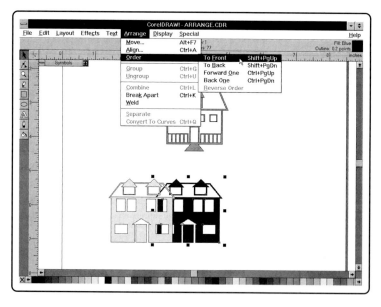

Figure CR6.8. One object selected, Order highlighted from the Arrange menu, and To Front highlighted from the cascading menu.

Order, To Front

Selection

Keyboard shortcut: Alt+A, O, Alt+F or Shift+PgUp

Pointing device: **A**rrange, **O**rder, To **F**ront

Usage

1. Select object(s) that you want to bring to the front.
2. Select Order from the Arrange menu.
3. From the cascading menu, select To Front. The selected object(s) will now be moved to the front (see Figure CR6.9).

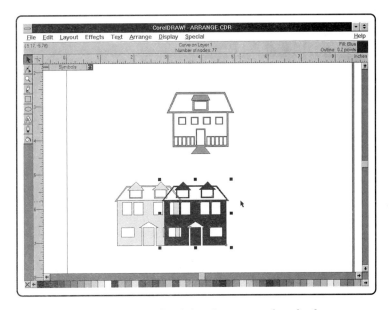

Figure CR6.9. The selected object after it has been moved to the front.

Order, To Back

Selection

Keyboard shortcut: Alt+A, O, Alt+B or Shift+PgDn

Pointing device: **A**rrange, **O**rder, To **B**ack

Usage

1. Select object(s) that you want to send to the back.
2. Select Order from the Arrange menu.
3. From the cascading menu, select To Back. The selected object(s) are moved to the back.

Order, Forward One

Selection

Keyboard shortcut: Alt+A, O, Alt+O or Ctrl+PgUp

Pointing device: **A**rrange, **O**rder, **F**orward One

Corel*NOTE!*

> When you select Forward One or Back One, the selected object(s) will move forward or back by one position. For example, if there are three objects and the object that you have selected is the third from the front, selecting Forward One will make it second from the front.

Usage

1. Select object(s) that you want to bring forward one.
2. Select Order from the Arrange menu.
3. From the cascading menu, select Forward One. The selected object(s) will now be moved up by one position.

Order, Back One

Selection

Keyboard shortcut: Alt+A, O, Alt+N or Ctrl+PgDn

Pointing device: **A**rrange, **O**rder, Back **O**ne

Usage

1. Select the object(s) that you want to send back.

2. Select Order from the Arrange menu.

3. From the cascading menu select Back One. The selected object(s) will be moved back by one position.

Order, Reverse Order

Selection

Keyboard shortcut: Alt+A, O, Alt+R

Pointing device: **A**rrange, **O**rder, **R**everse Order

Usage

1. Select the objects that you want to change the order of.

2. Select Order from the Arrange menu.

3. From the cascading menu, select Reverse Order. The selected objects will now be in reverse order.

Group

This option allows you to group selected objects, including text. This will help you when you have already created and placed objects in the order you require. You can select those objects and group them, allowing you to move the grouped objects as if they were one single unit (see Figures CR6.10 and CR6.11). For more information about grouping, see Skill Session 14.

Selection

Keyboard shortcut: Alt+A, G or Ctrl+G

Pointing device: **A**rrange, **G**roup

Usage

1. Select the objects that you want to group.

2. Select Group from the Arrange menu.

3. These objects will be grouped and can be moved as a unit.

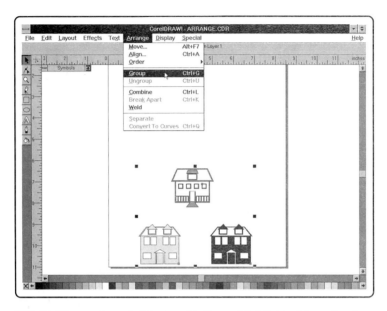

Figure CR6.10. Three selected objects with Group highlighted from the Arrange Menu.

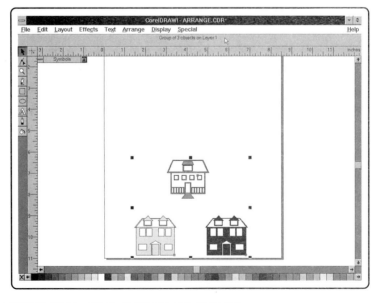

Figure CR6.11. Three selected objects now grouped.

Ungroup

Select this option to ungroup objects that are grouped (see Figures CR6.12 and CR6.13). For more information about Arrange Ungroup, see Skill Session 14.

Selection

Keyboard shortcut: Alt+A, U or Ctrl+U

Pointing device: **A**rrange, **U**ngroup

Usage

1. Select a group of objects that you want to ungroup.
2. Select Ungroup from the Arrange menu. The objects are now ungrouped and can be moved independently.

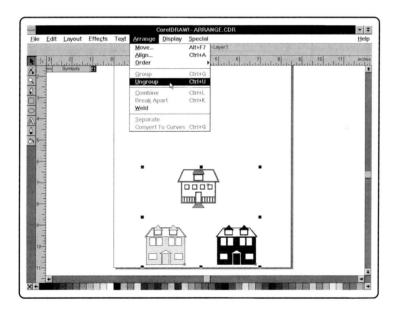

Figure CR6.12. Group of three objects selected with Ungroup highlighted from the Arrange menu.

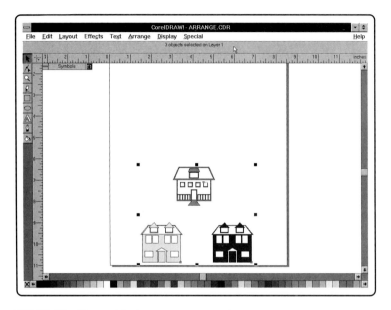

Figure CR6.13. The three objects now ungrouped.

Combine

To use the Combine command, select two or more objects. These objects can overlap each other or have space between them. The last object selected is what the other objects will default to. For example, suppose you have a yellow circle, a red square, and a blue rectangle. If you select the blue rectangle last and then combine the objects, the yellow circle and red square will now be blue (see Figures CR6.14 and CR6.15). For more information about combining, see Skill Session 15.

Corel*NOTE!*

When you combine text, it has the same effect as converting it to curves. Your text is now a curve and will not be editable. For more information about converting text to curves, see Skill Session 25.

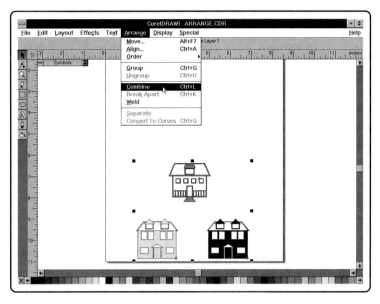

Figure CR6.14. Three objects selected with Combine highlighted from the Arrange menu.

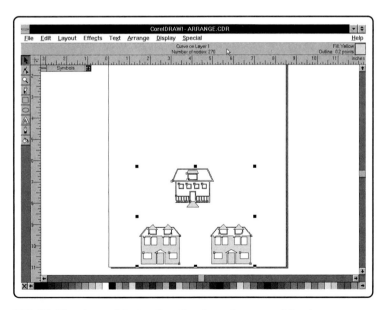

Figure CR6.15. The three objects after they have been combined.

Selection

Keyboard shortcut: Alt+A, C or Ctrl+L

Pointing device: **A**rrange, **C**ombine

Usage

1. Select objects that you want to combine.
2. Select Combine from the Arrange menu. The status line now reflects one object, with *x* number of nodes.

Break Apart

Select the Break Apart option to break combined objects into separate objects (see Figures CR6.16 and CR6.17). For more information about breaking combined objects apart, see Skill Session 15.

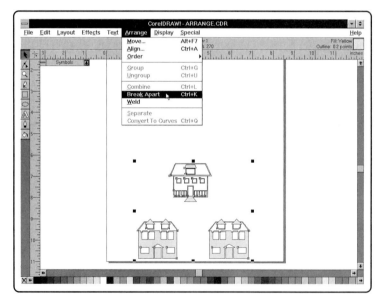

Figure CR6.16. The selected object with Break Apart highlighted from the Arrange menu.

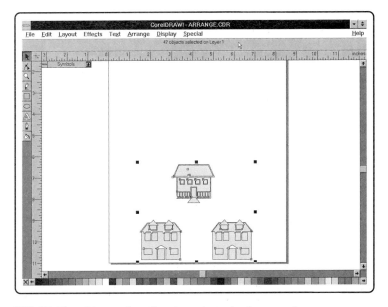

Figure CR6.17. The objects after they have been broken apart.

Selection

Keyboard shortcut: Alt+A, K or Ctrl+K

Pointing device: **A**rrange, Brea**k** Apart

Usage

1. Select the object that you want to break apart.
2. Select Break Apart from the Arrange menu. The object is now broken down into separate parts.

Weld

This command will weld several objects to create an entirely new shape. A complex shape such as a key can be made rather quickly by placing elements like a couple of ellipses together with a few rectangles. You can create odd shapes by combining and then node editing, but welding cuts down on the amount of time spent to do so.

An object will cut a hole through a larger object if it is engulfed by the large object. Two objects will form a new object if they overlap each other (see Figures CR6.18 and CR6.19). For more information about Arrange, Weld, see Skill Session 24.

Selection

Keyboard shortcut: Alt+A, W

Pointing device: **A**rrange, **W**eld

Usage

1. Select the objects that you want to weld.
2. Select Weld from the Arrange menu. Your objects will now be welded into one shape.

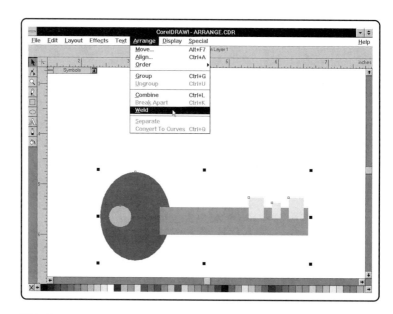

Figure CR6.18. The selected objects with Weld highlighted from the Arrange menu.

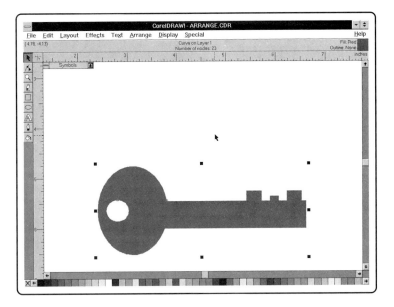

Figure CR6.19. The welded object.

Separate

The Separate option is used to break apart objects that have such effects
as blends, contours, extrudes, and so on applied to them (see Figures
CR6.20 and CR6.21). For more information about separating, see Skill
Sessions 5 and 23.

Selection

Keyboard shortcut: Alt+A, S

Pointing device: **A**rrange, **S**eparate

Usage

1. Select the object that has an effect applied to it, such as a blend.
2. Select Separate from the Arrange menu.
3. Your object is now separated into three separate parts.

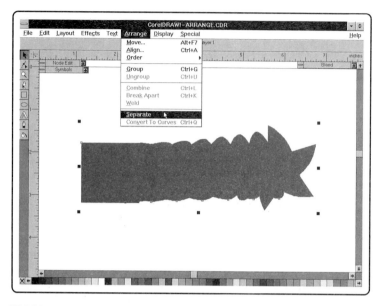

Figure CR6.20. A blend group selected with Separate highlighted from the Arrange menu.

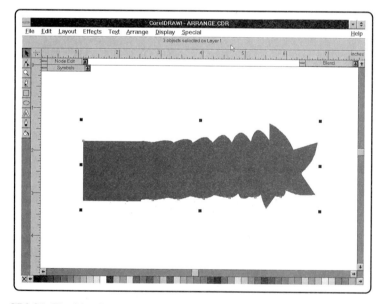

Figure CR6.21. The blend group separated into three objects.

Corel*NOTE!*

For blends, the three parts resulting from the Separate command include the starting and ending objects that were blended. The steps between, which created the blend, will be a group of *x* number of objects, where *x* is the number of steps in the blend.

Convert To Curves

This option is used to convert your text or fonts to curves (see Figures CR6.22 and CR6.23). This comes in handy when you want to output your file through a service bureau that does not have the fonts you are using. Although this eliminates providing the service bureau with the fonts, it may increase the size of your file. For more information about converting text to curves, see Skill Session 25.

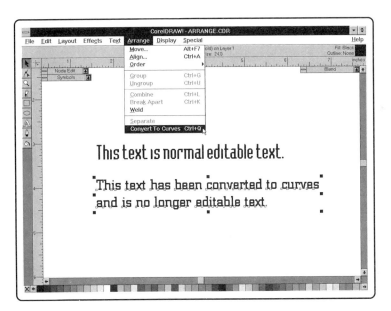

Figure CR6.22. The selected Artistic text with Convert To Curves highlighted from the Arrange menu.

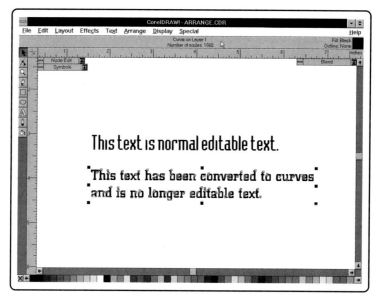

Figure CR6.23. The converted text.

Corel *NOTE!*

Paragraph text cannot be converted to curves.

Selection

Keyboard shortcut: Alt+A, V or Ctrl+Q

Pointing device: **A**rrange, Con**v**ert To Curves

Usage

1. Select the Artistic text you want to convert to curves.
2. Select Convert To Curves from the Arrange menu. Your Artistic text is now converted to curves.

7

Display Menu Commands

The Display menu provides various commands for displaying several tools (see Figure CR7.1). They include the rulers, status line, color palette, and the floating toolbox. This menu also allows you to control the display of objects in various modes including how, when, and what objects are displayed in your document.

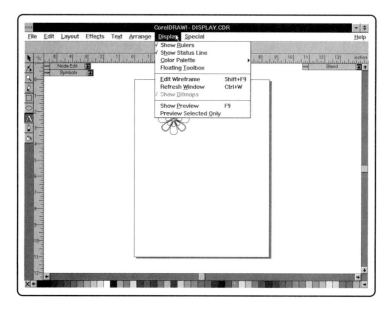

Figure CR7.1. The Display menu.

Show Rulers

Select Show Rulers from the Display menu, and the rulers will appear on-screen. A check mark appears next to the Show Rulers option when they are enabled (see Figures CR7.2).

Selection

Keyboard shortcut: Alt+D, R

Pointing device: **D**isplay, Show **R**ulers

Usage

1. Select Show Rulers from the Display menu. Rulers appear on-screen.

2. Select Show Rulers from the Display menu a second time. The rulers disappear from the screen.

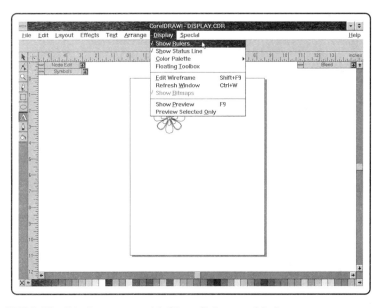

Figure CR7.2. The Display menu with Show Rulers enabled.

Show Status Line

When Show Status Line is enabled, the status of selected object(s) is displayed in the area below the menu bar. The upper left of the status line reflects the location of your cursor in your file. The status line reads "Leave Original" below the cursor location when you duplicate an object by pressing the secondary mouse button or the plus sign (+) on your keypad. The selected object's fill, outline size, and color are displayed on the far right of the status line (see Figures CR7.3).

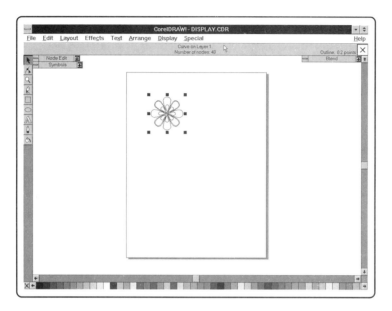

Figure CR7.3. Object selected with its information displayed in Status Line.

Corel*NOTE!*

> If you have the Snap To Grid option enabled, the status line reflects this in the same area below the cursor location.

Selection

Keyboard shortcut: Alt+D, H

Pointing device: **D**isplay, **Sh**ow Status Line

Usage

1. Select Show Status Line from the Display menu.
2. When the status line is enabled, a check mark will appear next to it in the menu (see Figure CR7.4).
3. Select Show Status Line when it is enabled to turn it off.

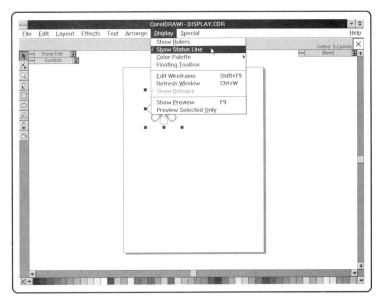

Figure CR7.4. Display menu with Show Status Line selected.

Color Palette

To change or disable the Color Palette at the bottom of the screen, select Color Palette from the Display menu (see Figure CR7.5). For more information about palettes, see Skill Session 12.

Selection

Keyboard shortcut: Alt+D, C

Pointing device: Display, Color Palette

Usage

1. Select Color Palette from the Display menu.
2. Choose a palette from the cascading menu. The enabled palette will be indicated by a check mark.

851

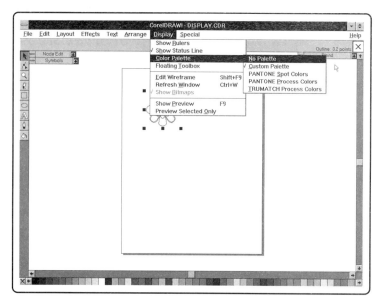

Figure CR7.5. The Display menu with Color Palette enabled and the Color Palette cascading menu displayed.

Color Palette, No Palette

Selection

Keyboard shortcut: Alt+D, C, N

Pointing device: **D**isplay, **C**olor Palette, **N**o Palette

Usage

1. Select Color Palette from the Display menu.
2. Choose No Palette from the cascading menu. The Color Palette is disabled.

852

Color Palette, Custom Palette

Selection

Keyboard shortcut: Alt+D, C, C

Pointing device: **D**isplay, **C**olor Palette, **C**ustom Palette

Usage

1. Select Color Palette from the Display menu.
2. Choose Custom Palette from the cascading menu. The default palette is displayed at the bottom of the screen.

Color Palette, PANTONE Spot Colors

Selection

Keyboard shortcut: Alt+D, C, S

Pointing device: **D**isplay, **C**olor Palette, PANTONE **S**pot Colors

Usage

1. Select Color Palette from the Display menu.
2. Choose PANTONE Spot Colors from the cascading menu. The PANTONE Spot Colors palette is displayed at the bottom of the screen.

Color Palette, PANTONE Process Colors

Selection

Keyboard shortcut: Alt+D, C, P

Pointing device: **D**isplay, **C**olor Palette, PANTONE **P**rocess Colors

Usage

1. Select Color Palette from the Display menu.
2. Choose PANTONE Process Colors from the cascading menu. The PANTONE Process Colors palette is displayed at the bottom of the screen.

853

Color Palette, TRUMATCH Process Colors

Selection

Keyboard shortcut: Alt+D, C, T

Pointing device: **D**isplay, **C**olor Palette, **T**RUMATCH Process Colors

Usage

1. Select Color Palette from the Display menu.
2. Choose TRUMATCH Process Colors from the cascading menu. The TRUMATCH Process Colors palette is displayed at the bottom of the screen.

Floating Toolbox

Select this command to turn the standard, static tool box into one that can be placed anywhere on the page (see Figure CR7.6).

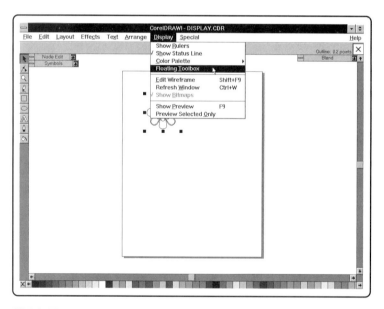

Figure CR7.6. The Display menu with Floating Toolbox selected and the Floating Toolbox positioned in the center of the screen.

Selection

Keyboard shortcut: Alt+D, T

Pointing device: **D**isplay, Floating **T**oolbox

Usage

1. Select Floating Toolbox from the Display menu. The floating toolbox will appear on-screen.
2. Drag the toolbox anywhere on-screen.
3. To return to the standard toolbox, select Floating Toolbox from Display menu.

Corel *NOTE!*

You can also click on the close button in the upper left corner of the toolbox to disable the Floating Toolbox.

Edit Wireframe

Select this option to work in wireframe mode. When editing objects with complex fills and attributes, this option allows for faster screen redraws (see Figures CR7.7 and CR7.8).

Selection

Keyboard shortcut: Alt+D, E or Shift+F9

Pointing device: **D**isplay, **E**dit Wireframe

Usage

1. Select Edit Wireframe from the Display menu. This toggles you between preview mode and wireframe mode.

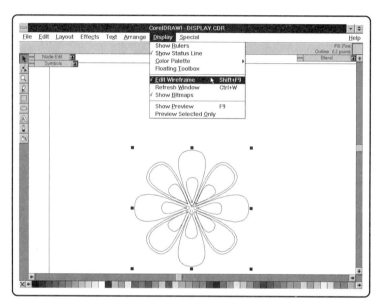

Figure CR7.7. The Display menu with Edit Wireframe selected and the object displayed in wireframe mode.

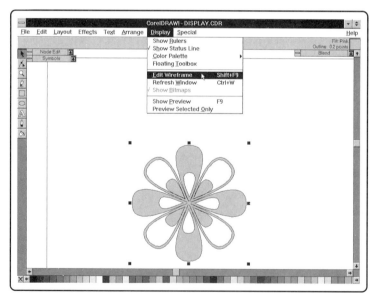

Figure CR7.8. The Display menu with Edit Wireframe selected and the object displayed in preview mode.

Display Refresh Window

Sometimes, when zooming in and out of your window or when working close up with your shape tool, remnants from your altered object(s) remain on-screen. To remove these remnants, select Refresh Window from the Display menu.

Selection

Keyboard shortcut: Alt+D, W or Ctrl+W

Pointing device: **D**isplay, Refresh **W**indow

Usage

1. Select Refresh Window from the Display menu.
2. The remnants from your altered object(s) will disappear.

Show Bitmaps

Select this option to hide any bitmaps in your file. This is another method of speeding up screen redraw. When Show Bitmaps is disabled, you will see only the bounding box around the bitmap on-screen (see Figures CR7.9 through CR7.11).

Corel*NOTE!*

> Show Bitmaps cannot be enabled or disabled in preview mode.

Selection

Keyboard shortcut: Alt+D, B

Pointing device: **D**isplay, Show **B**itmaps

Usage

1. Select Show Bitmaps from the Display menu. A check mark appears next to Show Bitmaps.
2. Any bitmaps in your file will display on-screen.
3. To hide bitmaps, reselect Show Bitmaps and the check mark will disappear.

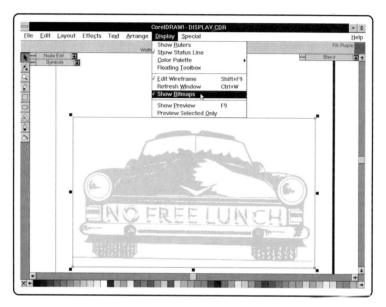

Figure CR7.9. The Display menu with Show Bitmaps enabled and a bitmap displayed.

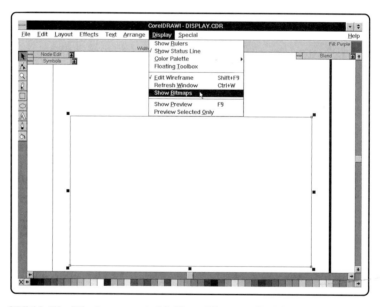

Figure CR7.10. The Display menu with Show Bitmaps disabled and the bounding box of the bitmap displayed.

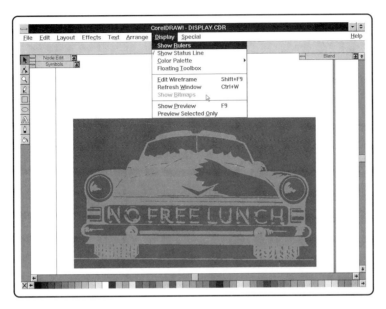

Figure CR7.11. Bitmap shown in preview mode.

Show Preview

Select this option to see a full preview of the current page(s) in your file. The toolbox, all status lines, and palettes will not be displayed. You can show a preview whether you are zoomed in close to an object, viewing the full page, or anywhere in between. See Figures CR7.12 and CR7.13.

Selection

Keyboard shortcut: Alt+D, P or F9

Pointing device: **D**isplay, Show **P**review

Usage

Select Show Preview from the Display menu. A preview of the current file appears on-screen.

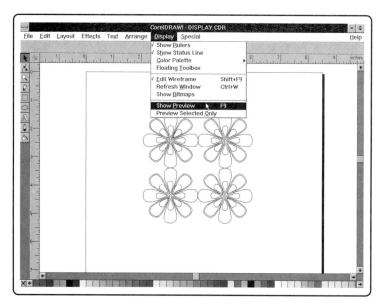

Figure CR7.12. Show Preview selected from the Display menu.

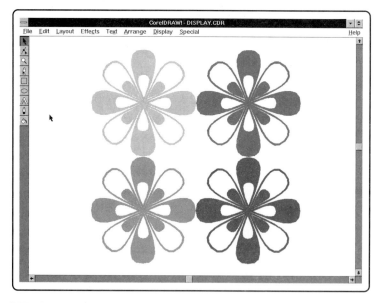

Figure CR7.13. A preview of how this file currently appears.

Preview Selected Only

If you want to view only certain objects in your file, select them and then enable the Preview Selected Only option from the Display menu (see Figures CR7.14 and CR7.15).

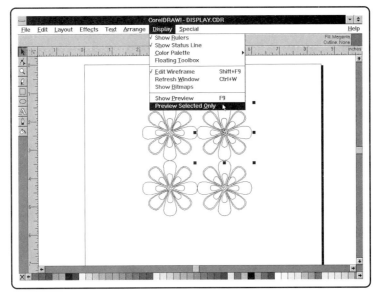

Figure CR7.14. Selected object with Preview Selected Only highlighted in the Display menu.

Selection

Keyboard shortcut: Alt+D, O

Pointing device: **D**isplay, Preview Selected **O**nly

Usage

1. Select the object(s) to be previewed.
2. Select Preview Selected Only from the Display menu. The file will now display selected objects.

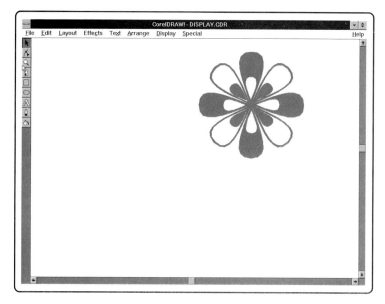

Figure CR7.15. The preview of the selected object.

8

Special Menu Commands

The Special menu (see Figure CR8.1) provides commands for creating patterns, arrows, and symbols. You can also select the commands Extract and Merge Back for text. You can change Corel Draw preferences by selecting Preferences from this menu.

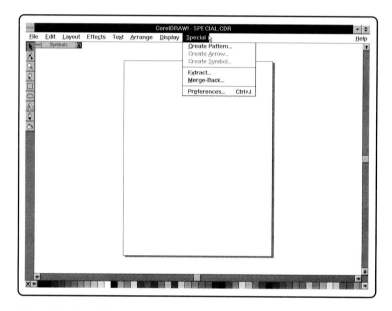

Figure CR8.1. The Special menu.

Create Pattern

To create a pattern, draw an object and select Create Pattern from the Special menu. You can choose to use the entire object or sections of it to create the pattern.

The Create Pattern dialog box appears on-screen (see Figure CR8.2). Select the Two Color option to change the color of the foreground and background of the pattern. Create your pattern with a black-and-white object. To change the color of a Two Color pattern, select the Color icon from the Fill tool fly-out menu. Selections for foreground and background colors in that dialog box are available. There are three settings for the Resolution for Two Color patterns: Low, Medium, and High.

Figure CR8.2. The Create Pattern dialog box.

Select the Full Color option to create a pattern that retains the object's colors. When creating a Full Color pattern, you will be asked to name the pattern. For more information about patterns, see Skill Sessions 12.

Selection

Keyboard shortcut: Alt+S, C

Pointing device: **S**pecial, **C**reate Pattern

Usage

1. Open a file or draw an object with which to create a pattern.
2. Select Create Pattern from the Special menu. The Create Pattern dialog box appears.
3. Select Two Color or Full Color.
4. Click on the OK button. The cursor becomes a large cross hair (see Figure CR8.3).
5. Marquee-select the area you want to use for your pattern.
6. If the area you selected is what you want to use, click on OK in the Create Pattern dialog box (see Figure CR8.4).

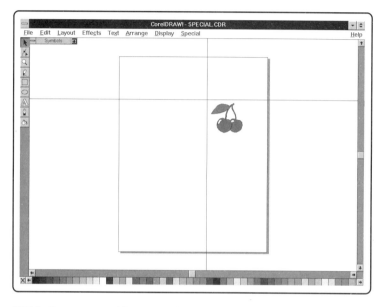

Figure CR8.3. Cursor turned into cross hair for marqueeing object for creation of pattern.

Figure CR8.4. The Create Pattern dialog box prompt.

7. Name your pattern in the Save Full-Color Pattern dialog box (see Figure CR8.5).

Figure CR8.5. The Save Full-Color Pattern dialog box.

8. Select an object to fill with the new pattern.

9. Select the Two Color or Full Color icon from the Fill tool fly-out (see Figure CR8.6).

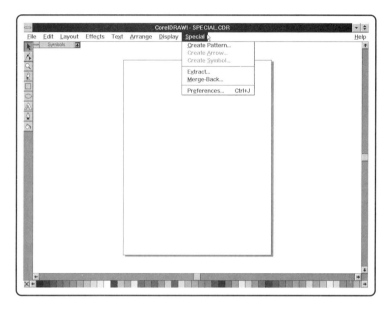

Figure CR8.6. An object selected for filling with the new pattern with the Full Color icon from the Fill Tool fly-out selected.

10. Select the newly created pattern from the bottom of the Pattern dialog box (see Figure CR8.7). The selected object is now filled with the new pattern (see Figure CR8.8).

Create Arrow

Use this command to create an arrow. You must first have an object selected. Then select Create Arrow option from the Special menu. You will be prompted, "Create arrow with selected object?" Click on OK if the object selected is what you want to create an arrow with. Draw a line and select the Outlinepen tool.

867

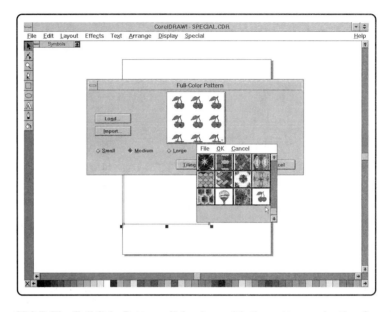

Figure CR8.7. The Full-ColorPattern dialog box with the pattern selection fly-out and the newly created pattern located at the bottom of the fly-out.

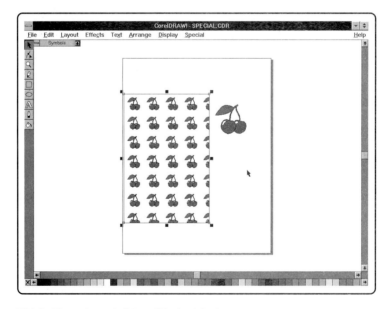

Figure CR8.8. The selected object filled with the new pattern.

The newly created arrow is added to the very bottom of the arrows section in the Outline Pen dialog box. The new arrow is located at the end of the Arrows Options fly-out. The line you previously selected now displays the new arrow. You cannot see the arrow in Wireframe mode. For more information about creating arrows, see Skill Session 11, "The Outline Tool."

Corel *NOTE!*

> When creating arrows, you cannot use objects that are grouped. Objects that have been combined or welded can be used.

Selection

Keyboard shortcut: Alt+S, A

Pointing device: **S**pecial, Create **A**rrow

Usage

1. Select an object.
2. Select Create Arrow from the Special menu (see Figure CR8.9).
3. Click OK in the Create Arrow dialog box prompt (see Figure CR8.10).
4. Draw a line on-screen.
5. Invoke the Outline Pen dialog box.
6. Select the newly created arrow from the end of the Arrows Options fly-out (see Figure CR8.11).
7. The line now displays the new arrow added to it (see Figure CR8.12).

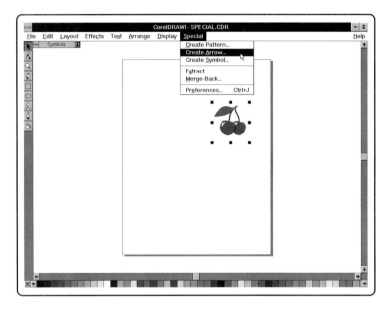

Figure CR8.9. An object selected and the Special menu with Create Arrow highlighted.

Figure CR8.10. The Create Arrow dialog box prompt.

Create Symbol

The next item in the Special menu is Create Symbol. You must have an object selected when creating a symbol. Select Create Symbol from the Special menu. The Create Symbol dialog box appears on-screen. Select the category into which you want to place the new symbol, or type a name to create a new category. Invoke the Symbols roll-up and find the category into which you placed the symbol. The symbol is located at the end of that category's list. For more information about creating symbols, see Skill Session 10.

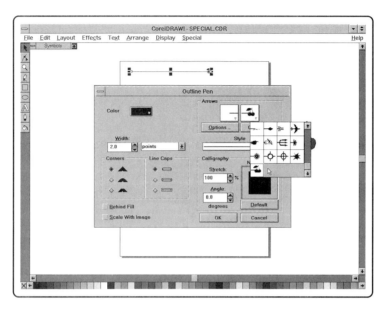

Figure CR8.11. A line selected and the new arrow displayed in the Outline Pen dialog box.

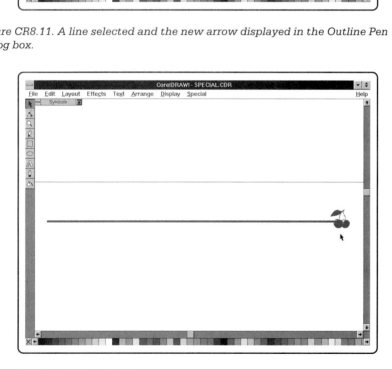

Figure CR8.12 The line with the new arrow.

Corel *NOTE!*

> When creating symbols, you cannot use objects that are grouped.
> Objects that have been combined or welded can be used.

Selection

Keyboard shortcut: Alt+S, S

Pointing device: **S**pecial, Create **S**ymbol

Usage

1. Select the object you want to create a symbol with.
2. Select Create Symbol from the Special menu (see Figure CR8.13).

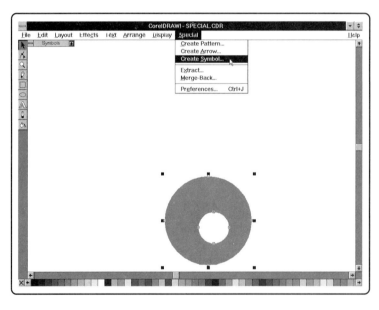

Figure CR8.13. The selected object with Create Symbol highlighted in the Special menu.

3. Select a category for the symbol in the Create Symbol dialog box (see Figure CR8.14) or create a new category.

Figure CR8.14. The Create Symbol dialog box.

4. Click the OK button.

5. In the Symbols roll-up, find the category where the new symbol was placed (see Figure CR8.15).

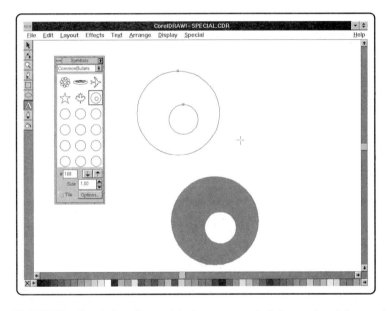

Figure CR8.15. The Symbols roll-up with the new symbol dragged and dropped onto the screen.

Extract

You can take any text created in a Corel Draw file and edit it in a word processing program. This is especially handy when you have a very large text file to edit. Select the text and then select the Extract option from the Special menu. The Extract dialog box appears. You can give your file a name that will be saved with the .TXT extension. You can also choose which directory to place the text in. In this example, the extracted text was edited in Windows Notepad. For more information about extracting text, see Skill Session 33.

Selection

Keyboard shortcut: Alt+S, X

Pointing device: **S**pecial, E**x**tract

Usage

1. Select the text you want to edit.
2. Select Extract from the Special menu (see Figure CR8.16).

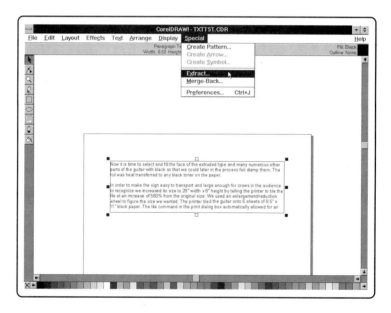

Figure CR8.16. Text selected with Extract highlighted in the Special menu.

3. In the Extract dialog box, name the file (see Figure CR8.17).

Figure CR8.17. The Extract dialog box.

4. Click the OK button.

5. Open the file in a word processing program and make your edits (see Figure CR8.18).

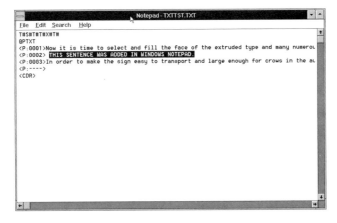

Figure CR8.18. The extracted text file edited in a word processing program.

6. Save your file.

Merge-Back

To place text that has been edited in a word processing program back into your Corel Draw file, select Merge-Back from the Special menu. The Merge Back dialog box appears. Select the filename and directory of the text file you want to merge into your document. After you click on OK, the edited text file appears on-screen. For more information about merging text, see Skill Session 33.

Selection

Keyboard shortcut: Alt+S, M

Pointing device: **S**pecial, **M**erge-Back

Usage

1. Select Merge-Back from the Special menu (see Figure CR8.19).

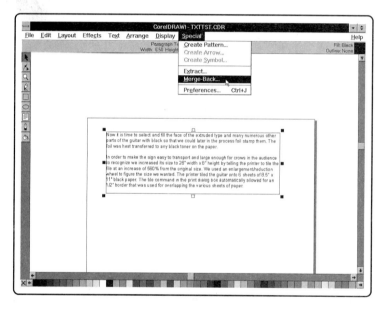

Figure CR8.19. Text selected and Merge-Back highlighted in the Special menu.

2. In the Merge Back dialog box, select the text file (see Figure CR8.20).
3. Click the OK Button.
4. The text will appear in your document (see Figure CR8.21).

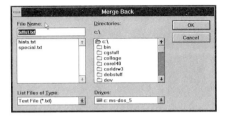

Figure CR8.20. The Merge Back dialog box.

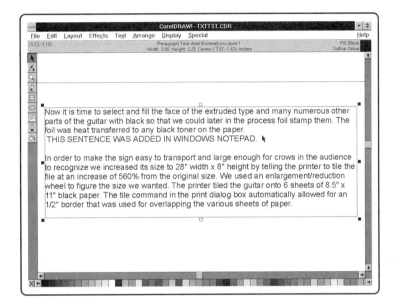

Figure CR8.21. The text file on-screen.

Preferences

The last selection in the Special menu is Preferences. Select this option to invoke the Preferences dialog box. Within the box, you can change the placement of duplicates and clones. Nudge, Restrain Angle, and Miter Limit can be assigned new values if needed. You can set Undo Levels from 1 to 99. You can also enable the Auto-Panning, Cross Hair Cursor, Interruptible Display and 3.0 Compatibility Message options from this box.

In the upper right corner of the Preferences dialog box are the buttons Curves, Display, Mouse, Roll-Ups, and Dimension. Clicking any of these buttons invokes new dialog boxes where you can change the default settings of each Preference. For more information about setting preferences, see Skill Session 60.

Selection

Keyboard shortcut: Alt+S, E or Ctrl+J

Pointing device: **S**pecial, Pr**e**ferences

Usage

1. Select Preferences from the Special menu (see Figure CR8.22).

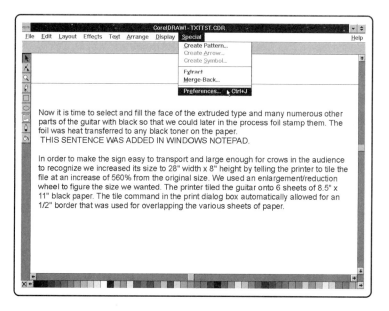

Figure CR8.22. The Special menu Preferences highlighted.

2. Change the appropriate settings in the Preferences dialog box (see Figure CR8.23).

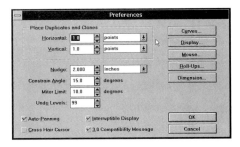

Figure CR8.23. The Preferences dialog box.

3. Click the OK button. Your new settings will take effect immediately.

Preferences, Curves

Selection

Keyboard shortcut: Alt+**S**, **E**, Alt+**U** or Ctrl+J, Alt+U

Pointing device: **S**pecial, Pr**e**ferences, **C**urves

Usage

1. Select Preferences from the Special menu.
2. Click the Curves button in the Preferences dialog box.
3. In the Preferences - Curves dialog box (see Figure CR8.24), change the required settings.

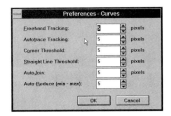

Figure CR8.24. The Preferences - Curves dialog box.

4. Click the OK button.

Preferences, Display

Selection

Keyboard shortcut: Alt ⎮ S, E, Alt+D or Ctrl+J, Alt+D

Pointing device: **S**pecial, P**r**eferences, **D**isplay

Usage

1. Select Preferences from the Special menu.
2. Click the Display button in the Preferences dialog box.
3. In the Preferences - Display dialog box (see Figure CR8.25), change the required settings.

Figure CR8.25. The Preferences - Display dialog box.

4. Click the OK button.

Preferences, Mouse

Selection

Keyboard shortcut: Alt+S, E, Alt+M or Ctrl+J, Alt+M

Pointing device: **S**pecial, P**r**eferences, **M**ouse

Usage

1. Select Preferences from the Special menu.
2. Press the Mouse button in the Preferences dialog box.
3. In the Preferences - Mouse dialog box (see Figure CR8.26), change the required settings.

Figure CR8.26. The Preferences - Mouse dialog box.

4. Click the OK button.

Preferences, Roll-Ups
Selection
Keyboard shortcut: Alt+S, E, Alt+R or Ctrl+J, Alt+R

Pointing device: **S**pecial, Pr**e**ferences, **R**oll-Ups

Usage
1. Select Preferences from the Special menu.
2. Click the Roll-Ups button in the Preferences dialog box.
3. In the Preferences - Roll-Up dialog box (see Figure CR8.27), change the required settings.
4. Click the OK button.

Figure CR8.27. The Preferences - Roll-Ups dialog box.

Preferences, Dimension

Selection

Keyboard shortcut: Alt+S, E, Alt+E or Ctrl+J, Alt+E

Pointing device: **S**pecial, P**r**eferences, Dim**e**nsion

Usage

To change dimension line defaults:

1. Select Preferences from the Special menu.
2. Click the Dimension button in the Preferences dialog box.
3. In the Preferences - Dimension dialog box (see Figure CR8.28) change the required settings.

Figure CR8.28. The Preferences - Dimension dialog box.

To change the dimension line format:

1. Click the Format button. The Format Definition dialog box appears (see Figure CR8.29).

Figure CR8.29. The Format Definition dialog box.

2. Change the format for your dimension lines.

3. Click the OK button.

Appendix

Glossary

A

A sizes   Paper sizes measured in metric units. You can choose from A3, A4, and A5 sizes through the Page Setup command in the Layout menu.

.ABK   The filename extension for backup files created by Corel Draw for drawings you are working on. These files are created at regular intervals and deleted when you exit Corel Draw or choose the File New command. You can control the time between backups and the directory in which they are saved by editing the CORELDRAW.INI file. These files are created in the event of a system crash. You can retrieve the file you were working on the the state the file was in the last time it was backed up. *See also* Backup.

Active window   The window in which you are working.

.AI   The filename extension for Adobe Illustrator files. A vector graphic file format that Corel Draw can import and export.

Artistic text   Text that can be fitted to a path and manipulated with commands in the Effects menu. Selecting the Text tool and then clicking in the drawing window allows you to add text up to 250 characters long. *See also* Paragraph text.

Ascender   The part of a letter that extends above the main body (x-height) in certain lowercase letters, for example, *d* and *h*. *See also* Descender.

ASCII   American Standard Code for Information Interchange. A standard code for representing characters and nonprintable control codes, such as carriage returns and page breaks.

Aspect ratio   The ratio of the width of an image to its height. You can change the aspect ratio of an object in Corel Draw by stretching it in one direction. You do this either by selecting it and dragging a middle control handle or by using the stretch command in the Effects menu.

Attributes   Characteristics assigned to objects using the Outline and Fill tools. Outline attributes include thickness, color, and line style (solid, dashed, dotted, or arrowheads). An object's Fill attribute can be a solid color, fountain fill, pattern, or texture. Text objects also have attributes, including typeface and character spacing.

Auto-panning   A feature in Corel Draw that automatically lets you scroll the drawing window when you drag beyond its borders. You can turn Auto-panning off or on in the dialog box that is displayed when Preferences is selected from the Special menu.

Autotrace   A feature in Corel Draw that automatically generates a vector drawing from an imported bitmap image.

B size   Paper size measured in metric units. You can choose the B5 size through the Page Setup command in the Layout menu.

Backup   Files in Corel Draw with a .BAK or .ABK extension. Corel Draw creates a backup of the drawing you are working on at preset intervals and whenever you use the Save or Save As commands to save it. You can open a backup file by changing the extension to .CDR. You can change the period between backups by editing the CORELDRW.INI file.

.BAK   The filename extension for backup files that Corel Draw creates of open drawings. These files are created each time you save a drawing using the Save or Save As commands. You can eliminate this backup file by editing the MakeBackupWhenSave line in the CORELDRW.INI file. *See also* Backup.

Baseline   The imaginary line to which characters in a line of type align.

Bézier curves   A method computer graphics programs use to represent curved surfaces. A Bézier curve has two endpoints and a set of control points that allow you to change the shape of the curve.

Bézier drawing mode   One of two ways you can draw lines and curves using the Pencil tool. Bézier mode lets you draw in a point-to-point style by clicking once and then clicking again on another spot on the page. A line is then drawn between the two points.

Bitmap   An image composed of a series of dots (pixels). Scanners and paint programs, such as CorelPHOTO-PAINT! and Fractal Design's Painter, generate this kind of image.

Bleed   Part of a printed drawing that extends beyond the edge of the page.

Blend   The process of mixing one object of one color with another of a different color through a series of intermediate steps. The Blend command in the Effects menu does this automatically.

.BMP   The filename extension for Windows Bitmap files. Corel Draw can import and export files in BMP format.

Calligraphic   An effect created with the Outline tool, in which objects are given an outline that varies in thickness. This gives curved objects a hand-drawn appearance. *See also* PowerLines.

Cap height   The distance from the baseline to the top of an uppercase character.

.CDR   The filename extension for files created in Corel Draw.

Center of rotation   A circle with a dot in the center that appears in the middle of a selected object when you double-click on it. Moving this marker changes the axis around which the object rotates.

.CGM   The filename extension for Computer Graphics Metafile, a vector graphics file format that Corel Draw can import and export.

Character attributes   Characteristics such as typeface, style, and point size that are assigned to characters in a block of text, using the Edit Text command in the Text menu.

Character set   The letters, punctuation marks, and special characters in a particular font. A © symbol or mathematical symbols are examples of special characters.

Check box   A square box in a dialog box used to turn options on or off. An option is on when an × appears in the check box and is off when the check box is empty.

Child object   An object created when an object within a group of objects is selected while holding down the Ctrl key. This child object can now be transformed separately without affecting the other objects in the group. A child object has round handles when selected rather than the normal square handles.

Click   The action of quickly pressing and releasing the mouse button.

Clip art   Predrawn images that can be brought into Corel Draw and edited or used as is. Corel supplies a Clip Art directory.

Clipboard   A temporary storage area provided by Windows to store information. This information then can be pasted back into the same or different applications.

Clipping holes   The process of combining two objects using the Combine command from the Arrange menu. This creates a transparent hole so that underlying objects are visible. Also known as masking.

Clone   A duplicate of an object, created with the Clone command in the Edit menu. Most changes made to the original object will also be made in the Clone image.

CMYK   An acronym for Cyan, Magenta, Yellow, and Black, the ink colors used in four-color process printing. Corel Draw allows you to specify colors using CMYK values.

Color palette   The color bar along the bottom of the Corel Draw screen that allows you to choose outline and fill colors for selected objects. Choosing Color Palette in the Display menu opens a fly-out menu with commands for turning the palette on and off or displaying other types of palettes.

Color proof   The preliminary step in the color printing process. Sometimes called a prepress proof, it shows how an image will look when it's printed. Proofing provides an opportunity to make corrections and adjustments before final printing.

Color separation   The process of separating the colors in an image into the primary printing colors: cyan, magenta, yellow, and black.

Command   A word or phrase in a menu that starts an action.

Command button   A button in a dialog box used to start an action, such as displaying another dialog box.

Composite   A preliminary version of a design combining all image, line art, and text elements. Also known as comp.

Constrain   The effect that occurs when your movements are limited, for example, when you hold down the Ctrl key while transforming an object with the mouse. Holding down the Ctrl key while rotating an object forces it to rotate in 15-degree increments. The number of degrees can be changed in the Preferences dialog box found in the Special menu.

Continuous tone   An image represented by graduated tones from black to white as in a photograph.

Contour   A feature in Corel Draw that allows you to apply contour lines to an object. Contour can be accessed by opening the Contour roll-up in the Effects menu.

Control object   A term used in Corel Draw to differentiate the original objects from those that are created when you apply the Blend or Extrude command.

Control point   Points extending from nodes along a curved object that determine the angle at which the curve passes through the node. Control points appear when you select a node or segment with the Shape tool. Nodes associated with straight lines do not have Control points.

CorelCHART! A program that comes with Corel Draw for creating charts and graphs.

CORELDRW.INI A text file with configuration information about Corel Draw. This file is in the Config subdirectory of Corel40 and can be edited by double-clicking on it in File Manager. Changes you can make include the interval between backup files for open files that Corel Draw creates and the directory in which these backup files are stored.

CorelMOSAIC! A file management program that displays thumbnail views of your Corel Draw files. You also can use CorelMOSAIC! for doing batch operations, such as printing and exporting, and to archive files.

CorelMOVE! A program that comes with Corel Draw for creating and editing animations.

CorelPHOTO-PAINT! A program that comes with Corel Draw for creating and editing bitmap images.

CorelSHOW! A program that comes with Corel Draw for preparing presentations.

CorelTRACE! A program that comes with Corel Draw that automatically traces bitmap images. The result is a vector graphic that you can import into Corel Draw for editing. CorelTRACE! also supports Optical Character Recognition (OCR), which allows you to scan in text and then import the text into Corel Draw and other word processing applications.

Crop The process of using the Shape tool to remove part of an area of an imported bitmap. The parts that are not displayed on-screen or printed are still stored in the bitmap file so that your file size will not be reduced.

Crop marks Alignment marks at the corners of a page printed on a PostScript printer. Used as aids for trimming the paper to the proper size, crop marks are turned on in the Options dialog box accessed from the print dialog box. They appear only if the page size in Corel Draw is smaller than the paper size of the printer.

Cross hairs Marks at the corners of a sheet of paper or film used for aligning color separations. Corel Draw automatically adds cross hairs when printing color separations to a PostScript printer. Also refers to the pair of intersecting lines that can be dragged from the spot where the rulers meet and to the cursor, which can be displayed through the Preferences command in the Special menu. Also known as registration marks.

Cursor   The on-screen, arrow-shaped pointer controlled by the movement of the mouse or pen. The shape of the cursor changes depending on the tool or command selected. Also called the mouse pointer.

Curve object   An object with nodes and control points which can be manipulated to change its shape. Curved objects are created when you draw with the Pencil tool. You also can convert text and objects drawn with the Rectangle and Ellipse tools into curved objects using the Convert To Curves command in the Arrange menu.

Cusp   A type of node that permits a curve to pass through it at a sharp angle. Node types are selected from the Node Edit menu and are revealed when you double-click on a node or segment with the Shape tool.

Default printer   The printer that Corel Draw automatically uses to print a drawing when you choose the Print command from the File menu. Choose the printer you want as the default printer by clicking on the printer icon in the Windows Control panel.

Default settings   Preset options built into a program.

Descender   The part of a letter that extends below the main body (x-height) in certain lowercase letters, for example, *j* and *q*. *See also* Ascender.

Deselect   The process of removing the selection handles from the object you have currently selected. The best way to make sure you do not select another object when deselecting the first object is to click somewhere *off* the page area.

Destination file   The file into which an embedded or linked object is being inserted. *See also* Embedded object and Linked object.

Dialog box   A window displayed when additional information is needed to perform an action.

Direction keys   The arrow keys and the Home, End, PgUp, and PgDn keys. The arrow keys nudge objects in small steps. They also move the insertion point when entering or editing text on-screen or in a dialog box. The Home and End keys select the start and end nodes on a curved object. They also move the insertion point in a block of text to the beginning or end of a line.

Directory   Part of a structure used to organize files on a disk the same way separate folders keep certain files. Directories are given names and can be divided into subdirectories. For example, you can create a directory called CDRFILES for storing most of your files created in Corel Draw and a subdirectory called CDRFILES\SPECIAL for special files you create in Corel Draw.

Dithered color   Dots of one or more different colors placed very close together to simulate the desired color. Windows uses dithering to display colors that the graphics adapter is unable to display. *See also* Pure color.

Double-click   The action of pressing and releasing the mouse button twice in quick succession.

Downloadable fonts   Fonts that are stored on disk for transmission to a printer. If you have purchased downloadable PostScript fonts from Adobe, you can use them instead of Corel Draw's fonts by selecting All Fonts Resident in the Print Options dialog box.

DPI   An acronym for dots per inch. A measure of a printer's resolution. Typical desktop laser printers print at 300 dpi; image setters are capable of printing at resolutions of 1,270 or 2,540 dpi. The more dots per inch, the smoother the output.

Drag   The action of moving the mouse while holding down the mouse button. Releasing the button completes the action.

Drawing window   The portion of the Corel Draw screen available for drawing (usually defined by a rectangular outline with a drop shadow). Although you are free to draw anywhere on the screen, only objects on the Printable Page will print.

Drop-down list box   A list box that appears in dialog boxes and opens to display a list of choices when you click on the arrow. If the list cannot accommodate all available options, scroll bars are provided. *See also* List box.

.DXF   The filename extension for AutoCAD files. Corel Draw can import and export in this format.

Edit   The process of changing an object using commands in the Edit, Layout, Effects, Text, and Arrange menus or the Pick, Shape, Outline, and Fill tools.

Editable preview   One of two ways to view objects in the drawing window. In editable preview (the default view), you see the outlines and fills of objects as you create them. In the wireframe view, objects are displayed in skeleton form. Because objects redraw more quickly without outlines and fills, you may find it quicker to edit complex drawings in wireframe view. You can switch freely between views by choosing Edit Wireframe from the Display menu.

Em   A unit of measurement used primarily in typesetting to specify the space between characters and words. An em is equal in width to the point size being used. For example, in 12-point type, an em is 12 points wide.

Embedded object   Information from a file created in one application that's been inserted into a file in another application. For example, you can embed a graphic created in Corel Draw into a Microsoft Word document. The embedded information can be edited from within the application in which it is embedded.

Emboss   An effect created in Corel Draw by using two offset duplicates of the original and coloring one duplicate light and one dark to give the illusion of the original being recessed. Also, an effect automatically created in Corel Photo-Paint, accessed through the Effects menu.

En   A unit of measurement equal to half the width of an em.

End node   The small square at the end of an open path which appears when you select the path with the Shape tool. The end node is distinguishable from the start node by its smaller size. You can toggle between the start and end nodes with the Home and End Keys.

Envelope   A feature in the Effects menu that allows you to distort the shape of an object by manipulating the bounding box that contains the object. You can use predefined shapes or use the freehand method.

.EPS   The filename extension for Encapsulated PostScript files. Corel Draw can import EPS files created in Adobe Illustrator. It also can export to EPS format, but it cannot import the resulting file. The EPS files CorelTRACE creates can be imported by Corel Draw and other PC programs, such as Ventura Publisher and Aldus PageMaker. An Adobe Illustrator file can be imported into Fractal Design's Painter program as a Frisket.

Export A command found in the File menu of Corel Draw allowing you to export all or part of a image on the Corel Draw screen to formats other than .CDR.

Extension Characters preceeded by a period in a filename that identify the type of information in the file. The extension .TIF, for example, indicates the file contains a bitmap.

Extrude A feature in the Effects menu that allows you to give objects a three-dimensional effect.

File previewer In the Open Drawing dialog box, a small bitmap representation that lets you see what the selected file contains before you open it.

Film Photosensitive sheets on which images are transferred either as positives or negatives. These sheets are then used to create printing plates. An option in the Print Options dialog box lets you create film negatives for printing on an image setter.

Film Recorder A device that reproduces images from a computer screen on film. The film can then be developed into slides or prints using conventional photographic processes.

Filter A program that translates information from one format to another. Corel Draw's import filters, for example, allow you to open graphics created in CorelPHOTO-PAINT!, Fractal Design's Painter, and many other applications.

Fly-out menu An extra menu that appears to the side of certain selections in drop-down menus and dialog boxes within Corel Draw.

Font A set of characters in a given typeface and point size, for example, 12-point Helvetica. Some fonts are also available in different weights or styles, such as bold and italic.

Fountain fill A fill that fades gradually from one color to another. Corel Draw now lets you use as many different colors as you want in a fountain fill. Also called a gradient or graduated fill. Corel Draw lets you create linear, radial, and conical fountains using the Fountain Fill icon in the Fill tool menu and the Fill roll-up window.

Four-color process The process of reproducing color artwork using four separate sheets of film that represent the cyan, magenta, yellow, and black content of the artwork.

Frame The rectangle that encloses a block of paragraph text created with the Text tool. Also, a command in the Text menu used to format Paragraph text.

Freehand drawing mode One of two ways you can draw lines and curves using the Pencil tool. In Freehand mode, you draw by moving the mouse pointer as you would a pencil on paper. *See also* Bézier mode.

.GDF The filename extension for vector graphics files used by IBM mainframe computers. Corel Draw imports and exports these graphics as PIF files. PIF files can be translated to GDF format by the mainframe computer.

GEM Acronym for Graphics Environment Manager. A menu-driven interface used by programs such as Xerox Ventura Publisher. Also a filename extension for files created by programs such as GEM Artline. Corel Draw can import and export files in this format.

.GIF The filename extension for files in a bitmap format that is commonly used to store digitized color photographs. Corel Draw imports and exports files in this format.

Gray component replacement (GCR) A technique in which equal amounts of cyan, magenta, and yellow are removed and replaced with black ink. This produces better color saturation and contrast and may save on ink costs. Corel Draw allows you to custom-configure these settings by clicking on the PrePress button in the Color options dialog box in the Print dialog box. Also called undercolor removal.

Grayscale image An image, typically created from a scanner, in which continuous tones are represented as uniform shades of gray. Corel Draw can import and display .TIF images with up to 256 levels of gray and print them on a PostScript printer.

Grid A series of evenly spaced horizontal and vertical lines used to align objects. The spacing is specified through the Grid Setup command in the Layout menu. You also can display the grid using this command and have objects snap to the grid by turning on Snap to Grid in the Layout menu.

Grid markers Points on the screen that help you lay out your drawing. The grid markers are normally turned off. You can turn the grid markers on by choosing Grid Setup from the Layout menu and selecting Show Grid.

Group The process of making one or more objects into a single select-able object with the Group command in the Arrange menu. Grouping is useful when you want to keep individual elements in a graphic from being accidentally moved or otherwise altered.

Guidelines Nonprinting lines used to align objects. Guidelines can be placed anywhere in the drawing window by clicking and dragging on the rulers or by using the Guidelines Setup command in the Layout menu. By turning on Snap To Guidelines in the Layout menu, you can force objects to a guideline when they are drawn or moved near it.

Gutter The space between columns of Paragraph text.

Halftone The process of reproducing a continuous tone image, such as a black-and-white photograph, using dots of various sizes. On laser printers that cannot print different sized dots, the halftone is produced by printing different numbers of dots in a given area.

Halftone screen A method of representing an image made up of gradually changing shades into a series of dots so that when they are printed, they will look like the original. Corel Draw allows you to set the type and frequency of dots as well as the screen angle to eliminate moiré patterns when printing to PostScript devices. By changing the type, frequency, and angle, you can create different looks to Corel Draw PostScript fills (see page 80 of Corel Draw's user manual).

Handles Small squares that appear on the corners and sides of an object's highlighting box when the object is selected. You use these handles to resize and stretch an object. When you click on an already selected object, the handles change to arrows. Use the arrows to rotate and skew the object.

Hanging indent A format applied to Paragraph text in which the first line of text begins further right than subsequent lines.

Highlighting box The invisible rectangle with eight handles that encloses a selected object. When you move, scale, or otherwise trans-form an object, a dotted rectangle representing the highlighting box appears instead of the object.

Hints Information included with fonts to improve their appearance when printed in small point sizes. TrueType and Adobe Type 1 fonts are hinted.

Hourglass cursor   The mouse pointer during an operation such as printing. No other actions can be performed until the pointer reappears.

HPGL   An acronym for Hewlett-Packard Graphics Language. A file format created by programs such as AutoCAD for printing drawings on plotters. Corel Draw can import and export HPGL files with the extension .PLT.

HSB   An acronym for hue, saturation, and brightness, the components in the HSB color model. HSB is one of three color models Corel Draw provides for creating process colors.

Hue   In the HSB color model, hue is the main attribute in a color that distinguishes it from other colors. Blue, green, and red, for example, are all hues. *See also* Saturation.

Icon   A small graphic symbol that represents various elements in Windows and Corel Draw. For example, the tools in Corel Draw are represented by icons.

Image header   An optional bitmap image created when you save a Corel Draw file or export it in .EPS format.

Image setter   A generic term for printers capable of printing text and graphics (line art and photographs) at resolutions of about 1,200 dots per inch and more.

Import   A command found in the File menu of Corel Draw allowing you to import different file formats into Corel Draw. This command lets you import file formats like PCX or TIF and even CDR for use in your Corel Draw images.

Insertion point   A flashing vertical bar that indicates where text will be inserted when you type. The insertion point appears when you click on a text block with the Text tool and in dialog boxes that require you to type information.

Inter-character spacing   The amount of spacing between characters of text. You can adjust inter-character spacing interactively with the Shape tool or by entering numeric values in a dialog box.

Inter-line spacing   The amount of spacing between the baselines of text. It is also called leading. You can adjust inter-line spacing interactively with the Shape tool or by entering numeric values in a dialog box.

Inter-paragraph spacing   The amount of spacing between blocks of Paragraph text separated by pressing the Enter key. You can adjust inter-paragraph text by entering numeric values in a dialog box.

Interruptible Display   A feature in Corel Draw that stops the screen during a redraw whenever the primary mouse button or a key is pressed. If you are working on a complex drawing, Interruptible Display can save time by allowing you to select tools and commands without waiting for the screen to redraw completely. You can turn Interruptible Display on and off with the Preferences command in the Special menu.

Inter-word spacing   The amount of spacing between words of text. You can adjust inter-word spacing interactively with the Shape tool or by entering numeric values in a dialog box.

Jaggies   A stairstep effect that often occurs when a bitmap image is enlarged.

JPEG   A file format that compresses bitmap images into smaller file sizes than the standard formats like PCX and TIF.

Justification   A term referring to the alignment of text. You can choose from several justification options in Corel Draw, including left, right, and center.

Kerning   The process of reducing the spacing between pairs of letters. With certain letter pairs, such as AV, moving the letters closer together improves their appearance when printed. You can kern text interactively with the Shape tool or by entering numeric values in a dialog box.

Landscape   A page that is oriented so that it prints from left to right across its longest dimension.

Layer   A plane on which objects are placed. You can control how objects in your drawing overlay one another by moving the layer and the objects they contain up or down in relation to other layers. Moving and editing layers is done in the Layers roll-up accessed from the Layout menu. You also can make layers invisible and nonprintable.

Leading   The amount of spacing between baselines of text. Referred to as inter-line spacing in Corel Draw. You can adjust the amount of leading interactively with the Shape tool or by entering numeric values in a dialog box.

Limit check error   A PostScript printing error that occurs when a drawing contains too many line segments for the printer to reproduce. Corel Draw provides a Flatness control in the Print Options dialog box that helps to overcome this problem.

Line art   In traditional graphic arts, an illustration containing only black and white.

Line style   Solid, dashed, or dotted-line types selected from the Outline Pen dialog box or the Pen roll-up window.

Linked object   A reference or placeholder for information inserted into a file. Changes made to the information from the application that created the linked object are reflected automatically in the destination files.

Lino   Short for Linotronic, a line of PostScript image setters used for high-resolution printing.

List box   Boxes that appear in dialog boxes and display a list of options. If the list cannot accommodate all available options, scroll bars are provided. *See also* Drop-down list box.

LPI   An acronym for lines per inch.

Marquee box   The dashed box created by dragging around objects with the Pick tool or around nodes with the Shape tool. Enclosing objects and nodes with a marquee box selects them.

Marquee-select   A method of selecting multiple objects with the Pick tool or multiple nodes with the Shape tool by dragging a dotted rectangle around them.

Masking   The combining of two objects, using the Combine command from the Arrange menu, to create a transparent hole through which underlying objects are visible. Also known as clipping holes.

Maximize   The process of enlarging an application window to full-screen size.

Menu   A list of commands that appears when you choose a name in the menu bar. The menu bar appears below the title bar that is at the top of the window.

Menu bar   The bar near the top of the window that contains the names of the program menus.

Mirror   The process of creating a mirror reflection of an object by using the Stretch & Mirror command in the Effects menu. You also can mirror the object by dragging on a middle handle of the selected object.

Moiré pattern   Undesirable patterns in an image printed from color separations with incorrect halftone screen angles.

Multiple select   A method of selecting multiple objects with the Pick tool or multiple nodes with the Shape tool by holding down the Shift key and clicking on the objects or nodes one at a time.

Negative   An image in which the values in the original are reversed so that black areas appear white, white appears black, and colors are represented by their complements. Corel Draw can print color separations as negatives if Film Negative is selected in the Print Options dialog box.

Nodes   The points at the ends of line and curve segments in a curve object. Also refers to the small hollow squares along the outlines of objects drawn with the Rectangle and Ellipse tools and those next to characters in a text object.

Nudge   The action of moving objects in small steps by using the arrow keys. The incremental amount of movement can be set in the Preferences dialog box in the Special menu.

One-point perspective   The process of lengthening or shortening one side of an object's Perspective bounding box to create the impression that the object is receding from view in a single direction.

Orthogonal extrusion   Projecting an object using the Extrude feature so that opposite sides are parallel to one another. Contrasts with Perspective extrusion in which opposite sides recede toward a vanishing point.

Overprint   The process of printing over an area that has already been printed. Overprinting is used in Corel Draw to create traps in color separated artwork. You also can use it to overprint selected Spot colors for certain visual effects. *See also* Trap.

Page border   In the drawing window, the rectangle with the drop shadow that represents the printable area. It is also called the printable page. You can turn the Page border on and off through the Preferences command in the Special menu.

Paint program   A generic term referring to computer illustration programs that create graphics as bitmaps. CorelPHOTO-PAINT! and Fractal Design's Painter are examples of paint programs. *See also* Vector graphics.

Palette   A collection of colors displayed along the bottom of the Corel Draw screen and in the Uniform Color and Outline Color dialog boxes.

PANTONE   A standard color matching system in which solid (spot) colors are specified using color sample books. You can use this system in Corel Draw to specify colors.

Paragraph text   Text in blocks of characters. Selecting the Text tool then dragging to create a bounding box allows you to add text in blocks of up to 4,000 characters. Paragraph text is designed for adding text to ads, brochures, and other text-intensive applications. You also can add text in strings of up to 250 characters. *See also* Artistic text.

.PAT   The filename extension for files containing Full-Color patterns used to fill objects in Corel Draw. You can open these files and edit the patterns just as you can other objects.

.PCT   The filename extension for vector graphics files used by Macintosh computers. Corel Draw imports PICT 1 (black-and-white) and PICT 2 (color) files and exports PICT 2 files.

.PCX   The filename extension for bitmap files created by CorelPHOTO-PAINT! and other paint programs, such as Fractal Design's Painter. Corel Draw can import and export files in this format, including those containing color and grayscale information.

Photo CD   A process developed by the Eastman Kodak company that converts 35mm film negatives or slides into digital format and stores them on a compact disc (CD). CorelMOSAIC! can open Photo CD images and convert them into formats that Corel Draw and CorelPHOTO-PAINT! can import.

.PIC   The filename extension used by two different vector graphic file formats. One format is created by Lotus 1-2-3 and can be imported by Corel Draw. The other format is used by slide-making equipment, such as VideoShow or Slidemaker, and can be exported by Corel Draw.

Pica   A unit of measurement used primarily in typesetting. One pica equals approximately 1/6 of an inch.

.PIF   The filename extension for vector graphics files that Corel Draw can import and export. PIF is an intermediate format which IBM mainframe computers translate to GDF format for use in mainframe applications.

Pixels   Dots on a computer or television screen that combine to form an image. Short for picture elements.

.PLT   The filename extension for vector graphics files conforming to the HPGL format. These are primarily files created by programs such as AutoCAD for printing drawings on plotters. Corel Draw can import and export HPGL files with the extension .PLT.

Point   A unit of measurement used primarily in typesetting for designating type sizes. There are 72 points to an inch and 12 points to a pica.

Portrait   A page size that is less wide than it is high.

Positive   An image in which dark, light, and color values are the same as the original. *See also* Negative.

PostScript   A page description language with which a program can describe the text and graphics it wants the printer to output. Several features in Corel Draw require the use of a PostScript printer.

PostScript textures   Variable pattern fills that require the use of a PostScript printer to print. Textures are selected through the PS icon in the Fill tool menu.

PowerLines   A feature in Corel Draw that allows you to draw predefined shapes with the pencil tool. The PowerLines feature is accessible through the PowerLines roll-up in the Effects menu.

Preview screen   A viewing option that uses the entire screen to display your drawings. You can switch to the Preview screen by choosing Show Preview from the Display menu or by pressing F9. Pressing any key returns you to the drawing window.

Primary mouse button   Usually the left mouse button.

Printable page   The rectangle with the drop shadow that appears in the drawing window.

Process color   The primary colors used in four-color process printing: cyan, magenta, yellow, and black. *See also* Four-color process.

Proof   The trial print of a graphic that shows how it will look when output in its final form.

Pure color   Any color that individual pixels on a computer screen can assume. On a monochrome screen, there are only two pure colors, black and white. Color screens typically may display 8, 16, 256, or 16 million pure colors. *See also* Dithered color.

Radio button   A rectangular, square, or round button in a dialog box that turns an option on or off. When two or more options are available, only one can be selected. They are also called option buttons.

Rasterizer   A program that converts vector graphics into bitmaps for printing on a non-PostScript printer.

Registration marks   Marks on paper or film used for aligning color separations. Corel Draw automatically adds registration marks when printing color separations to a PostScript printer. Also known as cross hairs.

Resident fonts   Typefaces permanently stored in the printer's memory. PostScript printers typically have 35 resident typefaces, such as Times and Helvetica. You can print using these typefaces rather than Corel Draw's by selecting an option in the Print Options dialog box.

Resolution   In printing, a term referring to the number of dots per inch (dpi) the printer is capable of printing. Typical laser printers have resolutions of 300 dpi; image setters have resolutions of approximately 1,200 or 2,400 dpi. The more dots per inch, the smoother the output.

RGB   An acronym for Red, Green, and Blue. The component colors in one of three color models Corel Draw provides for creating process colors.

Roll-up windows   A special type of window with controls for choosing and applying fills, outlines, text attributes, and options associated with the Extrude, Blend, Layers, PowerLines, Contour, and Fit Text to Path commands. Roll-up windows contain many of the controls found in dialog boxes: command buttons, text boxes, drop-down list boxes, and so on. But unlike most dialog boxes, the window stays open after you apply the selected options. This lets you make adjustments and experiment with different options without having to continually reopen a dialog box.

Rotate   The process of turning an object around its center axis using the Rotate & Skew command in the Transform menu. You also can rotate by dragging a corner handle with arrows revealed when you click twice on the outline of an object.

Ruler cross hairs The pair of intersecting lines that can be dragged from the spot where the rulers meet. Used to check the alignment of objects and to reset the 0,0 points on the rulers.

Rulers Measuring tools displayed on the left side and along the top of the drawing window. You can choose the unit of measurement the rulers use by choosing Show Grid from the Layout menu and changing the Grid Frequency. To show or hide the rulers, choose Show Ruler from the Layout menu.

Sans serif A typeface, such as Helvetica, that lacks serifs. *See also* Serif.

Saturation In the HSB color model, the component that determines the purity or intensity of a color.

Scale The process of resizing an object by equal amounts horizontally and vertically using the Stretch & Scale command in the Effects menu. You also can scale by dragging a corner handle on the object's highlighting box.

Scanner A device that converts images on a page or transparency into digital form. Corel Draw can import scanned images in PCX, TIFF, TARGA, and JPEG formats. *See also* Bitmap.

SCODL A file format used by film recorders for making slides.

Screen angles When printing color separations, the angles at which each of the four process colors are printed to avoid undesirable moiré patterns. These angles can be specified in Corel Draw. *See also* Halftone screen.

Scroll To shift the view in the drawing window to see portions of a drawing outside the current viewing area. Corel Draw provides scroll bars along the edges of the drawing window and an Auto-panning feature which scrolls the drawing window automatically whenever you drag beyond its borders. *See also* Auto-panning.

Secondary mouse button Usually the right mouse button.

Segments Lines or curves between nodes in a curved object.

Select The process of choosing an object with the Pick tool or a node or segment with the Shape tool.

Serif   The short strokes at the ends of individual letters in some typefaces, such as Times Roman. Sans serif typefaces, such as Helvetica, lack these strokes.

Service bureau   A commercial business that prints customer-provided documents or artwork, usually on high-resolution PostScript devices.

Skew   The process of slanting an object using the Rotate & Skew command in the Effects menu. You can also skew by dragging a side handle that is revealed when you double-click on an object.

Snap   To force an object being drawn or moved to a grid line, guideline, or another object. You can turn Snap on and off by choosing commands in the Layout menu.

Source file   The file that contains information being embedded or linked. *See also* Embedded object and Linked object.

Spot color   In offset printing, solid colors commonly specified using the PANTONE color matching system. Spot color is used whenever exact colors are required. Corel Draw also uses the PANTONE system to specify spot colors.

Start node   The small square at the beginning of an open path revealed when you select the path with the Shape tool. The start node is distinguishable from the end node by its larger size.

Status Line   An area below the menu bar that shows information about the currently selected object or node and the action in progress. Use the Show Status Line command in the Display menu to turn the Status Line on and off.

Stretch   The process of resizing an object either horizontally or vertically using the Stretch & Scale command in the Effects menu. You also can stretch by dragging a side handle on the object's highlighting box.

Subscript   Characters smaller than and positioned below the baseline of other characters in a word or line of text.

Superscript   Characters smaller than and positioned above the x-height of other characters in a word or text string.

Symbol   A predrawn graphic selected from Corel's Symbol Library. You access the library by holding the mouse down on the Text tool and clicking on the star icon from its fly-out menu.

Texture Fills   Fills made up of predefined texture patterns that are fully editable. Texture fills are accessed from the Fill dialog box and the Fill roll-up.

.TGA   The filename extension for files in Targa format, which is a bitmap format that is commonly used to store digitized color photographs. Corel Draw imports and exports files in this format.

.TIF   The filename extension for Tag Image Format, which is a bitmap graphic format that Corel Draw can import and export. You can import and export color and grayscale .TIF files.

Tile   The process of printing a drawing larger than the printer's paper size on multiple pages. You can print drawings in tiles from Corel Draw by choosing Tile in the Print Options dialog box. You also can tile bitmap, vector, and texture fills into an object created in Corel Draw.

Title bar   The bar along the top of a Windows application that contains the name of the application, the Control menu box, and the Maximize and Minimize boxes. In Corel Draw, the title bar also contains the name of an open file.

Toggle   The action of alternately turning a program function on and off. For example, the Show Rulers, Show Status Line, and Color Palette commands in Corel Draw's Display menu toggle on and off.

Tool box   The collection of icons on the left side of the Corel Draw screen used to perform tasks from selecting and transforming objects to choosing outline and fill attributes.

Trap   The process of adding a slight overlap between adjacent areas of color to avoid gaps caused by registration errors. You can create traps in Corel Draw if you are printing color separations. Also referred to as chokes or spreads.

TrueType fonts   Fonts that print as vectors or bitmaps, depending on the capabilities of your printer. TrueType fonts print as they appear on-screen and can be resized to any height.

TRUMATCH   A color matching system for specifying Process Colors. This system is available in Corel Draw.

Two-Color pattern   Fill made up of bitmap images. Corel Draw supplies a collection of bitmap patterns. You can even make your own and save them as new patterns.

Type style   Variations within a typeface. Some common styles include roman (regular or normal), bold, italic, and bold italic.

Typeface   Characters of a single type design, such as Avante Garde or Bookman. Most typefaces are available in different variations or styles. Some common styles include roman (regular or normal), bold, italic, and bold italic.

Uniform color   A solid color, black, white, or shade of gray used to outline or fill objects. You can select uniform fills from the Outline and Fill tool menus, their respective Roll-Up windows, the Outline Color and Uniform Fill dialog boxes, and the on-screen color palette.

Vector graphics   Graphics created in programs such as Corel Draw in which shapes are represented as a series of lines and curves. These contrast with bitmap graphics, which are created pixel-by-pixel in paint programs and by scanners. Also referred to as object-based graphics. *See also* Rasterizer, Paint program.

Weight   The thickness of outlines assigned to objects using the Outline tool. Sometimes used to refer to different type styles (normal, light, bold, and so on).

.WFN   The filename extension for files containing symbols supplied with Corel Draw.

Window   A rectangular area on the screen in which applications are displayed. Every application window has a title bar and menu bar along the top and one or two scroll bars along the sides or bottom.

Wireframe view   One of two ways of viewing objects in the drawing window. In wireframe view, objects display in skeleton form without fills or outlines. Because the screen redraws faster in this view, you may want to use it for editing complex drawings. In the other view, editable preview, you see the outlines and fills of objects as you create them. You can switch freely between views by choosing Edit Wireframe from the Display menu.

.WMF   The filename extension for Windows Metafile, which is a vector graphic format that Corel Draw can export.

.WPG   The filename extension for WordPerfect's graphics files, which is a vector graphic format that Corel Draw can export.

WYSIWYG   An acronym for What You See Is What You Get. A term describing a program's ability to provide an accurate on-screen representation of what an image or document will look like when printed.

X-height   The part that makes up the main body of a lowercase letter, equal to the height of a lowercase *x*.

B

The Companion CD-ROM

You'll find a treasure chest of software on the CD-ROM included with this book. Here's a sample of the types of software you'll find:

- Commercial demos
- Clip art
- Graphics
- Fonts
- Programs and utilities
- Sound clips
- Video and animation clips
- Corel tech support files

In addition, you'll find a special offer from the CompuServe Information Service, including a free copy of Windows CompuService Information Manager software.

Categories of Software

Under each listing in this appendix, the software is broken down into these categories:

- Commercial software demos
- Samplers of commercial products
- Shareware and freeware

Commercial Software Demos

Many retail software publishers produce demonstration disks that contain limited versions of their programs. Each of these programs is limited by the publisher in some manner. For example, the software publisher may disable the save and print functions within the demo version. Software that fits into this category is referred to as a *working demo*.

Some of the software publishers represented here do not have special demo versions. They have contributed sample graphics that show off the capabilities of their programs. Software that fits into this category is referred to as *demo graphics*.

The working demo programs and sample graphics provided on this CD-ROM are intended to provide a glimpse of the full program's capabilities.

Obviously, the software publishers who created these demonstrations hope you will be impressed enough with the demonstration to order their full product. If you would like to order any of these products, you can either visit your local computer store or contact the software publisher directly.

Samplers of Commercial Products

A wide variety of sample software—clip art, photos, music, sounds, and videos—are included on this book's CD-ROM. These files have been provided by software publishers to expose you to their collections. You'll find everything from CDR, TIFF, and EPS files to video and MIDI files. If you would like more information on any of these products, please contact the software publisher.

Read the .TXT or .WRI files in the product's directory for information on usage rights, or contact the software publisher directly if you have any questions.

What Is Shareware?

Shareware is a software distribution method that provides users a chance to try software before buying it. If you try a shareware program and continue to use it, you need to register the program with the author.

Shareware products are not free. They are marketed by companies (usually small ones) that cannot afford the time and frustration of packaging and distributing a software product through other means. This gives users the chance to test many fantastic programs before paying for them. The key factor to keep shareware developers working is that you do pay for the software you use. The suggested price is usually much lower than commercial software or the cost of developing a similar product yourself.

You should always remember that copyright laws apply to both shareware and retail software, and the copyright holder retains all rights, except as already noted.

Registering Your Shareware

Shareware is a distribution method, not a type of software. You should find software that suits your needs and pocketbook, whether it's retail or shareware. The shareware system makes fitting your needs easier because you can try before you buy. And because the overhead is lower, prices are lower. Shareware has the ultimate money-back guarantee—if you don't use the product, you don't pay for it.

If you decide to use one or more of the shareware programs distributed with this book, you should write, call, or send electronic mail to the appropriate shareware author. Each of the shareware programs included with this book is accompanied by a text file that describes how to register the software.

What Is Freeware?

Freeware is similar to shareware, except that there is no registration charge. The author still retains all copyrights to the software, but has decided that it can be distributed free of charge. The files included with the freeware may include information on how to contact the author, and you may wish to do so, for instance, if you want to see if you have the latest version of the software.

Unlike shareware, however, you should not expect any additional help or materials with the software. Freeware is generally distributed on an "as is" basis. If you like the software, you are free to use it with no additional requirements.

CompuServe Information Service

More than one million computer users are a part of CompuServe Information Service, and for good reason. CompuServe has special interest areas for nearly any subject you're interested in. And you'll find users from across the United States and around the world.

Joining and using CompuServe is now a lot easier, because CompuServe is offering readers of this book a free membership and $15 of free connect time. Plus, a free copy of Windows CompuServe Information Manager (WinCIM) software is included on the CD-ROM.

Two other good reasons for joining CompuServe are the Corel and PHCP forums. The Corel Forum is run by the Corel Corporation to support CorelDRAW! and its other products. In this forum, you'll find product updates, technical information, useful utilities, hints and tips, and more. Once you're on CompuServe, you can enter this forum by selecting

WinCIM's traffic light icon and entering COREL. If you're using modem communications software, type GO COREL.

The PHCP forum is the Prentice Hall Computer Publishing forum. Sams Publishing is a part of PHCP, and you'll find Sams Publishing areas in the files libraries and message areas. This forum contains information on our books, tips and information, programs and utilities, and technical support information. Once you're on CompuServe, you can enter this forum by selecting WinCIM's traffic light icon and entering PHCP. If you're using modem communications software, type GO PHCP.

Behind the CD-ROM in the back of the book, you'll find a special registration card for CompuServe with your temporary user number and password. This number and password is unique for every copy of this book.

To learn how to sign up and receive your free connect time, read the file SIGNUP.WRI in the \WinCIM directory of the CD-ROM.

Windows CIM

CompuServe International
P.O. Box 20212
Columbus, OH 43220

Location on CD-ROM: \WINCIM

Documentation: SIGNUP.WRI

Command to install the program: SETUP

Windows CompuServe Information Manager (WinCIM) is the communications software that makes being on-line easy. Instead of typing commands, you can click icons or choose from menu items to explore forums, download files, read and create messages, send and receive electronic mail, and much more.

Instructions on how to install and configure WinCIM are contained in the SIGNUP.WRI file in this directory.

After installing the software, you'll need to configure WinCIM for your modem. Then, you'll need to enter your special user number and password, which are on the CompuServe behind the CD-ROM.

WinCIM contains extensive online help, which is always available by pressing the F1 key. You can even browse through a list of the forums on CompuServe without being on-line.

Commercial Demos

Most of the demos in this section are special versions of commercial programs. In most cases, they operate like the full version, with some features (such as saving your work) disabled. These are referred to as *working demos*.

Some of the software publishers represented here do not have special demo versions. They have contributed sample graphics that show off the capabilities of their programs. Software that fits into this category is referred to as *demo graphics*.

All of the working demos need to be installed to your hard drive before they will work. The install program is listed for each demo.

Fractal Design Painter

> Fractal Design Inc.
> P.O. Box 2380
> 335 Spreckels Drive
> Aptos, CA 95003
>
> *Category:* Working demo
>
> *Location on CD-ROM:* \DEMOS\FDPAINT
>
> *Documentation:* README.TXT
>
> *Command to install the program:* INSTALL

This working demo of Fractal Design Painter 2.0 allows you to experiment with the full program, but you cannot save or print images. Fractal Design Painter is described in depth in Companion Software Workshop 4.

Follow these steps to install the program to your hard drive:

1. From File Manager or Program Manager, select **F**ile + **R**un from the menu.
2. Type *<drive>*\DEMOS\FDPAINT\INSTALL and press Enter (*<drive>* is the drive letter of your CD-ROM).
3. The installation program starts—click Continue.
4. At the next screen, you will see Install from Drive\Directory:. Type the path where the install program is stored: *<drive>*\DEMOS\FDPAINT.

5. After you finish selecting any other options, click Continue.

6. When the install program asks you to insert disk number two or three, press Enter and the installation will continue.

PhotoStyler

Aldus Corporation
411 First Avenue South
Suite 200
Seattle, WA 98104
(800) 333-2538

Category: Working demo

Location on CD-ROM: \DEMOS\PSTYLER

Documentation: README.TXT

Command to install the program: TVSETUP

This working demo of PhotoStyler 2.0 allows you to experiment with all the image processing features of the software, but you cannot print or save images. PhotoStyler offers photo-realistic image enhancement for processing color, grayscale, and B&W images.

Adobe Photoshop

Adobe Systems, Inc.
PO Box 7900
1585 Charleston Rd.
Mountain View, CA 94039-7900
(800) 333-6687
(415) 961-4400

Location on CD-ROM: \DEMOS\PSHOP

Command to install demo: SETUP

This working demo of Adobe PhotoShop allows you to experiment with all the image processing features of the software, but you cannot print or save images. PhotoShop offers photo-realistic image enhancement for processing color, gray scale and B&W images.

Photoshop offers a number of professional features, including color correction, prepress and darkroom systems. Created files are binary-compatible with the same version for the Macintosh, enabling users to freely exchange files between platforms.

915

PhotoMorph

North Coast Software
P.O. Box 459
265 Scruton Pond Road
Barrington, NH 03825

Category: Working demo

Location on CD-ROM: \DEMOS\PMORPH

Documentation: README.TXT

Command to install the program: INSTALL

PhotoMorph is the easy-to-use Windows-based morphing software from North Coast Software. PhotoMorph can easily create morphs of various types and in different formats, including Video for Windows .AVI format. The quality of morphs created with this software can rival what you see in movies and on television.

This demo has most of the functionality of the retail version, with some restrictions. Read the documentation file for more details. See the section "Morphing Videos" later in this appendix for information on some sample morphs included on the CD-ROM.

Kai's Power Tools

HSC Software
1661 Lincoln Blvd.
Suite 101
Santa Monica, CA 90404
(310) 392-8441

Category: Demo graphics

Location on CD-ROM: \DEMOS\KAITOOLS

Documentation: KAITOOLS.WRI

Format: TIFF

These sample graphics were created with Kai's Power Tools for Windows, the new add-in software that works with CorelDRAW!, Fractal Design Painter, PhotoStyler, and PhotoShop. Kai's Power Tools provides 33 tools and plug-in filters, which can create a nearly infinite variety of gradients, textures, fractal textures, and fills.

Kai's Power Tools also includes fractal creation tools, a glass lens feature to create spherical sections of objects, sharpen and intensity tools, and a cyclone filter to capture 24-bit color animations of images.

Typestry

Pixar
1001 W. Cutting Blvd.
Point Richmond, CA 94804
(510) 236-4000

Category: Demo graphics

Location on CD-ROM: \DEMOS\TYPESTRY

Command to start the program: PIXAR

The sample graphics in this presentation were created with Typestry, Pixar's software that turns your Type 1 and TrueType fonts into three-dimensional text. Typestry includes Pixar's RenderMan, so the images will have the same professional quality you've seen in many movies.

To make a Typestry picture, you simply type in the characters, select the font and bevel style and Typestry turns your word into a 3-D object. You can then rearrange the letters, apply surface appearances and lighting effects. This demo also includes examples from One Twenty Eight, Pixar's collection of photographic textures.

Part of this presentation plays an AVI video file. To view this file, you must first install the Video for Windows drivers, located in the \VFW directory. Read the file VIDEO.WRI in the root directory for more information.

Fontographer

Altsys
269 West Renner Parkway
Richardson, TX 75080
(800) 477-2131

Category: Demo graphics

Location on CD-ROM: \DEMOS\ALTSYS

Documentation: README

Format: Type 1 Fonts

917

These sample fonts were created with Fontographer, the outline font design and editing program. Fontographer creates high-resolution PostScript and TrueType fonts, downloadable and bitmap fonts, and logos or designs with interchangeable parts. It reads and writes standard TrueType and PostScript fonts.

Fontographer provides three drawing planes for character construction and a tool palette for precise control and handling of points and paths. The software has a number of powerful features, including a pen tool for freeform drawing of strokes, three types of control points for smooth curves, and autotracing of images.

Vistapro 3.0

Virtual Reality Laboratories, Inc.
2341 Ganador Court
San Luis Obispo, CA 93401

Category: Working demo

Location on disk: \DEMOS\VP3

Documentation: VPDEMO.TXT

Command to install the program: INSTALL

This is an interactive tutorial and a working demo for version 3 of Vistapro, the three-dimensional landscape simulation program. Using U.S. Geological Survey (USGS) Digital Elevation Model (DEM) data, Vistapro can accurately re-create high-resolution real world landscapes in vivid detail. As a fractal landscape generator, Vistapro can create landscapes from a random seed number.

The save and animation functions, as well as a few advanced features, are disabled in this demo.

Corel*NOTE!*

This is a DOS-based program. You will need to exit Windows to run it properly.

Master Trax Pro 4

Passport Designs
100 Stone Pine Road
Half Moon Bay, CA 94019

Category: Working demo

Location on CD-ROM: \DEMOS\TRAX

Documentation: README2.TXT

Command to install the program: SETUP

This is a full-featured demo of Passport Design's Master Trax Pro 4 MIDI
sequencer for Windows. The demo has the same functionality as the full
version, although the saving to disk function is disabled. Read the file
README.TXT for more information on installing the demo.

Encore

Passport Designs
100 Stone Pine Road
Half Moon Bay, CA 94019

Category: Working demo

Location on CD-ROM: \DEMOS\ENCORE

Documentation: README2.TXT

Command to install the program: SETUP

This is a demo of Encore, the MIDI/music notation program from Passport Designs. It has the same functionality as the full version, although
the saving to disk and printing functions are disabled. Read the file
README.TXT for more information on installing the demo.

Music Time

Passport Designs
100 Stone Pine Road
Half Moon Bay, CA 94019

Category: Working demo

Location on CD-ROM: \DEMOS\MUSICTIM

Documentation: README2.TXT

Command to install the program: SETUP

This is a demo of Passport Designs' music notation editor, MusicTime for Windows. It has the same functionality as the full version, although the saving to disk and printing functions are disabled. Read the file README.TXT for more information on installing the demo.

Distant Suns

Virtual Reality Laboratories, Inc.
2341 Ganador Court
San Luis Obispo, CA 93401

Category: Working demo

Location on cd-rom: DEMOS\DSUNS

Documentation: DSDEMO.TXT

Command to install the program: INSTALL

Distant Suns is the Windows-based desktop planetarium that displays the night sky from anywhere on the planet from 4173 BC to 10000 AD. One of the new features in Distant Suns 2.0 is the off earth mode that can display the heavens from anywhere in the solar system.

The complete version of the software includes NASA images of the planets.

Clip Art

These sample clip art images cover a wide range of subjects, from background textures and medical images to business graphics and southwestern images.

Masterclips—The Art of Business

Masterclips, Inc.
5201 Ravenswood Road, Suite 111
Fort Lauderdale, FL 33312
(800) 292-CLIP (orders only)
(305) 983-7440
(305) 967-9452 (fax)

Category: Commercial sampler

Location: \CLIPART\MCLIPS

Format: CGM

These clip art samples are from The Art of Business collection from Masterclips, Inc. This collection is available on CD-ROM and diskettes, and it contains more than 6,000 full-color images, all drawn by professional artists. More than 100 categories are represented, and the images are available in CGM or WPG format.

Masterclips also offers Custom Clips, a service for converting your logos or images into electronic clip art images. These images are hand drawn from your original camera-ready art, which guarantees an exact reproduction of the original.

Your Custom Clips can be produced in full color and in black-and-white, in a variety of graphics formats. Contact Masterclips for more information; you can also fax your logo or image for a free estimate. Be sure to see the ad for Masterclips at the back of this book.

Artbeats

Artbeats
Box 1287
Myrtle Beach, OR 97457
(503) 863-4429

Category: Commercial sampler

Location on CD-ROM: \CLIPART\ARTBEATS

Format: TIFF and EPS

Artbeats offers a number of unusual graphics collections, including:

Full Page Images Library. EPS background images of marble and wood textures, landscapes, paint splatters, 3-D textures, and more.

Backgrounds for Multimedia, volumes I and II. 8-bit and 24-bit high quality images designed with video, animation, and texture mapping applications in mind.

Marble & Granite. An extensive and varied library of high-resolution digitized of marble and granite textures.

Marbled Paper Textures. Dramatic and unusual digitized images of marbled paper, such as that found inside antique book covers.

You'll find samples of all of these products in this directory. The full collections of these products are available on CD-ROMs.

Mountain High Maps

Digital Wisdom
Box 2070
Tappahannock, VA 22560
(800) 800-8560

Category: Commercial sampler

Location on CD-ROM: \CLIPART\MAPS

Documentation: README.TXT

Format: TIFF

Mountain High Maps is a CD-ROM collection of relief images of the world's continents, countries, and ocean floors. Each dimension and contour of our planet is portrayed in a detailed and accurate topographical view.

In addition to the sample image in this directory, you'll find the complete Mountain High Maps catalog. Follow these directions to run the catalog application:

1. From File Manager or Program Manager, select **File Run**.

2. Type *<drive>*\CLIPART\MAPS\TBOOK.EXE CATALOG.TBK and press Enter. Substitute the letter of your CD-ROM drive for *<drive>*; for example, E:.

This will start the catalog application, which will show you a sample view of all the images in the Mountain High Maps collection.

MEDSET Medical Clip Art

Ray Litman Photographics
P.O. Box 5031
Glendale, AZ 85312-5031

Category: Shareware

Location on CD-ROM: \CLIPART\LITMAN

Documentation: README1.WRI and README2.WRI

Format: CDR

These images are designed to help artists, medical professionals, or anyone who needs to prepare graphics related to health care and the medical community. The complete sets are available on floppy disks.

Some of the images are located in subdirectories, such as FIRE, PEOPLE, SAFETY, and so on.

Sante Fe Collection

RT Computer Graphics
602 San Juan de Rio
Rio Rancho, NM 87124
(800) 245-7824

Category: Commercial sampler

Location on CD-ROM: \CLIPART\RTGRAPH

Format: EPS

The complete Sante Fe Collection (Professional Version) contains native American and southwest clip art—more than 500 images and 125 borders in EPS format.

Image By McCormick

Image By McCormick
13726 W. Aleppo Dr.
Sun City West, AZ 85375
(602) 584-8403

Category: Shareware

Location on CD-ROM: \CLIPART\IMAGE

Documentation: README.TXT

Format: CDR

These original images were created by Pete McCormick, one of the authors of this book.

Hot Clips

Eagle Software

Category: Commercial sampler

Location on CD-ROM: \CLIPART\HOTCLIPS

Documentation: README.TXT

Format: BMP

These stock photos, patterns, and textures are free for your own per-sonal use. Read the files AGREEMNT.TXT and LICENSE.TXT for more information on how you can use these files.

The PHOTOS subdirectory contains the photographs and the PATTERNS subdirectory contains the patterns and textures. Read the files PHOTOS.TXT and PATTERNS.TXT for details in the files included in these directories.

Stock Photos

The graphics in this section are stock photographs from commercial stock companies. These sample photos will give you an idea of the wide range of photos that are available electronically.

Most of these companies offer their photos for sale on a limited use basis—once you've purchased their disk of photos, you can use the photo in several projects without additional fees, but subject to certain restric-tions. Check with each individual company for more details.

Digital Zone

Digital Zone, Inc.
P.O. Box 5562
Bellevue, WA 98006
(800) 538-3113

Category: Commercial sampler

Location on CD-ROM: \PHOTOS\DIGIZONE

Documentation: DIGIZONE.WRI

Format: TIFF

The Digital Zone offers CD-ROMs of dramatic and colorful photography from some of the world's top professional photographers. The pictures on the CD-ROMs are in Kodak PhotoCD format.

The five samples on this disk are from different collections and they have been converted to TIFF format. In addition, there are images that show the complete range of photographs in each of the CD-ROM collections. These thumbnail images are named for the photographer represented on the disk.

For more information on the complete collection, see the file DIGIZONE.WRI.

Photos on Disk

Cantrall's Photos on Disk
7070 Fisherman Lane
Pilot Hill, CA 95664
(916) 933-1260

Category: Commercial sampler

Location on CD-ROM: \PHOTOS\CANTRALL

Documentation: README.WRI

Format: TIF

Cantrall's Photos on Disc is a set of CD-ROMs, each containing more than 100 digitized photographs. Subjects include Western United States, Flowers and Trees, Wild and Domestic Animals, Coastal and Ocean Themes and Patterns, Textures and Cloud Formations.

The more than 200 files in this sampler are low resolution versions from various collections. They are located in different subdirectories; for example, \PHOTOS\CANTRALL\SCENIC. For more information on the complete collections, see the file CANTRELL.WRI.

Fonts

TrueType and Type 1 fonts are represented in the font samplers on this disk. Some of these fonts are samples from commercial companies, while others are shareware and freeware offerings.

925

Corel *TIP!*

To preview any of these fonts before installing them, try using the Font Monster or TrueType Install utilities, which are included on this disk. You'll find more information in the "Programs and Utilities" section of this appendix.

The Font Company

The Font Company
7850 E. Evans Rd., Suite 111
Scottsdale, AZ 85260
(800) 442-3668
(602) 998-9711
(602) 998-7964 (Fax)

Category: Commercial sampler

Location on CD-ROM: \FONTS\FONTCO

Documentation: None

Format: TrueType

Twenty TrueType fonts from The Font Company's collection of over 2,000 faces is included on the CD. Also, see The Font Company's ad in the back of this book.

TypeTreats Sampler

Raynbow Software Inc.
P.O. Box 1541
Rapid City, SD 57709
(800) 456-5269

Category: Shareware sampler

Location on CD-ROM: \FONTS\RAYNBOW

Documentation: RAYNBOW.TXT

Format: TrueType, Type 1, and Corel WFN

Type Treats is a CD-ROM collection of more than 500 public domain and shareware fonts. The fonts are stored in a variety of formats:

- PC TrueType
- PC Type 1 and Type 3
- Corel WFN
- Mac TrueType
- Mac Type 1 and Type 3
- Next Type 1 and Type 3
- Nimbus-Q

The Type Treats font finder program is included on this disk to give you a peek at all the fonts that are included in the complete collection. To start the font finder, run the WFONTFIN.EXE program found in this directory.

The FONTS subdirectory contains 10 sample fonts from the collection in TrueType, Type 1, and WFN formats. The file AUTHORS.TXT contains information on the creators of these fonts.

The complete package includes a book of samples for all the fonts in the collection, as well as information on their designers. The collection also includes more than 100 public domain and shareware type-oriented utilities.

35Fonts Collection

Thomas E. Harvey
420 N. Bayshore Blvd., #206
Clearwater, FL 34619

Category: Shareware

Location on CD-ROM: \FONTS\FONTSAM

Documentation: 35README.TXT

Five TrueType fonts are included here from the 35 Heads font collection. To view the fonts in the full collection, run Windows Cardfile, found in the Accessories group of Program Manager. Open up the file SEE35HDS.CRD, which contains cards showing each font in the collection, as well as additional technical information.

Carr's Fonts

Alan Carr

Category: Freeware

Location on CD-ROM: \FONTS\CARR

Documentation: CARR.WRI

These TrueType fonts are sets of symbols, arrows, and special characters. Read the file CARR.WRI for more information about these fonts.

Publisher's Paradise Sampler

Publisher's Paradise BBS
(205) 882-6886 (modem)

Category: Commercial sampler

Location on CD-ROM: \FONTS\PUBPARAD

These sample fonts were created by the Publisher's Paradise bulletin board system (BBS). This BBS is created for people with interests in desktop publishing and graphics. You can call this BBS at the number listed above.

Programs and Utilities

Most of these utility programs are distributed as shareware. Be sure to read the section on shareware earlier in this appendix.

The software represented here ranges from utilities that enhance CorelDRAW! to programs that enhance the new multimedia capabilities of CorelDRAW!. You'll also find workhorse utilities that you'll find yourself using every day.

SetDRAW

Shooting Brick Software
P.O. Box 549
Moss Beach, CA 94038

Category: Shareware

Location on CD-ROM: \UTILS\SETDRAW

Documentation: README.WRI

Command to install the program: INSTALL

This software is intended exclusively to help you configure and tune your CorelDRAW! 4 program. SetDRAW loads five INI files that affect the performance and operation of DRAW. The settings in these files are checked, then read and presented for you to review and edit. These INI files control many options and important features that have a significant effect on DRAW 4 performance and output capability.

QwikDRAW! v2.1

Smart Typesetting
6835 E. Phelps Rd.
Scottsdale, AZ 85254-1539
(602) 443-3282

Category: Shareware

Location on CD-ROM: \UTILS\QWIKDRAW

Documentation: QDMANUAL.CDR

Command to install the program: INSTALL

QwikDRAW! adds an icon box containing as many as 50 icons to CorelDRAW! v4. The icons are all shortcuts for commands in CorelDRAW!. This way you don't have to remember what menu a particular function is in or what keyboard shortcut to use. The icon box floats above CorelDRAW! so that you can still work on your drawing at all times. Over 80 commands and icons are included for you to choose from or let your imagination run wild by creating your own commands and icons.

CDR Check and WFN Map

Rus Miller

Category: Freeware

Location on CD-ROM: \UTILS\CDRCHECK

Documentation: CDRCHECK.WRI and WFNMAP.WRI

Command to install the program: INSTALL

The CDR Check utility may be used to determine what fonts, if any, are used by a particular CDR file. It will read any CDR file created by any version of CorelDRAW! (up to and including 4). WFN Map is used to set up WFN font files for use with CorelDRAW!.

PRN Viewer

Rus Miller

Category: Freeware

Location on CD-ROM: \UTILS\PRNVIEW

Documentation: PRNVIEW.WRI

Command to install the program: INSTALL

PRN Viewer is used to peek into PostScript PRN files created by CorelDRAW!. It is useful in determining exactly what fonts are required to be resident in or downloaded to the output device, although it also displays other information that you may find useful.

ROM Cat

Paul Schaefer

Category: Freeware

Location on CD-ROM: \UTILS\ROMCAT

Documentation: README.TXT

Command to install the program: INSTALL

Rom CAT is a searchable database of the graphics images included on the two CorelDRAW! 4 CD-ROMs. You can look for particular images and automatically load them into CorelDRAW! for viewing and editing.

PSCorel

Costas Kitsos
P.O. Box 64943
Los Angeles, CA 90064

Category: Shareware

Location on CD-ROM: \UTILS\PSCOREL

Documentation: PSCOREL2.WRI

Command to install the program: INSTALL

PSCorel is a PostScript Font Downloader designed to work with CorelDRAW! 4 and PSCRIPT.DRV—the Windows PostScript printer driver. PSCorel works by monitoring CorelDraw's output to PSCRIPT.DRV.

WaldoPS

Costas Kitsos
P.O. Box 64943
Los Angeles, CA 90064

Category: Shareware

Location on CD-ROM: \UTILS\WALDOPS

Documentation: WALDOPS2.WRI

Command to install the program: INSTALL

WaldoPS helps you manage the PSResidentFonts section of CorelDraw!'s CORELFNT.INI file. With WaldoPS you can update the PSResidentFonts section when you add new fonts to ATM and/or edit any of the fonts installed in this section.

Printer's Apprentice

Bryan T. Kinkel
Lose Your Mind Development
506 Wilder Square
Norristown, PA 19401

Category: Shareware

Location on CD-ROM: \UTILS\PRINTAPP

Documentation: PA.HLP

Command to install the program: INSTALL

Printer's Apprentice is a font management utility that helps you manage all your TrueType and Adobe Type 1 fonts by printing three different types of inventory sheets, ANSI charts, keyboard layouts, and specimen sheets.

Font Monster

Leaping Lizards
7F, No. 8, Lane 197
Chuang Ching Road
Taipei 110
Taiwan, R.O.C.

Category: Shareware

Location on CD-ROM: \UTILS\FMONSTER

Documentation: FMONSTER.HLP

Command to install the program: INSTALL

Font Monster is a powerful utility that allows you to view, edit, and examine TrueType and Type 1 fonts. You can rename any font, edit internal font data, preview Preview TrueType fonts before installing, create font groups which you install by clicking on a Program Manager icon, and much more.

Corel *NOTE!*

When you register Font Monster, be sure to send only cash to the author—no checks or money orders. See the help information in the program for more information.

TrueType Font Installer

Kai Kaltenbach
15015 Main Street
Suite 103-137
Bellevue, WA 98007

Category: Shareware

Location on CD-ROM: \UTILS\TTINST

Documentation: TTINST.HLP

Command to install the program: SETUP

TrueType Font Installer allows you to easily preview fonts before installing them. This is something that Windows Control Panel cannot do, and something that is difficult to do with most other font utilities.

Picture Man

Igor Plotnikov, Mike Kuznetsov, Alex Bobkov
c/o Igor Plotnikov
519 Barry Court,
Mechanicsburg, PA 17055

Category: Shareware

Location on CD-ROM: \UTILS\PICTMAN

Documentation: PMAN.WRI

Command to install the program: INSTALL

Picture Man is a powerful true color image processing tool. It offers a large variety of 46 different bitmap operations, including geometrical transforms, halftone/color correction, filtering, and color fills. Seven types of selected areas are available, including rectangle, ellipse, polygon, text, freehand, pen, and magic wand.

Paint Shop Pro

JASC, Inc.
10901 Red Circle Drive
Suite 340
Minnetonka, MN 55343
(612) 930-9171

Category: Shareware

Location on CD-ROM: \UTILS\PSPRO

Documentation: PSP.HLP

Command to install the program: SETUP

Paint Shop Pro 2.0 is a Windows program that will display, convert, alter, and print graphics images. It works with files in these formats:

TIFF	GIF	TGA
WPG	BMP	PCX
MAC	MSP	IMG
PIC	RAS	RLE
DIB	JAS	

Altering includes resizing, trimming, applying filters, dithering, palette manipulation, and much more. Paint Shop Pro also does screen capturing.

Mandel

Phillip Crewes
cerious software
5424 Chedworth Drive
Charlotte, NC 28210

Category: Shareware

Location on CD-ROM: \UTILS\MANDEL

Documentation: MANDEL.HLP

Command to install the program: INSTALL

This program produces displays of the Mandelbrot fractal set. It has a wide variety of options and features, including the ability to apply 3-D special effects and easily save fractal images.

Makin' Waves

Geoff Faulkner
11664 Silvergate Drive
Dublin, CA 94568-2208

Category: Shareware

Location on CD-ROM: \UTILS\MAKEWAVE

Documentation: MAKEWAVE.WRI

Command to install the program: INSTALL

Makin' Waves is a sound file converter and wave file player. It can convert .VOC, .SOU, and .SND to .WAV format.

Wave Editor

Keith W. Boone
c/o ASG Inc.
11900 Grant Place
Des Peres, MO 63131

Category: Shareware

Location on CD-ROM: \UTILS\WAVEEDIT

Documentation: WAVEEDIT.WRI

Command to install the program: INSTALL

Wave Editor is an application that allows you to input, create, modify, and analyze wave files. You can also add special effects to the sounds.

WinJammer

WinJammer Software Limited
69 Rancliffe Road
Oakville, Ontario
Canada L6H 1B1

Category: Shareware

Location on CD-ROM: \UTILS\WINJAMM

Documentation: WJREADME.WRI

Command to install the program: SETUP

WinJammer is a fully featured MIDI sequencer for Windows 3.1. It uses standard MIDI files, giving you access to a huge number of songs. WinJammer also contains a companion program called WinJammer Player, which is used to play MIDI song files in the background.

WindJammer Pro Demo

WinJammer Software Limited
69 Rancliffe Road
Oakville, Ontario
Canada L6H 1B1

Category: Shareware

Location on CD-ROM: \UTILS\WJPRO

Documentation: WJPRO.WRI

Command to install the program: SETUP

WinJammer Professional is a MIDI sequencer for Windows 3.1. It uses standard MIDI files, giving you access to a huge number of songs. This is a demonstration version of the software—it will not save files.

Corel*NOTE!*

> The help file for this software has been downsized by removing the pictures that would appear in the normal help file. Throughout this help file you will see boxes that say "unable to display picture" whenever a picture has been removed.

WindSock Performance Monitor

Chris Hewitt

Category: Freeware

Location on CD-ROM: \UTILS\WINDSOCK

Documentation: WINDSOCK.HLP

Command to install the program: SETUP

WindSock 3.20 is the latest version of this Windows performance analysis utility. WindSock tests your machine's CPU, Video, Disk, and Memory speed from the point of view of Windows, using API calls where appropriate. It includes a version of Intel's iCOMP index and an overall index.

WindSock Resource Monitor

Chris Hewitt

Category: Freeware

Location on CD-ROM: \UTILS\WINDSKRM

Documentation: WNSKSRM.HLP

Command to install the program: INSTALL

WindSock SRM is a Windows resources monitor. It tracks your system's usage of memory, User, GDI, Menu, and String Resources. It also includes the ability to track and record GDI object usage. WindSock SRM runs either in the foreground or background and allows you to set resource thresholds and sounds an alarm if these are exceeded.

Drag and View

Dan Baumbach
Canyon Software
1537 Fourth Street Suite 131
San Rafael, CA 94901

Location on CD-ROM: \UTILS\DRAGVIEW

Documentation: DVHELP.HLP

Command to install the program: DVSETUP

Drag and View allows you to drag files from File Manager to an icon, and view files in a variety of formats. You can view most popular graphics, word processor, spreadsheet and database formats, plus also ASCII and HEX. Has search and goto functions. You can also open multiple windows and compare files.

WinZip

Nico Mak
P.O. Box 919
Bristol, CT 06011
CompuServe 70056,241

Category: Shareware

Location on CD-ROM: \UTILS\WINZIP

Documentation: WINZIP.DOC

Command to install the program: SETUP

WinZip brings the convenience of Windows to the use of ZIP, LZH, ARJ, and ARC files. It features an intuitive point and click interface for viewing, running, extracting, adding, deleting, and testing files in archives. Optional virus scanning support is included.

PKZip

PKWare, Inc.
9025 N. Deerwood Dr.
Brown Deer, WI 53223-2437

Category: Shareware

Location on CD-ROM: \UTILS\PKZIP

Documentation: PKZIP.DOC

Command to install the program: INSTALL

PKZip is the predominant standard when it comes to file compression programs. Version 2.04g improves upon the previous versions with improved compression, added features, and more speed.

Once the file PK204G.EXE has been installed to your hard drive, you must run this program from a DOS prompt. This file is a self-extracting archive, and it will automatically decompress the individual PKZip files.

EDI Install Pro

Eschalon Development Inc.
110-2 Renaissance Square
New Westminster, BC
V3M 6K3 CANADA

Category: Shareware

Location on CD-ROM: \UTILS\INSPRO

Documentation: INSTALL.HLP

Command to install the program: INSTALL

EDI Install Pro is a complete Windows installation utility that you can use "right out of the box" or configure to your needs. Features include dithered and bitmap background, selectable components, Program Manager groups, modifying .INI files, viewing text files, version checking, file compression, and more.

The registered version of this program was used to create a number of the installation routines for the programs on this book's CD-ROM.

Time Keeper v3.2

Smart Typesetting
6835 E. Phelps Rd.
Scottsdale, AZ 85254-1539
(602) 443-3282

Category: Shareware

Location on CD-ROM: \UTILS\TIMEKEEP

Documentation: TIMEKEEP.WRI

Command to install the program: INSTALL

TimeKeeper is great for keeping track of how much time has been spent on a project, phone call, or even to time how long it takes a particular program to load! If you bill your time out to clients, it can help you bill for all the time you spend on a project. It is very easy to run multiple copies of TimerKeeper and give each copy a separate name for those who are constantly juggling many different things.

Sound Files

This section highlights a variety of sounds. Most of the sounds come from commercial sound libraries and are offered as a sample of the complete library.

Hollywood Sound Library

New Eden Multimedia
7652 Hampshire Avenue
Minneapolis, MN 55248

Category: Commercial sampler

Location on CD-ROM: \SOUNDS\HSLIB

Documentation: HSLINFO.WRI or HSLINFO.TXT

Command to install the program: INSTALL

The Hollywood Sound Library is the world's largest library of digital computer sound files. Unlike other suppliers, which sell CD-ROM based collections of only a few hundred sound clips, the Hollywood Sound Library sells individual sound files from its library of more than 10,000 sounds. Because this massive collection requires more than 50 gigabytes of storage, it will never be sold at your local computer store (at least not in this century).

The sound effects are all high-quality, 16-bit, 44k stereo wave files licensed from some of the world's leading sound studios, including The Hollywood Edge and Sound Ideas. These sounds have been used in everything from radio and TV commercials to Academy Award-winning movies. See the ad in the back of this book for more information.

Also included is New Eden's WAVEVIEW sound browser application, which allows you to play sounds from the library and view descriptions for each of them. Run the INSTALL.EXE program in this directory to install it to your hard drive. The file HSLCAT.WRI is a catalog of the complete sound effects library.

The 16-bit versions of the WAV files are located in the \SOUNDS\HSLIB\DEMO16 directory. If you have an 8-bit sound card, you'll find 8-bit versions of the sounds in the \SOUNDS\HSLIB\DEMO8 directory.

MIDI Collection

Voyetra Technologies
333 Fifth Ave.
Pelham, NY 10803
(800) 233-9377

Category: Commercial sampler

Location on CD-ROM: \SOUNDS\VOYETRA

Format: MID

These samples are from Voyetra's complete collection of multi-track MIDI sequences. The collection contains more than 150 songs and drum patterns. The MIDI format allows users to modify songs to make them shorter, change key, reassign instruments, and tailor to individual needs. Contains full performance including drums, bass, piano, and solos.

Hot Clips

Eagle Software

Category: Commercial sampler

Location on CD-ROM: \SOUNDS\HOTCLIPS

Documentation: README.TXT

Format: WAV

These sound effects and music clips are free for your own personal use. Read the files AGREEMNT.TXT and LICENSE.TXT for more information on how you can use these files.

The MUSIC subdirectory contains the music clips and the SOUNDFX directory contains the sound effects. Read the files MUSIC.TXT and SOUNDFX.TXT for details on the files included in these directories.

Wave Library

Graphica Software
CIS Address 100026,2317

Category: Freeware

Location on CD-ROM: \SOUNDS\WAVELIB

Documentation: SOUNDS.TXT

Format: WAV

This is a collection of 8-bit sounds, created by John Hartley of England.

Video and Animation Files

In this section, you'll find a number of different video and animation clips that can be used with CorelDRAW's new multimedia capabilities. The AVI files are Microsoft's Video for Windows format and FLC files are in Autodesk Animator format.

The video for Windows runtime files and drivers are located in the /VFW directory. This directory also contains subdirectories for the Indeo 2.0 and Cinepak video drivers. Read the file VIDEO.WRI for more information.

Canyon Action

The San Francisco Canyon Company
150 Post Street
Suite 620
San Francisco, CA 94108

Category: Commercial sampler

Location on CD-ROM: \VIDEO\CANYON

Format: AVI

Canyon Clipz and Canyon Action are CD-ROM collections of video clips. Clipz is in Video for Windows format, and Action is in QuickTime for Windows format.

The movie categories include historical, modern, and music videos. The Canyon collections contain everything from Laurel and Hardy to Nils Lofgren and Bruce Springsteen, from weird science of the fifties to vintage cartoons in the Canyon collections.

See Canyon's ad in the back of this book for a special offer on these CD-ROM video collections. The ad is for Canyon Action, but you can also order the Canyon Clipz collection.

CUCUMBER.AVI/MOV—"Everything Goes," by *The Cucumbers.* ©1985 Fake Doom Records, Publisher (ASCAP). Jon Fried and Deena Shoshkes, Composers.

ARCANUM3.AVI/MOV—©1992 N.C. Gorski.

VEGETABL.AVI/MOV—© 1992 Lamb & Company, courtesy Doug Pfeifer.

SRL1.AVI/MOV—© 1992 N.C. Gorski. Additional footage courtesy Survival Research Laboratories, circa 1982.

Corel *NOTE!*

The directories AVI and OTIME contain Video for Windows and QuickTime for Windows versions of the videos.

PC Video Madness!

Ron Wodaski

Category: Commercial sampler

Location on CD-ROM: \VIDEO\PCMAD

Format: AVI

The videos in this section are a sample of more than 150 video clips featured in the book *PC Video Madness!* (Sams Publishing, 1993). The book includes a special edition of *Nautilus,* the multimedia magazine on CD-ROM. The CD contains more than 150 video clips, video applications, a full-length music video, NASA videos, and much more.

PC Video Madness! shows you how to do everything from creating and editing simple videos to adding special effects. If you ever wished you could be Steven Spielberg, here's your chance to learn how to create films on your own PC!

These sample videos from the book's CD-ROM show off a variety of video techniques and methods. See the file README.WRI for more details on how the videos were created.

Morphing Videos

North Coast Software
P.O. Box 459
265 Scruton Pond Road
Barrington, NH 03825
(603) 664-7872 (fax)

Category: Commercial sampler

Location on CD-ROM: \VIDEO\MORPHING

Format: AVI

These sample video files are examples of morphing, created with PhotoMorph, the Windows-based morphing software from North Coast Software. PhotoMorph can easily create morphs in Video for Windows .AVI format.

See the section on PhotoMorph earlier in this appendix for information on the demo version of this software.

VistaPro FLC Files

Sams Publishing

Category: Commercial sampler

Location on CD-ROM: \VIDEO\VISTAPRO

Format: FLC

These animated fly-bys of landscapes were created with VistaPro 3, from Virtual Reality Laboratories, Inc. The .FLC files in this directory can be played from within CorelDRAW!.

You'll find a demo of this DOS-based software on the CD-ROM. See the "Commercial Demos" section of this appendix for more details.

Corel Corporation Files

The Corel Corporation has provided a number of tech support documents that cover a number of subjects. In addition, you'll find the winning entries from Corel's fourth annual $1,000,000 design contest.

Tech Support Documents

Corel Corporation

Location on CD-ROM: \COREL\TECHSUPP

In this directory, you'll find a number of Windows Write (.WRI) documents that were created by the technical support department of the Corel Corporation.

Design Contest Winners

Corel Corporation

Location on CD-ROM: \COREL\WINNERS

Documentation: WINNERS.WRI

Format: SHW (Corel SHOW)

These are the winners of Corel Corporation's fourth annual Corel World Design contest. You'll find details on the winning artists in the file WINNERS.WRI.

Graphics

Many of the CorelDRAW! files created for this book are included on this disk. You'll even find award-winning compositions. In addition, there are landscape graphics created with VistaPro.

Authors' Graphics

Location on CD-ROM: \GRAPHICS\AUTHORS

Format: CDR, EPS, and TIFF

These graphics were created by the authors of this book. You'll find these files used in the book cover, the color insert, and other spots in the book.

VistaPro Landscapes

Location on CD-ROM: \GRAPHICS\VISTAS

These TIFF files were created with VistaPro 3.0. See the section on VistaPro earlier in this appendix for information on the demo version.

Many of these graphics are from the book *Virtual Reality Madness!* by Ron Wodaski (Sams Publishing, 1993). Read the file VRMAD.WRI for more information on this book.

Textures

Location on CD-ROM: \GRAPHICS\TEXTURES

This directory contains a variety of textured backgrounds that were created by Sams Publishing. These TIFF files were created using a number of applications.

C

Production Notes

The production of this book spanned many different software packages running on both the Macintosh and PC platforms. This may be disconcerting to those who see no reason why a Macintosh should be used to produce a book on the leading PC graphics product. Simply put, it was used due to convenience and not in any way due to its superiority or inferiority.

Most of the writing was done in Microsoft Word for Windows version 2.0c, although Windows Write and Microsoft Works for Macintosh were used at various times. All the editing was done in Microsoft Word version 5.5.

The screen shots throughout the book were captured in Collage. Most of the other figures were drawn in CorelDRAW! versions 2.0, 3.0, and 4.0. The color pages contain many images that were composed using a combination of other software, such as Adobe Photoshop, Fractal Design Painter, Pixar Typestry, and the various Corel products. These products provide for a very versatile toolbox when used in conjunction with each other. Other artwork was scanned on a combination of an HP Scanjet IIc, Agfa Arcus Plus, and Nikon LS-3510AF scanners. They all did a fantastic job with the artwork we threw at them.

The typeface used for the layout of the book is The Font Company's FC-Serifa family and Prentice Hall Computer Publishing's MCPdigital. Layout was done in PageMaker for Macintosh version 4.2.

The large amount of files needed for the CD-ROM were transferred using SyQuest 44MB removable cartridges. Because many of the files exceeded the size of floppy disks even when compressed, the SyQuest cartridges proved to be lifesavers.

Biographies

Foster D. Coburn III

Foster D. Coburn III got into the field of electronic publishing while attending the University of Kansas. In 1990, he started his own business, Smart Typesetting.

Smart Typesetting specializes in CorelDRAW! and Ventura Publisher related production and consulting. In fact, Coburn was the first Certified Ventura Professional in Arizona. Smart Typesetting's projects have included everything from business cards to magazine advertisements appearing in such publications as *PC World, Publish,* and *Computer Shopper.* Smart Typesetting's logo won an Award of Excellence in Corel Corporation's 1993 World Design Contest.

In 1991, he teamed with The Font Company to help them produce and support products for the PC. This association has been very successful, as all of their more than 2000 PostScript typefaces are available on both the Macintosh and the PC. The Font Buyer software was also successfully converted from the Macintosh to the PC, enabling users to unlock the fonts of their choice from a CD-ROM. He also helped produce some fonts for inclusion in Microsoft's TrueType Font Pack 2.

In 1992, Smart Typesetting entered the software business by introducing two Shareware packages. TimeKeeper enables users to track the time spent on a particular project and the amount billable to clients. QwikDRAW! is a CorelDRAW! add-on that provides a floating icon box with 50 different functions represented. Both have been an overwhelming success with users around the world.

He can be reached on CompuServe at 70274,3072, on the Internet at 70274.3072@compuserve.com, or by mail at 6835 E. Phelps Rd., Scottsdale, AZ 85254-1539.

Carlos F. Gonzalez

Carlos F. Gonzalez began his artistic career after receipt of an Associate of Arts degree in Graphic Design with Honors in 1989 from Al Collins Graphic Design School. In 1993, he started his own business, Running Changes.

Gonzalez was employed part-time by *Help Wanted Weekly Magazine* as Assistant Production Manager. Besides assisting with the weekly production of the magazine, he was their spokesperson in radio commercials and was instrumental in the creation of a television pilot to inform the public of employment availability.

Gonzalez was also employed part-time by Mike Byrnes & Associates. That later grew into a full-time position as Creative Director, wherein he excelled in the usage of PC programs such as CorelDRAW!, Ventura Publisher, and other programs. Award-winning design, illustration, and layout of numerous books published resulted thereafter. Text book guides were produced for Barron's Educational Series, Inc. and the Ministry of Ontario, Canada. Most memorable was *Bumper-To-Bumper, The Complete Guide to Tractor-Trailer Operations*, which was used on the television show "Roseanne" as a prop.

Gonzalez is a charter member of the Phoenix PC Users Group CorelDRAW! SIG and led it from 1990 to 1992. He continues to write monthly columns in the Phoenix PC Users Group Newsletter regarding CorelDRAW!, is a member of the board of directors of Phoenix ACAD, and continues to demonstrate his support and admiration for CorelDRAW! by writing numerous "How To" articles for the Phoenix ACAD newsletter and *Corelation* magazine. At work or at home, you can find him using CorelDRAW! on a daily basis.

Gonzalez can be reached by mail at 1307 E. Oregon Avenue, Phoenix, AZ 85014.

Peter McCormick

Peter McCormick became involved with art and computers late in life. At age 40, he discovered a latent talent for painting. This discovery began a career in the field of fine art that lasted until the age of 53. It was then that he discovered computers. After experimenting with several graphics programs, he concentrated on CorelDRAW! In 1992, he was awarded Grand Prize World in the Landmarks division of Corel Corporation's World Design Contest.

McCormick creates art for software developers, ad agencies, and others. He is currently President of the Phoenix chapter of the Association of CorelDraw Artists and Designers and was a guest presenter at ACAD's first annual convention in Burbank, California, in June of 1993.

McCormick writes for the real-world user of CorelDRAW! Instead of showing samples of what the advanced user is capable, he wants the reader to understand the complexities and functionalities of working in CorelDRAW! With a thorough understanding of CorelDRAW!, the reader can then create drawings that bring to the page his or her own unique talents.

McCormick can be reached on CompuServe at 72172,1761, on the Internet at 72172.1761@compuserve.com, or by mail at 13726 W. Aleppo Drive, Sun City West, AZ 85375-5207.

Index

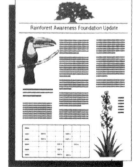

Top Ten Reasons to buy the *Canyon Action!* CD-ROM

for your multimedia equipped computer

1. Comes with *QuickTime for Windows*, Apple Computer's digital video standard now available for Microsoft Windows (so you can play any QuickTime for Windows movie).

2. Playable on both the Macintosh and IBM-compatible PC.

3. Contains a wide variety of exciting QuickTime movies (see below).

4. Also available in Video for Windows format (AVI) as *Canyon Clipz*.

5. Easy to install—playable right out of the box.

6. Tested on all major brands of video and audio hardware.

7. Featured in *PC Magazine*, *Variety*, *PC Week*, *Publish!*, *PC World*, etc.

8. Includes high-level browser program for easy movie watching.

9. Demonstrates the power of cross-platform technology.

10. Software-only operation—no special hardware required.

Retail Price: *$29.95*. Call 415-398-9957 to order.

Visa/Mastercard accepted. Also available for bundles.

Description of Product: *Canyon Action!* is a cross-platform CD-ROM designed to showcase QuickTime for Windows. Along with a movie player and associated DLLs, the user gets a wide selection of QuickTime movies to enjoy, including full length MTV-style music videos (nationally known performers), vintage Hollywood animation and old movie clips, high quality computer graphics shorts, and segments from contemporary documentaries.

Canyon Action! is a production of The San Francisco Canyon Company, a Bay Area Multimedia corporation specializing in CD-ROM publishing and contract software development.

Add to Your Sams Library Today with the Best Books for Programming, Operating Systems, and New Technologies

The easiest way to order is to pick up the phone and call
1-800-428-5331
between 9:00 a.m. and 5:00 p.m. EST.
For faster service please have your credit card available.

ISBN	Quantity	Description of Item	Unit Cost	Total Cost
0-672-30318-3		Windows Sound FunPack (Book/Disk)	$19.95	
0-672-30310-8		Windows Graphics FunPack (Book/Disk)	$19.95	
0-672-30249-7		Multimedia Madness! (Book/Disk/CD-ROM)	$44.95	
0-672-30322-1		PC Video Madness! (Book/Disk/CD-ROM)	$39.95	
0-672-30391-4		Virtual Reality Madness! (Book/CD-ROM)	$39.95	
0-672-30248-9		FractalVision: Put Fractals to Work for You (Book/Disk)	$39.95	
0-672-30305-1		Computer Graphics Environments (Book/Disk)	$34.95	
0-672-30315-9		The Magic of Image Processing (Book/Disk)	$39.95	
0-672-30361-2		Virtual Reality and the Exploration of Cyberspace (Book/Disk)	$26.95	
0-672-30345-0		Wasting Time with Windows (Book/Disk)	$19.95	
0-672-30301-9		Artificial Life Explorer's Kit (Book/Disk)	$24.95	
0-672-30352-3		Blaster Mastery (Book/Disk/CD-ROM)	$34.95	
0-672-30320-5		Morphing Magic (Book/Disk)	$29.95	
0-672-30308-6		Tricks of the Graphics Gurus (Book/Disk)	$49.95	
0-672-30362-0		Navigating the Internet	$24.95	
0-672-30373-6		On the Cutting Edge of Technology	$22.95	
		Shipping and Handling: See information below.		
		TOTAL		

❏ 3 ½" Disk

❏ 5 ¼" Disk

Shipping and Handling: $4.00 for the first book, and $1.75 for each additional book. Floppy disk: add $1.75 for shipping and handling. If you need to have it NOW, we can ship product to you in 24 hours for an additional charge of approximately $18.00, and you will receive your item overnight or in two days. Overseas shipping and handling adds $2.00 per book and $8.00 for up to three disks. Prices subject to change. Call for availability and pricing information on latest editions.

201 West 103rd Street, Indianapolis, IN 46290 USA

1-800-428-5331 — Orders   1-800-835-3202 — FAX   1-800-858-7674 — Customer Service

Book ISBN 0-672-30371-X

Corel DRAW! UNLEASHED

UNLEASHED

Software Demos
Stock Photos
Utility Programs
Backgrounds & Textures
Sound Clips
Unique Clip Art
Video Clips

SAMS
PUBLISHING

The CorelDRAW! 4 Unleashed CD-ROM

Here's a taste of the sample programs and files you'll find on the CD-ROM.

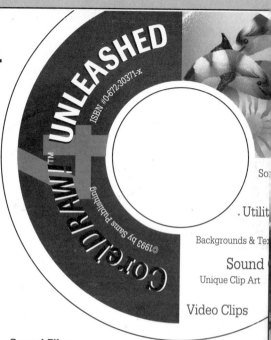

Demos and Samples of Commercial Products

Fractal Design Painter
PhotoStyler
PhotoShop
PhotoMorph
Master Trax Pro 4
and more...

Clip Art—More than 300 Selections!

Masterclips—The Art of Business
ArtBeats
Santa Fe Collection
Mountain High Maps
and more...

Stock Photos

Digital Zone
Hot Clips
Photos on Disk

Programs and Utilities

SetDRAW
Printer's Apprentice
QwikDRAW!
Font Monster
Paint Shop Pro
ROM Cat
and much, much more...

Fonts

The Font Company
TypeTreats Sampler
and more...

Sound Files

Hollywood Sound
Library
Voyetra MIDI Collection
and more...

Video and Animation Files

Canyon Clipz
and more...

CompuServe Information Service

Free CompuServe membership
and $15 of free connect time
Free Windows CompuServe
Information Manager

Corel Corporation Files

Tech support documents
Winning entries from Corel's fourth
annual design contest

To explore the details of what's on the CD-ROM, read Appendix B in the book. The special registration card for free connect time on CompuServe is behind the CD-ROM.